# The Black-capped Chickadee

# The Black-capped
# CHICKADEE

*Behavioral Ecology and Natural History*

# Susan M. Smith

Department of Biological Sciences
Mount Holyoke College

**Comstock Publishing Associates**

*a division of*

**Cornell University Press**

*Ithaca and London*

*For May Annetts Smith*

Copyright © 1991 by Cornell University

All rights reserved. Except for brief quotations in a review, this book, or parts thereof, must not be reproduced in any form without permission in writing from the publisher. For information, address Cornell University Press, 124 Roberts Place, Ithaca, New York 14850.

First published 1991 by Cornell University Press.

International Standard Book Number 0-8014-2382-1 (cloth)
International Standard Book Number 0-8014-9793-0 (paper)
Library of Congress Catalog Card Number 91-55072

Printed in the United States of America

*Librarians: Library of Congress cataloging information appears on the last page of the book.*

Epigraph: Henry David Thoreau, *The Journal of Henry D. Thoreau*, ed. Bradford Torrey and Francis H. Allen (1906; reprint [14 vols. in 2], New York: Dover Publications, 1962), 2: 1386–1387.

# Contents

The fields are bleak, and they are, as it were, vacated. The very earth is like a house shut up for the winter, and I go knocking about it in vain. But just then I heard a chickadee on a hemlock, and was inexpressably cheered to find that an old acquaintance was yet stirring about the premises, and was, I was assured, to be there all winter. All that is evergreen in me revived at once.

—Henry David Thoreau
November 7, 1858

# Preface

Familiar to many and immensely popular, the Black-capped Chickadee is one of the best-studied species in North America. When I set out to write this book, I simply wanted to produce a compilation of everything I could find published about these remarkably interesting birds. As my work progressed, however, I realized I had underestimated my task.

First, two other species—the Willow Tit of the Old World and the North American Carolina Chickadee—have been considered by some to be the same species as the Black-capped Chickadee. I have therefore included as close to complete coverage as I can of the literature on Carolina Chickadees and much of the recent literature on Willow Tits. This in turn has forced me to attempt to summarize the recent (and enormous) literature on European tits, at least as it pertains to our knowledge of chickadees: a rather daunting task.

One of my goals in writing this book was to encourage people to write more about chickadees. Although I have tried to present all the information published so far, as fairly and clearly as possible, I am well aware that not all my interpretations or conclusions are necessarily correct—just that they do fit the data currently available to me. Science constantly strives to get closer to the truth, and I hope this book will encourage people with unpublished information about chickadees to write it up. From the review of the relevant literature provided here, they can easily see how their data fit in with what else is known about the subject.

The book opens with an introductory chapter that brings together some basic information on the natural history of Black-capped Chickadees. Next, Chapter 2 discusses some of the more common study techniques used in work with chickadees. Chapters 3 and 4 deal with two important daily activities of chickadee life: food and feeding (Chapter 3) and communication (Chapter 4). The next three chapters follow Black-capped Chickadees through their annual cycle, paying particular attention to behavior and social organization throughout the year. Chapter 8 deals with various aspects of chickadee physiology, focusing on an exploration of how such tiny birds can withstand the long winter nights without freezing to death. Chapter 9 explores survivorship and population dynamics. Finally, Chapter 10 discusses some of the more exciting areas for future research.

I have tried to make each chapter able to stand alone, since some readers may wish to go straight to the chapters that interest them most. To this end, I have given the scientific names of other chickadees and titmice the first time I mention them in each chapter. To minimize overlap of information, I refer readers to the place where a topic is covered most fully.

Throughout the book I have been careful to identify the locality of each study. Some readers may wonder why I bothered to include this information. The Black-capped Chickadee is a non-migratory bird that occupies an unusually large geographic range. Population differences in morphological characteristics such as wing and tail length or plumage coloration have been well documented. It is likely that other consistent differences, including some in behavioral ecology, also occur; indeed, a few have already been discovered. I find such differences particularly exciting because comparative studies between two differing populations of a single species seem to have enormous potential for allowing us to discover how and why such differences arise and are maintained.

I recently read a review by Charles Blem (1989) in which he mentioned a complaint he had heard about today's "chart- and table-studded articles" on bird behavior, and it occurred to me that some readers might be dismayed by the profusion of charts and tables in this book. With that in mind, I tried to make all the general points in the text itself; the tables and graphs merely provide illustrations of the data on which those points are based.

The tables and graphs are there for readers who wish to use them, but my hope is that readers who choose not to will be able to read right on with comprehension but without distraction.

Studying chickadees can be addictive—I've been hooked for years. I can't imagine ever getting tired of working with them. They are endlessly fascinating, endlessly intriguing. Each new bit of information discovered simply brings up important new questions to pursue. I hope this book not only conveys but also explains my excitement in working with these truly marvelous birds.

During the writing of this book, much of my thinking has been shaped and clarified by conversations with other biologists. Even those who did not necessarily agree with my interpretations (and still don't!) were extraordinarily generous in taking time to talk over ideas and data with me. I am particularly grateful for discussions with Christopher P. L. Barkan, André Desrochers, André A. Dhondt, Jan Ekman, Millicent Sigler Ficken, Thomas C. Grubb, Jr., Svein Haftorn, Jack P. Hailman, Christine L. Hitchcock, Olav Hogstad, James L. Howitz, Donald E. Kroodsma, D. Archibald McCallum, Alison M. Mostrom, Stephen Nowicki, Craig D. Orr, Christopher M. Perrins, Laurene Ratcliffe, David F. Sherry, and Charles M. Weise.

Many people shared unpublished data and manuscripts with me; I especially thank Christopher Barkan, André Dhondt, Jan Ekman, Thomas C. Grubb, Jr., Christine Hitchcock, Olav Hogstad, Lloyd Kiff, Donald Kroodsma, Archibald McCallum, Alison Mostrom, and Stephen Nowicki.

It is a pleasure to thank Christopher and Mary Perrins for their hospitality in Oxford; I am grateful for their generosity and kindness while I was there. The discussions we had during that short time were most helpful.

Special thanks go to my friends Muriel W. Harris and Janice A. Gifford for lending me negatives of their photographs to use in this book, to Marjorie Kaufman for tracking down the particulars on the quotation from Thoreau's journal, and to Doris S. Atkinson for help with many of the figures as well as for continued support throughout the preparation of the manuscript.

SUSAN M. SMITH

*South Hadley, Massachusetts*

## The Black-capped Chickadee and Related Species

These sketches of the main species discussed appear on figures throughout the book to identify the species on which the study was done.

**Black-capped Chickadee**
(*Parus atricapillus*)

**Mountain Chickadee**
(*Parus gambeli*)

**Tufted Titmouse**
(*Parus bicolor*)

**Carolina Chickadee**
(*Parus carolinensis*)

**Willow Tit**
(*Parus montanus*)

**Crested Tit**
(*Parus cristatus*)

**Great Tit**
(*Parus major*)

**Blue Tit**
(*Parus caeruleus*)

# The Black-capped Chickadee

# 1

# General Natural History

The Black-capped Chickadee (*Parus atricapillus*) is one of the most familiar and popular of North American birds. Found from coast to coast, including much of Canada and approximately the northern two-thirds of the United States, chickadees readily approach people's houses and show little fear of humans. Flocks of chickadees crowd to feeders in areas where most other songbirds, especially those as small as chickadees, have left for the winter. Who has not gladly stopped to watch the antics of these birds on a cold winter day?

Another factor contributing to their popularity is that chickadees, unlike many other common birds, do not cause any serious nuisance to people. In fact, their summer diet is primarily insectivorous, making their presence all the more welcome.

Chickadees make ideal research subjects. They are resident year-round, so field studies can be done in any season. They come readily to feeders, making certain kinds of observations easier to get. They are easily caught for banding. Relatively unafraid of humans, they can be approached closely for behavioral observations. And even wild-caught adults adapt readily to captivity. For such reasons, there is a vast and growing literature on the biology of these birds. But, as Gill and Flicken (1989) pointed out, research opportunities on chickadees are nowhere close to being exhausted—more information simply generates new and fresh questions about chickadee biology.

The more than 40 species of chickadees and titmice (genus *Parus*), found in most habitats in the Northern Hemisphere, provide ideal subjects for comparative studies. Moreover, many, including the Black-capped Chickadee, inhabit enormous and diverse geographical ranges, permitting within-species comparisons as well (something that is essential to any understanding of between-species data). Some of the most exciting work on avian learning and memory is being conducted today on Black-capped Chickadees (see Food Storage and Memory, Chapter 3); this work, along with certain other chickadee studies (e.g., Nowicki and Capranica 1986a, 1986b), helps to increase our understanding of how the avian brain actually operates. Research on how chickadees respond to cold temperatures has helped further our understanding of the winter physiology of warm-blooded vertebrates. Long-term studies on chickadees and titmice continue to provide the basis for many of our insights into vertebrate population ecology. Chickadees have already taught us a great deal and will surely continue to do so in the foreseeable future.

## Appearance and Behavior

All North American chickadees have the same basic pattern of dark cap and bib; white cheeks; unstreaked dark back, wings, and tail; and pale underparts with a darker wash along the flanks and under the tail (the crissum). The cap and bib of Black-capped Chickadees are solid black, the back is usually some shade of greenish gray, there is at least some white edging on the gray wing feathers (including the wing coverts), and the wash on the flanks and crissum is often a warm buff color (Fig. 1-1). Occasionally, chickadees with some form of aberrant plumage have been reported (Fig. 1-2; also see, for example, Wetherbee 1933, Tanner 1934, Low 1969, and Tallman 1987). Often such birds have either too much or too little dark pigment (melanin) in their feathers. Some have been known to grow normally colored feathers after going through a molt (Tallman 1987; see below).

Chickadees are small. Most Black-capped Chickadees weigh between 10 and 14 grams, with northern individuals being perhaps somewhat heavier than their southern counterparts. By contrast, House Sparrows (*Passer domesticus*) weigh about 30 grams, and

Fig. 1-1. The Black-capped Chickadee. Note the prominent pale edgings on both the upper wing feathers (secondaries) and the wing coverts. (© Alan Cruickshank / VIREO.)

American Robins (*Turdus migratorius*) often weigh well over 80 grams.

Chickadees are most definitely not known for their fast flight. Evidently, their ordinary flight speed is approximately 11 miles

Fig. 1-2. This partial albino Black-capped Chickadee had much white on the top of its head. Curiously, although the rest of the feathers had normal coloration, its beak and feet were pink, rather than dark as in normal chickadees. (Photograph courtesy of Janice Gifford.)

per hour (just under 20 km per hour), a speed they typically achieve after only four or five wingbeats (Greenewalt 1955). By contrast, the White-breasted Nuthatch (*Sitta carolinensis*) has slower acceleration but a faster terminal velocity.

Like all birds, chickadees must preen frequently to maintain their feathers in good condition. Oil from the uropygial, or preen, gland, located at the base of the tail, is spread over each feather, increasing its flexibility and insulative properties. Where conditions permit, chickadees also bathe frequently. When taking a bath, a chickadee typically jumps into the water, rolls its body and flicks its wings, then retires to the bank or to a low perch to vibrate its wet feathers and preen before returning for another plunge

(Slessers 1970). In times of drought, chickadees may use dew for bathing, fluttering repeatedly among wet leaves (Verbeek 1962); they have also been known to take baths in new-fallen snow (Mitchell 1950).

Some of the most interesting and readily observed chickadee behavior relates to their feeding. Chickadees are seldom still; they seem to be in almost constant motion in their never-ending search for food. They and their relatives are well known for being particularly acrobatic, often hanging upside down from the tips of twigs and larger branches as they forage. The fact that chickadees' legs are both somewhat longer and stronger than those of most other birds of similar weight (Perrins 1979, Moreno 1990) may account for their impressive acrobatic abilities.

If a chickadee catches something that needs manipulation before it can be eaten (such as a large caterpillar or even a sunflower seed), the bird typically holds the food down with one or both feet and pounds away with its short but stout bill. This use of the feet is fairly unusual among birds, but is characteristic of virtually all members of the genus *Parus*.

Chickadees' appearance changes little as they age; that is, they have no distinct immature plumage. Newly hatched Black-capped Chickadees are sparsely covered with grayish natal down, but this is soon pushed out by the growing contour feathers of their juvenal plumage, which is virtually identical to that of adults, although the feathers are softer and fluffier than those of older birds.

Young chickadees next undergo a partial postjuvenal molt about midsummer, in which essentially every feather except the larger wing and tail feathers is replaced. Once past the postjuvenal molt, every chickadee undergoes a single annual molt, typically beginning in July and August and continuing into autumn, in which each feather is replaced (Bent 1946; see Postbreeding Molt, Chapter 6).

When you stop to think about it, the consequences of this simple fact are quite remarkable. Since chickadees molt only once a year, the feathers that keep them warm through the cold winter are the same ones in which they must survive the summer's heat. Of course, some wear occurs over time, so the feathers are not quite so thick by the time summer arrives (see Physical Adjustments Chapter 8); nevertheless, the ability of such small birds to maintain a fairly constant body temperature throughout the year with one set of feathers is indeed amazing.

## Life History

Black-capped Chickadees live in nonbreeding flocks in the fall and winter, then shift to monogamous, territorial breeding pairs during the spring and summer. Chickadees in winter flocks are hard to miss, but during the breeding season chickadees are relatively silent and inconspicuous, as they go quietly about the business of nesting and rearing offspring.

As do most other members of the genus, Black-capped Chickadees nest in holes, although they are far less likely to use nest boxes than are many of their European relatives (Perrins 1979), preferring instead to excavate their own cavities in stumps or rotting branches. Both sexes excavate nest cavities, but the female alone builds the nest and incubates the eggs. Once the eggs hatch, however, both parents share the duties of feeding the young. Such feeding typically continues for up to four weeks after the young have left the nest. Each young chickadee then disperses independently from its natal area, often moving several kilometers away. Chickadees rarely have a second brood; by the time the fledglings disperse, the adults will generally have begun their postbreeding molt.

The dispersing young soon settle and join newly forming flocks. These flocks typically consist of local breeding pairs together with unrelated young birds that hatched some distance away. The flocks, which persist through the nonbreeding season, typically exhibit stable, linear dominance hierarchies (peck orders) in which every member has its own particular position, or rank. A chickadee's rank within the flock can profoundly affect both its behavior and its chances of survival (see Chapters 3 [Foraging Niche], 7 [Dominance Hierarchies], and 9 [Predators and Antipredator Behavior]).

Throughout most of its range, the Black-capped Chickadee is usually resident; that is, individuals inhabit the same area year-round. Many of the most northerly chickadee populations don't migrate, even in the absence of feeders (Taverner 1949, Kron 1975). Nevertheless movements can and do occur. Some are simply vertical: chickadees inhabiting mountainous areas may descend to lower, warmer localities for the winter, then return to higher altitudes the following spring (Smith and Van Buskirk 1988). These migrants may well be mostly young birds; Dixon and Gilbert (1964) found that altitudinal migration by Mountain

Chickadees (*Parus gambeli*) is done almost exclusively by immature birds. Other movements, such as the more familiar pattern of temperate zone migration, are apparently latitudinal—several banding studies contain reports of birds captured in fall and (to a somewhat lesser extent) in spring that were not seen again (e.g., Loery and Nichols 1985). Moreover, in many winters, Black-capped Chickadees occur farther south than they do during the breeding season. Little is known about these apparent migrants; however, two important features emerge. First, again, the vast majority are young birds. Second, the number that moves in this manner varies markedly from year to year; in some years apparently few to none move, while in others, called irruption years, very large numbers may be involved (Bagg 1969; see Migration and Irruptions, Chapter 9).

### Longevity and Natural Enemies

The oldest known Black-capped Chickadee to date was at least 12 years and 5 months old (Kennard 1975). A bird of such age, while not unique, is quite unusual. The average life span of a chickadee is far shorter—approximately 2.5 years or less according to most studies (Smith 1967c, Elder and Zimmerman 1983).

Throughout the year, chickadees must withstand the attacks of several natural predators. Among avian predators, hawks of the genus *Accipiter*, such as Sharp-shinned (*A. striatus*) and Cooper's (*A. cooperii*) Hawks can be particularly efficient at capturing chickadees. Other predators, such as American Kestrels (*Falco sparverius*) and Merlins (*F. columbarius*), and more locally, Northern Pygmy Owls (*Glaucidium gnoma*) and Northern Shrikes (*Lanius excubitor*) can also take their toll (Bent 1946). Often, however, a healthy chickadee is agile enough to escape such predators; the individuals that are caught often turn out to have been weakened by age, disease, or some other factor (Geer 1982).

The house cat, an introduced species, is most dangerous to chickadees around that human-constructed item, the feeder. Natural nonavian predators are more likely to catch chickadees at nest or roost sites. Nest predators must be able to fit, either partially or entirely, into the entrance hole of the nest cavity. Many such holes are small enough to exclude all but the smallest squirrel (e.g., *Tamiasciurus* sp.) or chipmunk (*Tamias* or *Eutamias* sp.), although

certain weasels (*Mustela* sp.) and climbing snakes still pose a danger
(Bent 1946, Perrins 1979; see the section on predators and antipredator behavior in Chapter 9 for a discussion of these and other
nest predators).

Brown-headed Cowbirds (*Molothrus ater*) occasionally manage to
lay eggs in Black-capped Chickadee nests (Friedmann et al. 1977;
Lowther 1983). However, the cavity entrances of most chickadee
nests are too small for female cowbirds to enter, so such instances
are rare.

As cavity nesters go, chickadees support a relatively low level
and diversity of external parasites (see Parasites and Diseases,
Chapter 9)—perhaps because they seldom reuse a nest site, preferring to excavate a new cavity each time they nest.

## Relationships

All Northern American chickadees and crested titmice are currently placed in the genus *Parus*, within the family Paridae. The
Paridae is a family of the suborder Oscines (songbirds) within the
order Passeriformes, or perching birds. This huge order contains
over half of all living bird species. Within this order, parids are
generally thought to be fairly closely related to the families Sittidae
(nuthatches) and Certhiidae (creepers and their allies) (Sibley et al.
1988). Members of the family Paridae inhabit more or less wooded
areas over most of North America, Eurasia, and much of Africa,
but are absent from both South America and Australia. Evidently
the North American parids are all descended from Eurasian lin-
eages that crossed the Bering land bridge during the Pleistocene
(Mayr 1946, Parkes 1958).

The Black-capped Chickadee's scientific name, *Parus atricapillus*,
was coined in 1766 by Linnaeus; roughly translated, it means "titmouse with a black crown." The type specimen was collected in
Québec City, Canada. At one time, the Black-capped Chickadee
was considered to be conspecific with the Eurasian Willow Tit.
However, they are now considered separate species, because of,
among other things, considerable differences in voice and, to some
extent, in plumage (Snow 1956). Although some biologists still
question this split (e.g., Desfayes 1964), recent work has provided
solid evidence that the two are separate species (Gill et al. 1989; see
below). The Willow Tit is now known as *Parus montanus*.

Among North American chickadees (all of which are in the subgenus *Poecile*), two groups have traditionally been recognized (e.g., Mayr and Short 1970): the "brown-capped" chickadees, including the Boreal Chickadee (*Parus hudsonicus*), the Chestnut-backed Chickadee (*P. rufescens*), and the Siberian Tit (*P. cinctus*); and the "black-capped" group, consisting of the Black-capped Chickadee, the Carolina Chickadee (*P. carolinensis*), the Mountain Chickadee (*P. gambeli*), and the Mexican Chickadee (*P. sclateri*). Both Mountain Chickadees, of western Canada and the United States, and Carolina Chickadees, of the southeastern United States, are known to hybridize with Black-capped Chickadees. While Mountain/Black-capped hybrids are relatively scare, Carolina/Black-capped hybrids are fairly common in certain areas, and the whole problem of interaction at the interface of these two chickadees' ranges has received much attention (e.g., Brewer 1963, Rising 1968, Johnston 1971, Braun and Robbins 1986, Gill et al. 1989). Everyone recognizes that there are substantial differences between Mountain and Black-capped Chickadees; nobody has seriously suggested lumping them. However, there is definite disagreement over whether Carolina and Black-capped Chickadees are really sufficiently different to be regarded as separate species or just races of a single species. This question is not easily resolved.

Many of the existing data have been interpreted as supporting each side of the debate. The breeding ranges of Carolina and Black-capped Chickadees are for the most part contiguous but nonoverlapping; indeed, actual narrow gaps often exist between the two ranges where no chickadee breeds. Those favoring two separate species suggest that these gaps may be the result of interspecific competitive exclusion (Tanner 1952). Others, who dispute the two-species theory, see the gaps as merely habitat of such poor quality that no chickadee would settle and breed there (Robbins et al. 1986).

Whatever the causes of these narrow gaps, contact is made in several places within the midwestern states (from Kansas east to Illinois) and in the southern Appalachians, where interbreeding apparently is fairly regular. In such contact zones, it is not unusual to find chickadees that can sing the two-note fee-bee of Black-capped Chickadees, the four-note fee-bee, fee-bay of Carolina Chickadees, and several intermediate whistled vocalizations as well (Johnston 1971, Merritt 1981; see Fig. 1-3). Ward and Ward (1974)

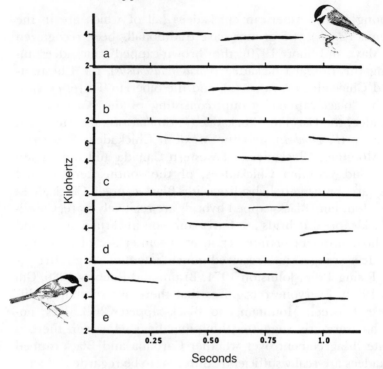

Fig. 1-3. Tracings of spectrograms of Missouri chickadee vocalizations, showing a normal Black-capped
Chickadee song (a); a normal Carolina Chickadee song
(e); and two-, three-, and four-note songs, all sung by a
single individual, of unknown affinities, from the contact
zone (b–d). Kilohertz scale is logarithmic. (From Robbins
et al. 1986, courtesy of *Auk*.)

interpreted this apparent convergence in song pattern as evidence
of interspecific competition between the two kinds of chickadees,
suggesting it represents vocal mimicry between members of two
different species. There is much to support the Wards' views.
Whistled songs can be involved in repelling rivals (Ficken 1981b).
Moreover, chickadees do imitate; in fact, each young Black-
capped Chickadee probably must learn (by imitation) what to
whistle (Ficken 1981b). When Donald E. Kroodsma played taped
whistled songs to mixed groups of hand-reared nestling Black-
capped and Carolina Chickadees (all from nests well outside the
contact zone), he found that each kind readily learned to imitate
elements of the other's whistled songs (D. E. Kroodsma, pers.

comm.). Furthermore, a chickadee may be able to continue to add new notes it hears to its repertoire throughout its life. A chickadee in the contact zone would hear both songs, and could well experiment with various combinations of the notes, using whatever combination is most effective in driving off any given rival. With such imitative abilities, a chickadee's song should not, as Robbins et al. (1986) seem to claim, necessarily indicate the genetic makeup of the singer.

Black-capped and Carolina Chickadees differ behaviorally in many ways. For example, their precopulatory vocalizations, by both males and females, are very different (see Copulation, Chapter 5). Another area of divergence is their winter social organization: Carolina Chickadee flocks can have markedly less stable dominance hierarchies than those of typical Black-capped Chickadee flocks, and not infrequently have unbalanced sex ratios, even when first formed (Mostrom 1988), a decidedly unusual phenomenon in Black-capped Chickadee flocks over most of their range (see Flock Formation and Flock Composition, Chapter 7). In addition, the mechanisms underlying whistled song production in the two chickadees may be quite different. In the whistled fee-bee of Black-capped Chickadees, relative pitch seems to be far more important than the absolute pitch of the song; that is, a bird may show considerable variability in how high the first note of a song is, but far less variability in the pitch interval between adjacent notes (Weisman et al. 1990). By contrast, Carolina Chickadees seem to rely much more on absolute pitch of their songs (Lohr et al. 1991). Such behavioral differences, while not constituting proof, nonetheless support the idea that the two chickadees are different species.

Recently, an entirely new approach, involving biochemical analysis, has been used. One such method entails the analysis of tissue samples for protein (and, more specifically, enzyme) similarity. The enzymes studied are referred to variously as allozymes, isozymes, or electromorphs. The idea behind this analysis is that the structure of these enzymes can give information concerning the genetic material that codes for the enzymes' manufacture within the cells. The greater the difference in the allozymes, the greater the genetic difference, and hence the more likely the samples are from two different species. Conversely, if few or no differences are found, the samples may represent only one species.

While the reasoning seems clear, there are evidently many pitfalls associated with interpretation and analysis of the data. Results can vary depending on which enzymes were examined and even on which computer program was used (e.g., Gill et al. 1989, Springer and Krajewski 1989). Nevertheless, although an early study (Braun and Robbins 1986) indicated that there was virtually no difference between Black-capped and Carolina Chickadees, a somewhat more extensive analysis by Gill et al. (1989), involving most of the same allozymes and analyzed by the same computer program, suggested fairly substantial differences between the two. Indeed, this later study seems to indicate that the Black-capped Chickadee is genetically closer to the Mountain Chickadee and even the Mexican Chickadee than to the Carolina Chickadee, and that it is closer to the Chestnut-backed and Boreal Chickadees than it is to the Eurasian Willow and Marsh Tits (Fig. 1-4).

Using a somewhat different approach, Mack et al. (1986) examined nucleotide sequences in the mitochondrial DNA of Black-capped and Carolina Chickadees and found considerable dif-

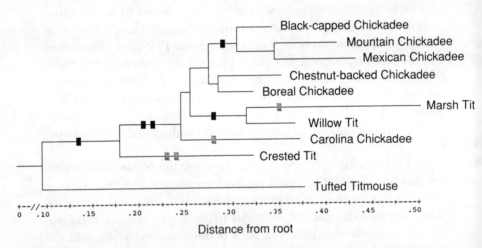

Fig. 1-4. Genetic relationships among chickadees and titmice of the subgenus *Poecile*, portrayed as a distance Wagner tree. Black rectangles indicate shared, derived alleles (suggesting closeness); pepper rectangles indicate alleles unique to species (suggesting distance). According to these data, the Black-capped Chickadee is more closely related to Chestnut-backed and Boreal Chickadees than to either Willow Tits or Carolina Chickadees. This tree is a subset of a fuller set of species rooted with the nuthatch genus *Sitta*. Total length of the full tree = 2.86; percent SD = 10.99. (From Gill et al. 1989, courtesy of *Wilson Bulletin*.)

ferences between the two. In light of this study and the one by Grill et al., and with a note of caution based on Braun and Robbins's data and the fact that hybridization undoubtedly occurs, I will follow the lead of the latest (1983) AOU checklist, and treat these two chickadees as closely related but distinct species.

## Subspecies

The Black-capped Chickadee is nonmigratory, and its enormous geographic range encompasses a wide variety of climates and habitats. For these reasons, Black-capped Chickadees show marked local variation in size and, to some extent, plumage. Where recognizably different populations occur, especially if they seem to show little geographical overlap, they are often described as subspecies.

There is some disagreement as to how many valid subspecies of Black-capped Chickadees there actually are. For example, Snow (1967) recognized only seven subspecies, although both Duvall (1945) and the 1957 AOU checklist (the last one to include subspecies) recognized more. The nine subspecies of Black-capped Chickadees listed by the 1957 AOU checklist (see Fig. 1-5) are described below.

The eastern black-capped chickadee, *Parus atricapillus atricapillus* Linnaeus, ranges from west of the Great Lakes to the Atlantic, and from James Bay in the north down to central Missouri and northern New Jersey in the south. The back is olive-gray, and the wings have broad white edgings on the secondaries and wing coverts. The flanks are strongly tinged with buff, especially in early fall. Measurements (from Duvall 1945): adult males (36 specimens), wing 60–67.5 mm (average, 65.1 mm), tail 58.5–66 mm (average, 62.1 mm); adult females (31 specimens), wing 60–67 mm (63.4 mm), tail 57–64 mm (60.5 mm). See also Glase 1973 and Gochfeld (1977 for further measurement data.

The Appalachian black-capped chickadee, *P. a. practicus* Oberholser, lives from Ohio and southwestern Pennsylvania south along the Appalachian Mountains to the Great Smokies. It is somewhat smaller than the eastern black-capped chickadee and has a shorter tail; the upper parts are darker and less green, and the white edgings on the wing coverts and tail feathers are less broad. Measurements (from Duvall 1945): adult males (12 specimens), wing 61.5–67 mm (64 mm), tail 57–61.5 mm (59.9 mm);

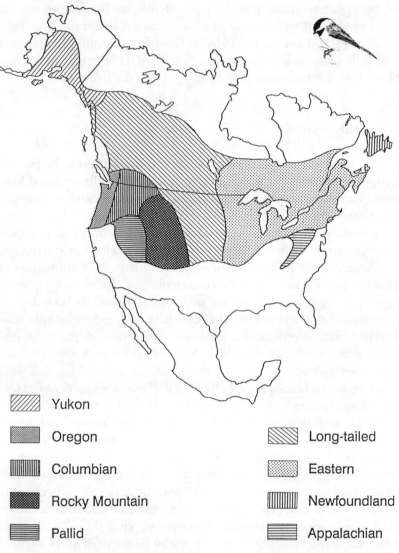

| | |
|---|---|
| ▨ Yukon | |
| ▦ Oregon | ▧ Long-tailed |
| ▥ Columbian | ▦ Eastern |
| ▰ Rocky Mountain | ▥ Newfoundland |
| ▤ Pallid | ▤ Appalachian |

Fig. 1-5. Breeding range of the Black-capped Chickadee, showing the distribution of the nine subspecies recognized by the 1957 AOU checklist. Of these, Snow (1967) recognized all but the Columbian and Rocky Mountain forms, which he lumped with the long-tailed chickadee (Columbian) and pallid chickadee (Rocky Mountain). The boundaries between the subspecies' ranges are probably far less clear-cut than they appear here.

adult females (12 specimens), wing 59.5–65.5 mm (63 mm), tail 57–60.5 mm (59.3 mm).

The Newfoundland black-capped chickadee, *P. a. bartletti* Alrich and Nutt, is restricted to the islands of Newfoundland and Miquelon. It is darker and slightly larger than the eastern black-capped chickadee, browner above, and has darker buff on the sides and flanks. Measurements (from Duvall 1945): adult males (7 specimens), wing 65–68 mm (66.4 mm); tail 59–64 mm (62.4 mm); adult females (6 specimens), wing 61–64.5 mm (62.3 mm), tail 57.7–61.5 mm (60 mm).

The long-tailed chickadee, *P. a. septentrionalis* Harris, inhabits west central Canada and central United States. It has markedly longer wings and tail than the eastern black-capped chickadee, and still broader white edgings on the wing and tail feathers. Measurements (from Duvall 1945): adult males (62 specimens), wing 64.5–73 mm (68.7 mm), tail 63–72.5 mm (67.4 mm); adult females (30 specimens), wing 64–71 mm (67.2 mm), tail 64–71 mm (64.2 mm).

The Oregon chickadee, *P. a. occidentalis* Baird, is the West Coast form of the Black-capped Chickadee, ranging from southwestern British Columbia (excluding Vancouver Island) south to northwestern California. It is a particularly distinctive form, being decidedly smaller than the eastern black-capped chickadee and considerably darker. The back tends to be dark gray-brown, and the sides and flanks are much richer buff than in most other races, especially in autumn and early winter. The white edgings on the wings and tail are narrower than in many other races, also contributing to the overall dark appearance of these western birds. Measurements (from Duvall 1945): adult males (41 specimens), wing 57.5–64 mm (61.2 mm), tail 53.5–60.5 mm (57.1 mm); adult females (35 specimens), wing 57.5–63.5 mm (60 mm), tail 53–59.5 mm (56 mm).

The pallid black-capped chickadee, *P. a. nevadensis* (Linsdale), inhabits the Great Basin area, ranging south to northern Arizona and Utah. The birds are about the same size as the long-tailed chickadee, but are even paler and have broad white edgings on the wing and tail feathers. Measurements (from Duvall 1945): adult males (22 specimens), wing 64–72.2 mm (68 mm), tail 64–71.6 mm (67.5 mm); adult females (13 specimens), wing 63.5–70.5 mm (66.9 mm), tail 63.5–70.5 mm (67 mm).

The Rocky Mountain black-capped chickadee, *P. a. garrinus*

Behle, inhabits much of the Rocky Mountain area of the United States. It is a fairly large, buffy chickadee, about the same size as the long-tailed chickadee, but with a brown back and strongly buff rump. Both the wing and tail feathers have quite broad pale edgings. It was lumped by Snow (1967) with the Pallid black-capped chickadee. Measurements (from Behle 1951): males (10 specimens), wing 64.3–70.6 mm (68.6 mm), tail 61.5–69.8 mm (66.7 mm); females (10 specimens), wing 63.4–76.7 mm (67.6 mm), tail 63.1–70.0 mm (65.6 mm).

The Columbian black-capped chickadee, *P. a. fortuitus* (Dawson and Bowles), lives in southern British Columbia (except on the coast) and in Washington and Oregon east of the Cascades. A decidedly buffy race, it is very similar to the Rocky Mountain form, but is somewhat smaller, and the back and rump are essentially the same shade. Snow (1967) lumped it with the long-tailed chickadee. Measurements (from Duvall 1945): adult males (27 specimens), wing 60–67 mm (64.1 mm), tail 57.5–65 mm (62.1 mm); adult females (23 specimens), wing 59–67 mm (63.2 mm), tail 57–65 mm (61.4 mm).

The Yukon chickadee, *P. a. turneri* Ridgway, inhabits Alaska, extreme northwestern British Columbia, the Yukon and western Northwest Territories north to the tree line. It is a fairly large, pale form with a pale gray back, sides and flanks very pale buff, and with very broad white edgings on the wing and tail feathers. Measurements (from Duvall 1945): adult males (20 specimens), wing 61–68 mm (65.4 mm), tail 62–70.5 mm (65.7 mm); adult females (15 specimens), wing 61–66.5 mm (63.6 mm), tail 61–66 mm (63.7 mm).

# 2

# Some Study Techniques

This chapter discusses a few of the more common techniques applied in the study of chickadees and titmice along with a few that seem to have especially exciting potential for use in future research.

## Banding

Banding is essential for many areas of chickadee research. The most common ways to catch chickadees are with mist nets (Fig. 2-1), often using playbacks of vocalizations to help attract chickadees into the nets, and with wire traps (McCamey 1961). Very young chickadees can be banded before they leave the nest, preferably when they are about ten days old; that is, old enough to have legs the right size but too young for handling to cause early fledging.

Much important information can be obtained through the use of aluminum bands alone (see, for example, Loery and Nichols 1985, Loery et al. 1987). For many kinds of research questions, however, it is necessary to be able to identify individuals from a distance. Sight identification is typically achieved by the use of auxiliary markers such as color bands. When each individual is

Fig. 2-1. A Black-capped Chickadee caught in a mist net. Mist nets are particularly effective for catching every flock member, including those that are relatively shy.

given its own set of colors, it can easily be distinguished by sight, making further handling unnecessary.

Investigators have been using color bands on chickadees for many years (e.g., Butts 1931; Odum 1941a, 1941b). Few questioned the effect of this technique until Burley (1981) reported that mate choice of Zebra Finches (*Poephila guttata*) can be influenced to a measurable extent by color bands: both males and females apparently preferred to spend time with birds wearing red bands rather than with birds wearing bands of any other color, or even with unbanded finches. Not too surprisingly, Burley's data caused quite a stir among researchers. Although Burley's interpretation of her original data was challenged (Immelmann et al. 1982), she and her colleagues later published additional data that support her claims (Burley et al. 1982; but see also Ratcliffe and Boag 1987). The fact that the bills of juvenile Zebra Finches are black and those of adults are orange-red may explain the apparent preference for red bands, red being a signal of sexual maturity in this species. Similarly, Metz and Weatherhead (1991) discovered that both red and black color bands, when placed on male Red-winged Blackbirds (*Agelaius phoeniceus*), can act as social signals.

Will a chickadee's chances of obtaining a mate be influenced by the colors it happens to be given when it is banded? For several reasons, I suspect the answer is no. Unlike Zebra Finches, chickadees do not have any natural color changes that signal sexual maturity. Moreover, since much of pair formation occurs during flock formation (see the section on pair formation in Chapter 5), most chickadees will already be paired before they are banded. Nevertheless, some pair formation does occur at other times of the year. Because it remains to be proven that a chickadee's color bands have no effect whatsoever on its relations with other chickadees, banders should randomize colors among birds.

When handling wild birds, banders should take precautions to guard against ticks that might carry the spirochete that causes Lyme disease, because several avian species are now known to harbor carrier ticks (Anderson et al. 1990, Burgess 1990; see Parasites and Diseases, Chapter 9).

## Aging and Sexing Techniques

Chickadees that are less than a year old can be distinguished from older birds relatively easily. Two methods can be used. One is to check for skull pneumatization. As a chickadee develops, the growing bones (in this case, those of the skull) become thicker and typically come to include many very small pockets of gas; hence the term *pneumatization*. Young chickadees' darker, less pneumatized skulls can easily be told apart from the paler, more pneumatized skulls of the older birds. However, this technique is effective only in late summer and early fall because most young chickadees' skulls are fully pneumatized by mid-October (Yunick 1980, 1981; Meigs et al. 1983). The other technique involves examining the tail feathers. In autumn, when most banding is done, juvenile chickadees' tail feathers, which start to grow in the nest, are actually older and thus more worn than those of adults, which are grown during the postbreeding molt of late summer and early fall. Owing in part to this differential wear, first-year chickadee tail tips are more pointed and have less pale edging than those of adults (Fig. 2-2). This difference, described for Black-capped Chickadees by Meigs et al. (1983), is easily seen after a bit of practice and can be used to age chickadees with well over 90 percent accuracy. Moreover, it remains useful throughout the fall and early winter.

Sexing chickadees accurately presents more of a problem. A few years ago Mosher and Lane (1972) suggested that males and females could be told apart by the shape of their caps and bibs: males, they thought, had bibs that were fairly broad just below the bill, with poorly defined lower margins, while females' bibs were

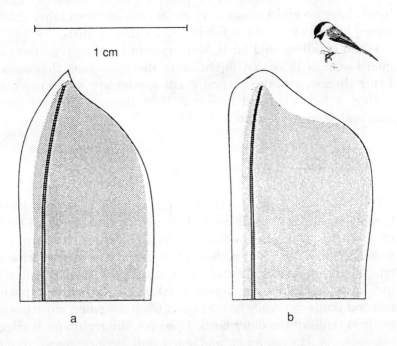

Fig. 2-2. The age of Black-capped Chickadees can be determined by examining the tail feather (rectrix) tips. (a) Representative immature (first basic) outer rectrix. The feather is pointed and worn, showing no white on the tip of the inner vein. (b) Representative adult (basic) outer rectrix. The feather is less worn than that of an immature and usually shows some white on both edges of the feather tip. (Modified from Meigs et al. 1983.)

Table 2-1. Plumage categories of Black-capped Chickadees

| | | | Males | | Females | |
|---|---|---|---|---|---|---|
| Bib shape | Bib margin | Cap margin | Adult | Juvenile | Adult | Juvenile |
| Wide | Rough | Truncate | 6 | 1 | 5 | 2 |
| | | Pointed | 2 | 0 | 1 | 0 |
| | Smooth | Truncate | 11 | 2 | 2 | 3 |
| | | Pointed | 8 | 3 | 6 | 0 |
| Pinched | Rough | Truncate | 4 | 1 | 5 | 1 |
| | | Pointed | 3 | 1 | 1 | 1 |
| | Smooth | Truncate | 4 | 3 | 4 | 3 |
| | | Pointed | 2 | 1 | 4 | 0 |

Statistical comparison (adult and juveniles combined)

| | Males | Females | | Males | Females |
|---|---|---|---|---|---|
| Wide | 33 | 19 | Rough | 18 | 16 |
| Pinched | 19 | 19 | Smooth | 34 | 22 |
| | FEP2 > .30 | | | FEP2 > .50 | |

| | Males | Females | | Males | Females |
|---|---|---|---|---|---|
| Truncate | 32 | 25 | Wide-pointed | 12 | 7 |
| Pointed | 20 | 13 | Pinched-truncate | 13 | 13 |
| | FEP2 > .30 | | | FEP2 > .30 | |

Source: Gochfeld 1977.
Note: Mid-April to mid-September plumages. FEP2 = Fisher exact probability test (two-tailed, designated).

supposed to be narrower right under the bill and to have sharper, more clear-cut lower margins. As for caps, they claimed that the hind end, where the cap joins the back, was neatly squared in females and more pointed in males (Mosher and Lane 1972). Gosler and King (1989) found similar sex-related differences in bib shape in a British population of Coal Tits (*Parus ater*). Unfortunately, this method, even if accurate in a small population of Black-capped Chickadees, seems not to be of general use. The careful work of Gochfeld (1977) showed that, while variability in these characters does exist, it is not broadly correlated with sex differences in this species (Table 2-1). No consistent differences were found either between males and females or between adult immature birds.

Several morphological measures can help determine the sex of a chickadee in the hand once the subspecies is known; as shown at the end of Chapter 1, the nine subspecies of the Black-capped Chickadee exhibit markedly different measurements. One important measure is wing length. In general, males have longer wings than do females (Glase 1973, Weise 1979). This indicator must be used with caution, however, because chickadee wings get longer with age (Blake 1956, Stewart 1963, Glase 1973). It is therefore necessary to know a chickadee's age before using wing length to determine its sex. Furthermore, in most populations there is at least some overlap in wing length, so individuals with intermediate-length wings must be sexed by some other means. Another measure is tail length. Males typically have longer tails than do females, although here again there is considerable overlap. Most males also weigh more than most females—yet chickadee weights (or mass) vary from season to season, and also with time of day (Lawrence 1958), so both season and time must be standardized before such data will be useful. Perhaps the best way to sex chickadees is to use a combination of wing and tail length and weight. Indeed, Desrochers (1990) found that by using a discriminant analysis of these three measures, he could accurately sex over 90 percent of both males and females in his population.

Besides such morphological clues, various behavioral indices, such as how often a bird gives gargle vocalizations, can also give some indication of sex. Males are far more likely to give this call, particularly in the nonbreeding season (Ficken, Ficken, and Witkin 1978; Weise 1979).

Laparotomy, a surgical procedure in which a bird is anesthetized, cut open, and the gonads examined, can give unequivocal data on the sex of birds in the hand (Risser 1971). Ketterson and Nolan (1986) showed that laparotomized individuals of larger species, such as sparrows and juncos, had just as good long-term survival as did unlaparotomized controls. Nevertheless, even these experienced investigators reported that a few birds died while they were improving their technique in giving the anesthetic and in performing the operation itself. Chickadees, being quite a bit smaller, would be still harder to laparotomize. Recently a new and related technique, known as laparoscopy, was used on passerines (Richner 1989). This process uses fiber optics, specifically a diagnostic arthroscope, to observe the gonads of the birds. Richner (1989) claimed that this technique is faster and less harmful than laparotomy; however, it has yet to be tested on birds as small as chickadees. Perhaps someday researchers (who can afford it) may sex chickadees using some of the new high-technology methods of DNA analysis. These include sex-specific DNA probes from blood samples, a method recently developed for geese (Quinn et al. 1987, 1990), and flow cytometry (fluorescence-activated cell sorting), in which the DNA content of blood or other nucleated tissue samples is compared with that of reference cells (Nakamura et al. 1990, Tiersch et al. 1991). Meanwhile, sexing chickadees on the basis of behavioral observations, while taking longer to confirm, seems preferable to subjecting them to the risks of tissue sampling, laparotomy, or even laparoscopy, especially in studies where survivorship is being measured.

### Nest Boxes

Black-capped Chickadees do not readily accept nest boxes, nor do the closely related Willow Tits (*Parus montanus*) of Europe. In contrast, several other European titmice, such as Great (*P. major*) and Blue (*P. caeruleus*) Tits, actually seem to prefer such nest sites (Perrins 1979).

Nevertheless, a rather simple trick can markedly increase the chances of a box's being used by chickadees. Kluyver (1961) found that nest boxes can be made far more acceptable by filling them half-full of sawdust. The sawdust provides the chickadees with something they can excavate. Kluyver used boxes that had entrance holes of 3.0–3.5 cm (about 1¼ inches) in diameter.

Because so many European tits use nest boxes readily, most of the really interesting techniques involving boxes have been devised for these species; only a few of these techniques have been applied to Black-capped Chickadees so far. Mechanical devices can be attached that can record each time a bird enters or leaves the nest (Fig. 2-3). Boxes with one or more glass sides have been constructed, allowing inside activities to be monitored, either by a video camera or by an observer in a blind close-by. The perch at the entrance of a box can be rigged to a scale so that the weight of the entering bird (plus any food it might be carrying) can be measured (Perrins 1979). Nest boxes have even been converted into metabolic chambers so that precise physiological measurements can be made of the occupants (Haftorn and Reinertsen 1985).

Fig. 2-3. A Black-capped Chickadee with food for its nestlings at a nest box that has contact apparatus. The entering parent moves a hanging strip, which makes the chronograph operate, yielding a record of each time an adult enters or leaves the nest. (From Kluyver 1961, courtesy of *Auk*.)

Grundel (1987, 1990) applied some of these techniques very effectively to nesting Mountain Chickadees (*Parus gambeli*). He got his chickadees to nest in cement nest boxes (see also Dahlsten and Copper 1979) and then constructed three automated camera systems around cement nesting boxes identical to those used by the chickadees. Each was mounted with a movie camera and an electronic flash. When a brood was ready to be recorded, he could transfer it from the regular nest box to the camera box. A photocell activated by a bird passing through the nest entrance triggered the camera shutter and flash. The camera then photographed each bird as it entered (showing kind, number, and size of food being carried) and again as it left. A watch mounted near the entrance allowed precise timing data to be taken. Dots painted on each parent's forehead allowed each bird to be distinguished on the film.

Several of the nest box techniques might profitably be applied to nesting Black-capped Chickadees. Areas where nest boxes are most likely to be accepted by chickadees include suburban settings: places that have plenty of canopy to provide food for the offspring but relatively few unpruned older trees, where natural cavities might occur.

## Ptilochronology

Ptilochronology, a technique recently pioneered by Thomas C. Grubb, Jr., is based on the fact that as each feather grows, it produces marks, termed *growth bars,* that reflect daily growth. These bars are most visible in the larger feathers of the wings and tail; they run more or less at right angles to the length of the feather. There is somewhat of a knack to seeing these bars. It is best to tilt the feather back and forth under a bright light to pick them out; they will appear as a series of alternating darker and paler bands. Evidently the darker bands are derived from material laid down during the day, and the paler bands, from material laid down during the night (Grubb 1989). Of greatest importance to researchers is that the breadth of the growth bars apparently reflects the bird's nutritional status when the feather was being grown.

Grubb (1989) suggested that researchers experimentally induce the growth of new feathers to learn more about the nutritional ecology of a species. One can capture a bird, mark it for future identification, then pluck, label, and save one standard feather, such as the right outer tail feather. After the bird has grown a replacement feather (in about six weeks or so), recapture the bird, collect the induced feather, and compare it with the one removed earlier.

Ptilochronology has already been applied to parid ecology (see, for example, Grubb and Cimprich 1990a, 1990b and Hogstad 1990b). It seems to be a particularly sensitive method for measuring the effect of various events or conditions on the nutritional ecology of free-living birds.

## Telemetry

One of the most exciting new techniques to be used on parids is radio telemetry. Various kinds have been developed, some of which have been used in studies of European tits.

Reinertsen and Haftorn (1983) implanted small (0.75-gram) transmitters into the bodies (intraperitoneal cavities, to be precise) of Willow Tits. This technique allowed them to obtain continuous recordings of deep body temperatures of undisturbed birds. Indeed, their setup permitted continuous recordings for almost 500 hours. However, because the strength of the signal is not very great, this kind of recording is best done on captive birds.

East and Hofer (1986) did a pilot study on radio-tracking free-living Great Tits in England. They considered various methods of attachment for the transmitters, including direct adhesion, harnesses, and tail clips. Direct adhesion has the advantage of being lighter than the other two, since the glue is lighter than either a harness or a tail clip; nevertheless, East and Hofer rejected this method because removal of the transmitter could result in dangerous reduction of the insulative properties of the feathers it had been attached to. They avoided harnesses for fear of disrupting the birds' balance and because the harnesses might have become tangled in vegetation. In the end they decided that the least disruptive attachment was tail clips, placed close to the body on the two or three central tail feathers.

East and Hofer, using special receiving equipment, found that the signal from their birds was detectable at distances of up to 50 meters (almost 55 yards) in woodland habitat. The technique allowed them to follow the movement of relatively undisturbed birds, giving information on home range size and movement patterns. In fact, their data led them to speculate that standard observations on free-living Great Tits may be somewhat biased by observer proximity. Although this is potentially an exciting and important technique, some problems remain to be solved before it can easily be applied to Black-capped Chickadees. One is weight. The combination of East and Hofer's radio transmitter plus the tail clip weighed 1.8 grams. For a 29–30-gram bird such as the Great Tit, this is well within the recommended limit of 10 percent of a bird's body mass (Brander and Cochran 1969, Amlaner and MacDonald 1980). For a 10–14-gram bird such as a Black-capped Chickadee, however, this weight is unacceptably high. Another problem is that the batteries East and Hofer used in their transmitters had a mean life of only seven days. Still, as radio miniaturization and the production of superior batteries improves, the day may not be far off when a transmitting device small enough to fit without harm on a Black-capped Chickadee may be developed. Indeed, researchers in Europe recently developed a 0.9-gram transmitter that is suitable for use on Blue Tits (Arie J. van Noordwijk, pers. comm.). Moreover, the life of this transmitter is said to be considerably longer than just one week. Transmitters this small would seem to be perfectly suitable for use on Black-capped Chickadees. If so, it may even now be possible to obtain accurate data on the movements and behavior of undisturbed chickadees in the field.

# 3

# Food and Feeding

One thing a chickadee must do every day of its independent life is find and eat food. Some people assume that in particularly bad weather chickadees do not feed at all. While it is true that they might curtail their activity somewhat and stay in sheltered areas as much as possible, they do have to eat—and the worse the weather, the more they have to eat. Birds are warm-blooded animals, and they need the energy provided by food to keep warm. Additionally, small animals spend more energy in staying warm than do large animals, because the smaller the individual, the greater its ratio of surface area to volume. Put in practical terms, very small creatures such as chickadees have a proportionally greater amount of surface area (over which body heat can be lost) with respect to the volume of warm core where heat can be stored. Various studies on European titmice have shown that birds the size of Black-capped Chickadees need approximately 10 kcal of energy each day (Perrins 1979). One gram of stored fat yields about 9 kcal. But, especially in bad winter weather, all fat reserves are typically depleted by the end of the long night, so the bird must get out the next morning and forage for that day's fuel.

Not only food but also water is essential for Black-capped Chickadees (Fig. 3-1). Although chickadees must have water in some

Fig. 3-1. Chickadees frequently visit water to drink and to bathe. (© Alan Cruickshank / VIREO.)

form throughout the year, probably their greatest need for water comes with the summer's heat. Simple metabolism in the summer can produce about 0.24 kcal in just one hour, even in a resting bird; flight adds to the amount of heat produced. Much of this heat must be dissipated through evaporative cooling (Rising and Hudson 1974). Clearly, the need for evaporative cooling is far lower in cooler seasons, but water must still be obtained. During the winter, Black-capped Chickadees can occasionally be seen eating snow (Bent 1946).

## Diet

Throughout the year, about 70 percent of Black-capped Chickadees' food is animal and 30 percent is vegetable matter (Bent 1946). These proportions vary with the season: most plant material is eaten in the fall and winter, and the chickadees' typical summer diet is almost entirely animal material. Martin et al. (1951) reported that the winter diet of Black-capped Chickadees was approximately 50 percent animal and 50 percent plant material, while in the summer, 80–90 percent of their food was animal.

Plant matter eaten is mostly seeds and berries. Chickadees seem particularly fond of small wax-covered berries such as those of poison ivy (*Rhus radicans*) and bayberry (*Myrica* sp.). In autumn they also eat seed of ragweed (*Ambrosia* sp.), goldenrod (*Solidago* sp.), and staghorn sumac (*Rhus typhina*), as well as other things such as blueberries (*Vaccinium* sp.), blackberries (*Rubus* sp.), wild cherries (*Prunus* sp.), and, where available, fruits of the tulip tree (*Liriodendron tulipifera*) (Bent 1946, Brewer 1963, Baird 1980). In winter, the bulk of their plant food is seeds of coniferous trees. Hemlock (*Tsuga* sp.) seeds are particular favorites (Odum 1942a).

The two animal groups eaten most by Black-capped Chickadees are lepidopterans (moths and butterflies, especially in the form of caterpillars) and spiders (Robinson and Holmes 1982). Chickadees will also eat beetles, true bugs, katydids, cicadas, plant lice, and scale insects. They are even known to eat bees. Other animals, such as centipedes and small snails and slugs, are sometimes also eaten (Bent 1946).

On occasion, chickadees will actually eat some of the hairy caterpillars so often rejected by most other insectivorous birds. These include both gypsy moth (*Limantria dispar*) and tent caterpillars (*Malacosoma americanum*). The only gypsy moth caterpillars I have seen Black-capped Chickadees eating were very tiny, having not yet dispersed from the egg patch. A pair of chickadees fed on the emerging caterpillars, taking turns visiting the patch to get billfulls. I have also seen chickadees repeatedly tearing open "tents" to get at tent caterpillars. Although the caterpillars I have seen chickadees eating were all an inch (2.5 cm) or less in length, reports exist of Black-capped Chickadees eating even larger tent caterpillars (Terres 1940).

Perhaps the most unexpected type of animal food that chickadees eat naturally is animal fat. If a chickadee flock finds a dead mammal, even one as large as a white-tailed deer (*Odocoileus virginianus*), the birds may peck through the skin to get at the subcutaneous fat, returning again and again until the source is depleted. Black-capped Chickadees are also known to eat dead fish—very likely for the fat stored under the fish's skin (Southern 1966). The largest group of chickadees that Hamerstrom (1942) ever saw away from human habitation was feeding on the fat of a dead skunk (*Mephites mephites*). Similarly, Glase (1973) reported aggregations of more than one flock feeding on the fat of a dead deer. Small wonder that chickadees visit suet feeders so readily!

Finally, at least in eastern North America, within the range of sugar maple trees (*Acer saccharum*), chickadees show strong evidence of a fondness for sweet substances. In early spring when the sap runs, icicles of maple sap can form where branches have broken during the winter. Black-capped Chickadees regularly visit these icicles, both to drink if the sap is melting (Fig. 3-2) and to eat the frozen sap. Some hover below and snatch mouthfuls; some actually hang from the larger sap icicles. I have watched a chickadee knock a small sap icicle off a branch, catch it in midair, carry it to a branch, and eat the whole thing. European titmice also show evidence of similar taste preferences. Warren and Vince (1963) found that Great Tits (*Parus major*) prefer sweet to salty, sour, or bitter solutions, and Perrins (1979) reported that Blue Tits (*P. caeruleus*) are known to visit hummingbird-type feeders in England.

At certain times in their lives, chickadees may need extra amounts of particular sorts of foods. One such time is during nestling and early fledgling periods—that is, during posthatching growth and development. Kluyver (1961), working in Massachusetts, recorded 65 food items brought by parent Black-capped Chickadees to their offspring. These were 35 caterpillars, 11 spiders, 10 small insect larvae, 6 termites, 1 white moth or butterfly, 1 pupa, and 1 fly. The points to stress here are that all were animal foods (high in protein to meet growth requirements) and that almost 70 percent were larvae, which are usually softer than adult insects, and thus easier to digest.

Another time of particular nutrient requirements occurs every spring for breeding females. Eggs are costly to produce, being packed with nutrients for the embryos' development during in-

Fig. 3-2. A Black-capped Chickadee drinking sugar maple sap (photograph © Marie Reed).

cubation. Females must obtain food that is particularly rich in protein just before the onset of egg laying (see Factors That Affect the Onset of Breeding, Chapter 5). Moreover, female chickadees must also obtain enough calcium to form strong egg shells. Females of some European tits are known to store bits of snail shell in their gizzards during egg laying (Perrins 1979). A few reports exist of Black-capped Chickadees eating small snails (Bent 1946), and Ficken (1989) reported a case of Boreal Chickadees (*Parus hudsonicus*) that repeatedly ate ash high in calcium (clearly preferring that to ash low in calcium). It is not clear, however, how the preference was related to egg laying because Ficken's observations were made in October, well past the breeding season. I know of no study that focuses directly on how any chickadee species solves the problem of obtaining sufficient calcium for egg-shell production. This remains an interesting area for future research.

## Food Selection and Optimal Foraging

Optimal foraging models are based on the idea that an animal collects food in a manner that will maximize its rate of energy intake (Pyke et al. 1977, Krebs et al. 1978). The animals is assumed to do this by discriminating among alternative sources of energy (Grubb 1979). Foraging animals are expected to "figure" into the equation not only rates of energy intake, but also rates of energy expenditure (usually measured by human investigators in terms of search time, pursuit time, and handling time) (Grubb 1979).

Foraging theory typically assumes a hierarchy of feeding decisions: foragers first choose among habitats, then among patches within habitats, and finally among food items within patches (Stephens et al. 1986). One of the predictions of optimal patch choice theory has to do with a forager's giving up-time. The foraging bird should leave a patch when its rate of food intake there has

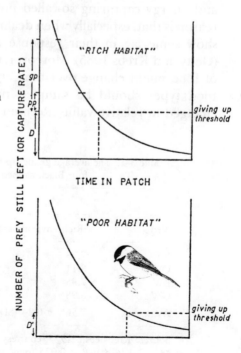

Fig. 3-3. A graphical representation of an optimal foraging model of patch use. The graphs show the number of prey (or food) that survived in a patch plotted against the time the predator (or forager) spent searching in the patch. The two curves show the change in capture rate with time spent searching in a patch (assuming that the capture rate within a patch is proportional to the number of prey present). The predator leaves a patch when its capture rate drops to a critical level, called the giving-up threshold. This model predicts that the giving-up threshold is equal to the average rate of food intake for the habitat. The giving-up threshold is thus higher in the rich habitat (upper graph) than in the poor one. D, prey surviving after predator has left; gp, good patch; pp, poor patch. (From Krebs et al. 1975, courtesy of *Animal Behaviour*.)

dropped to the average rate for that habitat; therefore, the giving-up time should be shorter in rich patches and relatively longer in poorer ones (Fig. 3-3). The behavior of Black-capped Chickadees foraging in aviaries fitted this prediction very well (Krebs et al. 1975): the birds' giving-up time was inversely related to the average capture rate of the environment (Table 3-1). In a study on wild-caught Great Tits, Krebs et al. (1978) found that when given two different patch types of differing profitability, the Great Tits would first sample each one, then exploit the more profitable patch. Although Plowright and Plowright (1987) criticized the interpretation of these data by Krebs et al., Kamil et al. (1988) later demonstrated remarkably similar foraging behavior by Blue Jays (*Cyanocitta cristata*).

Early versions of optimal foraging models predicted that foraging birds would never exhibit partial preferences; rather, for any encounter with food, the response should be either always attack or always ignore (Pyke et al. 1977). Later, however, several studies (all on Great Tits) showed that at least this species does indeed exhibit partial preferences, occasionally rejecting profitable food and taking less profitable items. Why would these birds spend time and energy capturing so-called nonoptimal kinds of food? One reason is that, especially when dealing with cryptic prey, Great Tits show some lag in their response to newly available food types (Getty and Krebs 1985). Moreover, the actual value of a given sort of food might change over time, in which case the "nonoptimal" food types should be sampled periodically in case they have changed in relative value (Rechten et al. 1983).

Table 3-1. The average giving-up times (for all patch types) of four Black-capped Chickadees

| Bird | Giving-up time (s) | |
|---|---|---|
| | Rich environment | Poor environment |
| YY | 7.73 | 11.69 |
| OW | 8.11 | 15.57 |
| BW | 7.45 | 9.94 |
| GW | 6.98 | 8.30 |
| AVERAGE | 7.56* ± 0.24 (SD) | 11.38* ± 1.56 (SD) |

*Source:* Krebs et al. 1975, courtesy of *Animal Behaviour.*
*$t = 2.4$ (6 $df$); $P < 0.025$ (one-tailed).

A theory related to optimal foraging is the optimal diet theory (e.g., Stephens et al. 1986). Barkan and Witham (1989) performed some interesting experiments on prey choice by captive Black-capped Chickadees. They were concerned with what would happen if two sorts of food were available—one more profitable but smaller than the other. One version of the optimal diet model predicts that a predator would maximize its long-term rate of food intake by specializing on the larger but less profitable prey if the encounter rate was sufficiently low. However, Barkan and Witham's chickadees did not behave as this model predicts; they always preferred the higher profitability food type, regardless of encounter rate. Barkan and Witham reasoned that their birds could have been choosing food so as to either minimize pursuit time or maximize profitability; evidently, from the results of their second experiment (Fig. 3-4) the chickadees chose food so as to maximize profitability.

Apparently, foraging chickadees tend to prefer a sure thing over a more uncertain one. Barkan (1990) demonstrated this preference in the field with free-living Black-capped Chickadees. He gave the birds a choice of two food types, each hidden in holes in a feeder. The two types of food had equal expected values but different variances. That is, the two food types had the same energy content and were presented in equal total amounts (equal expected values), but one kind (the low-variance type) was placed in the feeder's holes such that every hole contained the same amount of food, while the other kind (the high-variance type) was distributed such that some holes contained a large amount of food and other holes contained nothing. The chickadees showed a clear, significant preference for the low-variance food (that is, the sure thing). In this regard, the chickadees' behavior fits the predictions of still another variant on optimal foraging, known as the risk-sensitive foraging theory (see, for example, Stephens and Krebs 1986).

Lucas (1987) and others (e.g., Grundel 1990) have pointed out that actual (as opposed to theoretical) foraging by birds in nature is regularly influenced by a wide variety of constraints, each of which may influence different birds in different ways. Some of these constraints are predation (Lima 1985), rank and the presence of more dominant individuals (Pierce and Grubb 1981, Schneider 1984), and the individual's need at that moment for the expression of other sorts of behavior, such as defense of territory

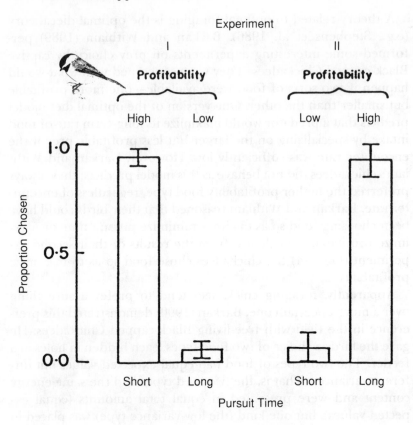

Fig. 3-4. A comparison of the proportion of each food type chosen by four Black-capped Chickadees under two sets of conditions. The chickadees consistently chose high-profitability food, regardless of pursuit time. Error bars indicate ± 2 SE. (From Barkan and Witham 1989, courtesy of *American Naturalist,* © 1989 by The University of Chicago.)

(Ydenberg 1987). Clearly, chickadee food selection, at least that of captive birds, does fit well with some of the predictions of optimal foraging theory and some of its later derivatives. Nonetheless, Lucas (1987) may well have been right when he concluded that foraging by any wild bird is an extremely complex, dynamic process that may never fit very well with sweeping general models.

## Foraging Niche

Exactly where Black-capped Chickadees feed can vary with the individual, the weather, the season, and what is available in the local habitat. Several studies have described this species' feeding niche and compared it with that of other species that have overlapping ranges (e.g., Brewer 1963; Smith 1967b; Sturman 1968a, 1968b). Many of these studies reported on the plant species used, foraging height, and where within the tree or shrub each bird obtained its food (Table 3-2).

More recently, Grubb (1975, 1977, 1978) demonstrated that for at least three parids—Black-capped Chickadees, Carolina Chickadees (*Parus carolinensis*), and Tufted Titmice (*P. bicolor*)—weather (particularly temperature and wind speed) significantly affects many measured aspects of these birds' foraging niches, especially in the winter. Thus in cold and windy conditions, all three species fed at significantly lower heights (where friction results in lessened wind speed) than in warmer, calmer conditions; some of these data are shown in Figure 3-5. Grubb (1975) also found that either cold or wind could cause significant reduction in the number of tree species used in foraging. Actually, this finding may simply reflect the fact that chickadees move significantly less in cold, windy weather (Odum 1942a, Grubb 1978). (The behavioral responses of chickadees to severe winter weather are discussed more fully in the last section of Chapter 8.) In light of Grubb's findings, however, the data from the earlier studies must be viewed with some caution.

Another factor that may affect where a chickadee forages is its rank within the flock's dominance hierarchy (Glase 1973, Desrochers 1989). Glase found that rank has measurable effects on apparent foraging niche of both male and females Black-capped Chickadees. Essentially what he found was that the lower the rank, the smaller the trees used for foraging and the more toward the outer branches of these trees the birds foraged. Desrochers (1989) also found rank-related niche differences among Black-capped Chickadees, although in his study area, the higher ranked birds fed higher and farther from the trunks than did the lower-ranked chickadees. Desrochers (1989) related this apparent difference to differences in local predators, suggesting that in both his and Glase's populations, the dominant birds fed preferentially in the safest foraging sites (see Predators and Antipredator Behavior, Chapter 9). Certain areas will be more profitable than others in terms of energy intake as well as safety. Recently, Gustafsson (1988) showed that older, and presumably more dominant, Coal Tits (*P. ater*) in Sweden occupy the most profitable foraging sites.

Besides studying *where*, one can also ask *how* chickadees forage.

Table 3-2. Percentage of free-living Black-capped and Carolina Chickadees found in foraging locations during autumn/winter and spring/summer

| Foraging position | Black-capped Chickadee | | Carolina Chickadee | |
|---|---|---|---|---|
| | October–March (%) | April–September (%) | October–March (%) | April–September (%) |
| Ground | 9.6 | 0.0 | 7.5 | 0.0 |
| Herb | 13.2 | 5.2 | 5.8 | 4.0 |
| Shrub | 2.9 | 0.0 | 7.0 | 7.0 |
| Vine | 6.6 | 3.4 | 4.8 | 6.0 |
| Tree | 67.6 | 91.4 | 75.0 | 83.0 |
| Small branches | 43.6 | 39.9 | 42.2 | 24.3 |
| Large branches | 12.4 | 11.7 | 14.1 | 12.0 |
| Bole | 11.6 | 18.7 | 15.0 | 12.0 |
| Fruits and flowers | 0.0 | 7.0 | 3.8 | 16.6 |
| Foliage | 0.0 | 14.1 | 0.0 | 18.1 |
| TOTAL NUMBER OF OBSERVATIONS | 136 | 58 | 172 | 100 |

Source: Brewer 1963, courtesy of Auk.

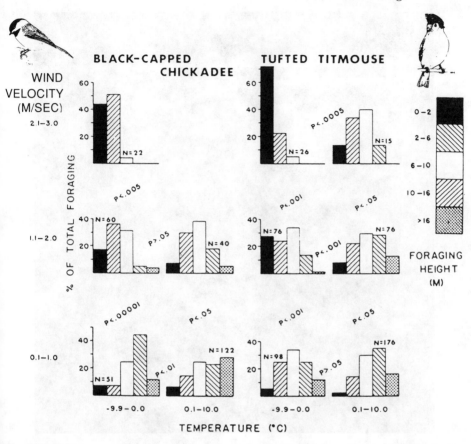

Fig. 3-5. Influence of temperature and wind velocity on foraging heights of Black-capped Chickadees and Tufted Titmice. Both chickadees and titmice foraged lower under windy conditions, especially when the temperature was cold. Probabilities of randomness from two-sample chi-squared tests are shown between adjacent plots. (Modified from Grubb 1975, courtesy of *Condor*.).

Some of the best data on how they forage were obtained by Robinson and Holmes (1982) during the breeding season in New Hampshire. They recognized five major foraging maneuvers used by Black-capped Chickadees: gleaning, hanging, hovering, probing, and hawking. These they defined as follows. Gleaning involves a standing or hopping bird taking a stationary prey item from a substrate. In hanging (Fig. 3-6), the chickadee flies to a leaf or twig, hangs from it, then either takes a prey item directly from the substrate or, more often, manipulates it (for example, uncurls the leaf to get at a caterpillar or spider hidden inside the curl).

Fig. 3-6. Chickadees and their relatives have unusual leg muscles, which enable them to hang upside down while foraging. (Photograph by David G. Allen, courtesy of Bird Photographs, Inc.)

Hovering includes all attacks in which a food item is taken from a substrate while the chickadee is flying. Probing constitutes the maneuvers with the bill when a chickadee explores for hidden insects. And hawking entails a chickadee flying out to catch insects in midair. Of 658 chickadee foraging maneuvers recorded by Robinson and Holmes during the summer, 57 percent were gleaning and 28.7 percent were hanging, while only 8.8 percent were hovering, 3.5 percent were probing, and 2.4 percent were hawking. Hence, at least under the conditions of this study, gleaning and hanging are by far the most important of the Black-capped Chickadee's foraging methods.

The actual proportions of the five maneuvers may well vary with such factors as season, year, and location. Sturman (1968a) found that Black-capped Chickadees in Washington State shifted their foraging position with the kind of tree they foraged in, spending significantly more time hanging in deciduous trees than in conifers. Now that Robinson and Holmes (1982) have shown that the vast majority of chickadee foraging behavior is encompassed by five basic maneuvers, it will be interesting to see how the proportion of these five varies with different ecological conditions.

One important factor that can affect how a chickadee forages is often overlooked by researchers: individual differences. Partridge (1976) found that hand-reared Great Tits developed different preferred feeding methods; each individual had at least one method that it preferred and performed better than other methods. More recently, Sherry and Galef (1984) published data suggesting that foraging Black-capped Chickadees may also show individual specializations. This seems a particularly interesting area for future research.

Chickadees are strongly inquisitive, tending to explore any new material they encounter. As new food items become locally common, chickadees will increase the frequency of the maneuver most appropriate for the new food type. Actually, learning plays a large role in the foraging behavior of chickadees and their relatives. When some enterprising European titmice, including both Blue and Great Tits, discovered that they could open English milk bottles and obtain rich cream from just below the foil caps, the habit spread rapidly (Hinde and Fisher 1952). Although some of the spread of this practice was undoubtedly due to naive birds that found and fed from milk bottles already opened by other tits, as was demonstrated convincingly with wild-caught Black-capped Chickadees (Sherry and Galef 1984, 1990), some of the spread could also have been attributable to imitation. Indeed, social learning, both within and between species, is common among chickadees. John Krebs, studying mixed groups of hand-reared captive Black-capped and Chestnut-backed (*P. rufescens*) Chickadees, found that individuals kept a close eye on the behavior and success of other members of the group. When any group member was successful, the others modified their foraging behavior by increasing the frequency of the successful maneuver. On the other hand, observed persistent lack of success resulted in nearby chickadees lowering their own frequency of the unsuccessful maneuver. By such learning, the chickadees increased their own foraging efficiency (Krebs 1973).

Chickadees must also learn to avoid noxious sorts of food. Not all food items available to chickadees are of the same quality. Among animal prey, certain brightly colored, conspicuous insects are unpalatable or carry stings; among plant foods, some shelled seeds may have failed to develop. Obviously, it is to a chickadee's advantage to be able to discriminate between these various quality foods, thus spending as little energy as possible on unsuitable items (Alcock 1970).

If Black-capped Chickadees are presented with sunflower seeds whose shells are dyed such that one color indicates full seeds and the other color, empty seeds, the chickadees rapidly learn to distinguish between them and to choose primarily seeds of the appropriate (full) color. This ability has been demonstrated both for free-living Black-capped Chickadee flocks as a whole (Hawks 1983) and for color-banded individuals (Hutchins 1989). When first presented with a mixture of full and empty seeds, the birds carried off both colors about equally and hammered the seeds open before discovering that some were empty. Soon afterward, the chickadees picked up seeds at the feeder regardless of color, but dropped the empty ones back into the feeder (using either weight differences or possibly auditory cues); eventually the chickadees came to pick up mostly seeds of the "full" color, to a great extent ignoring seeds of the other color (Hawks 1983, Hutchins 1989).

Still more learning may be involved in selecting among available good-tasting food. Tinbergen (1960) formed a hypothesis to explain his observations on such prey selection by European titmice. He had found that if a prey species ignored by titmice when at low densities increased in abundance, the tits' responses to it also increased, but not in a linear fashion. There appeared to be a critical prey density, beyond which titmice suddenly shifted their feeding patterns and started taking considerable numbers of the prey (Fig. 3-7). Tinbergen suggested that the titmice might be forming what he called a search image. At very low densities, the birds concentrate on other, more common types of prey. As the prey density increases, titmice start to encounter the prey item more and more simply by accident. At a critical encounter rate, the birds shift their hunting patterns to search specifically for this newly common prey

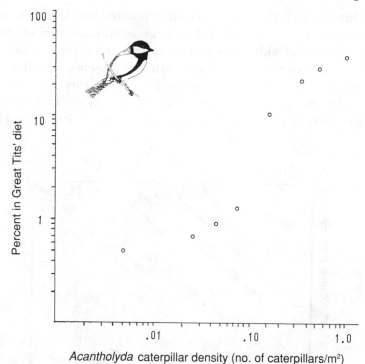

Fig. 3-7. Relationship between the density of a particular food type (*Acantholyda* caterpillars) and the percentage of those caterpillars in the diet of nestling Great Tits. The birds did not start taking many of the larvae until they had become quite common; moreover, the proportion in the diet leveled off at about 80 percent. (Data from Perrins 1979, based on Tinbergen et al. 1960.)

type. More recently, Lawrence (1986) found that hand-reared young Great Tits can in fact develop search images, and he concluded that the development process, while probably very complex, is likely a fundamental characteristic of vertebrate predation.

In an elegant series of experiments, Heinrich and Collins (1983) demonstrated that the foraging behavior of wild-caught Black-capped Chickadees kept in seminatural conditions in large outdoor aviaries is amazingly complex. When presented with 10 birch "trees" (actually large branches), of which 2 had leaf damage and contained hidden insect food, the newly caught chickadees all rapidly learned to use experimentally provided leaf damage as a foraging cue, even though they had shown marked individual differences in foraging behavior when initially caught (which is in itself interesting). Heinrich and Collins pointed out, however, that in nature, the reliability of leaf damage as an indication of food availability varies with tree species. On some trees, such as birches (*Betula* sp.), damage is associated with the presence of palatable caterpillars; on others (e.g., red maples, *Acer rubrum*), it is associated with noxious caterpillars typically rejected by chickadees; and on still others (e.g., alders, *Alnus* sp.), leaf damage bears no correla-

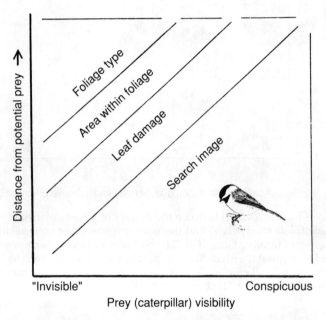

Fig. 3-8. Model showing possible hierarchy of cues used by insectivorous birds such as chickadees to locate prey (caterpillar) on broad-leaved trees as a function of prey visibility. Conspicuous prey can be seen from farther away than can cryptic ("invisible") prey; it is also expected that prey visibility to a bird would increase with experience. Birds may use innate or learned preferences or both for particular kinds of foliage and sites; then when they are closer, leaf damage may lead them to approach either to where they can catch the prey or to where search images can be useful. (From B. Heinrich and S. L. Collins, "Caterpillar Leaf Damage and the Game of Hide-and-Seek with Birds," *Ecology* 64 (1983): 592–602. Copyright © 1983 by the Ecological Society of America. Reprinted by permission.)

tion with the presence of any kinds of caterpillars at all. Hence in order for chickadees to use plant damage information effectively, they should be good plant taxonomists—and indirect evidence so far available suggests that they are (Heinrich and Collins 1983). Clearly Black-capped Chickadees are even more sophisticated foragers than previously imagined.

Heinrich and Collins (1983) developed a model depicting a hierarchy of cues that a foraging chickadee might use in its search for food (Fig. 3-8). As chickadees approach a new area, the first thing they respond to is foliage type (tree species). As they come closer, they will concentrate on a particular area within the foliage, which itself can give some information regarding prey availability. When still closer, the chickadee can use information provided by leaf damage, and finally, it can use whatever search image(s) it may have formed. The model also indicates that each of these cues can be used at a greater distance if the prey is conspicuous than if it is well camouflaged (Fig. 3-8). Heinrich and Collins point out that several factors affect precisely how each individual chickadee fits into this picture. An experienced chickadee may well be able to detect cryptic prey from farther away than can a less experienced bird. Also, as summer progresses, even sedentary caterpillars will pupate or get eaten, thus lowering the reliability of the leaf damage cue. Nevertheless, this is still an excellent overview of chickadee foraging behavior.

## Food Handling

Having considered how and where chickadees search for food, and the kinds of maneuvers and cues they use to obtain it, we can now give some thought to what chickadees do with food once they have it. Chickadees sometimes eat food right where they find it. Often, however, they will carry it off to eat elsewhere; this is the usual pattern seen at bird feeders. Lima (1985) investigated factors that might affect whether free-living Black-capped Chickadees carry off food before eating it. His study was done on winter flocks. He found two factors that affect the choice of eating site: size of the food item, which directly affects handling time (largest items take the longest to handle); and distance to cover, which affects a chickadee's degree of exposure to predators. When distance from cover was held constant, chickadees tended to eat small items where they found them, but as the size of the food increased, so did the chickadees' tendency to carry it away (Fig. 3-9). For food of a given size, the closer it was to cover, the more likely the chickadees were to carry it off before eating.

Having chosen the eating site, chickadees may have to process food before it can be eaten. Chickadees and titmice often hold food with their feet during this procedure (Fig. 3-10). Interestingly, both European titmice (Perrins 1979) and Black-capped Chickadees (pers. observ.) show evidence of "handedness" in this regard—that is, individuals will typically use one foot more readily than the other to hold down or manipulate food. An item thus held is hammered. Some European tits use only the upper mandible for hammering (Perrins 1979); this may also be true for chickadees. While seeds simply need opening, large insects may require considerable attention: heads, legs, wings, and guts may have to be removed before the rest is eaten.

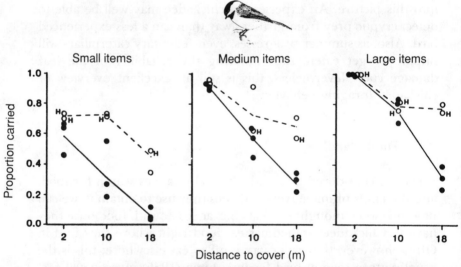

Fig. 3-9. The proportion of items eaten by Black-capped Chickadees that were carried to cover for each item size–distance combination. For each distance to cover, the bigger the food item, the more likely the chickadees were to carry it off before eating it. Moreover, the likelihood of carrying an item off (as opposed to eating it in situ) was greater in high-risk situations (open circles) than in low-risk situations (solid circles), especially at sites farthest removed from cover. The high-risk sessions, during which a hawk model was flown, are indicated with an *H*. The solid and dashed lines indicate the weighted average of the proportions for each combination for the low- and high-risk segments, respectively. (From Lima 1985, courtesy of *Oecologia*.)

Fig. 3-10. Black-capped Chickadees typically hold down seeds with their feet while pounding them open with their bills. This use of feet is widespread among chickadees and their relatives.

## Food Storage and Memory

Many members of the genus *Parus,* including Black-capped Chickadees, are known to store or cache food of all kinds. The bulk of the items they store seems to be seeds, but chickadees also store animal matter, including insects (Heinrich and Collins 1983) and spiders (Lawrence 1958). Insect material is usually prepared before storing: the head is removed, and sometimes other parts as well. Besides natural food, food provided at feeders, such as sunflower seeds and small pieces of suet, are also readily stored where available. Chickadees typically remove the shell from sunflower seeds before caching them (Petit et al. 1989).

Most food storage is done in the fall. Odum (1942a) found for Black-capped Chickadees in New York that the peak of food storage occurred in October and November; he saw none after December. However, given favorable conditions, low levels of food caching probably occur at any time of year. Heinrich and Collins (1963) reported that breeding chickadees stored insects in midsummer, and Brewer (1963) found a Black-capped Chickadee storing a seed in late February. At peak activity, chickadees can store hundreds or even thousands of food items in a day (Sherry 1984a, 1989). Haftorn (1959) estimated that a typical food-storing tit in his study area in Norway stores between 50,000 and 80,000 spruce seeds each autumn.

Storage sites can be practically anywhere. Most commonly, food items are stored in small cracks or crevices in vegetation, including under bits of bark (especially curling birch bark), in curled leaves, in needle clusters of conifers, wedged in the ends of broken branches, or in knotholes (Sherry 1984a). Petit et al. (1989) found that both Black-capped and Carolina Chickadees in the field tend to store food on relatively slender twigs, branches, and trunks; more than 85 percent of the observed caching substrates were less than 8 cm (just over 3 inches) in diameter. When storing in vegetation, both Black-capped and Carolina Chickadees show a strong preference for caching on the undersides of branches (Petit et al. 1989). Chickadees are also known to store food items in the ground and even in the snow. Less natural storage sites include under roof shingles, in gutters, and in drainpipes. Although some parids are known to cover their stored food with a piece of bark or lichen (Sherry 1989), there seems to be no evidence as yet that either Black-capped or Carolina Chickadees ever do this (Petit et al. 1989). Each item is stored in a separate location; this sort of caching is termed *scatter hoarding,* as opposed to *larder formation,* a system in which many items are stored together. Larders are made by a few corvids (crows, jays, and their relatives) and woodpeckers, but are more typical of mammals (Smith and Reichman 1984).

Very likely there is a geographical gradient in frequency of food storage. While hoarding by Black-capped Chickadees is common in more northern populations such as in Ontario (Lawrence 1958) and upstate New York (Odum 1942a), Brewer (1963), working in southern Illinois, saw it on only one occasion. This apparent correlation of hoarding frequency and winter severity is hardly surprising (see Behavioral Adjustments, Chapter 8).

An important advantage of scatter hoarding is that if a competitor discovers a cache, all is not lost. There is a corresponding disadvantage, however: the storer must remember hundreds of storage sites. Hoarding costs energy; Odum (1942a) reported that a single chickadee made 16 trips in six minutes while storing hemlock seeds. For the bird that invested all that energy in storing those food items to have any advantage over pilferers in recovering its stored food, it must have excellent spatial memory. Recent work both on Black-capped Chickadees and on European Marsh Tits (*Parus palustris*) indicates that such memory capabilities are indeed well developed among parids.

David Sherry (1984a, 1984b, 1989) of the University of Toronto has investigated this memory in wild-caught Black-capped Chickadees. His results demonstrate that his birds could accurately relocate their cache sites 24 hours after storage. After having stored food, the chickadees spent significantly more time and visits at hoard sites than at nonhoard sites, but prestorage times and visits had not differed significantly between sites, suggesting that the birds could accurately find the cache sites. (Fig. 3-11). In addition, if they either emptied a site themselves (by recovering and eating

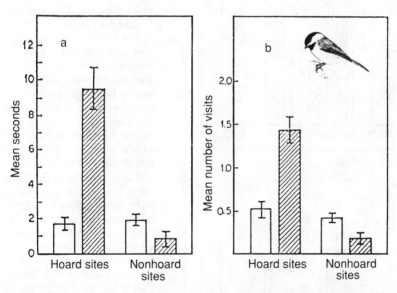

Fig. 3-11. Time spent (a) and frequency of visits (b) by Black-capped Chickadees, both at locations where they had stored food (hoard sites) and where they had not or would not (nonhoard sites). Open bars indicate behavior before food was stored (prestorage), and shaded bars indicate behavior after storage ("search" behavior). (From Sherry 1984a, courtesy of *Animal Behaviour*.)

the stored food) or found a site already emptied (pilfered), they spent significantly less time searching the now-empty site than sites that still contained food (Fig. 3-12). Sherry's chickadees also showed evidence of being able to recall what was stored where. Not all food items have the same energy content, ease of handling, or palatability. When given food items of varying quality to store, chickadees spent most of their subsequent search time at the sites where they had stored the best kinds of food (Fig. 3-13).

What happens if a potential pilferer is watching while a chickadee is busily storing seeds? Recent evidence suggests that very

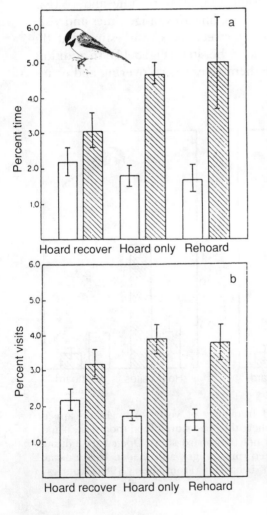

Fig. 3-12. Percent of time spent (a) and percent of visits (b) by Black-capped Chickadees at three sites: hoard-recover, hoard only, and rehoard. Open bars indicate prestorage behavior, and shaded bars indicate search behavior. In the hoard-recover situation, the chickadee had removed its stored food before the experiment; in the other two situations, stored food was still available. Both the time spent and number of visits were much greater in the latter two situations than at sites from which food had already been removed, suggesting that a chickadee can remember which hoard sites it has used and which it has not. Prestorage levels did not differ significantly among themselves for either time or visits. (From Sherry 1984a, courtesy of *Animal Behaviour*.)

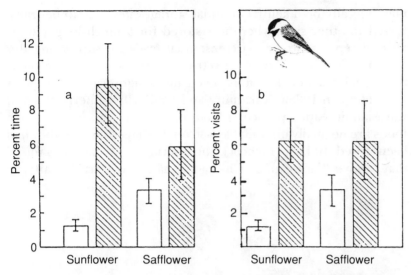

Fig. 3-13. Search levels by Black-capped Chickadees at sunflower and at poorer-quality safflower seed storage sites. Compared with prestorage levels (open bars), chickadees increased their search (shaded bars) time and visit frequency significantly at sunflower seed sites, but not significantly at the safflower seed sites, suggesting that quality of stored food has a marked effect on subsequent recovery efforts. (From Sherry 1984a, courtesy of *Animal Behaviour.*)

little happens at all. Working with wild-caught Black-capped Chickadees, Baker et al. (1988) showed that simply watching another bird store seeds does not help the watcher find those seeds (Figs. 3-14, 3-15), even though the same watcher has no difficulty in recovering its own cached food. Apparently, the perceptual and motor experience of carrying the food to a hiding place and storing it there may be necessary to establish spatial memory in these birds. The presence of other chickadees nearby, however, can affect a given chickadee's hoarding behavior (Stone and Baker 1989, Baker et al. 1990). Individual captive Black-capped Chickadees, when kept with many other chickadees, stored significantly fewer seeds and initiated hoarding later than when kept alone or with just one other chickadee (Stone and Baker 1989). Evidently under natural circumstances a great deal of pilfering may occur, both by other birds and by rodents (Sherry 1989).

Sherry's (1989) work on parids indicates that most individuals recover stored food within a few days of depositing it. As Sherry pointed out, however, this may not be the complete picture—food

may typically be taken from initial storage sites only to be trans-
ferred to other sites, where it is stored for a much longer time.
Several reports provide circumstantial evidence supporting this
view. Parids in captivity often retrieve stored seeds only to cache
them again in new locations. Even more significant are reports
(e.g., Haftorn 1988a, Nakamura and Wako 1988, Sherry 1989) of
Eurasian tits eating particular kinds of foods at seasons when such
foods are normally unavailable—strongly suggesting that they had
been stored. In fact, Hitchcock and Sherry (1990) have now found
that captive Black-capped Chickadees can recover caches after at

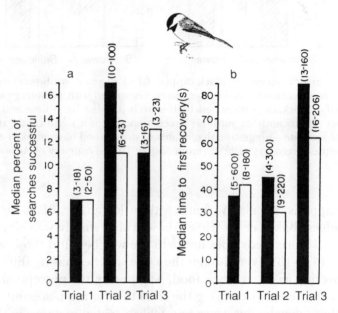

Fig. 3-14. Recovery performance of observer Black-capped
Chickadees two hours after watching demonstrator chickadees
store seeds (black bars) compared with the performance of the
same birds searching for unobserved caches (open bars) made
randomly by the experimenter. Median (range in parentheses)
percent of searches that were successful (a) and the time re-
quired to find the first seed (b) in three trials ($n = 8, 8, 8$), are
shown. If observational learning had occurred, then the recovery performance of birds at observed caches would have been
better than that of birds at unobserved caches. The fact that no
significant differences occurred suggests that there was no
benefit gained from watching a demonstrator. (From Baker et
al. 1988, courtesy of *Auk*.).

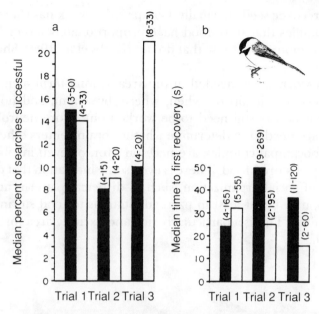

Fig. 3-15. A shorter-term experiment than that shown in
the preceding figure: percent of searches successful (a) and
time to first recovery (b) by Black-capped Chickadees only 6
minutes (range 5–12 min) after watching demonstrator
chickadees cache seeds (black bars) with the performance of
the same birds searching for unobserved caches (open bars)
made randomly by the experimenter ($n = 8, 7, 7$). Again no
evidence of observational learning can be seen; actually, the
only significant difference between the long- and short-
term experiments is that in the short-term the percent of
successful searches at the unobserved sites is higher than at
observed sites. (From Baker et al. 1988, courtesy of *Auk*.)

least 28 days' delay, again suggesting that long-term food storage
may be far more important to parids than had once been thought.

Some important recent research concerns work on the structures of the brain in which memory actually functions. One such
structure is the hippocampus, which is well known to be involved
in the spatial memory of mammals (Sherry 1989). Experiments on
Black-capped Chickadees show that individuals with a damaged
hippocampus recover cached seeds much more poorly than do
undamaged, control birds (Sherry and Vaccarino 1989); that is, a
functional hippocampus may be necessary for a chickadee to be

able to recover seeds normally. Comparative work has shown that avian families that store food have proportionately larger hippocampal regions than those that do not (Krebs et al. 1989, Sherry et al. 1989).

Much work is still needed in the area of long-term memory. It clearly occurs; details on when, where, by whom, and how frequently it occurs still need to be worked out. More neurological studies are needed to determine whether brain centers other than the hippocampal complex are necessary for, or even involved in, recovery of stored food. There is even some indication that certain aspects of social organization, such as dispersal patterns and site tenacity, may be, at least in part, adaptations to food storing (Ekman 1989b). This is a particularly rich and exciting area for future research.

# 4

# Communication

Communication, the transfer of information from one individual to another, is an essential feature of a chickadee's daily life. Naturally, information can be transmitted only by signals that are preceivable to the intended recipient. Chickadees, like most other birds, probably have a fairly poor sense of smell, and their sense of taste is likely no better than our own. Tactile communication by Black-capped Chickadees is essentially unstudied. Most of the chickadee communication that investigators are aware of is vocal and visual. This chapter therefore deals only with displays involving one or both of these sensory modalities.

## Vocalizations

The greatest amount of information published on chickadee communication so far concerns vocal displays. Over the years, many people have tried to describe the "vocabulary" of Black-capped Chickadees. The early attempts (e.g., Forbush 1929, Odum 1942a) were limited to the authors' efforts to render noises, uttered by birds and filtered through human ears, into human syllables. While this method works well for certain vocalizations (virtually everybody recognizes which vocalization the "whistled fee-bee" is meant to indicate), it is not very effective for some of the other, more complex calls.

Later, analysis of vocalizations was made possible through the use of improved recording equipment and the sound spectrograph machine. This machine produces sonograms, which are actually a kind of graph of a sound, with frequency (a measure of pitch) on the vertical axis and time on the horizontal axis (Fig. 4-1); on occasion amplitude (volume) can also be shown. The amount of detail a sound spectrograph machine can give to a sonogram is far greater and more accurate than any human rendering could possibly be.

Studies on the vocal repertoires of several chickadee species have been published: for example, S. T. Smith 1972 on Carolina Chickadees (*Parus carolinensis*), Dixon and Martin 1979 and Gaddis 1985 on Mountain Chickadees (*P. gambeli*), McLaren 1976 on Boreal Chickadees (*P. hudsonicus*), and Ficken 1990b, 1990c on Mexican Chickadees (*P. sclateri*); see Hailman 1989 for a review. For the purposes of this chapter, however, I will focus almost exclusively on the information available on Black-capped Chickadees.

By far the best survey of the vocal repertoire of the Black-capped Chickadee was published in 1978 by Millicent Sigler Ficken and her colleagues at the University of Wisconsin (Table 4-1). This excellent sonographic analysis lists 13 different vocalizations (Ficken, Ficken, and Witkin 1978). To these I have added the flight, or restless, note and the distress call, which were discussed by Odum (1942a) and are also recognized for Black-capped Chickadees by Susan T. Smith (1972). Wherever possible, I have used the terminology of Ficken, Ficken and Witkin 1978.

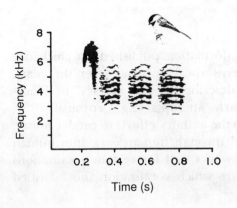

Fig. 4-1. Example of a sonogram: a typical chick-a-dee call as shown by a narrow-band (frequency resolution = 90 Hz) sound spectogram, showing one introductory syllable and three dee syllables. (From Nowicki 1983, courtesy of *Behavioral Ecology and Sociobiology*.)

Table 4-1. Usages of vocalizations of adult Black-capped Chickadees

| Vocalization | Context | Distance[a] between signaler and recipient | Sex[b] | Probable function |
|---|---|---|---|---|
| Fee-bee | On territory or some distance from others during nonbreeding season | L | ♂ | Territorial advertisement? Stimulates female? Leads flock |
| Faint fee-bee | Caller is separated from mate | S, M | ♂, ♀ | Feeding interactions at nest hole; parent-young |
| Gargle | Territorial encounters, agonistic encounters during flocking | S, M | ♂ | Increases distance between caller and recipient in agonistic situation, but not in sexual situation |
| Chick-a-dee call complex | Composition of call varies according to context; given in a variety of situations | M, L | ♂, ♀ | Alerts group members; attracts male or flock; coordinates group movements |
| Broken dee | Reproductive period only | S, M | ♀ | Cements pair bond; may elicit feeding |
| Variable see | Reproductive period only, often precopulatory | S, M | ♀ | Attracts mate; may facilitate copulation |
| Hiss | Surprised at nest hole (usually by predator) | S | ♀ | Deters predation |
| Snarl | Fights | S | ♂ | Increases distance between caller and recipient |
| Twitter | Bird is startled, often at nest hole by mate | S | ♀ | Probably same as above; may also inhibit an attack |
| High zee | Predator present | S, M | ♂ | Alerts group members and induces immobility |
| Tseet | Agonistic encounters | S | ? | ? |

Source: Ficken, Ficken, and Witkin 1978, courtesy of Auk.
[a]S = < 5 m, M = 5–20 m, L = > 20 m.
[b]Indicated as one sex if > 90 percent of calls recorded from one sex.

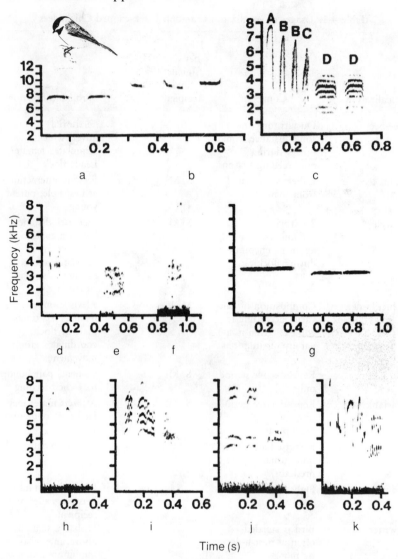

Fig. 4-2. Sonograms of Black-capped Chickadee vocalizations: high zees (a); variable sees (b); chick-a-dee call complex showing A, B, C, and D syllables (c); twitter (d); hiss (e); snarl (f); fee-bee (g); tseets (h); begging dee (i); broken dee (j); and gargle (k). (from Ficken, Ficken, and Witkin 1978, courtesy of *Auk*.)

*Fee-bee.* Most fee-bees (Fig. 4-2g) consist of two clear whistled notes, with the second lower in pitch. Actually, the second note is often composed of two components separated by a very slight pause (about 0.05 second, according to Ficken, Ficken, and Witkin 1978). Moreover, the second of these last two components can be slightly higher than the first, producing a fee-beeyee. Where three tones are involved, the pitch of the third is usually intermediate between the first and second tones. Fee-bees are remarkably uniform over most, and perhaps all, of the Black-capped Chickadee's range.

Fee-bee calling can start in late December, right around the winter solstice, and typically builds to a peak in spring. It is generally fairly frequent in early to midsummer, almost nonexistent (by adults) in late summer, and sporadic in fall and early winter (Dixon and Stefanski 1970).

Although both males and females can give fee-bees, the majority are given by males. Birds giving this vocalization are typically some distance from the nearest other chickadee; Ficken, Ficken, and Witkin (1978) estimated this distance to be at least 10 meters (11 yards). Most fee-bees are given by perched birds (Fig. 4-3); how-

Fig. 4-3. The loud fee-bee songs of male Black-capped Chickadees are a familiar sound in springtime. Note this bird's vertical posture and expanded throat.

ever, chickadees can also give fee-bees in flight, usually while flying toward the site of a territorial confrontation.

Not all of the fee-bees given by a particular chickadee necessarily start on the same pitch; occasionally a chickadee will give
fee-bees that start elsewhere in the scale. Furthermore, these frequency shifts are all apparently in the same direction—that is, the
rarer version, or shifted song, seems always to be lower than the
individual's ordinary fee-bee (Table 4-2). These shifted songs have
been studied using Black-capped Chickadees both in captivity
(Ratcliffe and Weisman 1985) and in the field (Hill and Lein 1987).
Both sexes can give shifted songs (Hill and Lein 1987), but because
males sing so much more frequently, most of the work has been
done with that sex. Although their results were not statistically
significant, Ratcliffe and Weisman (1985) found that their captive
chickadees sang shifted songs more often during playback of recorded chickadee songs than they did when singing alone. This
difference suggests that the shifted song conveys a message of
somewhat increased aggression. Hill and Lein (1987) confirmed
this interpretation, finding that shifted songs occur particularly
frequently after a singing bird has approached to within 10 meters

Table 4-2. Frequency characteristics of normal and shifted
fee-bee songs of Black-capped Chickadees

| Male | | Normal song (kHz) | | Shifted song (kHz) | |
|---|---|---|---|---|---|
| | | *Fee* | *Bee* | *Fee* | *Bee* |
| 1 | $\bar{x}$ | 3.87 | 3.31 | 3.28 | 2.89 |
| | SE | 0.01 | 0.01 | 0.02 | 0.03 |
| | *n* | 6 | 6 | 5 | 5 |
| 2 | $\bar{x}$ | 3.90 | 3.34 | 3.42 | 3.00 |
| | SE | 0.04 | 0.03 | 0.02 | 0.02 |
| | *n* | 5 | 5 | 5 | 5 |
| 3 | $\bar{x}$ | 3.73 | 3.18 | 3.30 | 2.92 |
| | SE | 0.04 | 0.01 | 0.01 | 0.01 |
| | *n* | 4 | 4 | 5 | 5 |
| 4 | $\bar{x}$ | 3.74 | 3.19 | 3.32 | 2.88 |
| | SE | 0.01 | 0.01 | 0.01 | 0.01 |
| | *n* | 5 | 5 | 5 | 5 |

Source: Hill and Lein 1987, courtesy of *Condor*.
Note: *n* = number of songs measured.

of a rival and during countersinging with a rival. Hill and Lein concluded that the frequency-shifted song indicates a higher probability of agonistic behavior, and is thus a more aggressive signal than the normal fee-bee of Black-capped Chickadees. More recent work now suggests that each male Black-capped Chickadee may sing two or more distinct fee-bee vocalizations, which differ from each other only in their pitch (Horn et al. 1989).

For the past three years I have had a banded male chickadee in my study area that sings a truly aberrant version of fee-bee. The first note is whistled normally (fee), but it is seemingly always followed immediately by two notes that sound like the end of a typical chick-a-dee call: fee-dee-dee. When I first heard this, I thought I was hearing two chickadees calling simultaneously—it was a while before I was finally convinced that a single bird was giving all three notes. This chickadee regularly sings fee-dee-dee in vocal duels with other fee-beeing chickadees.

In most parts of North America, Black-capped Chickadees involved in playback experiments respond aggressively only to their own song type rather than to either artificial combinations of notes (Ratcliffe and Weisman 1986, Weisman and Ratcliffe 1987) or the songs of other chickadee species such as Carolina Chickadees. On the other hand, chickadees from the contact zone between Black-capped and Carolina Chickadees do respond aggressively to either song type (Robbins et al. 1986).

The one definite function that Ficken, Ficken, and Witkin (1978) attributed to the fee-bee was that of leading flocks (see Table 4-1). However, Ficken (1981b) later showed that fee-bees also serve to advertise territories and to repel rivals. Recently Weisman et al. (1990) and Ratcliffe (1990) showed that fee-bees may serve to provide information for individual recognition as well, primarily on the basis of the relative pitch of adjacent notes (see Relationships, Chapter 1). S. T. Smith (1972) stated that the whistled song of Carolina Chickadees has similar functions, conveying readiness to perform aggressive and bond-limited behavior.

*Faint fee-bee.* The faint fee-bee is very similar to the fee-bee, but its volume is much lower. Moreover, both its context and message are very different from those of the regular fee-bee.

Faint fee-bees are apparently given only during the breeding season. Both sexes give faint fee-bees, which appear to act as a close-range signal that attracts the mate when it is not in sight.

They are most commonly given during incubation or while the young are still in the nest. The male feeds the female regularly during this period; when he comes to call for her, he typically gives faint fee-bees, after which the female leaves the nest cavity and receives his food. Occasionally, after the female has been on the nest for some time, she will give faint fee-bees, and usually her mate will appear quickly in response (Ficken, Ficken, and Witkin 1978). Faint fee-bees may also be used between parents and fledged young (Dixon and Stefanski 1970).

*Gargle.* The gargle (Fig. 4-2k), which Odum (1942a) referred to as the dominance note, is one of the two most complex calls in the repertoire of the Black-capped Chickadee (the other is the chick-a-dee call complex). Ficken and Weise (1984) studied the gargle in detail and came up with very interesting results. They recognized up to 23 different syllables that chickadees can combine in various ways to make up a complete gargle. Each individual in their study areas probably uses at least 15 different syllable types, which can be given in various combinations. A gargle can consist of from 2 to 13 syllables, and the birds have the ability to produce at least 15 gargle types using these syllables. However, many gargle types are quite rare; the majority are a few more or less standard varieties. What is amazing is the microgeographic variation in this call; indeed, Ficken and Weise discovered that birds at sites less than four miles (roughly 6 km) apart showed major differences in how frequently they used various syllables (Table 4-3). Perhaps even more

Table 4-3. Number of and percentage of total (in parentheses) of the two most common gargle types given by Black-capped Chickadees at various field station sites in Wisconsin

| | Gargle type[b] | |
| --- | --- | --- |
| Site[a] | EKVRFSQ | VRP2Q |
| D7 | 525 (19.7) | 208 (7.8) |
| A8 | 48 (12.2) | 83 (21.0) |
| F9 | 84 (9.2) | 196 (21.6) |
| Riveredge | 0 | 2 (4) |
| Grafton | 0 | 0 |

*Source:* Ficken and Weise 1984, courtesy of *Auk.*
[a]Sites D7, A8, and F9 were all within 650 meters (about 700 yards) of one another. Riveredge was 5.7 km (about 3.5 miles) north of them, while Grafton was 9.8 km (roughly 6 miles) south-east of them.
[b]Each letter represents a separate syllable.

Table 4-4. Occurrence of the 12 most common Black-capped Chickadee gargle types at one particular feeder in different years

| Gargle type | 1970–74 | 1974–77 | 1977–78 | 1978–79 | 1979–80 | 1980–81 |
|---|---|---|---|---|---|---|
| C2RKVP1P2SJ | 18 | 15 | 14 | 42 | 53 | 0 |
| RKIFSQ | 6 | 16 | 13 | 18 | 24 | 1 |
| EKVFP1P2SQ | 2 | 7 | 7 | 31 | 29 | 0 |
| EKVFSQ | 0 | 4 | 4 | 22 | 43 | 0 |
| EKVR | 0 | 3 | 11 | 10 | 31 | 4 |
| LEKVFSQ | 0 | 0 | 0 | 27 | 18 | 5 |
| LHRF | 0 | 2 | 1 | 1 | 16 | 6 |
| LHRFP1P2SJ | 0 | 43 | 0 | 7 | 65 | 5 |
| LHRFSJ | 0 | 0 | 51 | 7 | 1 | 0 |
| KIFSQ | 34 | 16 | 0 | 2 | 0 | 0 |
| EKVRFSQ | 30 | 30 | 75 | 130 | 184 | 38 |
| VRP2Q | 58 | 13 | 14 | 29 | 85 | 6 |

*Source:* Ficken and Weise 1984, courtesy of *Auk.*

amazing, local gargle repertoires apparently change from year to year (Table 4-4).

Although the frequency of occurrence of the gargle types may vary over time, apparently the actual makeup of the gargles themselves is unusually stable. Ficken and Weise (1990) sampled local gargles for 20 years and reported that all 15 major note types persisted, essentially unchanged, as did the most common call types. This persistence was evident both in the intricate fine structure of the notes (as seen in sonographic analysis) and in several precise combinations of notes. Ficken and Weise suggest that such persistence could lead to great stability of local gargle dialects.

Gargles, with their enormous variety, can be used to encode several different messages. Over most of a year, males give gargles far more often than do females. Especially in winter, gargles frequently are given during agonistic encounters. Ficken, Ficken, and Witkin (1978) stated that gargles were a threat display. Later Ficken et al. (1987) concluded that gargles signified a willingness to escalate the encounter: the signaler has no intention of fleeing and will escalate its agonistic behavior if approached. S. T. Smith (1972) pointed out that the message conveyed by rasps (the Carolina Chickadee's equivalent of gargles) differed depending on whether they were directed toward a flockmate or a stranger. Captive Black-capped Chickadees studied by Baker et al. (1991) showed a variable response to gargles, depending on the familiarity of the call: they were noticeably more deterred by unfamiliar

gargles than by more familiar ones. Baker and his colleagues also
found that gargles, while usually involved, were not necessary in
the initial establishment of dominance between two stranger
males.

Ficken et al. (1987) directed their studies to the relationship
between the gargle vocalizations and rank of free-living Black-
capped Chickadees. They found that dominants did not have any
larger or more diverse repertoires of gargles than did subordinates (Table 4-5). Moreover, dominants had essentially the same
amount of sharing of gargle types as did subordinates, and apparently dominants did not address particular syllable combinations
to specific individuals.

Gargles given in aggressive interactions in nonbreeding flocks
or when one chickadee invades another's breeding territory are
directed toward one particular bird (the subordinate or invader).
Juvenile males in late summer and young birds of either sex in
early spring, however, can be heard giving highly repetitive
gargles that are apparently not directed at any bird in particular
(pers. observ.); such repetitive gargling may convey a somewhat
different message from the more common, directed notes. Gargles
can also be used in sexual contexts, in which they are seldom, if

Table 4-5. A comparison of Black-capped Chickadee dominance rank, individual
repertoires of gargle notes, and Shannon-Wiener (S-W) diversity index

| Site no. | Year | Dominance rank | No. of gargle types | No. of gargles | S-W index |
|---|---|---|---|---|---|
| D7 | 1978–79 | 1 | 14 | 40 | 3.35 |
| | | 2 | 12 | 50 | 2.37 |
| | | 3 | 7 | 54 | 0.88 |
| | | 7 | 8 | 22 | 2.17 |
| | | 11 | 8 | 26 | 2.47 |
| | | $\rho s = -0.68, P > 0.05$ | | $\rho s = -0.30, P > 0.05$ | |
| D7 | 1979–80 | 1.5 | 5 | 30 | 1.64 |
| | | 1.5 | 11 | 52 | 2.88 |
| | | 3 | 18 | 34 | 3.75 |
| | | 4.5 | 7 | 32 | 2.31 |
| | | 4.5 | 20 | 83 | 3.60 |
| | | 6 | 22 | 42 | 4.35 |
| | | 11 | 15 | 65 | 3.28 |
| | | $\rho s = 0.52, P > 0.05$ | | $\rho s = 0.46, P > 0.05$ | |

Source: Ficken et al. 1987, courtesy of Condor.

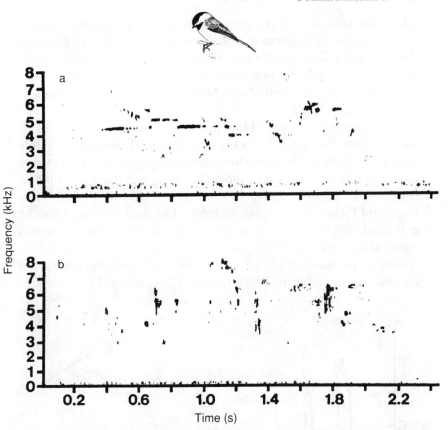

Fig. 4-4. Sonograms of subsong of young Black-capped Chickadees. The upper example (a) has a preponderance of fee-bee elements, while in the lower example (b) gargle elements predominate. (From Ficken, Ficken, and Witkin 1978, courtesy of *Auk*.)

ever, followed by aggression (Dixon et al. 1970; Ficken, Ficken, and Witkin 1978). In a sexual context, still a third kind of message may be conveyed. Much remains to be learned about this remarkable vocalization.

*Subsong*. The subsong is an unusual chickadee vocalization, given only by young birds (Fig. 4-4). Subsongs are rarely noticed because they are so soft that one must be extremely close to hear them. When I hand-reared several broods of Black-capped Chickadees one summer, I particularly enjoyed listening to their long, rambling, and surprisingly musical subsongs. Ficken, Ficken, and Witkin (1978) found that the subsongs of free-living young chickadees that they recorded were made up of some syllables reminiscent of those incorporated into a variety of adult vocalizations. This is hardly surprising, since, as Nottebohm (1975) pointed out, subsongs are probably not true communication at all, but are instead a kind of practice that is important in the vocal development of most young birds.

*Chick-a-dee call complex.* The chick-a-dee call complex, a set of variations on the familiar chick-a-dee-dee-dee theme, is commonly uttered by both sexes throughout the year (Fig. 4-2c). It is actually made up of one to four note types (Fig. 4-5), and these can each be repeated a variable number of times in a given call (Ficken, Hailman, and Ficken 1978; Nowicki 1989). The four notes can also be arranged in various combinations (Hailman et al. 1985; see also Nowicki and Nelson 1990).

Several fascinating and important studies have been conducted on this call complex in Black-capped Chickadees. In an elegant

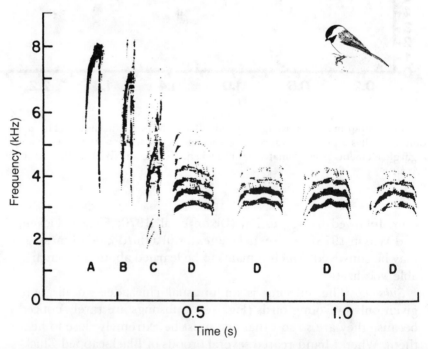

Fig. 4-5. Sound spectrogram of a chick-a-dee call of a Black-capped Chickadee, showing the three different introductory note types (A, B, and C) followed by four D notes. This call might be transcribed as *chick-k-ka-dee dee dee dee*. (From Hailman et al. 1985, courtesy of *Semiotica*.)

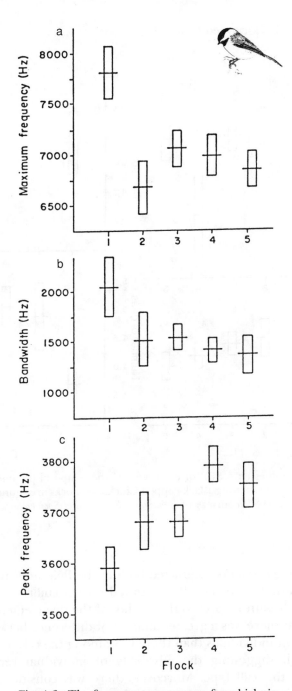

Fig. 4-6. The frequency parameters for which significant differences among Black-capped Chickadee flocks are found, showing mean values ± 1 SE. (From Mammen and Nowicki 1981, courtesy of *Behavioral Ecology and Sociobiology*.)

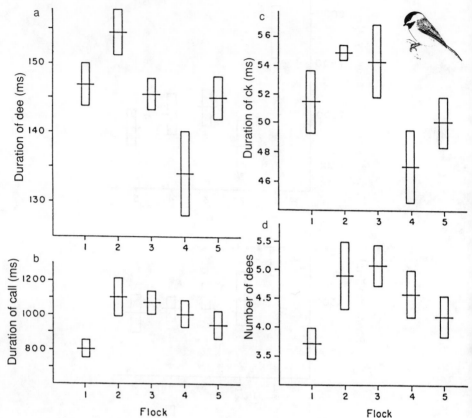

Fig. 4-7. Mean values (± 1 SE) for each flock of the temporal parameters for which significant differences among Black-capped Chickadee flocks are found. (From Mammen and Nowicki 1981, courtesy of *Behavioral Ecology and Sociobiology.*)

series of experiments conducted both in the field and in aviaries, Mammen and Nowicki (1981) worked on variability in this call, particularly with respect to the quality of the dee elements. They found that there was a greater amount of difference between calls of different individuals than there was among the calls of a single individual, suggesting the possibility of individual recognition based on this call type. Moreover, there was considerable convergence in the dee elements of chick-a-dee calls among members of a given flock, both in frequency parameters (Fig. 4-6) and in temporal parameters (Fig. 4-7). This convergence suggests that

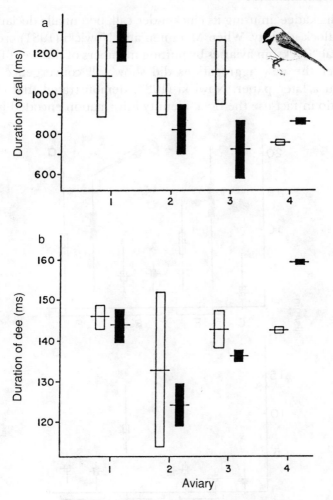

Fig.4-8. Mean duration of call (a) and mean duration of dee (b), each ± 1 SE, of the Black-capped Chickadee flocks formed experimentally in aviaries, using calls recorded in the field before exposure to each other (open bars) and calls recorded at least one month after the experimental flocks were formed (closed bars). (From Mammen and Nowicki 1981, courtesy of *Behavioral Ecology and Sociobiology*.)

70    The Black-capped Chickadee

each chickadee, in using its chick-a-dee call, potentially declares its home flock identity. When Mammen and Nowicki (1981) created artificial "flocks" in aviaries by putting members of different flocks together the new aggregations did show call convergence (Fig. 4-8). In a later paper, Nowicki (1983) demonstrated that chickadees do in fact use the flock-identity information encoded in the

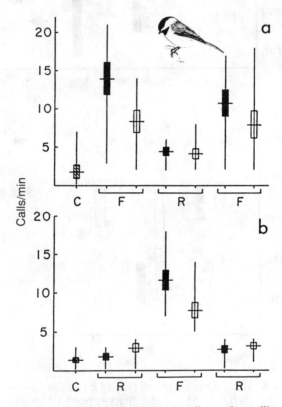

Fig. 4-9. Effects of playback stimuli on the calling rate of Black-capped Chickadee flocks during playback of tapes of foreign (F) and resident (R) flock calls. C = baseline control. Closed bars are data during the minute when the stimulus was played, and open bars are data from the minute immediately following playback. In situation *a* (above), the birds were given foreign/resident/foreign tapes, while in *b* (below) they received resident/foreign/resident tapes. Regardless of the sequence, the birds consistently increased their calling rate whenever the foreign calls were heard. Depicted are means (horizontal lines), ranges (vertical lines), and one standard error on either side of the mean (vertical bars). (From Nowicki 1983, courtesy of *Behavioral Ecology and Sociobiology*.)

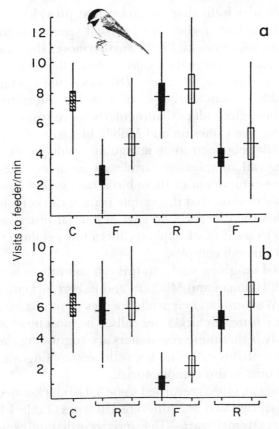

Fig. 4-10. Effects of playback stimuli on the visitation rate of Black-capped Chickadees to a feeder during playback of tapes of foreign (F) and resident (R) flock calls. C = baseline control. Whether the birds were given tapes in the sequence F-R-F (a) or R-F-R (b), the flock visitation rate decreased whenever foreign calls were heard. Means, ranges, and standard error are indicted as on Fig. 4-9. (From Nowicki 1983, courtesy of *Behavioral Ecology and Sociobiology.*)

chick-a-dee calls. Using test flocks living at least 1½ miles (2.4 km) apart, Nowicki conducted playback experiments and noted the birds' reactions. When presented with foreign calls, that is, those from another flock, test flocks both increased their own calling rate (Fig. 4-9) and decreased their foraging rate (Fig. 4-10)—presumably while searching for the invaders. By contrast, the test flocks, on being played tapes of their own calls, showed no changes in either call or foraging rates (Figs. 4-9, 4-10). There appears to be no particular individual or group that provides a model that other birds imitate; rather, the birds all seem to converge on a common mean (Nowicki 1989). Furthermore, the rate at which chickadees can converge their calls to match those of others is now known to be very rapid indeed (Nowicki 1989). This ability to learn quickly to match other birds' calls has interesting implications for those chickadees that regularly move from flock to flock (Smith 1984; see Cohesion and Mobile Elements, Chapter 7).

Kelly (1988) obtained some intriguing results on the use of the chick-a-dee call complex by Carolina Chickadees. Kelly noticed that the dee component of these birds' calls varied in length, and she was able to show that this simple feature can contain information on what the caller will do next in a social situation. It will be interesting to see if Black-capped Chickadees exhibit a similar correlation in this call complex.

A detailed on-going study on this call complex is being carried out by Jack Hailman and Millicent and Robert Ficken, of the University of Wisconsin. Their study focuses in particular on the recombinant nature of chick-a-dee calls. The most innovative aspect of this study is that these researchers are comparing the recombinant nature of this call complex with written English, which, as they point out, is also combinatorial.

Hailman et al. (1985) recorded some 3,479 chick-a-dee calls, and their analysis revealed 362 different call types (Table 4-6). Most of these were extremely rare—154 were recorded only once, whereas their most common call type was recorded 174 times. They concluded that chick-a-dee calls are generative, that is, the larger the sample recorded, the more different types of calls will be found, as increasingly rarer call types are discovered. Hailman et al. (1985) believe that this generative quality is an important similarity to human language.

They also documented that the four types of notes involved in this call complex do not appear in random order; rather, there is a strong tendency for chickadees to use these notes in a distinct sequence. They referred to the four note types as A, B, C, and D, and found that while not all four were necessarily included in a given call, whichever types were included would most likely be given in the order A, then B, then C, then D (see Fig. 4-5). The ending (as suggested by Mammen and Nowicki's [1981] work) appears to be particularly important. Hailman et al. (1987) identified two constraints on this call complex: one operates to limit the

Table 4-6. Examples from the 362 call types recorded in 3479
Black-capped Chickadee chick-a-dee calls

| No. of notes | Call type example | No. of calls recorded |
|---|---|---|
| 1 | B | 8 |
| 2 | CC | 9 |
| 3 | DDD | 27 |
| 4 | BCBC | 3 |
| 5 | ACCDD | 1 |
| 6 | ABABCC | 1 |
| 7 | AAADDDD | 109 |
| 8 | BCBCBCDD | 1 |
| 9 | CCCCCDDDD | 1 |
| 10 | AAAABBCCDD | 1 |
| 11 | DDDDDDDDDDD | 2 |
| 12 | AAADDDDDDDDD | 2 |
| 13 | BBBBBBBAAAAAA | 1 |
| 14 | CCDDDDDDDDDDDD | 1 |
| 15 | AAAAABBBBBBBBBB | 1 |
| 24 | BCDDDDDDDDDDDDDDDDDDDDDDDD | 1 |

*Source:* Hailman et al. 1985, courtesy of *Semiotica.*

length of all chick-a-dee calls, while the other, opposing, tendency
operates to include at least one or two D notes at the end, regardless of overall length.

Hailman et al. (1987) have suggested that a chick-a-dee call
actually contains some characteristics of a spoken human sentence.
Moreover, Hailman and Ficken (1986), using Gross's (1972) definition of language, were able to construct an algorithm instructing a
Turing machine to distinguish strings of units that are "in the
language" (that is, something a Black-capped Chickadee might
give) from those that are not.

Different messages can apparently be encoded by different
forms of the chick-a-dee call. It is often used when one bird is
separated either from its mate, if in pairs, or from the rest of its
flock in winter. A long rapid string of dee notes is what Odum
(1942a) called the scold note, and it is typically given when someone or something gets too close to the nest or when a predator
such as an owl or a cat is discovered. High-ranked birds' chick-a-
dee calls, after danger has passed, can serve as an all-clear signal
(Ficken and Witkin 1977). A bird discovering a new food source
such as a newly filled feeder in the fall may give a chick-a-dee call,

thus attracting the attention of its mate and other flock members (Ficken 1981a).

Chick-a-dee calls probably encode information at several levels (Hailman et al. 1985). Some aspects, such as the quality of the dee notes, represent general information such as flock identity (Nowicki 1983). Another sort of general information conveyed by this kind of call is the direction the caller is facing with respect to the listener. Witkin (1977) showed that both fee-bees and chick-a-dee calls have properties that allow directional sound radiation, meaning they sound different in front of a calling bird from how they sound behind it.

At a more specific level, Hailman et al. (1985) proposed that each of the four note types that can make up a chick-a-dee call may represent a different internal state or behavioral tendency of the caller. If so, then the amount of repetition of each note type could encode the strength of these tendencies.

Finally, the context of the call may also be able to affect its message. A particular version of chick-a-dee uttered under one set of circumstances could mean one thing, while the same call in a different situation might mean something quite different. Clearly, a lot more work needs to be done before we can fully understand this complex and fascinating set of vocalizations.

*Begging dee.* Begging dees (Fig. 4-2i) are given only by young chickadees still dependent on their parents. Young chickadees may give this call a few days before they are old enough to leave the nest, but it is more commonly given after fledging. The begging dee reminds me of a rather raspy "feed me, feed me me." Begging dees apparently serve to get the parents to deliver food and may also serve as a location note after the young leave the nest (Ficken, Ficken, and Witkin 1978).

*Broken dee.* The broken dee call (Fig. 4-2j) had been lumped with the begging dee by many authors (e.g., Odum 1942a), and it wasn't until Ficken, Ficken, and Witkin (1978) applied sonographic analysis that the differences between them were demonstrated. Broken dees are given only by females during the breeding season, especially during nest building and early incubation. Males typically respond to this "demand behavior" by giving their mate some food. Ficken, Ficken, and Witkin (1978) stated that this call serves to cement the pair bond.

*Variable see.* The variable see (Fig. 4-2b) consists of repeated high-pitched syllables given rapidly in a string that often ends in a gargle. Variable sees are given by both sexes, primarily during the breeding season. Odum (1942a) reported that either or both members of a pair will give variable sees if they meet suddenly close to their nest. Variable sees can also be given by parents that are foraging while their fledged young are still in family groups (Ficken et al. 1985). Most commonly, however, this call is associated with copulation. When a female gives variable sees during the period of egg laying or early incubation, her mate typically approaches quickly, often from some distance away. If the male comes very close and gives a special form of gargle, the female often continues her variable sees and begins to quiver her wings. This is generally followed by copulation, during which the male often gives variable sees (Dixon et al. 1970).

Apparently this call must be learned. Ficken et al. (1985) found that hand-reared Black-capped Chickadees that had heard no adult chickadees after about 14 days posthatching gave only aberrant versions of variable sees, suggesting that they must hear the correct form of this call before they can produce it.

Ficken et al. (1985) found microgeographical variation in the gargle syllables that terminate the sequence of variable sees given by Black-capped Chickadees in three sites in southeastern Wisconsin. This variation is particularly interesting because variable sees are used primarily for within-pair interactions. Dialects of most birds are best known in vocalizations used in between-pair interactions, such as song.

*Hiss.* Odum (1942a) remarked that a Black-capped Chickadee's hiss (Fig. 4-2e) seemed to be the result of a forced exhalation rather than a vocal effort; Dixon (1983) transliterated it as *haaah.* It is typically given when a breeding chickadee is surprised at its nest by a potential predator, and it is widespread among parids in both North America and Europe (Gompertz 1967).

The full display is complex and has been called the "snake display" (S. T. Smith 1972), because the overall effect reminds some observers of a striking snake. The displaying bird rises up on its legs, lifts its head high above its shoulders, then brings the head sharply down and forward as it gives the hiss. Simultaneously the bird spreads its wings forcefully so they strike the walls of the nest cavity. It is the sound of the wings and head striking against the nest cavity, along with the vocal hiss, that gives such a strong impression of a snake strike (S. T. Smith 1972).

Occasionally, Black-capped Chickadees will give this display at times other than the breeding season if they are caught in an enclosed space such as a wire-mesh trap (Dixon 1983). Apel and Weise (1986) showed that nestling Black-capped Chickadees can also give hiss displays. When their hand-reared nestlings gave this display, they would lunge forward hissing, and sometimes ended up tipped forward on their beaks with their short tails pointing straight up in the air. These nestlings showed considerable grada- tions in the intensity of their hiss displays. Clemmons and Howitz (1990) found in their excellent field study that wild nestlings first gave hisses nine days after hatching.

The hiss, being given most frequently by adults suddenly con- fronted by a predator at the nest, probably signals thwarted escape combined with a strong attack tendency (S. T. Smith 1972). Being directed at the predator, hisses are unique among chickadee vo- calizations in that they are primarily for interspecific (between species), rather than intraspecific (within species), communication.

*Snarl.* The snarl (Fig. 4-2f) is given by male Black-capped Chick- adees during contact fights (a very rare occurrence among chick- adees). Sonographic analysis shows snarls and hisses are actually very similar and the calls may form a graded series (Ficken, Ficken, and Witkin 1978). Chickadees giving either hisses or snarls are probably experiencing both escape and attack tendencies, but with snarls the tendency for attack is greater than that for escape.

*Twitter.* The twitter, a rare call (Fig. 4-2d), like snarls and hisses, may serve primarily to increase the distance between the caller and other individuals. It is given in sudden unexpected confrontations with other chickadees and may possibly serve to inhibit attack (Ficken, Ficken, and Witkin 1978).

*High zee.* Odum (1942a) referred to the high zee (Fig. 4-2a) as the chickadee's "warning note." It is given primarily by males (Ficken and Witkin 1977) in response to a variety of bird and mammal predators, particularly those that are approaching rapidly. It conveys a strong message of fear—usually any other small bird, regardless of species, that hears this call will dive for cover or freeze instantly, staying immobile for up to several min- utes. The freeze among chickadees is typically broken when one member of the group gives a chick-a-dee call; almost instantly the entire group becomes active again (Odum 1942a, Ficken and Witkin 1977). High zees may actually vary with the kind of preda- tor the caller has spotted (Ficken and Witkin 1977)—suggesting that the call may convey a more specific message than simply "there is a predator" (Table 4-7). Similar information coding may occur in the alarm calls of Mexican Chickadees (*Parus sclateri*) as well (Ficken 1990a). The Black-capped Chickadee's high zee may actually have a directional radiation pattern such that it could be directed toward a particular flock member (such as the caller's mate) and could also be directed away from the predator (Witkin and Ficken 1979). The call has no sharp onset or ending, is high-pitched, and has only a narrow frequency range, all of which make it particularly difficult to locate—a useful attribute in a warning signal.

*Tseet.* The tseet is a high thin call that yields a chevron-shaped sonogram (Fig. 4-2h). Since the "recognition or contact notes" described for Black-capped Chickadees by Odum (1942a) and S. T. Smith (1972) are so common in nature, are not mentioned anywhere else by Ficken, Ficken, and Witkin (1978), and are in fact high thin calls that sound remarkably like *tseet*, I assume they are represented by this note. Odum (1942a) reported that contact notes are by far the most frequently uttered call in the Black-capped Chickadees' vocabulary, being given almost continually by both sexes at most times of year. It apparently functions to keep birds in close communication with each other, both in flocks and in pairs. Ficken, Ficken, and Witkin (1978) reported that tseets seem to lack features that would make them easily localizable; they are also given quite softly. Both these features are likely to be related to the fact that tseets are used most often at close range. Although Ficken et al. (1978) stated that the typical context for tseets is agonistic encounters (Table 4-1), neither Odum (1942a) nor S. T.

Table 4-7. Characteristics of high zees given by Black-capped Chickadees on seeing three species of potential predators

| Context | No. of calls measured | Highest frequency (kHz) | Frequency range (kHz) | Duration (s) |
|---|---|---|---|---|
| Sharp-shinned Hawk | 3 | 8.87 ± 0.2 | 0.28 ± 0.06 | 0.10 ± 0.03 |
| Saw-whet Owl | 11 | 8.55 ± 0.19 | 0.42 ± 0.11 | 0.10 ± 0.02 |
| Mink | 25 | 7.76 ± 0.17 | 0.35 ± 0.12 | 0.07 ± 0.01 |

*Source:* Ficken and Witkin 1977, courtesy of *Auk.*
*Note:* Amplitudes were analyzed with a B and K level recorder type 2305. The dB measured at 1 meter was $55.8 + 2.4, -3.3$ for 25 mink calls. Amplitudes in dB were converted to $N/m^2$ for calculation of mean and SD, then converted back to dB (re $0.00002\ N/m^2$).

Smith (1972) described tseets as being used in such circumstances, nor have I encountered this use in my banded birds.

*Flight, or restless, note.* The flight note, written as *tsleep* or *tsleet* for Black-capped Chickadees by S. T. Smith (1972), could perhaps be called the "let's go" call. It seems to be both somewhat louder and more rapid than the tseet, the contact note, and it appears to carry over much greater distances than do simple tseets. A chickadee about to move to a new location will give tsleets; after it has given tsleets for a short period, others evidently start giving them too, and the group moves off. Although both Odum (1942a) and S. T. Smith (1972) recognized the flight note in the Black-capped Chickadee's repertoire, Ficken, Ficken and Witkin (1978) did not mention it, so there are apparently no published sonograms of the call. And, to the best of my knowledge, nobody has yet studied whether there is any correlation between age, rank, or sex and the tendency to give this call.

*Distress call.* Young Black-capped Chickadees captured soon after leaving the nest give loud squeals (Odum 1942a, Clemmons and Howitz 1990). S. T. Smith (1972) reported similar calls given under similar circumstances by young Carolina Chickadees. Sudden loud squeals may well increase the possibility of a predator's dropping the young chickadee, thus enhancing its chances of escape. The call also serves to attract the attention of the bird's parents, and may possibly warn other fledglings as well.

Black-capped Chickadees thus have at least 15 major kinds of vocalizations, although Clemmons and Howitz (1990) suggest that at least 2 other, hitherto undescribed calls may also be given by adults in the vicinity of their nests. Two familiar vocalizations, gargle and chick-a-dee, are incredibly complex. Of the 15 described in detail above, perhaps only 14 actually function as communication, the exception being the subsong. Two (the begging dee and distress call) are given only by young chickadees. Fee-bee, gargle, and snarl are given primarily by males; while broken dee and, to a lesser extent, hiss and perhaps variable see are given mostly by females.

Until very recently, what little was known about vocalization development in young chickadees was derived from studies of birds hand-reared in laboratories (see, for example, Apel and Ficken 1981). Then Clemmons and Howitz (1990) published their superb field study of call development by free-living chickadees in

Minnesota. They observed 12 Black-capped Chickadee nests (containing a total of 74 offspring), placing microphones right in the
nest cavities as soon as the young hatched. (These microphones
easily picked up sounds from outside, including many adult vocalizations; such vocalizations have not always been provided to
developing young in hand-rearing studies.) Clemmons and
Howitz followed the birds from the day they hatched until they
dispersed, at about age 40 days. Although Clemmons and Howitz
were particularly interested in the development of the chick-a-dee
call, they obtained much useful information on other calls as well.

The nestlings gave faint, simple peeps the day they hatched. By
day 3, most vocalizations were clearly associated with feeding.
Gradually the calls changed: simple peeps became more complex
calls, such as the so-called parent-near notes and tee-ship calls (all
involved in feeding). Vocalizations given up to days 28–30 were
primarily associated with obtaining food from adults. Then between about day 30 and 36, the calls changed drastically. Many
adultlike vocalizations appeared, including tseets, fee-bees, and
chick-a-dees. Soon after, the young birds dispersed.

Interestingly, the chickadee families in Clemmons and Howitz's
study developed calls at different rates, even within a single year—
yet all 12 families showed the same changes in the same order,
even if the timing differed.

Haftorn (1990) did a similar study on free-living Willow Tits,
although he recorded vocalizations of young birds only after they
had fledged. He found that nonaggressive calls develop before
aggressive ones, a sequence that seems to be followed in the call
development of fledging Black-capped Chickadees as well (Clemmons and Howitz 1990).

The vocalizations of most songbirds can easily be placed into
one of two categories: songs or calls. Songs, often given primarily
by males, tend to be relatively long, complex, and musical, involving a comparatively high proportion of pure tones. Songs are
species-specific, although some species have local song dialects,
and each individual of many species may have its own personal
song repertoire. Songs are given mostly during the breeding
season and function in pair formation and territory defense.
Most songbirds (Oscines) must learn their songs when young
(Kroodsma 1982). By contrast, calls tend to be shorter, less musical, less variable, and relatively specialized for particular functions
such as alarm, increasing or decreasing the distance between indi-

viduals, and so on. Oscines generally do not have to learn their calls (Kroodsma 1982). Each individual, regardless of sex, can give and respond to a large number of calls, many of which are used year-round.

At first glance, the distinction between songs and calls of Black-capped Chickadees seems clear: fee-bees—the loud, pure tone vocalization given primarily by males—seem to be songs, while the rest of the vocalizations could be termed calls. However, the situation is not quite so simple.

As early as 1970, Dixon and Stefanski challenged the idea that fee-bees do, in fact, function uniquely as song. Both the gargle and chick-a-dee call complex, with their great variety and subtlety of meaning, are potentially longer and more complex than the whistled fee-bee. Unlike song in most birds, fee-bees are given in any month of the year. Moreover, while the peak of fee-bee use is indeed in the spring, most chickadee pair formation actually occurs in fall or winter (Ficken, Ficken, and Witkin 1978; Smith 1984). Ficken (1981b) discussed the problem of defining song for Black-capped Chickadees in detail. She pointed out that whistled songs of North American chickadees tend to be far simpler than those of European parids, and indeed some North American species such as the Chestnut-backed Chickadee (*Parus rufescens*), Boreal Chickadee (*P. hudsonicus*), and Mexican Chickadee (*P. sclateri*) evidently lack a whistled song altogether. On the other hand, the whistled song of Carolina Chickadees is both more complex and more variable than that of Black-capped Chickadees. Depending on context, both gargle and fee-bee now serve some of the functions traditionally ascribed to song. Ficken (1981b) suggested that the fee-bee vocalization may be gradually losing its importance for Black-capped Chickadees, and predicted that it will eventually be lost altogether.

The message of certain calls of some bird species, such as Eastern Kingbirds (*Tyrannus tyrannus*), varies with the calls' degree of harshness (Smith 1977). To the best of my knowledge, similar variations in meaning with call quality are not known in Black-capped Chickadees, with the exception of Mammen and Nowicki's (1981) work on information encoded in the distribution of energy among the frequency components of the dee note of chick-a-dee calls. It might be worthwhile to look for similar effects in other calls, especially in those as complex as gargles.

Sound quality in whistled parid vocalizations has received some

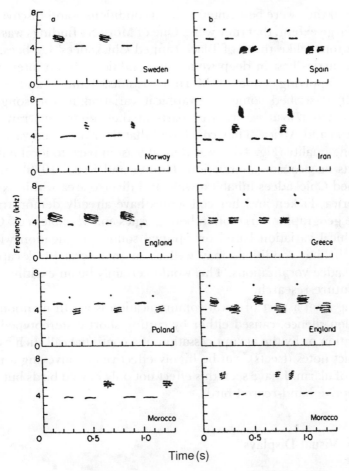

Fig. 4-11. Sonogram tracings of Great Tit songs from two kinds of habitats: deep forest (a) and more open areas (b). The songs recorded from populations living in deep forest conditions contain more pure tones (relatively narrow lines) than do those from more open habitats. (From Hunter and Krebs 1979, courtesy of *Journal of Animal Ecology*.)

study. This work builds on a study by Eugene Morton (1975), who created artificial bird "songs" having various sound properties (e.g., pure tones or more complex noises, high or low tones, and so on), then played them at a standard volume and measured how well each traveled under various ecological conditions (open fields, wood edge, or deep woodland). He found which kinds of noises propagated best in each area, then checked local bird vocalizations to see if they were best suited to local conditions—and discovered, to a large extent, that they were. One of Morton's findings was that pure tones, like those of Black-capped Chickadees' fee-bees, are what carries best in deep woodland conditions. In an interesting paper applying some of Morton's results, Hunter and Krebs (1979) described some geographical variation in the songs of Great Tits (*Parus major*) over parts of their enormous range in Eurasia and Africa. They concluded that their observed variation in song quality (Fig. 4-11) was due, at least in part, to local habitat effects on acoustic attenuation (Hunter and Krebs 1979). Black-capped Chickadees inhabit a wide and diverse area within North America. Ficken and her colleagues have already demonstrated some geographic variation in both gargles and variable sees. Geographical variation based on optimal sound propagation within local habitat conditions may well occur in several Black-capped Chickadee vocalizations. This would certainly be an exciting area for future research.

One final aspect of vocal communication is worth mentioning. Sudden silence, caused either by cutting short a stereotyped vocalization or by the abrupt cessation of a continual call such as the contact notes (tseets), can be highly effective at conveying a message of alarm. I have seen this effect not only in wild birds but also in captive hand-reared birds.

### Visual Displays

Remarkably little is known about the visual displays of Black-capped Chickadees. Brewer (1961) and Hartzler (1970), among others, have remarked on how infrequent and rapid such displays are. S. T. Smith (1972) stated that the really relevant part of Carolina Chickadee communication is the vocalizations, with the visual displays being essentially redundant: "It seems likely that for Carolina Chickadees there is no category of message that is encoded by visual displays that is not also encoded by one or more vocal displays" (S. T. Smith 1972:82). This might be true for Black-capped Chickadees as well.

S. T. Smith (1972) listed 14 visual displays for the Carolina Chickadee. No such careful analysis has yet been attempted for the visual displays of Black-capped Chickadees. Of the 14 Carolina Chickadee displays, at least 8 have been reported for Black-capped Chickadees as well. One more is uncertain, and the other 5 have not yet been reported for this species. These displays (using S. T. Smith's [1972] terminology) and one additional display recently described by Popp et al. (1990) are discussed below.

*Bill-up.* In the bill-up the chickadee suddenly tilts its head so that the bill is essentially vertical (Fig. 4-12). At its most extreme, the whole body swings back, and the tail points straight down, in a posture similar to the bill-up display of the Great Tit (Hinde 1952). The·bill-up display of Carolina Chickadees is sometimes associated with drooped wings and is often silent, although it may be accompanied by notes equivalent to gargles. The display is clearly directed toward a particular individual. In the case of Carolina Chickadees, the bird giving the bill-up display typically defers to the recipient (S. T. Smith 1972).

I have only been certain of seeing a Black-capped Chickadee perform this display a few times, perhaps because it is, at least in my experience, an extremely brief display. It is perhaps somewhat more common toward spring than at other times of year. On the occasion when I saw it best, the display was performed in an interaction between two color-banded males. It differed from the bill-up of Carolina Chickadees in that the displayer was the more

Fig. 4-12. Two interacting Black-capped Chickadees. The bird on the right is giving a bill-up display, and the one on the left is adopting the general sleeking posture. (Drawn from a photograph by S. M. Smith.)

dominant bird (an alpha male gave a bill-up display to the beta male of the flock). This display was silent, and the only apparent result was that the two birds moved farther apart. S. T. Smith (1972) saw no cases in which a bill-up display given by Carolina Chickadees resulted in an attack. It may well be that bill-up displays are given most often between two opponents that differ very little in rank.

*Gape.* When performing the gape display, the bird leans toward its opponent and opens its bill several times (Fig. 4-13). This display is well documented for Black-capped Chickadees, primarily through the photographs of Jon Glase (1973). Gaping is used as a threat both by Carolina Chickadees, which reportedly use it rarely, and by Black-capped Chickadees, which use it more often (Glase 1973). I have heard Black-capped Chickadees give gargles either before or right after gaping.

*General sleeking.* General sleeking involves pulling all the head and body feathers in tight to the body and leaning away from a higher-ranked individual (Fig. 4-14; see also Fig. 4-12). Chickadees showing this display are probably experiencing a strong tendency to escape, which is blocked by some other tendency, such as satisfying hunger (S. T. Smith 1972). Birds with general sleeking may arrive at a platform feeder and cling to the edge, rather than landing on top as a less hesitant bird would (Glase 1973). The display is usually silent.

Fig. 4-13. Black-capped Chickadee doing the gape display. The bird leans forward and directs its gape at an opponent. (Drawn from a photograph by Jon Glase.)

Fig. 4-14. Black-capped
Chickadee showing general
sleeking posture. In this figure,
the bird is displaying to a more
dominant chickadee to its left.
(Drawn from a photograph by Jon
Glase.)

*Ruffled crown.* Raising the crown feathers is very common in aggressive situations among both Black-capped and Carolina Chickadees. It is particularly frequent in interactions at feeders. A ruffled crown on a Carolina Chickadee probably indicates a sudden brief rise of aggressive tendencies (S. T. Smith 1972); the same is apparently true for Black-capped Chickadees. Ruffled crown displays are often accompanied by gargle notes.

*Body ruffling.* Body ruffling is probably the most noticeable of all visual threat displays of Black-capped Chickadees. Particularly common in autumn, it involves extreme fluffing of the rump and back feathers, and often wing drooping and tail spreading as well (Fig. 4-15). Birds showing body ruffling may face their opponent, or, if sideways, often lean toward the opponent. This display typ-

Fig. 4-15. Body ruffling by a Black-capped Chickadee.
This display is particularly common in interactions in
autumn. (Drawn from field sketches.)

ically occurs when individuals are 1 meter or less apart. Piaskowski et al. (1988) found that, while Black-capped Chickadees of all ages and sexes exhibit the display, juvenile males do so most frequently. While the display itself is usually silent, it may be preceded or followed by gargle notes, and it often results in an attack. Although it has been suggested that this display might play some role in pair formation by Black-capped Chickadees (Ficken et al. 1985), more recent data have shown that it is purely an aggressive display (Piaskowski et al. 1988).

*Wing quiver.* In the wing quiver the wings are drooped slightly, then quivered rapidly. Displaying birds usually crouch somewhat and may orient at a slight angle to, or directly toward, the recipient. This display may be used by Black-capped Chickadees in several different contexts. Dependent young quiver their wings when giving begging dees in soliciting food from their parents. Adult females may quiver their wings when giving broken dees, especially after incubation is underway. Both adult males and females may quiver their wings while giving variable sees just before copulation. Finally, males of both Black-capped Chickadees (pers. observ.) and Carolina Chickadees (S. T. Smith 1972) may quiver their wings just before chasing a rival. Wallace (1967) described wing quivering performed in a similar aggressive context by Tufted Titmice (*Parus bicolor*). Wing quivering in aggressive situations is widespread among other bird species as well (Smith 1973).

*Nest-site showing.* Nest-site showing (Fig. 4-16) is given early in the spring, during or right after flock breakup. The displaying bird clings to the entrance of a potential nest cavity, alternately looking into the entrance hole and looking back over its shoulder. After such a bout of looking, it may partially or completely enter the cavity. Often the mate then responds by coming over and exploring or excavating at the site or both. Apparently, only males of Carolina Chickadees do this display (S. T. Smith 1972). I have seen it done by Black-capped Chickadees of both sexes, although more commonly by males. On several occasions I have watched a male do this display, only to have his mate come over briefly to inspect his hole, then fly straight to another hole and do her own nest-site-showing display to him. Once I came across a pair, both members vigorously and simultaneously doing this display at two nest sites about 10 meters (about 11 yards) apart. I do not know which bird had started to display first, but the male was the first to

Fig. 4-16. Black-capped Chickadee at the entrance of a potential nest site, giving the nest-site-showing display.

stop and flew briefly to the female's nest site before flying up to a nearby tree and giving several loud fee-bees. The pair eventually nested in a third nest site (pers. observ.).

*Snake display.* The snake display—bringing the head sharply forward and down while strongly spreading the wings so they hit the nest cavity walls—is given with the hiss call described above. Its form is remarkably constant among a wide variety of parid species (Pickens 1928, Sibley 1955).

*Nest-site distraction.* The nest-site distraction is one of the most spectacular of the known displays of Black-capped Chickadees. It is typically given by adults that encounter a potential predator close to their nest or threatening a newly fledged young chickadee (Long 1982), although Hickey (1952) saw it given as early as April by an adult chickadee whose mate was in apparent danger. The displaying bird leans forward while slowly raising and lowering its fully extended wings (Fig. 4-17). It usually faces the predator and sways from side to side, sometimes twisting its body right and left; the tail is also widely flared (Long 1982). Although sometimes just one bird will perform this display, often both members of a pair will display simultaneously if their young are threatened. This display can also be accompanied by a loud vocalization, sounding a bit like a scream, and described by Long as *fzz*. Whether this is a modification of high zees, as suggested by Long (1982), or is perhaps related to some other vocalization, such as the distress call, awaits further investigation.

*Wing flick.* In the wing flick both wings are lifted quickly up over the back then returned to rest position. If given in strings, at least by Carolina Chickadees, the flicks are spaced about one second apart. Apparently this display is given, although rarely, by Black-capped Chickadees (Brewer 1961). By contrast, it is commonly given by Carolina Chickadees, where its message indicates that the signaler is hesitant, experiencing an escape tendency interfering with almost any other type of behavior (S. T. Smith 1972).

*Ballet.* The ballet, described by Popp et al. (1990), is frequently used in agonistic encounters by Black-capped Chickadees. It involves a series of movements resulting in changes in orientation

Fig. 4-17. Black-capped Chickadee performing a nest-site-distraction display. Occasionally the wings can be raised even more vertically than shown here; the bird can also tip forward until its head is down below the perch. (Drawn from field sketches.)

between the contestants. During this display, losers tend to face away from their opponents, while winners are more likely to face their opponents (Popp et al. 1990). Popp and his colleagues suggested that the ballet may provide an opportunity for chickadees to assess each other closely, perhaps with respect to sex, identity, and physical condition.

The remaining five visual displays described for Carolina Chickadees by S. T. Smith (1972) have not been reported for Black-capped Chickadees. These include the tail flick; general fluffing, in which all the body feathers, and in particular those of the head, are conspicuously fluffed; the ruffled bib; tail fanning; and the nape crest, in which the crown is sleeked and a crest is erected along the midline the entire length of the nape.

Black-capped Chickadees doubtless have other visual displays that Carolina Chickadees do not—displays that may never have been described in any detail. Since most chickadee displays are extremely rapid, videographic analysis seems necessary for accurate description.

# 5

# The Early Breeding Season

This and the next two chapters deal with the annual cycle of Black-capped Chickadees. Because it is a cycle, there is no one logical place to begin. I have started with the relatively simple social system of breeding pairs, leading up to the more complex social system found in wintering chickadees, to be dealt with throughout Chapter 7.

## Mating System

Like most other chickadee species (Bent 1946), the Black-capped Chickadee is strongly monogamous. The first published exception was a report I wrote in 1967 on a single instance of polygyny: in an area approximately twice that of adjacent territories, one male was mated to two females and helped take care of both broods. He was much more attentive to one of the females than to the other, and the second female bred with a new mate the following year (Smith 1967a). Recently Waterman et al. (1989) found evidence of an instance of polyandry in Black-capped Chickadees; one female was evidently mated simultaneously to two males. Given the number of investigators working on chickadees, the rate of nonmonogamy in this species is clearly very low indeed.

Alatalo and his colleagues described polygyny in Pied Fly-catchers (*Ficedula hypoleuca*) of Europe; again, males were typically more attentive to one mate (the primary female) than to the other (secondary female). Unlike chickadees, Pied Flycatchers are strongly migratory, and apparently females of that species are in such a hurry to mate when they get back to the breeding grounds in spring that males that defend very large territories can fool them into polygynous mating (Alatalo et al. 1981). Because chickadees are nonmigratory over most of their range, females have plenty of time to observe the males' true mating status, and thus could not be deceived in a similar way. I suspect that in the one observed case of polygyny in Black-capped Chickadees, the secondary female may have lost her mate very early in the breeding season, and one of the neighbor males simply expanded his territory to include that of the widowed female. I have seen similar expansion attempts by males in other years, but in each case they were repulsed. Mate-sharing is also rare among most European parids (Björklund and Westman 1986b). An apparent exception is the Blue Tit (*Parus caeruleus*), which is polygynous in just over 5 percent of reported nestings (Dhondt 1987a, 1987b).

### Pair Formation

Many migratory birds form pairs during a definite, rather short, time period in the spring. Black-capped Chickadees, however, being primarily resident, not migratory, most often form pairs in the fall as part of winter flock formation. It is perhaps not surprising that old birds pair at this time, but fall pairing apparently also occurs for young chickadees, often only two to three months posthatching (Smith 1984, 1990). Such early pair formation by parids is not uncommon—for example, Carolina Chickadees (*P. carolinensis*) (Dixon 1963), Willow Tits (*P. montanus*) (Hogstad 1987a), and Plain Titmice (*P. inornatus*) (Dixon 1949) form pairs in late summer as well.

While most pairs are formed in the fall, a few are formed during the winter, primarily in response to the mortality of high-ranking members of the winter flocks (Smith 1984). Finally, a second, smaller peak in pair formation occurs in the spring; generally at least one member of these spring-formed pairs ranked well down in its flock hierarchy during the previous winter (pers. observ.). Regardless of season, chickadees show essentially no recognizable courtship displays associated with pair formation.

## Spring Transition from Flocks to Pairs

Timing of flock breakup may vary with area, year, and other factors. On warm days in early spring, each chickadee pair may be well separated from the others, yet the same birds will rejoin into a flock immediately during a subsequent cold snap (Odum 1941a). Carolina Chickadees (Dixon 1963) and many European parids (Perrins 1979) are known to exhibit similar weather-related responses.

The period of flock breakup is characterized by increased aggressive interactions, as each pair tries to obtain a breeding territory (Fig. 5-1). In many of the areas where local survival has been good, more chickadees will try to get territories than the area will normally hold, and some pairs will be driven away. It is not easy to watch as a young chickadee pair defends an area that gets steadily smaller and smaller until one day the pair is gone—although not infrequently the same birds may obtain a territory, presumably on somewhat poorer quality habitat, nearby. Some of the unsuccessful pairs may split up once they have been driven off an area; others apparently stay together for another attempt elsewhere. In many banding studies, numerous unbanded chickadees, apparently driven from neighboring areas, appear during the period of spring flock breakup. Because unbanded chickadees arrive virtually every spring in my area, as opposed to every other spring or so, the influx is not correlated with return movements after irruption years (see Migration and Irruptions, Chapter 9). This finding suggests that the unbanded birds are low-ranked individuals from nearby flocks, driven out by the territorial behavior of higher-ranked birds. The spring movement of presumably unsuccessful pairs is common in many areas (Butts 1931, Odum 1941a, Smith 1967c, Glase 1973) and occurs in related species such as Carolina Chickadees as well (Brewer 1961).

Temporary aggregations of unsuccessful chickadees may form at this time in suboptimal habitat. These groups are typically made up of birds from two or more former flocks (Glase 1973). I have encountered such groups in six of the eleven springs during my

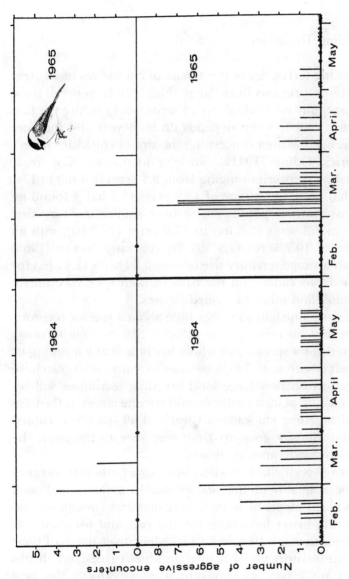

Fig. 5-1. Number of aggressive encounters among Black-capped Chickadees observed during the spring of two consecutive years. The top graphs represent the control area and the bottom graphs the study area. The two areas were about three miles (4.8 km) apart, in similar habitat. The study area had about 40 chickadees each winter; no count was possible in the control area because all the birds were unbanded. Note the distinct peak around the end of February or the beginning of March in each year. (From Smith 1967c, courtesy of *Condor*.)

current study, each time in the same general location. This observation in itself is interesting, because each year the birds forming
these groups have been less than a year old. Such groups do not
persist after nesting has begun.

### Breeding Territories

The breeding territories of most pairs of chickadees lie in areas
within the birds' previous flock range (Fig. 5-2). In general, these
territories are fully established five to seven weeks before the first
eggs are laid; exactly when depends on both year and location.

Much has been written concerning the size of chickadee breeding territories. Odum (1941a), working in upstate New York,
found breeding territories ranging from 8.4 acres (3.4 ha) to 17.1
acres (6.9 ha), with an average of 13.2 acres (5.3 ha). I found an
eastern Massachusetts population to have similar territory size,
ranging from 3.8 acres (1.5 ha) to 17.9 acres (17.2 ha), with an
average size of 10.7 acres (4.3 ha). By contrast, Brewer (1963)
arrived at an average territory size of only 3.64 acres (1.47 ha) for
Black-capped Chickadees, on the basis of both his own observations in Illinois and other published figures.

Actually, size alone tells us rather little about a species' territory.
John Wiens and his colleagues concluded that average territory
size measured for a species as a whole has little if any meaning or
value by itself (Weins et al. 1985), because so many factors can have
a marked effect on how large local breeding territories will be.

One such factor, at least under certain circumstances, is the local
numbers of breeding chickadees. Clearly, if all space is occupied
and breeding density goes up from one year to the next, the
average territory size must go down.

Other, more specific factors affect how big a particular territory
will be. One is quality of the real estate. To a chickadee, good
quality can mean plenty of suitable nest sites and enough vegetation to provide insect food both for the pair and for their offspring, at least through fledging. Chickadees, over much of their
range, set up territories well before deciduous trees and shrubs
have grown any leaves, so they cannot assess directly the local
insect populations that will occur later in the breeding season.
Sturman (1968a) found that in his study area in Washington State,

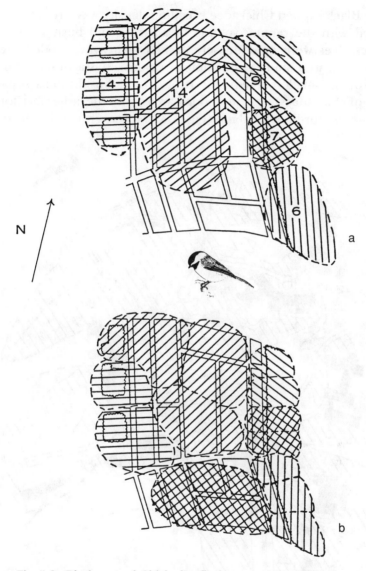

N

a

b

Fig. 5-2. Black-capped Chickadee flock ranges (a) and breeding territories (b) in a Vancouver study area in 1963–64. Numbers indicate the number of banded chickadees alive in each flock as of February 12, 1964. Shading in the lower map indicates flock membership of each pair. (From Smith 1967c, courtesy of *Condor*.)

the Black-capped Chickadee breeding density was strongly correlated with the canopy volume of all trees and bushes—that is,
chickadees were most densely packed in heavily wooded areas.
Similarly, in a study population in eastern Massachusetts (Smith
1976), the smallest breeding territories (and thus the densest pack-
ing of chickadees) were in wooded areas, with the larger territories
being in more open habitat (Fig. 5-3). Moreover, nestling feeding

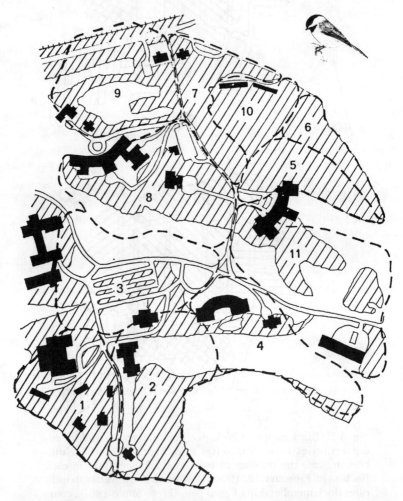

Fig. 5-3. Black-capped Chickadee breeding territories, showing boundaries (dashed lines) and relative amount of canopy (clear area, no canopy;
shaded areas, canopy). Territories in more open areas are larger than
those in areas with a greater proportion of canopy cover. Numbers refer to
particular pairs. (From Smith 1976, courtesy of *Auk*.)

rates were highest in the small, wooded territories (see Nestling Care, Chapter 6). Hence the best-quality territories are often smaller than poorer-quality territories. At first glance this might seem surprising, but it makes sense for two reasons: first, a pair will need less high-quality land than poor-quality land to satisfy all of its requirements; and second, more chickadees will try to incorporate high- rather than low-quality land into their breeding territory, so competition pressure will be considerably higher in the best areas, except in years having particularly low chickadee populations.

This picture is further complicated by another factor: the relative rank of the chickadees themselves. In my eastern Massachusetts study area, given equal habitat quality, alpha males tended to have somewhat larger territories than did beta males (Smith 1976). Glase (1973) also found that higher-ranked pairs obtained larger territories than did lower-ranked pairs. However, this effect may be lowered or even reversed if the alpha male is very old, at least in the case of certain European tits (Dhondt 1971a).

Finally, the actual time at which territory is measured can affect apparent territory size considerably, because the chickadees' use of their land changes markedly over the course of the breeding season. Territory use by Black-capped Chickadees was studied in detail by Stefanski (1967), who found that pairs used a very large area during nest building, but that the area used decreased markedly as nesting progressed (Fig. 5-4). Even after the young had hatched, Stefanski's chickadees did not expand their use to cover as much area as they had used during nest building. Similar changes in area use were found by Glase (1973).

Some European titmice have very complex territorial behavior. For example, Dhondt and Schillemans (1983) described three classes of breeding Great Tits (*Parus major*) in Europe: pairs that defend territories and nest in those territories; pairs that nest in another bird's territory while defending their own nearby ("territorial intruders"), and, incredibly, pairs that simply do not defend any territory, yet manage to nest in areas located within the territories of other Great Tits ("real intruders"). As far as is known, no North American parid has either of these last two classes; instead each nesting pair locates its nest within the boundaries of its own breeding territory.

Odum (1941a) claimed that the Black-capped Chickadee male

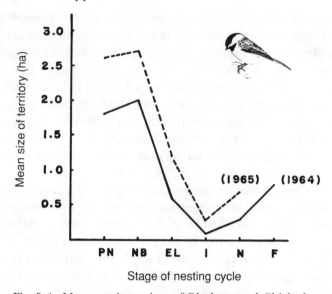

Fig. 5-4. Mean territory sizes of Black-capped Chickadees in different stages of the nesting cycle. While consistently high in the prenesting (PN) and nest-building (NB) stages, effective territory size dropped sharply during egg laying (EL), became smallest during incubation (I), then rose somewhat during the nestling (N) and fledgling (F) stages. (From Stefanski 1967, courtesy of *Condor*.)

assumes the leading role in breeding territory defense, although the female may join him on occasion. Other investigators, such as Glase (1973), have found that often the female will take an equal part in defense; my own observations support Glase's findings. Actually, defense varies not only with stage of nesting but also with individual chickadees. In a few pairs, before the complete clutch is laid, the female may take the lead in defense; I have seen this behavior even in a pair whose male was the alpha bird in last winter's flock (pers. observ.). Still, if one member of a pair takes a more active defensive role, it is usually the male. Frequently during an interaction between two neighboring pairs, three birds will be actively involved, with one bird quietly feeding some meters from the main confrontation. This quiet bird in most cases is a female.

Odum (1941a) recognized three potential stages in defensive

behavior: the challenge, the chase, and the fight. Every confrontation involves the first, most involve the second, but the third is extremely rare. In the challenge, the resident pair give loud calls (gargles, chick-a-dees, or loud fee-bees) directed at the intruder(s). If the intruders leave, the confrontation is over. Chases, again with loud calling of gargles, chick-a-dees and fee-bees, can be protracted affairs involving three or even more pairs, especially early in territory establishment. These can last for fifteen minutes or even longer. Contact fights among chickadees involve two birds flying together in midair, locking feet, and falling down to or near the ground. It is not surprising that such encounters are rare considering the danger involved; not only may a fighter be hurt by a rival, but also both fighters are made highly vulnerable to predators.

Behavior involved with territory defense is most common during the period when boundaries are being established. Afterward, defense behavior becomes far less common. Odum (1941a) reported that it continues until the young leave the nest, although intrusion and repulsion seldom occur so late in the nesting cycle. Where a pair raises a second brood, I have seen a brief increase in defense, but not to the early spring level.

Over most of their range, Black-capped Chickadees direct their defense only toward intruders of their own species. However, some interspecific defense has been reported between Black-capped Chickadees and Carolina Chickadees in the narrow area of range overlap (Brewer 1961, Robbins et al. 1986).

Ydenberg and his colleagues did some fascinating studies on territory defense by Great Tits (Ydenberg 1987, Ydenberg and Krebs 1987). Using captive males, Ydenberg (1987) offered the birds a choice of two foraging sites: a relatively poor one that afforded a view of an area where a simulated territorial invasion had taken place, or a rich site from which surveillance was impossible. After the males had seen the simulated intrusion, they chose to spend more time on the less profitable surveillance branch; that is, defense was worth some feeding cost to these birds.

Chickadees are likely to behave in a similar manner. I would like to see how age and former winter rank affect the birds' choices. It would be particularly interesting to see how females respond to such a setup, because their situation is rather more complicated than that of males: most females take an equal part in early territory defense, but at times of peak defensive behavior, females' nutritional needs are far greater than those of males, as they are about to lay eggs.

## Factors That Affect the Onset of Breeding

Many factors can affect the onset of breeding in chickadees and other parids. An obvious one is latitude: southern populations can start breeding well before more northern ones. Various aspects of local geography can also affect timing of breeding: for example, altitude can have a marked effect, with higher populations starting later than lower ones. The age of the female, at least of European tits, is known to affect the onset of breeding, with older birds beginning sooner than younger birds, up to a certain point—although very old birds lay later again (Great and Blue Tits: Dhondt 1989a). Size of the female may also have an effect—while the data are less clear, and there is some conflicting evidence, at least some studies indicate that smaller females may begin breeding before larger ones (Perrins 1979). Some small effects of local habitats are also known, especially for European species; for example, birds with woods-edge territories may breed a bit earlier than birds having deep-woods territories (Perrins 1979).

Even beyond simply varying with the factors just mentioned, strong yearly variations in the time of onset of breeding have been recorded both for European titmice (Perrins 1970, 1979, 1990) and for Black-capped Chickadees (Odum 1942b). These annual fluctuations have inspired a great deal of study.

As early as 1950, Gibb demonstrated that in his British population of Great and Blue Tits, the peak number of nestlings coincided with the peak levels of caterpillar abundance (Fig. 5-5). Is this evidence of amazing adaptation by these birds, with an almost magical predictive ability as well? Apparently not. Perrins (1970) and others have argued that the important part of Gibb's graph is not so much the timing of peak caterpillar abundance as the timing of the beginning of that curve, that is, the timing of first availability of caterpillars. Perrins (1970) proposed that the nestling stage is not the point at which young parids experience their greatest need for food—very likely this comes later—and others (e.g., van Balen 1973) agree. Thus if timing of breeding were based solely on food requirements of offspring, breeding should

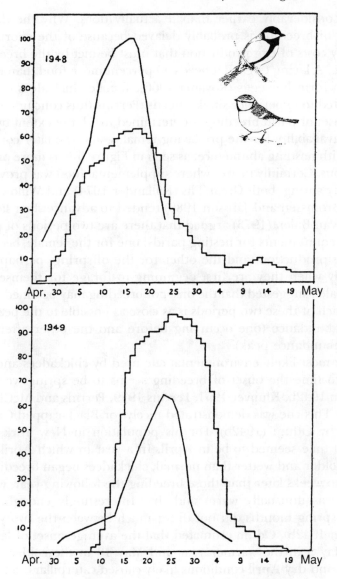

Fig. 5-5. Number of Great Tit broods and abundance of food caterpillars (1948 and 1949). Stepped graphs show daily combined total of Great and Blue Tit broods in nest boxes. Smoothed graphs show percentage abundance of caterpillars estimated from volume of fecal pellets. Figures on the vertical axis indicate percentage abundance of caterpillars and actual numbers of broods. Note that caterpillars are abundant for only a short period, the timing of which varies from year to year. (From Gibb 1950, *Ibis* 92: 507–539, courtesy of the British Ornithologists' Union.)

start considerably earlier than it actually does. Why the delay? Onset of breeding is probably delayed because of the enormous energy costs of egg production that must be met by the breeding female. A laying Great Tit needs 40 percent more food than usual just to form her eggs (Royama 1966); female chickadees can be expected to experience similar needs. Perrins thus concluded that the onset of parid breeding is determined to a large extent by the food availability for the pre-laying females, and the later correlation with nestling abundance, as seen in Figure 5-5, is more or less spurious. Certainly in ares where supplemental food was provided in early spring, both Great Tits (Källander 1974) and Willow Tits (von Bromssen and Jansson 1980) tended to advance their laying date. Van Balen (1973) argued that there are two periods of peak food requirements for nesting parids: one for the female, because of egg production, and the other for the offspring, perhaps especially when they are first beginning to forage for themselves. Van Balen suggested that the onset of breeding may be timed such that each of these two periods is as close as possible to the peak of food abundance (one occurring before and the other after the food abundance peak).

The most likely environmental cue used by chickadees and titmice to time the onset of breeding seems to be spring weather (Odum 1942b, Kluijver 1951, Perrins 1979, Perrins and McCleery 1989). This cue was demonstrated nicely for Black-capped Chickadees by Odum (1942b). For his population in New York, the critical time seemed to be in April. In a year in which April was both colder and wetter than normal, chickadees began breeding a full two weeks later than those breeding the following year, when April was unusually warm and dry. Interestingly enough, the other spring months did not differ much between the two years (Odum 1942b). Odum estimated that the average onset of laying was May 5 in the warmer year and May 18 in the colder year. Warm and dry April conditions likely caused caterpillars to hatch sooner, so female food requirements could be met earlier, thus leading to earlier onset of breeding.

Evidence supporting the theory that female food requirements are the most important factor affecting onset of breeding comes from looking at reactions to cold spells that occur just about the time when laying is to start. It take females about four days after the "decision" to start laying to produce the first egg and, because they lay eggs once a day, to continue the growth of the other eggs in various stages of development as well (Kluijver 1951, Kluyver 1961). Females that have already begun to lay, and thus have already invested this four-day period of energy expenditure, keep right on laying eggs during a cold spell, although if it lasts too long, they may stop early, thus producing unusually small clutches (Perrins 1979). However, females that have not yet begun to lay typically defer starting until warm weather returns. And, significantly, these birds do not start as soon as it gets warm; rather, they lay their first egg four days after warm weather returns. This has been shown not only for Black-capped Chickadees (Kluyver 1961) but for various European titmice (Perrins 1979) as well.

Hence, within limits set by latitudinal and geographical factors, females will begin breeding as soon as local food supply permits. One possible reason why older females begin before young ones is that old birds are usually dominant over younger ones in winter flocks (Dhondt and Hublé 1968; Smith 1976, 1984) and may thus end the winter with better fat reserves. Having such reserves may mean that the older birds do not need to spend as much time feeding to reach the energy level at which they can produce eggs, as do younger, lower-ranked females.

## Intrapair Dominance

Among chickadees, dominance relationships are easily documented in winter, when leaves are off the trees, food supplies are relatively low so competition is more readily seen, and birds come frequently to feeders. At this time, males are clearly dominant over most females. I used to think that the dominance of the male, so easily seen in winter, would continue throughout the year (e.g., Smith 1976). Earlier studies, however, had already provided some suggestive evidence to the contrary. The female Great Tit is usually dominant over her mate once nest building has started (Hinde 1952). Odum (1941a), being a bit more circumspect, pointed out that male Black-capped Chickadees were not seen to "exert their dominance" over females after flock breakup. More and more papers have now documented breeding female dominance in a variety of bird species (e.g., Willis et al. 1978, Smith 1980a, Dixon 1987). In fact, chickadee intrapair aggressive interactions during the breeding season are extremely rare. I have spent a good deal of time looking for them, and in ten years I saw only nine. One, which occurred at a feeder before nest building had begun, I would call a draw: the female landed on the feeder, then her mate dashed over and landed very close to her. She turned to face him and gaped, then both left without taking any food. Since he had been dominant over her all winter, her gape may have come as a surprise (see also Dixon 1987). All eight other interactions resulted in the female supplanting her mate (pers. observ.). Therefore, while seldom overtly expressed, female Black-capped Chickadees, like female Great Tits, evidently become dominant over their mates during the breeding season. This period of dominance is quite short, though. The transition back to male dominance may occur by late nestling period. Thus Brewer (1961) reported that when both members of a pair met at the nest bringing food for the nestlings, there was mutual wing quivering, but then the male fed first and left before the female delivered her food, suggesting that he had once more become the dominant member of the pair.

### Courtship Feeding

During the early part of the breeding season, males bring food items to their mates. Although this is generally referred to as courtship feeding, it is now known to have little to do with courtship in chickadees, beginning as it does well after most pairs have been formed (Orr and Verbeek 1984).

Courtship feeding behavior of both male and female Black-capped Chickadees changes gradually as the season progresses. Courtship feeding begins very early in the spring, before breeding territories are fully established (late March in Massachusetts). At this stage, courtship feeding is usually silent and happens so fast one is lucky to see it at all. Neither bird quivers its wings with the exchange of food. Typically the female forages quietly, then suddenly her mate flies over to her, she grabs food from him, and he flies away. On one such occasion, I heard one of the birds give a short gargle note at the moment of food exchange—unfortunately it happened so fast that I could not be sure which bird had given the call (pers. observ.).

The female's behavior is the first to change. By mid to late nest-building stage, she begins to quiver her wings and give broken dee calls to her mate, who responds by giving her food. At this stage, and through egg laying, the male is typically silent as he approaches and gives her the food. Finally, during incubation and into the nestling stage, the male approaches his mate with soft fee-bees, both at and away from the nest. She then gives broken dees, and he feeds her.

The rate of courtship feeding is highest during egg laying and incubation. This is also the time when females are most markedly dominant over their mates (Smith 1980a). Given this dominance, it seems rather odd to call the female's wing quivering begging, as so many published accounts do. For this and other reasons I have suggested that it would be more accurate to call this display de-mand behavior (Smith 1980b).

A female's energy requirements are greatest right before and during egg laying, when she is forming the eggs, and during in-cubation, when her foraging time is necessarily curtailed. The male's courtship feeding is of great importance in getting her through these periods. Krebs (1970) and others have shown that males of several European tits tend to eat relatively small food items at this time, while selecting the largest ones they find to bring to their mate. This, it has been suggested, minimizes the strain on males: they usually carry just one food item at a time, and the energy expended per trip is the same, regardless of prey size, so by bringing larger food items they lower the number of trips they must take for a given level of feeding of their mate. My own field notes indicate that male Black-capped Chickadees certainly manage to find remarkably large caterpillars to bring to females, even in March.

### Copulation

Very little display is associated with copulation by Black-capped Chickadees. Indeed, as Dixon et al. (1970) put it, this species', copulation is notable for the suddenness of its onset. It is most common in the period just before and during egg laying, but can occur even after the female has begun incubation (Odum 1941a). It can occur at any time of day (Dixon et al. 1970).

Both sexes may give variable sees just before, and during, copu-lation. Either sex can initiate the copulation sequence by starting the variable sees, usually while quivering the wings (Dixon et al. 1970, Ficken et al. 1985). The male may give a special gargle call either before or just as he mounts the female. The whole sequence is remarkably short: variable sees are seldom if ever begun more than one minute prior to mounting (Dixon et al. 1970). After mating, the male usually flies off a short distance; the female may continue wing quivering for a few seconds, then she usually preens, and the pair moves off quietly together.

The mating sequence of Carolina Chickadees appears to be rather different (Brewer 1961). The male Carolina Chickadee's four-note whistled song apparently initiates the sequence, and the female responds by giving broken dees, like those associated with courtship feeding, rather than the higher, thinner variable sees given by Black-capped Chickadees. Such differences in mating behavior should serve to lower the chances of hybridization between Carolina and Black-capped Chickadees.

Naturally, females of monogamous species such as chickadees copulate most frequently with their own mates. Nevertheless, extrapair copulations (EPCs) do occur. The study of so-called cuckoldry in birds is a fast-growing area of research. Bray et al. (1975) found that female Red-winged Blackbirds (*Agelaius phoeniceus*) that were paired with vasectomized males laid fertile eggs—suggesting that they must have mated with other, fertile, males. More recently, biochemical analysis of the genetic components found in blood samples has been used to demonstrate that the level of multiple paternity in a variety of avian species is remarkably high (e.g., Gavin and Bollinger 1985, Joste et al. 1985; see also Norris and Blakey 1989).

Clearly, any extrapair copulation by a female will decrease her mate's fitness, as it potentially lowers his own reproductive success and makes him spend time and energy raising a group of offspring that may not all be related to him. Paired males of most species apparently minimize the chances of cuckoldry by following their mates very closely, especially during the females' most fertile period (generally defined as the period from three days before the laying of the first egg to three days before the laying of the last one; e.g., Björklund and Westman 1986a). Chickadees and titmice practice such mate guarding at least to some extent. Orr and Verbeek (1984) reported some evidence that captive Black-capped Chickadees exhibited mate guarding, which resulted in increased male-male aggression during the period when females were most ready to copulate. Mace (1988, 1989), working with captive pairs of Great Tits, showed that mate guarding is most intense early in the morning, possibly the time of day when the female is most fertile. She also found that both sexes showed evidence of "guard-ing," or staying close to, the other. Björklund and Westman (1986a) did a detailed field study of mate guarding by Great Tits and reported that during the female's fertile period the distance between pair members decreased significantly (Fig. 5-6), males followed females more, and the proportion of site changes initi-ated by females increased markedly (Fig. 5-7). They also found that the intensity of mate guarding by Great Tits is definitely less than that of many other bird species. Evidently mate guarding by Black-capped Chickadees is not particularly intense either.

Over a total of 14 breeding seasons in three widely scattered

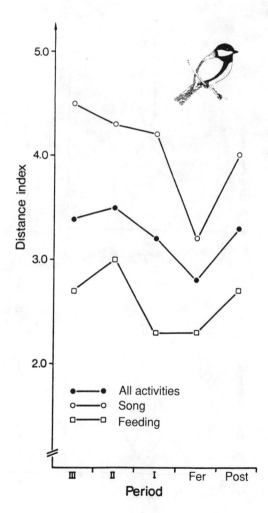

Fig. 5-6. Distance between members of Great Tit pairs during different activities through the breeding season. Distance index: 1 = less than 1 meter; 2 = 1–5 meters; 3 = 5–10 meters; 4 = 10–25 meters; and 5 = more than 25 meters. How close together a pair was depended on what the birds were doing, with birds being closest together during foraging (of the activities plotted here). Note that, regardless of activity, pair members were closest together during and immediately before the female's fertile period. Means of different pairs are shown. $N$ = 10 pairs for prefertile periods III and II; 9 pairs for prefertile period I and the fertile period (Fer); and 7 pairs for the postfertile period (Post). (From Björklund and Westman 1986a, courtesy of *Ornis Scandinavica*.)

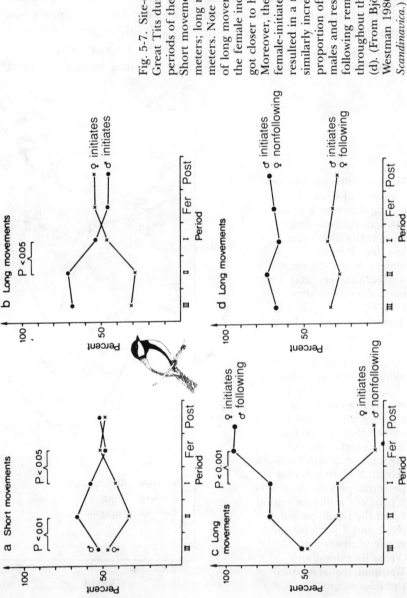

Fig. 5-7. Site-change initiation by Great Tits during different periods of the breeding season. Short movements, less than 25 meters; long movements, over 25 meters. Note that the proportion of long movements initiated by the female increased as the female got closer to her fertile period (b). Moreover, the proportion of female-initiated movements that resulted in a male following similarly increased (c), while the proportion of those initiated by males and resulting in a female following remained relatively low throughout the breeding season (d). (From Björklund and Westman 1986a, courtesy of *Ornis Scandinavica*.)

areas, I saw 13 extrapair copulations by color-banded Black-capped Chickadees (Smith 1988b). The great advantage of working with nonmigratory species like chickadees is that in color-banded populations, the social relationships and relative rank of each individual during the months leading up to the breeding season can be known—and known not only to the observer but also to the birds themselves. In other words, because chickadees are resident, essentially every breeding female will have had the opportunity to learn the relative rank of her own mate with respect to that of the other neighboring males. Seemingly, the females make use of this information. Of the 13 instances of extrapair copulation that I observed, every single one was with a male that had ranked above the female's own mate the previous winter (Table 5-1). Another interesting aspect of these data has to do with the location of the EPCs. A number of studies have either stated or implied that if a territorial male can just manage to prevent all male intrusion, he will have prevented the chance of his mate engaging in EPCs. The unstated, unexamined assumption here is that females never go beyond the boundaries of their own breed-

Table 5-1. Extrapair copulations (EPCs) by Black-capped Chickadees

| Year | Place[a] | Rank of mate[b] | Rank of other male | Location[c] | Time in breeding cycle | Time of day[d] |
|------|----------|-----------------|--------------------|-------------|------------------------|----------------|
| 1963 | BC | 2 | 1 | Other male | Nest building | D |
| 1963 | BC | 2 | 1 | Other male | Nest building | D |
| 1963 | BC | 2 | 1 | Other male | Egg laying | D |
| 1963 | BC | 3 | 1 | Own male | Incubation | D |
| 1964 | BC | 2 | 1 | Other male | Egg laying | D |
| 1964 | BC | 2 | 1 | Other male | Nest building | D |
| 1964 | BC | 3 | 2 | Own male | Nest building | D |
| 1971 | EM | 3 | 1 | Other male | Nest building | MM |
| 1982 | WM | 2 | 1 | Own male | Nest building | D |
| 1982 | WM | 3 | 2 | Other male | Egg laying | D |
| 1984 | WM | 2 | 1 | Own male | Egg laying | D |
| 1985 | WM | 3 | 1 | Other male | Nest building | D |
| 1986 | WM | 2 | 1 | Other male | Nest building | D |

*Source:* Smith 1988b, courtesy of *Behaviour.*
[a]BC = British Columbia; EM = eastern Massachusetts; WM = western Massachusetts.
[b]Rank refers to a male's position within the flock hierarchy: 1 is the top-ranked (alpha) male, 2, the beta male, and so on.
[c]Indicates the ownership of the territory where the EPC occurred.
[d]D = within an hour of dawn; MM = midmorning.

ing territory. Yet the data in Table 5-1 show a very different story: 9 of the 13 observed EPCs actually took place in the territory of the "other" male. This strongly suggests that these female chickadees were actively seeking out superior partners for EPCs. Since a large number of parids are essentially nonmigratory, and thus have the same opportunity for winter rank assessment, similar female initiation of EPCs may be a common pattern in other parids as well.

## Nest Site

Like most other parids, Black-capped Chickadees nest in cavities. Virtually all natural sites are in rotten wood: either stubs, knotholes where a branch formerly joined the main trunk, or in rotten limbs of living trees. Old woodpecker holes are used occasionally, especially in areas that have relatively few other natural nest sites. There is even a record of Black-capped Chickadees nesting in an old, unusually deep robin nest (Murie 1933).

As the pairs split off from the flocks in early spring, they spend more and more time investigating potential nest sites—entering old holes or digging at rotten wood in snags or heavy limbs. At first these explorations are sporadic and look almost like extensions of foraging for food. Nor is this activity restricted to pairs: I have seen banded single birds, clearly in search of mate and territory, engage in this kind of early spring exploration.

Later, as territories become more firmly established, digging begins in earnest. Many North American chickadee species show an interesting difference from European tits in this digging behavior. Both male and female Black-capped Chickadees, Carolina Chickadees, Boreal Chickadees (*Parus hudsonicus*), and others (Bent 1946, S. T. Smith 1972, McLaren 1975) excavate the nest cavities, while in European tits, the females do the vast majority of the excavation (Perrins 1979). This difference is even true for the Willow Tit (*Parus montanus*), once considered conspecific with Black-capped Chickadees.

Pairs of Black-capped Chickadees in rich habitat may explore half a dozen possible locations, but gradually they settle on one or two, which they then spend considerable time excavating fully. When a hole is just begun, chips fly. The digging bird usually flings the bits of wood over its shoulder, typically with a twist of the head that tends to scatter the chips so they don't pile up in a telltale heap below. Later, when the cavity gets larger, the digging birds will carry off mouthfuls of chips to drop some distance from the nest (Fig. 5-8). Not infrequently, one can see a chickadee carry off a mouthful of chips and then proceed to "kill" a larger chip by holding it down and hammering it before dropping it. Often each member of a pair will have its own favorite perches about 10–20 meters from the cavity; there they will go to drop bill-fulls of chips. As one bird leaves the nest with a load of chips, its mate will often enter and continue the digging, and so they take turns, often working for 30 minutes or more before taking a break.

This process of excavation is evidently important to Black-

Fig. 5-8. Black-capped Chickadee excavating a potential nest site. The bird will carry this beakful of wood chips some distance away before dropping it. (Photograph by Arthur A. Allen, courtesy of Bird Photographs, Inc.)

Fig. 5-9. Black-capped Chickadees can occasionally be induced to nest in bird boxes, particularly in suburban areas where natural cavities are scarce. (Photograph courtesy of Muriel Harris.)

capped Chickadees. Given a choice, they will virtually always dig out a natural cavity rather than take an empty hole such as a nest box—unless the box has been partly filled with sawdust (Kluyver 1961; see Nest Boxes, Chapter 2).

Of 192 Black-capped Chickadee nests whose eggs are deposited in the collection of the Western Foundation of Vertebrate Zoology in California, 152 were located in rotten stubs, 15 in dead limbs of living trees, 12 in fence posts, 6 where a large branch had fallen or been sawed from the main trunk of a tree, 3 in bird boxes (Fig. 5-9), 2 in large fallen branches (one wonders if this is how and why they were collected), 1 in a rotten part of an old telephone pole, and 1 in the underside of a wooden fence rail. Eighteen of these were in holes originally dug by woodpeckers. Softwood trees, such as alder (*Alnus* sp.), birch (*Betula* sp.), poplar (*Populus* sp.), cherry

(*Prunus* sp.), and willow (*Salix* sp.), provide especially popular locations for nest sites.

Chickadee nest sites range from ground level to 70 feet or more (over 20 meters), but most occur between 5 and 20 feet (approximately 1.5 to 7 meters) above the ground.

The entrance to most chickadee nest cavities is on the side of the tree or stub (Fig. 5-10). A small percentage of chickadee nests,

Fig. 5-10. Black-capped Chickadee at a typical natural cavity, with a side entrance (here through a knothole). (© Alan Cruickshank / VIREO.)

however, have entrances at the top (Fig. 5-11). Of 24 nests in my Vancouver population (Smith 1967c), 3 had top entrances; of 25 examined by Nickell (1956) from Michigan and Ontario, 4 had top entrances. I still remember my disbelief at finding my first such nest, in a rotten fence post. Vancouver is justly famous for its rain, yet the brood fledged successfully. Two factors may make these

Fig. 5-11. Black-capped Chickadee at a more unusual natural cavity nest, having a top entrance. (© Alan Cruickshank / VIREO.)

nests less vulnerable than they first appear. One is that chickadees often cover their eggs with nest material before leaving the nest, both during the laying period (Odum 1941b) and sometimes also during incubation (Nickell 1956). Secondly, these nests tend to be quite deep, so that even a slight amount of wind will slant rain sufficiently to keep it from pouring straight onto the nest and its contents.

Of 59 nests in the Western Foundation's collection with available data, depths ranged from a remarkable 18 inches (45.7 cm), in an old Hairy Woodpecker (*Picoides villosus*) cavity, to 4 inches (10.2 cm), with an average of 8.3 inches (21 cm). Odum (1941a) found cavity diameters ranging from 6.3 to 7 cm (2.5–2.8 inches). It is hardly surprising that such a variable structure takes a variable amount of time to excavate: anywhere from four days (Odum 1941a) to ten days or more (Bent 1946) being commonplace.

Typically, chickadees will excavate a new site each time they start a nest. However, sometimes they will use the same nest site over again. Butts (1931) reported a nest used by the same pair two years in a row; I know of a nest box in a suburban setting that was occupied for four consecutive years, three by the same pair. Doubtless longer strings of consecutive occupancy are also known. Such strings are most likely to occur in areas where alternative nest sites are scarce.

The Mountain Chickadee (*Parus gambeli*) of western North America, like the European Coal Tit (*P. ater*), may actually nest in the ground, in locations such as old mouse holes (Griffee 1961). Both species live in coniferous forests, where natural cavities may be relatively hard to find. Recently, Peck and James (1987) reported one record of a similar site used by Black-capped Chickadees in Ontario, where the actual nest was 11.4 cm (4.5 inches) below ground.

The most peculiar nest site I ever saw used by Black-capped Chickadees was a black metal pipe supporting a sign in an open parking lot. The pipe had an inner diameter of 2 inches (5 cm) and was completely open from above. The nest was 13 inches (33 cm) down, supported by the lower of two screws that held the sign. The pipe received no shade from the south and west, and was thus unprotected from the afternoon sun. It must have been incredibly hot for the occupants on sunny days; the incubating female frequently had to come to the top of the pipe to pant. The utterly amazing thing is that although that particular territory contained

many natural potential nest sites, the pipe was occupied for at least
two years in succession. The same male was involved both years,
but with a different mate each time. This observation suggests that
males, at least occasionally, have an important role in nest-site
selection. Clearly, the pipe was less than optimal as a nest site, and
at the end of each breeding season, the female that had bred with
this male deserted him and joined a different winter flock (Smith
1974b). Such "divorces" are quite uncommon among chickadees,
which frequently mate for life (Baldwin 1934, 1935a; see Mate
Fidelity and Divorce, Chapter 7).

## Nest Building

Very rarely, Black-capped Chickadees construct no nest—instead, they lay their eggs in unlined cavities (Peck and James 1987).
The vast majority of Black-capped Chickadees, however, having
found or constructed a suitable cavity, build a nest there before
laying their eggs. Although both sexes of some chickadees, such as
the Mountain Chickadee, participate in nest building (Dahlsten
and Copper 1979), the female Black-capped Chickadee builds the
nest herself, usually with her mate in close attendance. Females are
very secretive at this stage and typically search for building material some distance from their nest cavity. They gather great beak-
fuls of material, which sticks out on each side of their head like a
huge mustache. Occasionally I have seen the attending male find a
food item and fly over to present it to the female, only to be
rejected by a bird whose beak is bulging with moss.

Most nests are constructed in three to four days (Bent 1946),
although Odum (1941b) reported one that was completed in just
two days. Naturally, the nests, like the cavities they are in, are quite
variable in dimensions: Odum (1941b) weighed seven nests and
found they ranged from 1.6 to 10 grams in weight—and surely
took differing lengths of time to build.

Chickadee nests are usually made of both plant and animal
substances, although nests of both all plant and even all animal
material have been reported. Plant substances include fine bark
strips, pine needles, green moss, fern down, fluff from the fibers
attached to a variety of seeds, and even corn silk (in a late nest).
Animal materials include fur, hair, and wool from a wide variety of
mammals—and, occasionally, feathers as well. Typically a founda-

tion is made of some relatively coarse substance, such as moss, on which a soft cup is made of finer material such as rabbit fur (Nickell 1956). Often there is a pause of a day or so during which the female does little or no further nest construction before laying begins. However, at least some females apparently continue to add occasional small bits of fine lining material to the nest even after laying has begun (Nickell 1956). Usually by nest construction phase the female has begun roosting at night in the nest cavity, with the male roosting somewhere else close by (Odum 1941b).

### Egg Laying

With few exceptions, female chickadees lay one egg per day, usually early in the morning, until their clutch is completed (Odum 1941b, Kluyver 1961). Since the female is now roosting in the nest chamber, she is already in position to lay the egg; during the laying period, females leave their nests half an hour later than usual. Part of this half hour is spent by the female in covering the eggs with fine nest material, so to the casual glance of a would-be predator, the nest will appear to be empty (Kluyver 1961).

Chickadee eggs are rounded-ovate. Their ground color is white, and they are liberally spotted with fine dots of reddish brown, often concentrated about the larger end. They have little or no gloss and are very thin-shelled (as are the eggs of several European parids as well). Bent (1946) gave the average dimensions from 50 eggs as being 15.2 mm (0.60 inch) long and 12.2 mm wide (0.48 inch).

Courtship feeding is especially prominent during the egg-laying period, and members of the pair are seldom far apart. For the most part, they stay well away from the nest, feeding quietly together.

### Clutch Size

Black-capped Chickadee clutches range from just 1 egg (Smith 1974) to 13 eggs (Bent 1946). By far the most common clutch sizes are 6, 7, and 8 eggs (Fig. 5-12). Indeed, clutches of these three sizes made up almost 80 percent of the sample shown in Figure 5-12. The overall average from this sample is 6.64 eggs. Remark-

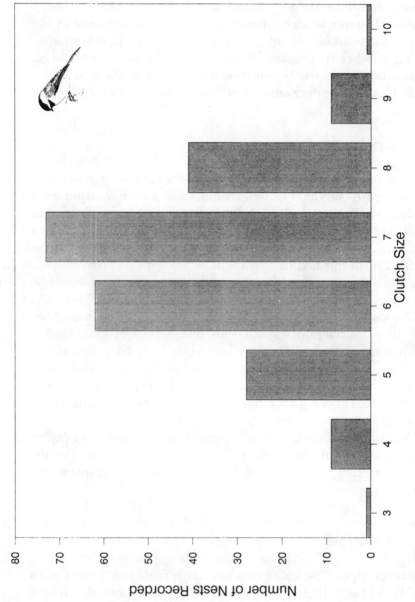

Fig. 5-12. Distribution of clutch sizes in a sample of 225 Black-capped Chickadee nests from all over North America. (Data courtesy of the Western Foundation of Vertebrate Zoology, Los Angeles.)

ably, Odum (1941b) reported an average of 6.7 eggs per clutch in his New York study area; Nickell (1956) found an average of 6.6 eggs per clutch in Michigan, and Kluyver (1961) found an average clutch size of 6.7 eggs in Massachusetts.

While this number of eggs may seem rather large for so small a bird, Black-capped Chickadee clutches are actually rather low in comparison with other parids. Brewer (1963) reported that Carolina Chickadees laid somewhat larger clutches than did Black-capped Chickadees living in the same area. And European titmice can lay positively enormous clutches: a single Blue Tit can lay up to 18 eggs in a clutch, and their average clutch size in Britain is about 11 eggs (Perrins 1979).

This brings up a curious point: Blue Tit nests containing more than 20 eggs have been found, but the eggs are thought to have been laid by more than one female. "Egg dumping," or the opportunistic laying of an egg in another bird's nest, is fairly widespread among European titmice (Perrins 1979). Recent studies involving biochemical analysis of broods has now shown that conspecific brood parasitism is possibly far more common than had once been thought (e.g., Gowaty and Karlin 1984, Wrege and Emlen 1987, Kendra et al. 1988, MacWhirter 1989). Whether any North American chickadee species also engages in such practices still awaits investigation.

One of the numerous factors that can affect how many eggs a chickadee or titmouse will lay is latitude: northern clutches are on average somewhat larger than those laid farther south. Brewer (1963) verified this difference for both Carolina and Black-capped Chickadees, and it holds true for many European titmice as well (Perrins 1979).

The chances that an egg will produce a successful offspring may also affect clutch size of parids. For example, Crested Tits (*Parus cristatus*), which suffer higher nest predation rates than Willow Tits, tend to lay smaller clutches than those of Willow Tits, thus minimizing losses if a whole nest fails (Ekman and Askenmo 1986).

A third factor is how late in the year a female begins to lay: the later the nest, the smaller the clutch (Kluyver 1961, Perrins and McCleery 1989, Perrins 1990). The caterpillar supply gets lower as the season progresses, and the reliability of such clues as leaf damage also decreases (Heinrich and Collins 1983), making the job of finding food for such late-growing offspring that much harder.

A fourth factor affecting clutch size is the age of the female: at least up to a certain point, older females tend to lay larger clutches. This has been found for both Black-capped Chickadees (Howitz 1986a) and several species of European tits as well (Perrins 1979, Dhondt 1989a).

Four other factors have been found to have quantifiable effects on the clutch size of European titmice, and probably affect the clutch size of chickadees as well. One is how early warm weather comes in the spring: early springs induce larger clutches. Another factor is the local habitat, which in turn affects territory quality. Clutches have been shown to be largest in the best quality habitat. A third factor, surprisingly enough, is the size of the nest cavity itself: females of Great, Blue, and even Willow Tits that used small nest cavities laid fewer eggs than those with larger chambers (Perrins 1979). Finally, Ekman and Askenmo (1986) found a positive correlation between average clutch size of Willow Tits and juvenile survival rate the following year (Fig. 5-13). This finding suggests

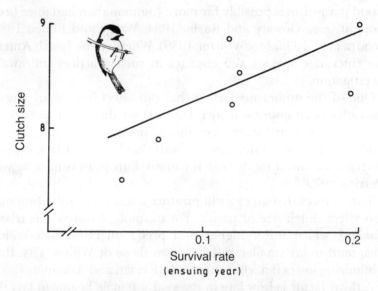

Fig. 5-13. Seven years' data showing the relation between average Willow Tit clutch size and survival rate of offspring during their first year. Survival variance components attributable to climate and predation pressure (presumably unpredictable) were removed. Offspring survival rates are Jolly-Seber estimates. ($y = 7.51 + 6.87x$; $r = 0.74$; $P < 0.05$). Note that as clutch size increased, so did subsequent survival of offspring, possibly suggesting adjustment of egg laying to cues predicting future conditions. (From Ekman and Askenmo 1986, courtesy of *Evolution*.)

that at least female Willow Tits may adjust clutch size in response to changing survival prospects for their offspring, possibly by using breeding density as a cue (Ekman and Askenmo 1986). Certainly local breeding density has a marked effect on the clutch size of a number of parids, with clutches being smaller in areas having particularly high population numbers (Perrins 1979, Perrins and McCleery 1989).

Perrins and Moss (1974) conducted some fascinating experiments involving manipulation of clutch size with Great Tits. By moving newly hatched nestlings, they compared overall survival of artificially enlarged broods with the survival of naturally occurring broods of the same size. Their results showed that natural large broods survived better than did artificial large broods, suggesting that females somehow lay clutches whose size is related to their own ability to raise young. Nur (1986), however, working with manipulated clutches of Blue Tits, claimed to have found evidence against the generality of this idea. He concluded that, at least in his population, clutch size apparently was not adjusted to the parents' ability to rear offspring and was perhaps regulated only by the earlier factors of differing ability to lay or to incubate the eggs themselves.

### Incubation

Incubation by Black-capped Chickadees, as by most parids, is done exclusively by the female. By the end of the laying period, the female's brood patch becomes well developed. Down feathers are shed from the belly region, and that area actually gets extra capillary vessels just below the skin. The heat carried by the blood in these surface vessels transfers easily to the eggs, facilitating their incubation. Because birds have voluntary control over the positions of their outer feathers, they can cover their brood patch at will, such as when they leave the nest. In this way even birds with fully developed brood patches can protect themselves from unnecessary heat loss.

All normal breeding females get fully developed brood patches. Some male Black-capped Chickadees also develop partial brood patches (Kluyver 1961). Development of brood patches by males of other bird species often indicates some male role in incubation; nevertheless, there is to date no known evidence of any incubation by male Black-capped Chickadees.

Ordinarily, a female will begin incubation on the day before she lays the last egg in the clutch. Because eggs do not begin development until incubation has begun, all the eggs will hatch on approximately the same date, so all the young will be able to leave the nest at about the same time. By contrast, a female beginning a replacement clutch late in the breeding season may begin incubation well before she lays the last egg (Perrins 1979); this will result in a brood of staggered ages. Later in the season, proper nestling food is much harder to find, and nestling starvation can be a problem. By having young of differing ages, the female will ensure that at least a few (the oldest) will beg more vigorously and get the most food, thus increasing the chances of at least some offspring surviving.

Incubating females must eat, and during the day they emerge periodically to forage for food. This foraging is often triggered by the male arriving with food for his mate. When he arrives he gives faint fee-bees; the female may answer with a soft twitter (Odum 1941b). Sometimes the male comes right to the nest hole to feed the female; at other times he just calls from near the nest until she emerges and joins him. If the male is late in coming, the female may leave the nest without him to feed on her own; usually this quickly brings the male over to her. Once emerged from the nest, the female moves around quietly, foraging for herself and eating food provided by her mate. Most pairs restrict their activity at these times to areas fairly close to the nest. Eventually the female will move back to the nest, enter, and resume incubation.

While the female incubates, the male patrols the territory, feeding quietly unless encountering a trespassing chickadee, and returning fairly regularly to feed his mate on the nest.

Various studies have measured the lengths of the female's attentive and off periods; Table 5-2 summarizes three such studies on Black-capped Chickadees. Average attentive (on) periods range around 20–25 minutes, but can be as short as six minutes or as long as an hour. Females generally stay off the nest for an average of seven or eight minutes, with extremes of 2–23 minutes. The result is that incubating chickadees spend about three minutes on the nest for every one minute off foraging, or as Brewer (1961) put it, they have a percent attentiveness of 75 percent.

Studies of European titmice, which nest in boxes far more readily than chickadees, have revealed that incubating females are quite active within the nest chamber (Perrins 1979). They move

Table 5-2. Black-capped Chickadee incubation behavior

| | | Attentive (on) periods | | | Inattentive (off) periods | | |
|---|---|---|---|---|---|---|---|
| Source | State | No. observed | Average length (min) | Range (min) | No. observed | Average length (min) | Range (min) |
| Odum 1941b | N.Y. | 29 | 24.0 | 6–61 | 33 | 7.8 | 2–23 |
| Brewer 1961 | Ill. | 10 | 18.0 | SE = 3.62 | 11 | 7.0 | SE = 1.07 |
| Kluyver 1961 | Mass. | [a] | 22.7 | 7–47 | [a] | 7.7 | 2–17 |

[a]Data taken on one brood for 30 hours over 3 days.

around within the chamber a fair bit, frequently fidgeting with the eggs. As a consequence all the eggs get turned fairly often, which is probably important for the proper development of the embryos. In very small cavities or extra large clutches, moreover, the female may not be able to warm all eggs equally, so moving the eggs is necessary to make sure that each one gets some warmth.

Incubation can be costly to the female, especially on cold nights. Because incubation typically begins quite early in the spring (Odum 1941b, Kluyver 1961), cold nights are to be expected. Svein Haftorn and his colleagues in Norway measured incubation costs in a variety of European titmice by converting nest boxes into metabolic chambers and measuring the birds' rate of oxygen consumption, first during the laying period and then during incubation itself. They found that incubation costs increased not only as temperature dropped but also with clutch size (Fig. 5-14), going up by about 6–7 percent for each additional egg (Haftorn and Reinertsen 1985). If one applies Haftorn and Reinertsen's figures for Blue Tits to Black-capped Chickadees, a female chickadee incubating a normal (seven-egg) clutch during a night with an air temperature around freezing would need to increase her metabolic rate by about 25 percent just to keep all her eggs sufficiently warm—quite a drain on a bird that has not only just spent all the energy needed to produce the eggs in the first place, but also now needs to spend at least three-quarters of her daylight hours incubating, rather than foraging. Clearly, incubation entails more than just resting in the nest cavity.

Normally, Black-capped Chickadee incubation lasts 12–13 days, after which the eggs begin to hatch. Some recent evidence shows that, at least in Blue Tits, larger clutches take longer to incubate

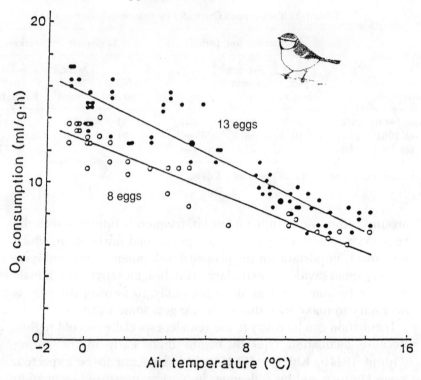

Fig. 5-14. The relationship of the female Blue Tit's oxygen-consumption rate to the air temperature, when incubating 13 eggs (solid circles) and after the clutch was temporarily reduced to 8 eggs (open circles). Each record represents the stable value of oxygen-consumption rate at a stable air temperature. Large circles represent several equal records. Upper regression line ($n = 71$): $y = 15.35 - 0.62x$. Lower regression line ($n = 32$): $y = 12.55 - 0.51x$. Note that incubation costs, as measured by oxygen-consumption rates, increased with clutch size and also as the temperature became colder. (From Haftorn and Reinertsen 1985, courtesy of *Auk*.)

(H. G. Smith 1989). When the onset of incubation by chickadees is normal, all the viable eggs typically hatch within 12–30 hours and tend to do so in the order in which they were laid (Odum 1941b). Brewer (1961) found that, at least in Carolina Chickadees, hatching can occur at any time of the day or night. Once an egg has hatched, the parents usually carry the shells some distance from the nest and either drop or eat them (Odum 1941b, Brewer 1961, Perrins 1979).

# 6

# The Later Part of the Breeding Season

## Nestling Care

It is not easy to determine exactly when chickadees hatch because even a few days after the eggs have hatched, the rhythmic behavior of the parents continues, with the female spending more time in the nest chamber than off foraging (Table 6-1). The main clue indicating that hatching has occurred is that, after the eggs have hatched, when the female returns to the nest, she usually carries very small food items back with her.

Instead of incubating, the female now broods her nearly naked young. Brooding is necessary, especially in cool or damp conditions, because young Black-capped Chickadees cannot thermoregulate (that is, maintain a high body temperature on their own) efficiently until they are at least 12 days old (Odum 1941b). Because the female must spend most of her time brooding, the bulk of early nestling feeding is done by the male (who does none of the brooding). He continues to bring food to the nest, giving it to the female if she is there, and entering the nest to feed the young directly if she is off (another good clue that the young have hatched). Courtship feeding declines rapidly after the eggs have hatched, and most of the male's efforts are spent gathering food for the offspring. Gradually, as the nestlings' need for brooding

Table 6-1. Characteristics of attentiveness during nest life of young Black-capped
and Carolina Chickadees and chickadees of the Vandalia population
(a Black-capped/Carolina Chickadee contact zone)

| Characteristic | Population | Days after hatching[a] | | | |
|---|---|---|---|---|---|
| | | 1–4 | 5–8 | 9–12 | 13–16 |
| Minutes | Carolina Chickadee | 308 | 300 | 300 | 211 |
| observed | Black-capped Chickadee | 205 | — | 198 | 175 |
| | Vandalia population | 330 | 89 | 423 | 45 |
| Percentage | Carolina Chickadee | 55.2 | 25.0 | 11.7 | 0.0 |
| attentiveness | Black-capped Chickadee | 71.5 | — | 9.3 | 0.0 |
| (brooding) | Vandalia population | 56.2 | 0.0 | 7.9 | 0.0 |
| Mean length | Carolina Chickadee | 11.4 | 5.3 | 8.9 | — |
| attentive period | | (3.0–25.5) | (2.5–11.5) | (2.5–15.0) | |
| (minutes) | Black-capped Chickadee | 10.5 | — | 6.2 | — |
| | | (1.0–8.0) | | (4.0–11.0) | |
| | Vandalia population | 11.1 | — | 3.0 | — |
| | | (3.0–79+) | | (1.0–7.0) | |
| Mean length | Carolina Chickadee | 8.2 | 16.4 | 21.0 | — |
| inattentive | | (3.0–13.8) | (5.0–33.0) | (3.0–79+) | |
| period | Black-capped Chickadee | 6.6 | — | 24.8 | — |
| (minutes) | | (2.0–7.5) | | (18.0–24+) | |
| | Vandalia population | 13.6 | — | 17.2 | — |
| | | (1.0–24.0) | | (2.5–87+) | |
| Feedings by | Carolina Chickadee | 2.6 | 2.5 | 2.8 | 3.8 |
| parents per | Black-capped Chickadee | 1.7 | — | 2.7 | — |
| young per hour | Vandalia population | 1.4 | 2.6 | 2.5 | 3.7 |
| Percentage of | Carolina Chickadee | 18 | 25 | 45 | 53 |
| feedings by ♀ | Black-capped Chickadee | 24 | — | 50 | — |
| | Vandalia population | 30 | — | 60 | — |
| Fecal sacs | Carolina Chickadee | 0.07 | 0.5 | 0.5 | — |
| removed per | Black-capped Chickadee | 0.08 | — | 0.5 | — |
| young per hour | Vandalia population | 0.01 | 0.5 | 0.5 | 0.7 |

Source: Brewer 1961, courtesy of Wilson Bulletin.
Note: Data are for Illinois except for 333 minutes of observation of Carolina Chickadees from
Baltimore, Md. (H. Brackbill, in litt.).
[a]Ranges are in parentheses.

decreases, the female can forage more and more, until by about
day 12 or 13 posthatching, both parents feed the young about
equally. Odum (1941b) documented this very nicely by recording
feeding rates by the two sexes at a nest when the young were 1, 4, 8
and 13 days old. He found that at the first two ages the male fed
the nestlings two to three times as often as did the female; even by

day 8 he still fed them about twice as much, but by day 13 the two parents fed their nestlings about equally, as brooding was no longer necessary. Brewer (1961) reported similar data for the Carolina Chickadee (*Parus carolinensis*).

A necessary by-product of all this feeding is nestling defecation. Actually, the feces of nestling chickadees are remarkably convenient in two major ways. First, they are enclosed in a neat mucous envelope, so they can easily be picked up without undue mess. Second, they are produced immediately after a nestling receives food, so the hard-working parent need only arrive, deposit food at one end, take up the resulting package from the other end, and the nest remains clean. Nestlings of a wide variety of other species share these same two characteristics. Usually, for at least the first two or three days after hatching, the adult chickadees will eat the nestlings' fecal packages. This is not as peculiar as it sounds—the food passes so rapidly through the digestive system of the newly hatched chickadees that a lot of nutrition remains, and the parents can use the extra energy. Later the adults typically fly off with the fecal packages (Fig. 6-1) and deposit them some distance from the nest. Thus such a sight confirms that the young have hatched, but does not indicate precisely when hatching occurred.

Brooding females of European parids can be quite active in the nest chamber. Besides frequently changing their position, they also commonly engage in nest fluffing: taking hold of part of the nest lining and shaking it vigorously (Perrins 1979). Fluffing likely serves both to increase the insulative properties of the nest and to shake any nest parasites there might be down to the bottom of the nest structure.

Brewer (1961) showed that the number of feedings per young per hour steadily increased as the nestlings of both Carolina and Black-capped Chickadees grew bigger (Table 6-1). This common pattern is hardly surprising, since larger individuals require more food for normal body maintenance. Kluyver (1961) succeeded in getting Black-capped Chickadees to nest in boxes fitted with chronographs, so that entry rates of the parents could be recorded mechanically. He too found that feeding rates increased overall with nestling age (Table 6-2), and he concluded that parental feeding rates may be largely regulated by the nestlings' own need for food, as conveyed by the intensity of their begging.

Not all eggs hatch or young survive after hatching. European titmice will pull out dead nestlings if they are small enough to be

Fig. 6-1. Adult Black-capped Chickadee removing a fecal package from the nest. The chickadee will take it some distance away, then either drop or eat it. (Photograph by David G. Allen, courtesy of Bird Photographs, Inc.)

carried, and will drop them some distance from the nest (Perrins 1979). Black-capped Chickadees probably do the same, although I have not found any published accounts of this behavior. Unlike dead nestlings, however, unhatched eggs provide no bill-hold and therefore must remain in the nest. Amazingly, although Odum

Table 6-2. Number of entrances (feedings per young) per day for breeding Black-capped Chickadees at Drumlin Farm

| Box 16, 6 young | | | Box 105, 6 young | | | Box 113, 5 young | | | Box 204, 5 young | | | Box 106, 3 young | | |
|---|---|---|---|---|---|---|---|---|---|---|---|---|---|---|
| Date | Age (d) | Feed p.y. | Date | Age (d) | Feed p.y. | Date | Age (d) | Feed p.y. | Date | Age (d) | Feed p.y. | Date | Age (d) | Feed p.y. |
| May 16 | 3 | 48 | May 21 | 2 | 22 | May 27 | 4 | 21 | June 20 | 1 | 29 | June 25 | 1 | 14 |
| 17 | 4 | 44 | 22 | 3 | 24 | 28 | 5 | 24 | 21 | 2 | 27 | 26 | 2 | 19 |
| 18 | 5 | 52 | 23 | 4 | 25 | 29 | 6 | 24 | 22 | 3 | 27 | 27 | 3 | 23 |
| 19 | 6 | 45 | 24 | 5 | 28 | 30 | 7 | (23) | 23 | 4 | 33 | 28 | 4 | 21 |
| 20 | 7 | 49 | 25 | 6 | 30 | 31 | 8 | (25) | 24 | 5 | 36 | 29 | 5 | (25) |
| 21 | 8 | 44 | 26 | 7 | 27 | June 1 | 9 | 26 | 25 | 6 | 35 | 30 | 6 | (30) |
| 22 | 9 | 43 | 27 | 8 | 24 | 2 | 10 | 23 | 26 | 7 | 40 | July 1 | 7 | 33 |
| 23 | 10 | (51) | 28 | 9 | (24) | 3 | 11 | 30 | 27 | 8 | 42 | | | |
| 24 | 11 | 59 | 29 | 10 | (24) | 4 | 12 | 31 | 28 | 9 | 42 | | | |
| 25 | 12 | 67 | 30 | 11 | 24 | 5 | 13 | 33 | 29 | 10 | 48 | | | |
| | | | 31 | 12 | 29 | 6 | 14 | 30 | 30 | 11 | 41 | | | |
| | | | June 1 | 13 | 31 | 7 | 15 | 36 | July 1 | 12 | 47 | | | |
| | | | 2 | 14 | 32 | 8 | 16 | 33 | | | | | | |
| | | | | | | 9 | 17 | 32 | | | | | | |
| | | | | | | 10 | 18 | 30 | | | | | | |
| | | | | | | 11 | 19 | 23 | | | | | | |

Source: Kluyver 1961, courtesy of Auk.
Note: Numbers in parentheses are estimates based on incomplete recordings.

(1941b) and others have remarked on how thin-shelled chickadee eggs are, the eggs somehow do not break, but instead get worked down into the soft lining of the nest itself. I have found several unhatched eggs in chickadee nests, but never any sign of eggs being broken by anything other than a predator.

I know of no published records of any chickadee having a helper at the nest (that is, a third individual that aids the parents in caring for a brood of nestlings), nor does Perrins (1979) report any record of helpers in any British titmouse. There are a few scattered reports of Tufted Titmice (*Parus bicolor*) having helpers (e.g., Brackbill 1970, Davis 1978, Tarbell 1983). The only other members of this genus known to have helpers are the Black Tit (*Parus niger*) of Africa and possibly the Varied Tit (*P. varius*) of Asia (Matthyson 1990). Certainly it seems safe to say that, given all the color-banding studies performed on chickadees and their relatives, such helpers are extremely rare among parids.

## Nestling Growth and Development

At hatching, chickadees are tiny, weighing not much more than a gram. Being altricial, their eyes are tightly shut, their legs and wings poorly developed, and they are essentially naked, having only six small patches of wispy juvenile down feathers, all on the upper (dorsal) surface (Odum 1941b). Their mouth is edged with bright yellow, and they can lift their head and gape for food when a parent arrives.

By the fourth day after hatching, the first signs of their new contour feathers appear as dark specks along the feather tracts, especially those along the nestlings' back. Shivering also appears at about day four. The eyes begin to open by about day 6 or 7, but are not fully opened until day 12. By day 9 the nestlings are in the "pinfeather stage," with their new contour feathers still covered with feather casings and poking out of the skin like short porcupine quills. Shivering is well developed by day 9, but not until day 12, when the feathers have burst through much of their casings, are the nestlings capable of true thermoregulation. By day 15 or 16 the nestlings look like short-tailed adults, except for the yellow corners of the mouth (Fig. 6-2). Odum 1941b) reported that the begging call of very young nestlings is a faint *eee*, gradually changing to a noisy clatter as they get older (see also Clemmons

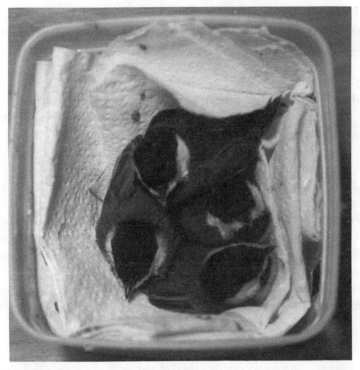

Fig. 6-2. These nestling chickadees are just about old enough to leave the nest.

and Howitz 1990). Typically they do not give begging dees regularly, until after they have left the nest.

At all ages, nestlings are quite active, and move about frequently in the nest chamber (Odum (1941b). There is often much scrabbling for position, with the hungriest nestlings usually managing to get the top positions; after these get fed, they generally sink down under the rest to digest for a while, then work their way back up for more food.

As the young continue to grow, the nest cavity becomes more and more crowded. The female roosts each night in the cavity until at least day 12 (the time at which the young become capable of thermoregulating on their own, and thus no longer need brooding). Soon after this, however, most females will find another quiet uncrowded place to roost, usually close to the nest (Odum 1941b, Perrins 1979).

Table 6-3 shows the data on nestling weights of Black-capped Chickadees obtained by Kluyver in Massachusetts. The young chickadees steadily increased in weight until about day 12, by which time most healthy nestlings weighed 10–11 grams. During the next few days less weight was added, and Kluyver's birds fledged (that is, left the nest) at just over 11 grams. Kluyver found no major difference in nestling growth rates between first and second broods, or between broods raised in deciduous habitat versus pine woods habitat (Kluyver 1961).

The growth of young birds typically can be described by a logistic curve, whose constant ($K$) reflects the rate at which a given species' young develop (Ricklefs 1968). For Black-capped Chickadees, Ricklefs (1968) calculated a $K$ value of 0.384, as opposed to a $K$ of 0.480 for Mountain Chickadees (*Parus gambeli*) (Grundel 1987). Thus nestling Black-capped Chickadees apparently develop faster than nestling Mountain Chickadees.

From about day 12 on, if anything disturbs the nest, the young chickadees may burst out, even though they are too young to fly

Table 6-3. Average weights (in grams) of nestling Black-capped Chickadees at Drumlin Farm, 1959

| Age (days) | \| First brood: No. of nestlings | | | | | | | All broods | \| Second brood: No. of nestlings | | | | All broods |
|---|---|---|---|---|---|---|---|---|---|---|---|---|---|
| | 3 | 3 | 5 | 6 | 6 | 7 | 7 | | 3 | 5 | 5 | 5 | |
| 0 | | | | | | | | | 0.9 | | | | 0.9 |
| 1 | | | 1.4 | | | | | 1.4 | | | 1.8 | | 1.8 |
| 2 | | | | | | | 2.2 | 2.2 | 1.7 | | | 2.6 | 2.2 |
| 3 | | | 3.3 | | | | | 3.3 | | 3.6 | 3.2 | | 3.4 |
| 4 | | | | | | | | | | | | 3.7 | 3.7 |
| 5 | | | 5.4 | | | | 5.6 | 5.5 | 3.7 | 5.6 | 5.0 | | 4.8 |
| 6 | 7.1 | 7.0 | | 6.9 | | | | 7.0 | | | | 5.8 | 5.8 |
| 7 | | | 6.9 | | | | 7.4 | 7.2 | 6.6 | 7.9 | 7.4 | | 7.3 |
| 8 | | | | 8.6 | | | | 8.6 | 8.2 | | | 7.6 | 7.9 |
| 9 | | | 8.8 | | 10.2 | | 8.9 | 9.3 | | 9.7 | | | 9.7 |
| 10 | | 9.8 | | | | | 9.1 | 9.5 | | | | | |
| 11 | 10.7 | | 10.2 | | | | 9.6 | 10.2 | | | 8.3 | | 8.3 |
| 12 | | | | | 11.5 | | | 11.5 | | | | 9.0 | 9.0 |
| 13 | | | 11.0 | | | 10.2 | 10.2 | 10.5 | | 10.4 | | | 10.4 |
| 14 | | | | 11.1 | | | | 11.1 | | | | | |
| 15 | | | | | | | 11.3 | 11.3 | | | | | |

Source: Kluyver 1961, courtesy of *Auk*.

properly. Since such young scatter, a few may escape the preda-tor's notice and thus survive the initial attack this way. Obviously, however, a young chickadee that fledges at the normal age will have a far better chance of survival than one forced to leave the nest early. It is therefore wise for people observing chickadee nests to be extremely careful not to get too close in the late nestling phase.

A few days before the nestlings are ready to leave the nest, they start exercising their wings and jumping up to look out of the nest entrance. They often cling to the edge and can put their entire head out the hole, turning to look out in as many directions as possible. At this stage, incoming parents usually do not enter the nest, but instead land on the outside and give their food to the first nestling that jumps up to get it.

### Fledging

In undisturbed chickadee nests, the young generally leave the nest when they are about 16 days old. Most broods of chickadees fledge fairly early in the day (Odum 1941b). Morning fledging is apparently the norm for many other parids as well (Brewer 1961, Perrins 1979). Perrins pointed out that morning fledging is likely adaptive, since it gives the young the rest of the day to learn their way about before dark.

Sometimes an adult will accompany a young chickadee in its first flight from the nest. Odum (1941b) observed a brood of seven Black-capped Chickadees fledge over a period of 40 minutes: first an initial group of four birds, then a pause, then the remaining three, each in rapid succession. I once watched a brood of eight fledge over a period of almost 75 minutes; five left quickly, then two more about 30 minutes later, and the last one, dithering in the entrance, almost three-quarters of an hour after that.

Once a few young have left the nest, the parents may try various ploys in an apparent attempt to get the rest to fledge too. Often they will carry food to the nest hole, then leave still carrying the food. One or both parents may perch some distance from the nest and give faint fee-bees (Butts 1931, Odum 1941b). Other species may go to even greater lengths. Walker (1972) observed one par-ent Great Tit (*Parus major*) going into its nest in apparent exas-peration and trying to pull out the last of its brood by brute force.

## Family Groups

Once all the young have left the nest, the group gathers together and starts to move away from the immediate vicinity of the nest. Just how far the brood can go depends on many factors such as when the group fledged and how well-developed the new fledglings are. Most British titmice do not wander far in the first few days after fledging (Perrins 1979). By contrast, Black-capped Chickadees that have fledged when they are no younger than 16 days posthatching may move considerable distances from their nest, even on the first day (Odum 1941b). (Young chickadees, once fledged, do not normally reenter their nest.) Odum (1941b) followed the brood of seven he had observed fledging. The family group all moved off in the direction in which the parents usually flew to get food; Odum reported that the young chickadees seemed to be following where their parents led them. That group, all of which had fledged by 10:00 A.M., were by nightfall at the opposite end of the breeding territory several hundred meters away from the nest, roosting well up in a clump of hemlock trees (Odum 1941b).

Newly fledged chickadees (Fig. 6-3) give frequent begging dees and are fed by both parents. There is no evidence of brood division, where each parent takes primary responsibility for feeding half the fledglings, as occurs in species such as Song Sparrows (*Melospiza melodia*) (Smith 1978) and Lapland Longspurs (*Calcarius lapponicus*) (McLaughlin and Montgomerie 1985). Hence the typical chickadee family group consists of both parents and all of their current brood of offspring.

Soon after leaving the nest, young chickadees show evidence of curiosity, pecking at twigs, small leaves, or any small moving object within reach. One fledgling from a hand-reared brood of four Black-capped Chickadees caught its first meal worm at 18 days posthatching, or about two days after it would have fledged in the wild; two others caught their first meal worms the next morning (19 days old), and the fourth did not pick up a meal worm until day 20 (Smith 1974a). Brewer (1961) reported that young hand-reared Carolina Chickadees also caught their first meal worms when they were 18 days old. In the wild, young Black-capped Chickadees can catch at least some of their own food within a week of fledging (Odum 1941b, Brewer 1961), although most of what they eat is still being provided by their parents. This proportion

Fig. 6-3. These seven fledgling Black-capped Chickadees have only just left their nest. Once out, they do not return, but instead travel as a family group with their parents. (© Alan Cruickshank / VIREO.)

gradually changes as the birds get older and more independent.

The family groups become more and more mobile as the fledglings get older. Once their young have fledged, most breeding pairs spend little energy in defending territorial boundaries, so the family groups can wander more or less freely across several adjacent territories. Evidently being accompanied by loudly begging young gives parent chickadees a sort of safe passage, permitting them to pass through areas where they might be attacked if alone. Nevertheless, tolerance by resident chickadees will vary to some extent with their particular stage in the breeding cycle— pairs occupied with second or replacement broods will naturally be more likely to attack invading family groups than will pairs with fledglings of their own (Brewer 1961). Family groups typically stay together from two to four weeks (Odum 1941b, Glase 1973).

## Family Group Breakup and Onset of Juvenile Dispersal

I learned about juvenile dispersal the hard way. As a graduate student, working on my first banding project, I knew that every fall my study area was flooded with unbanded young chickadees. I decided to be clever and band them all in the nest, thinking I would thus start the fall with an entirely banded study population. So I found every nest, climbed up, and banded every nestling. It was no easy task. Many of the nests were well over 20 feet (about 7 meters) up in rotten snags; some had bee nests only inches away from the chickadee nest cavity. For the next three weeks or so, everything was great—until family flock breakup, after which virtually all of my banded fledglings dispersed, to be replaced with the usual flood of unbanded chickadees dispersing from surrounding areas, and I was back to square one.

Dispersal itself is, with very few exceptions, a remarkably sudden event. I was lucky enough to observe dispersal of one family of six fledglings in British Columbia: on June 14 all six young were accompanying their parents in an apparently close-knit group, but the next day the parents were alone, and I was able to find only two of the young, each in a separate location some distance from their natal territory (Smith 1967c). Dispersal from the natal area within a few days is the rule not only for Black-capped Chickadees (Holleback 1974, Weise and Meyer 1979) but also for a wide variety of other parids (Goodbody 1952; Greenwood et al. 1979; Nilsson and Smith 1985, 1988; McCallum 1988).

As soon as the family groups dissolve, the young chickadees begin a period of relatively rapid long-distance movements. Of 96 chickadees banded as nestlings in British Columbia, only 9 joined winter flocks in my 65-ha (160-acre) study area (Smith 1967c). Similarly, of 88 banded nestlings in Wisconsin, only 12 joined winter flocks in a study area of almost 800ha (almost 2000 acres) (Weise and Meyer 1979). The direction the young chickadees take is apparently random (Fig. 6-4).

Evidently, young female Great Tits disperse somewhat farther than young males during the summer (Fig. 6-5), both in Britain (Greenwood et al. 1979) and in continental Europe (Dhondt 1979). Although Weise and Meyer (1979) reported no big difference in dispersal distance between male and female Black-capped Chickadees (Fig. 6-6), Robbins et al. (1986) reported that

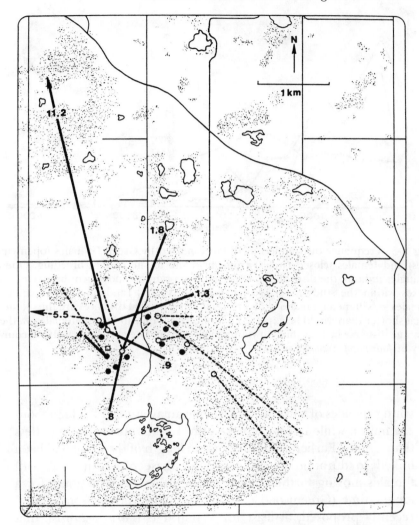

Fig. 6-4. Dispersal of Black-capped Chickadees banded as nestlings. Open square = 1970 nest; open circles = 1971 nests; closed circles = 1972 nests. Broken lines connect birthplace and winter location. Solid lines connect birthplace and breeding location. Numbers at ends of solid lines are distances in kilometers. All birds found breeding were located again in winter, but their winter locations are not shown. Note that the dispersal directions are essentially random. (From Weise and Meyer 1979, courtesy of *Auk*.)

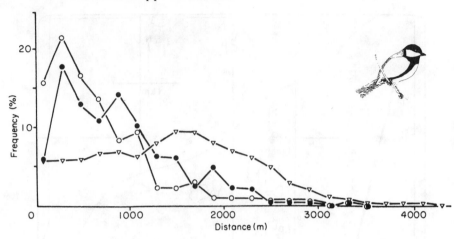

Fig. 6-5. Frequency distribution of distance moved by Great Tit males (open circles) and females (closed circles) from birth site to site of first breeding. Open triangles indicate the distribution expected from random movement between nest boxes within the study area. Median dispersal values: random = 1500 meters; females = 879 meters; males = 558 meters. The dispersal distances are thus somewhat shorter than would be expected if entirely random, and young females on the average disperse farther than do young males. (From Greenwood et al. 1979, courtesy of *Journal of Animal Ecology*.)

young females of this species disperse an average of 2.3 km (about 1½ miles), while males disperse only 1.3 km on the average (less than a mile). Earlier, this difference in length of dispersal had been linked to duration of the dispersal phase of Great Tits, with females moving farther simply because they keep on going for a longer time (Greenwood et al. 1979). However, Nilsson (1989a) recently proposed, at least for Marsh Tits (*Parus palustris*), that dispersal lengths shown by the two sexes may relate to levels of competition, brought on in part by differential survival of the two sexes. Nilsson suggests that dispersing males try to become established as soon as possible after independence, and hence, wherever possible, disperse as little as they can. By contrast, females, particularly early hatched ones, can more easily fit into the forming flocks, and thus can afford to assess several flock ranges before selecting one in which to settle.

Dhondt (1979) reported that summer dispersal of his first-brood Great tits in Sweden actually occurred in two periods: the birds moved farther between successive recapture sites in late July to early August and then again in September (Table 6-4). The pause between the two periods occurred when the young Great Tits were going through the most intense part of their postjuvenal molt. As Black-capped Chickadee fledglings also go through a postjuvenal molt in late summer, they might exhibit a similar pause in dispersal, although evidently none was detected by Weise and Meyer (1979).

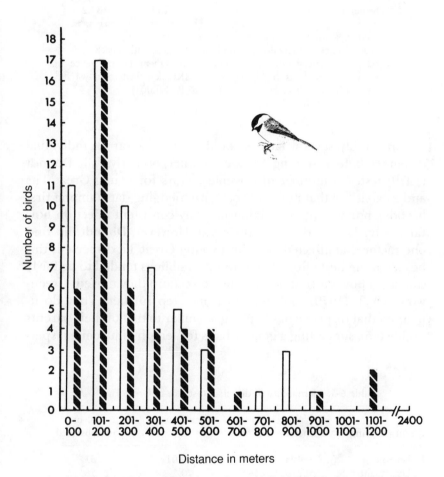

Fig. 6-6. Distances from the point where individual Black-capped Chickadees were banded as independent juveniles in July–August to their breeding sites in subsequent years. Open bars = males ($n = 58$; median = 211 meters); shaded bars = females ($n = 45$; median = 198 meters). No obvious difference in dispersal distance emerges between the sexes, although most of the closer distances seem to show a preponderance of males. (From Weise and Meyer 1979, courtesy of *Auk*.)

Table 6-4. Distance between successive recapture sites of
individual Great Tits retrapped 2–7 days apart

| Period of movement | No. captured | Mean distance (m) | Standard error |
|---|---|---|---|
| July 17–31 | 22 | 192 | 25.7 |
| August 1–15 | 46 | 67 | 11.0 |
| August 16–31 | 35 | 30 | 13.7 |
| September 1–10 | 51 | 157 | 34.2 |

Source: Dhondt 1979, courtesy of Oecologia.
Note: Males and females are combined, because within each period there was no significant difference between them. The difference between periods is highly significant (Kruskal-Wallis one-way analysis of variance: $H = 35.4$, $df = 3$, $P < 0.001$).

Conceivably several factors could affect how far an individual disperses before settling in late summer or early fall. Dhondt (1979) tested a number of possible factors for young Great Tits and established that neither brood size, fledging date (among first broods), nor weight at fledging had any consistent effect on how far the birds moved during dispersal. However, Dhondt did find one factor that affected how far a young Great Tit dispersed; this he called the nest effect. He found that siblings tended to be fairly similar in how far (but not in which direction) they moved. Greenwood et al. (1979) took this idea one step further. They documented that dispersal of offspring is similar to that of their parents (Table 6-5), suggesting a genetic basis for length of juvenile disper-

Table 6-5. Heritability of dispersal distance of Great Tits

| Parent-offspring | Regression coefficient ± SE | Significance (P) | No. of pairs observed |
|---|---|---|---|
| Father-son | 0.498 ± 0.149 | <0.01 | 31 |
| Father-daughter | 0.270 ± 0.145 | <0.1 | 56 |
| Mother-son | 0.237 ± 0.117 | <0.05 | 61 |
| Mother-daughter | 0.237 ± 0.098 | <0.05 | 86 |

Source: Greenwood et al. 1979, courtesy of Journal of Animal Ecology.
Note: Mean regression coefficient = 0.31; estimate of heritability = 62%. Mean regression coefficient weighted for sample size = 0.28; estimate of heritability = 56%.

sal. The effects of these factors on chickadee dispersal remain to be investigated.

The impressive 11-year study of British Great Tit dispersal conducted by Greenwood et al. (1979) also revealed that there were marked annual fluctuations in the distance traveled by both male and female fledglings (Fig. 6-7). Apparently the major consideration here is population density: at higher population densities, male dispersal especially tended to be farther than at lower densities (with their correspondingly lower competition levels), although the same trend did not seem to hold true for young females. Again, the relationship of population density to dispersal distance of Black-capped Chickadees has yet to be studied.

Fledgling Great Tits from second broods disperse considerably farther than those from first broods in both Belgium (Dhondt and Hublé 1968) and Holland (Kluijver 1951). Somewhat surprisingly, Greenwood et al. (1979) found no such difference between first and second broods of Great Tits hatched in Britain. For reasons stated in the first section of Chapter 7, I would expect that most second-brood Black-capped Chickadees would also disperse farther than those from first broods, thus following the continental, rather than the British pattern.

What causes dispersal? Holleback (1974), working with Black-capped Chickadees, suggested that it might be caused by increased aggression both of the parents toward their offspring and of the young toward each other. However, Weise and Meyer (1979), also working with Black-capped Chickadees, found no evidence of such increased aggression, nor have investigators working with other parids such as the Great Tit (e.g., Saitou 1979a). The effects of aggression on dispersal were investigated in more detail on Marsh Tits (*Parus palustris*) by Nilsson and Smith (1985). They manipulated brood size, reasoning that the hypothetical increased parental aggression, if it occurred at all, would most likely occur as a result of within-family competition for food; hence the largest families should show the most aggression and should disperse earlier than smaller broods. Regardless of brood size, however, Nilsson and Smith found only very low levels of parental aggression; moreover, experimental broods of increased and reduced size stayed equally long with the parents before they dispersed (Table 6-6). In addition, the level of aggression among the fledglings was so low that Nilsson and Smith were not able to work out the birds' dominance hierarchy in any detail. They therefore re-

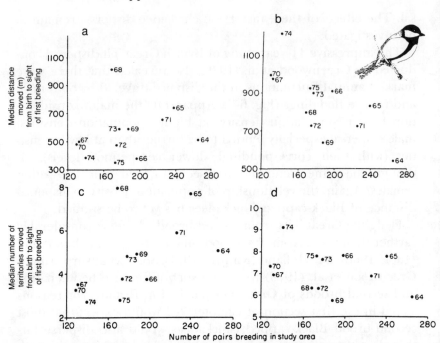

Fig. 6-7. The effects of population density on dispersal of young Great Tits. Upper two graphs: median distance moved from birth site to site of first breeding by males (a) and females (b) plotted against the number of breeding pairs in the study area. Lower two graphs: median number of territories moved from birth site to site of first breeding by males (c) and females (d) plotted against the number of breeding pairs in the study area. Numbers refer to year of breeding attempt. Note that young males especially (a, c) tended to move farthest, both in terms of actual distance and in terms of number of territories crossed, in years of highest population density; by contrast something of a reverse trend seems to be suggested for young females (b, d). (From Greenwood et al. 1979, courtesy of *Journal of Animal Ecology*.)

Table 6-6. Survival and day of dispersal of juvenile Marsh Tits
in family flocks in 1984

| Category | No. fledged | No. alive until 11 d after fledging | Days after fledging when at least one juvenile had dispersed |
|----------|-------------|-------------------------------------|-------------------------------------------------------------|
| Control | 6 | 6 | 13–14 |
| | 7 | 5 | 13 |
| | 8 | 8 | 12–13 |
| | 8 | 3 | 16 |
| TOTAL | 29 | 22 | |
| Enlarged | 9 | 6 | 14 |
| | 11 | 11 | 12 |
| | 10 | 9 | 14 |
| TOTAL | 30 | 26 | |
| Reduced | 4 | 4 | 14 |
| | 2 | 1 | 15 |
| | 5 | 4 | 13–14 |
| TOTAL | 11 | 9 | |

Source: Nilsson and Smith 1985, courtesy of Ornis Scandinavica.

jected the theory that increased aggression was instrumental in triggering the dispersal of Marsh Tits. Given the data of Weise and Meyer (1979), it seems unlikely that aggression plays a major role in the dispersal of Black-capped Chickadees either.

Nilsson and Smith did document one behavior that was correlated with the onset of dispersal of Marsh Tits: the parents brought markedly less food to their offspring. Similar decreases have been reported for both Great Tits (Davies 1978) and Black-capped Chickadees (e.g., Holleback 1974). Davies (1978) had suggested that such a decrease in parental care was what actually triggered dispersal: when self-feeding become more profitable than begging for food, the young birds should shift abruptly to foraging on their own. Field data, however, do not support this view; for example, levels of begging (begging dees) by young Black-capped chickadees evidently decrease continually, instead of dropping abruptly as predicted by Davies (Weise and Meyer 1979). Similar data were obtained for Marsh Tits by Nilsson and Smith (1985). Indeed, Nilsson and Smith suggest that decreased feeding by the parents may actually be the result of, rather than the cause of, decreased begging by their offspring.

Nilsson and Smith (1985, 1988) and Nilsson (1989a) found that more dominant Marsh Tit fledglings dispersed earlier than did more subordinate ones, regardless of sex. They suggested that since subordinate juveniles will probably have to travel farther than more dominant birds, they may require more energy to establish themselves; hence it is better to be more proficient at foraging before beginning dispersal.

Regardless of which proximate factor(s) causes juvenile dispersal, the evolutionary significance is clear: dispersal minimizes the chances of inbreeding. The distance moved serves to lower the chances of offspring breeding with their parents, and both the randomness of direction and the sex difference in distance moved act to lower the chances of brothers and sisters forming pair-bonds together. Greenwood et al. (1979) showed that inbreeding by Great Tits results in reduced breeding success; it is highly likely that a similar effect would also occur in Black-capped Chickadees.

After the late-summer dispersal phase, the young chickadees rapidly develop site attachments and tend to remain in place at least until the following spring, at which point further movement may occur. Only a few birds will be forced to go through this later spring dispersal, however, and the factors affecting it are very different. These are discussed more fully in the section on the fate of each class of chickadees after flock breakup, in Chapter 7.

## Replacement and Second Broods

If a pair loses a brood because of predation or disease, they will often begin a new nest, especially if it is not too late in the breeding season. Certain European titmice have been known to begin laying a replacement clutch less than a week after having lost their original brood (Perrins 1979); such data are usually from birds using nest boxes, where no time need be spent in excavating a new cavity. Odum (1941b) reported finding a Black-capped Chickadee replacement clutch in which the first egg was laid 10–11 days after the original brood was destroyed; this is remarkably rapid in light of the fact that Odum's pair did have to excavate a new site before they could nest in it.

Replacement nests are typically some distance from the original nest site. Odum (1941b) described one that was more than 300 meters (328 yards) from the earlier, failed nest, and Butts (1931) reported a replacement nest located almost 200 meters (219 yards) from the former site. Renesting a long distance from a failed nest makes a great deal of sense: any predator that destroyed the original nest might well return later, and if the first brood was lost to disease or parasites, these could still be infesting the original site. Nevertheless, in territories that have few natural sites, chickadees may be forced to renest close to, or even in, the old location. Kluyver (1961) reported that a pair that had lost its original brood actually renested in the same nest box, and another started a replacement nest in a box close to its former site. The fact that these birds were using nest boxes at all suggests that the area lacked many natural nest sites.

Once a replacement brood is begun, most features of parental care are identical with those for any other brood. However, certain European titmice may begin incubation of very late clutches before the last egg is laid, resulting in broods with staggered ages (Perrins 1979; see Incubation, Chapter 5). If there is enough food for every nestling, then it is likely that all will survive. However, if (as is often the case later in the summer) there is not enough food for all, then at least a few—the oldest—will have a good chance of surviving to fledging age (Lack 1954, Perrins 1979). It would be well worth looking to see if this behavior also occurs in Black-capped Chickadees.

Second broods are hard to document, because one must be sure that the original brood has not been killed in order to distinguish the second nest from a simple replacement clutch. True second broods of Black-capped Chickadees are apparently rare in most areas. Kluyver (1961) found that of his 20 study pairs in Massachusetts, only one had a second brood. Brewer (1961) found no second broods of either Black-capped or Carolina Chickadees in his study area in Illinois. One pair of Black-capped Chickadees raised two broods successfully in the same nest box two years running in British Columbia, yet 16 other pairs in the same general area produced no second broods over the same two-year period (Smith 1967c). Indeed, the best published accounts of second broods of Black-capped Chickadees are those of Odum (1941b, 1942b) for his New York population. In the first year of that study,

1 pair out of 11 raised two broods successfully, while the next year, 3 out of 7 pairs attempted second broods, at least two of which were successful (Odum 1942b).

Second broods are usually started well before the first brood has dispersed; indeed, some may be started within a few days of the first brood leaving the nest. For example, Peck and James (1987) reported one case in which a pair of Black-capped Chickadees began laying a second clutch in a nest box within a week of the initial fledging. The period just before beginning a new nest is marked by an increase in courtship feeding, or at least in demand behavior by the female. Perrins (1979) reported that more female European titmice begin demand behavior when the first brood begins fledging than ultimately begin second broods—evidently they may be assessing the degree of available male support before "deciding" whether or not to start a new nest. If this decision is made, the female builds, lays, and then incubates, while the male does virtually all the feeding of the first group of fledglings. After the first group disperses, he is then ready to help with the next batch of young.

Several factors have been identified as affecting the likelihood that chickadees and titmice will start second broods. One of these is date of first laying. In early springs, birds are far more likely to attempt second broods than in years when breeding begins later. This pattern is true not only for Black-capped Chickadees (Odum 1942b) but for many European titmice as well (Perrins 1979).

A second factor is the age of the breeding female. Older females, at least of European titmice, tend to begin breeding before younger ones do, and they are measurably more efficient at bringing off their first broods. Thus, even in normal years, they will have more time in which to attempt second broods than will younger, less experienced females (Perrins 1979). Very likely a similar effect also exists in Black-capped Chickadees. Certainly Glase (1973) found that alpha pairs (which are often older birds) begin nesting before beta pairs do.

A third factor is size of the first brood—the larger the original brood, the less likely a pair is to begin a second brood, at least in Great Tits (Tinbergen 1987).

A fourth factor is the density of the local breeding population—second broods of European titmice are evidently attempted more frequently in years when there are relatively few breeding pairs per unit area than when the local density is relatively high (Perrins

1979). However, Odum (1942b) reported that in his two-year study on Black-capped Chickadees, he found more second broods in the year with the higher population density. Clearly more work is needed to see if and how breeding density affects starting of second broods by Black-capped Chickadees.

A fifth factor is local food supply—not so much overall abundance as temporal distribution of food. Apparently second broods are more likely to be attempted in years or conditions in which food levels persist later in the season. For example, in Europe, caterpillars in pine woods are relatively abundant far later in the season than they are in oak woodland (van Balen 1973), and evidently second broods are more likely in pine woods. Even in oak woodland, however, food level and persistence can vary from year to year, and both Great Tits and Blue Tits (*Parus caeruleus*) are more likely to start second broods in years where food levels persist long enough to permit unusually high survival of late first broods (Perrins 1979). Recently, De Laet and Dhondt (1989) showed that weight loss of the female Great Tit during the first brood has a marked effect on whether or not that female will attempt a second brood. De Laet and Dhondt also found that Blue Tits, which seldom have second broods in their study area, typically lose more weight during the raising of their first broods than do local Great Tits, again suggesting a relationship between food availability and second brood production.

Given the fact that some pairs do manage to raise two broods in a season, why is this attempted so rarely? Successful raising of two broods per year should yield some selective advantage, since doing so seems certain to increase the proportion of the pair's offspring in the next generation. In most populations, however, attempting a second brood can bring several potential disadvantages as well. One of these is that survival of a second brood is not at all guaranteed. The best food for nestlings is caterpillars, most of which will pupate before the end of the summer. If the supply of food suitable for nestlings crashes too soon, there could well be no survivors from attempted second broods—and then all the time and energy invested in them is wasted. The survival of second broods of most European titmice is nearly always less than that of first broods, except in very unusual circumstances (Perrins 1979). Clearly such lower survival means lower gain for the parents.

Another potential disadvantage of attempting second broods is that the effort put into raising them takes time and energy away from the care of the first brood because of the time overlap. Females raising second broods do virtually no feeding of their first lot of fledglings, and the later courtship feeding done by the male in such circumstances also diminishes his time available for parental care. Hence having a second brood can actually lower the first brood's chances of survival.

Attempting second broods can also actually endanger the lives of the parents. Reproduction costs are not small—nonbreeding male Willow Tits (*Parus montanus*) survived better than males that simply attended a first brood (Ekman and Askenmo 1986). Perrins (1979) described three ways in which attempting to bring off a second brood could potentially lower the survivorship of parent titmice. First, breeding itself can increase the parents' chances of being caught at the nest and eaten by a nest predator; moreover, both parents are likely to concentrate so much on gathering food for their offspring that their general level of vigilance will be much lower than at other times of year. Bringing a second brood to fledgling stage will double the parents' exposure to this kind of predation risk.

A second way in which second broods might endanger the parents is by so exhausting them physically that they have lowered chances of being able to survive the rigors of winter weather so as to breed again the following year. This is an important point given the fact that first broods survive much better than do second ones. A pair that produces two broods in one season but dies over winter will have produced the same total of broods as a pair that brings off only one and thus survives to bring off another the following year, but the overall chances of offspring survival will be far better for the pair having two first broods.

Finally, having a second brood may force adults to delay the onset of their postbreeding molt (Perrins 1979). This complete molt is costly, and by delaying it the birds must molt when food levels are lower than they would have been earlier in the summer (Dixon 1962). Again, this delay can put adults into poor condition just before the onset of severe winter weather, lowering their chances of survival to the next breeding season.

Among European parids, second broods are far more common in continental populations than they are in Britain (Perrins 1979, Den Boer-Hazewinkel 1987). Clearly, where they can be successful, second broods will enhance a pair's offspring production. Perrins (1979) suggested that the best strategy for adults is plasticity of behavior and that they should attempt second broods only when conditions are particularly favorable. Black-capped Chickadees also seems to exhibit such plasticity of behavior with respect to second brood attempts (Odum 1942b).

## Reproductive Rates and Strategies

Various measures have been used to arrive at some estimation of reproductive success. Such measures include proportion of eggs that hatch, proportion of nestlings that fledge, and proportion of eggs that produce fledged young (e.g., Table 6-7). Van Balen et al. (1987) identified five components that had a major effect on the lifetime reproductive success of Great Tits: the lifespan of the bird; the number of clutches it produces per year; the number of eggs laid per clutch; the number of fledglings produced per egg laid; and the number of recruits per fledgling, or in other words the proportion of young produced that survive to become members of the breeding population. Van Balen and his colleagues

Table 6-7. Fertility rate and hatching success in a Vancouver population of Black-capped Chickadees

| Week ending | 1964 | | | 1965 | | |
|---|---|---|---|---|---|---|
| | No. of eggs laid | No. of nests | Proportion hatched | No. of eggs laid | No. of nests | Proportion hatched |
| April 30 | 0 | 0 | — | 7 | 1 | 0.86 |
| May 7 | 20 | 3 | 1.00 | 11 | 3 | 0.91 |
| May 14 | 25 | 5 | 0.96 | 7 | 1 | 1.00 |
| May 21 | 7 | 1 | 1.00 | 13 | 2 | 0.92 |
| May 28 | 3 | 1 | 1.00 | 0 | 0 | — |
| June 4 | 8 | 1 | 0.88 | 0 | 0 | — |
| June 11 | 0 | 0 | — | 0 | 0 | — |
| June 18 | 5 | 1 | 0.60 | 0 | 0 | — |
| June 25 | 0 | 0 | — | 0 | 0 | — |
| July 2 | 5 | 1 | 1.00 | 0 | 0 | — |
| Observed total | 73 | | | 38 | | |
| Fertility | | | 0.945 | | | 0.921 |
| Corrected total | 89 | | | 54 | | |
| Hatching success | | | 0.773 | | | 0.845 |

Source: Smith 1967c, courtesy of Condor.

found that for their population of Great Tits, recruits per fledgling was by far the most important component of overall lifetime
reproductive success, with lifespan being the next most important
component.

Several factors that can affect the components of reproductive
success are now known. Clutch size has already been discussed (see
Clutch Size, Chapter 5). Eggs may fail to hatch because they were
infertile, because they were eaten by some nest predator, or because something other than predation stopped the development
of a viable embryo. Since it is difficult to distinguish between infer-
tility and the death of an embryo in an intact egg without blowing
unhatched eggs, these are often lumped together (e.g., Smith
1967c).

Any factor that inhibits incubation by the female can potentially
reduce hatching success. One of the best studied of such factors is
weather. If conditions are particularly cold during incubation, the
females must eat more just to maintain their own body heat. Moreover, the food they must catch is harder to find, since cold insects
move far less than do warmer ones. In cold weather, therefore,
females must spend an unusual amount of time off the nest foraging, just when the eggs most need heat for incubation. Perrins
(1979) suggested that under such circumstances the top eggs in a
nest may cool to the point where the embryos inside are killed,
although Haftorn (1988a) later showed that the eggs of several
European tits can withstand fairly long periods of desertion at low
temperatures.

Similarly, in very late nests where the female has begun incubation well before the whole clutch is laid, later eggs may still need
incubation after both parents have begun to feed young hatched
from the earliest laid eggs in the clutch. In such cases, some of the
last eggs may not hatch at all (Perrins 1979).

Once the eggs have hatched, natural enemies (predators, parasites, and disease) can cause nestling mortality both directly, by
acting on the nestlings themselves, and indirectly, by removing one
or both of the parents. Nestling chickadees are particularly vulnerable to cold until they are approximately 12 days old and capable of maintaining a high body temperature on their own (Odum
1941b). Perhaps the most closely documented factor affecting nestling survival, however, is the amount of food provided by the
parents, usually measured in milligrams of food per nestling per
day.

Nestling feeding rates are extremely important. Studies (reviewed in Perrins 1979) have shown that weight at fledging has a major effect on subsequent survival: birds weighing most at fledging may have a better chance of surviving to reproductive age than do lighter birds (but see Nur 1984b).

Nestling feeding rates vary with the age of the nestlings, simply because the larger the individual, the more food it requires. Hence newly hatched chickadees need far less food than do older nestlings (Brewer 1961, Kluyver 1961). Just before fledging, at about day 14 or 15 posthatching, nestling feeding rates of Black-capped Chickadees may dip slightly (Smith 1976), but typically not enough to lower the nestlings' weights (Kluyver 1961). Both the increase in feeding rate with nestling age, and the dip right before fledging, have been nicely documented for Mountain Chickadees by Grundel (1987) (see Fig. 6-8).

Brood size itself can have a marked effect on how much food is available to each nestling (Lack 1954, Perrins 1979). Grundel (1987), working with natural broods of Mountain Chickadees, found that the food brought per nestling was far less in larger

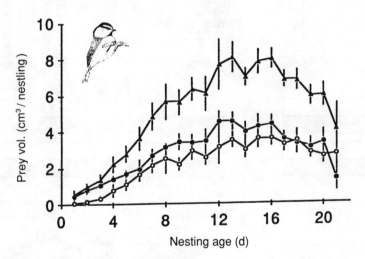

Fig. 6-8. Daily volume of prey (in cubic centimeters) delivered per nestling as a function of nestling age of Mountain Chickadees. Dark circles = males; open circles = females; dark triangles = combined male and female rates. Entries represent averages over all nests observed. Bars represent 1 SE. Note that the amount of food delivered steadily increased with age, but then dipped before fledging (about day 21). (From Grundel 1987, courtesy of *Condor*.)

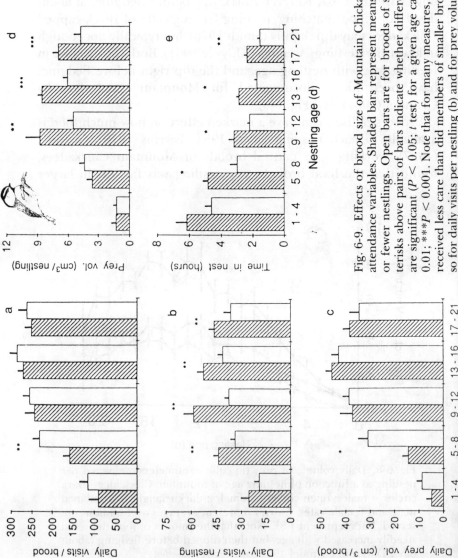

Fig. 6-9. Effects of brood size of Mountain Chickadees on feeding and nest attendance variables. Shaded bars represent means (±1 SE) for broods of six or fewer nestlings. Open bars are for broods of seven or more young. Asterisks above pairs of bars indicate whether differences between brood sizes are significant ($P < 0.05$; $t$ test) for a given age category: *$P < 0.05$; **$P < 0.01$; ***$P < 0.001$. Note that for many measures, members of larger broods received less care than did members of smaller broods. This was particularly so for daily visits per nestling (b) and for prey volume per nestling (d). (From

than average broods than it was in broods that were smaller than average (Fig. 6-9). This has also been documented nicely for Blue Tits using manipulated brood sizes (Nur 1984b). Nur was able to show that nestling weight significantly and consistently decreases with increasing brood size (Fig. 6-10); Orell and Koivula (1988) found the same for Willow Tits, and Smith et al. (1989) reported similar results for manipulated broods of Great Tits. Incidentally, as Perrins (1979) pointed out, large broods, being hungrier, will

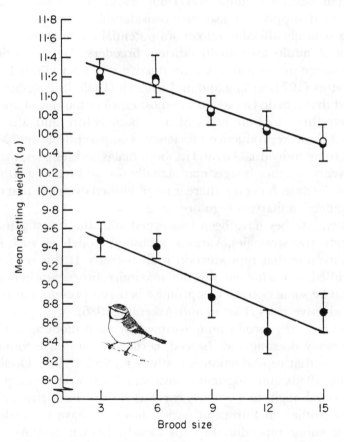

Fig. 6-10.  Mean nestling weight of young Blue Tits at day 10 (bottom curve) and day 13 (top curve) in relation to brood size in 1980. Solid circles indicate mean values for broods weighed both on day 10 and on day 13; bars indicate ± SEM. Open circles indicate mean values for all broods weighed on day 13, including those not previously weighed on day 10. (From Nur 1984b, courtesy of *Journal of Animal Ecology*.)

beg more, and such noisy broods may be more readily detected by predators than smaller, better-fed broods.

The amount of food available to foraging parents itself varies. One factor that affects food availability is territory quality. I found that Black-capped Chickadees living in the best quality territories (that is, those with the most canopy cover) had higher nestling feeding rates than did pairs living in poorer quality territories (Smith 1976). Local food availability also varies from month to month, so the timing of the nest in question can have a marked effect on nestling feeding rates (Dhondt and Olaerts 1981). Finally, local food supply can also vary considerably from year to year, again strongly affecting maximum potential feeding rates.

Not all adults are equally efficient breeders. Age in particular can change an individual's reproductive efficiency. Thus Perrins and Moss (1974) in England and Dhondt (1985) in Belgium both found that female Great Tits are most efficient parents at approximately three to four years of age: both before and after this period their reproductive efficiency is apparently lower. Moreover, some individual Great Tits, both males and females, that are five years or more in age, may actually forego breeding (Dhondt 1985). To date, however, there is no published evidence that older chickadees similarly forego breeding.

Recent studies have been concerned with the investigation of reproductive strategies. Various published models on such strategies assume that reproduction itself is costly. If this is so, then unbridled reproduction will not maximize fitness; rather, there should be some optimal compromise between present and future reproductive rates (Ekman and Askenmo 1986).

The cost of reproduction, assumed by most models, is not always easily documented. Indeed, certain studies have found no evidence that reproduction is costly (e.g., Smith 1981, Orell and Koivula 1988), and Högstedt (1980) actually suggested that parental survival might be positively correlated with clutch size. Several recent studies on European parids, however, have succeeded in documenting reproductive costs clearly. Ekman and Askenmo (1986) studied a population of Willow Tits in which certain males had lost their mates before the breeding season; as there were no available replacements, some of the resident males were reproducing while other were not. The nonbreeding male Willow Tits had significantly better annual survival rates than the breeding males

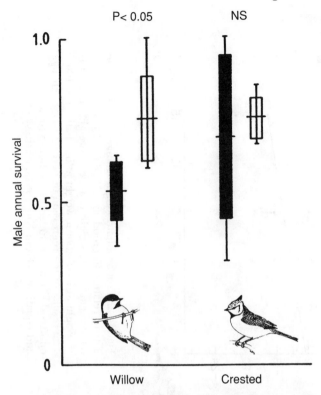

Fig. 6-11. Annual survival rates of breeding (dark) and nonbreeding (open) males based on complete surveys of the populations in spring. Horizontal lines give average rates for seven (Willow Tit) and six (Crested Tit) years; rectangle and vertical lines give 2 SE and range, respectively. The survival rate was significantly higher for nonbreeding Willow Tit males ($P < 0.05$; 135 breeding and 31 nonbreeding); there was a similar trend for Crested Tit males (74 breeding and 20 nonbreeding), but it is not statistically significant (NS). The interspecific difference in annual survival rate of breeding males is significant ($P < 0.05$). (From Ekman and Askenmo 1986, courtesy of *Evolution*.)

(Fig. 6-11). Ekman and Askenmo (1986) also reported a similar trend for breeding and nonbreeding male Crested Tits (*Parus cristatus*), but the difference was not significant.

Nur (1984a, 1984b, 1988) studied reproductive costs in detail by using manipulated Blue Tit brood sizes. By taking some newly hatched nestlings from some nests and introducing them into

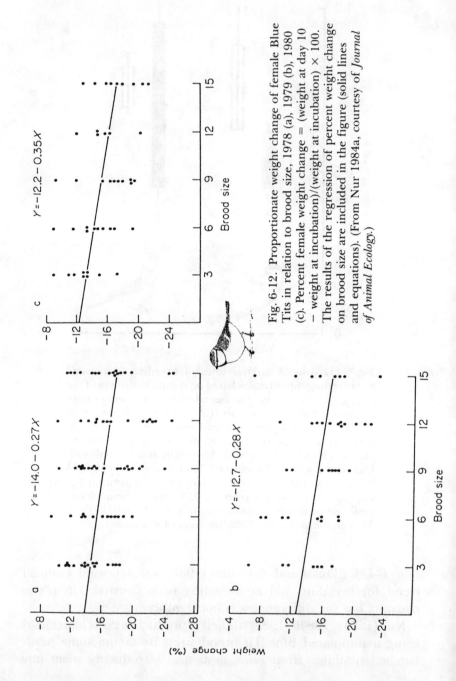

Fig. 6-12. Proportionate weight change of female Blue Tits in relation to brood size, 1978 (a), 1979 (b), 1980 (c). Percent female weight change = (weight at day 10 − weight at incubation)/(weight at incubation) × 100. The results of the regression of percent weight change on brood size are included in the figure (solid lines and equations). (From Nur 1984a, courtesy of *Journal of Animal Ecology*).

other nests, he created artificial broods of 3, 6, 9, 12, and 15 nestlings (the local average brood size was 9.3). One factor Nur (1984a) measured was the effect of manipulated brood size on parental weight. He found that the weights of females decreased with increased brood size (Fig. 6-12), whereas male weights were unaffected by brood size in two of the study's three years (Fig. 6-13). Female survival (as measured by recapture and resightings) decreased with brood size in two of the three years, with the three-year average showing a marked decrease with brood size (Fig. 6-14); by contrast, male survival seemed to be unaffected by brood size (Fig. 6-15) (Nur 1988). Orell and Koivula (1990), who did similar brood size manipulations on Willow Tits in Finland, found no overall correlation (in their three-year averages) between brood size and adult survival of either sex.

Nur (1984b) also looked at offspring survival—a measure of recruits per fledgling that has been shown to be so important in the lifetime reproductive success of Great Tits by van Balen et al. (1987). He found there was a clear fall-off in offspring survival of his Blue Tits with higher brood size in one year, but no such relationship in the next year. Other studies, such as that of Smith et al. (1989) on Great Tits, have shown a more consistent pattern of brood size and offspring quality, with nestling mass, wing length, and tarsus length all being inversely related to brood size: that is, the larger the brood, the smaller and poorer quality the offspring (and hence, quite possibly, the poorer the offspring survival). Orell and Koivula (1990) found similar relationships for their Willow Tits in Finland. Nevertheless, marked differences between years such as those found by Nur (1984b) and Orell and Koivula (1990) demonstrate how necessary long-term studies are in order to be able to draw any meaningful conclusions about such complex issues.

Finally, Nur (1988) looked at the number of surviving offspring produced in the year after he had done his manipulations in brood size, to see whether brood size in one year had any effect on reproduction in subsequent years. He found that for male Blue Tits, there was a significant negative correlation between number of surviving offspring produced and the size of the manipulated brood reared the previous year (Fig. 6-16). Oddly enough, although a similar trend appeared for females, the relation was not significant (Table 6-8). However, taken together, adults given broods of only 3–6 were almost four times as successful when

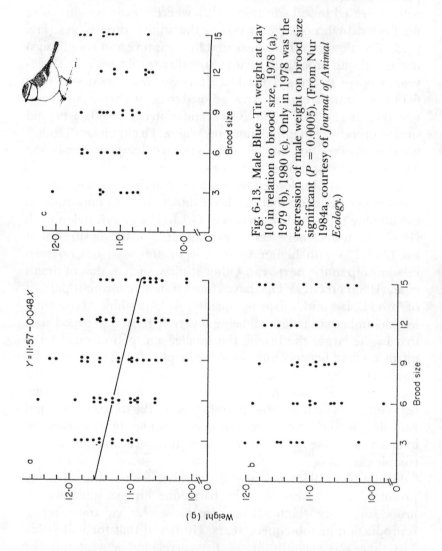

Fig. 6-13. Male Blue Tit weight at day 10 in relation to brood size, 1978 (a), 1979 (b), 1980 (c). Only in 1978 was the regression of male weight on brood size significant ($P = 0.0005$). (From Nur 1984a, courtesy of *Journal of Animal Ecology*.)

$Y = 11.57 - 0.048X$

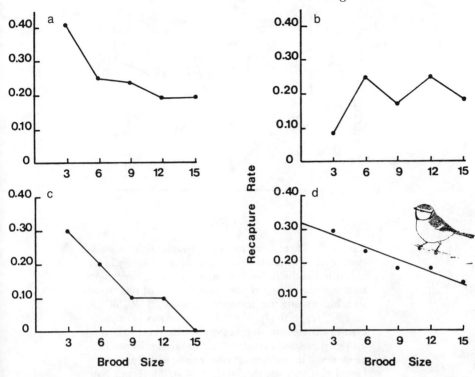

Fig. 6-14.  Proportion of female Blue Tits caught or identified in the following winter or spring in relation to manipulated brood size. 1978 (a), 1979 (b), 1980 (c), and the three-year average, weighted by sample size (d). Sample sizes are 43 ± 1 for each brood size. Note that the larger the brood size, the fewer the female parents found locally in subsequent years. The linear equation of best fit depicted in d is $y = 0.317 - 0.0119x$, where $x$ = brood size ($r = 0.928$; $P = 0.008$; SE of regression coefficient = 0.0019). (From Nur 1988, courtesy of *Evolution*.)

breeding the following year as those given broods of 15. Moreover, the effect is expressed not as differences in clutch size, hatching date, or brood size, but instead in the number of young that survived at least three months postfledging (Table 6-8).

Slagsvold (1984) manipulated Great Tit brood sizes shortly after hatching, then removed the nestlings before fledging in order to measure the timing and breeding success of replacement broods. The Great Tits were affected in two ways: parents of enlarged broods started their replacement nests later than did parents given normal or reduced broods; and parents of enlarged broods were

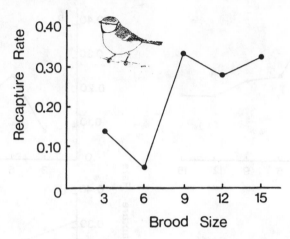

Fig. 6-15. Three-year average, weighted by sample size, of the proportion of male Blue Tits caught or identified in the following winter or spring in relation to manipulated brood size. Sample sizes of the brood sizes listed along the horizontal axis are 29, 36, 39, 33, and 31, respectively. Note that there was no significant linear relationship between male recapture rate and manipulated brood size, although significant heterogeneity in recapture rate exists with respect to brood size (chi squared test, $P < 0.05$). (From Nur 1988, courtesy of *Evolution*.)

more likely to desert replacement nests than parents given normal or reduced broods.

Slagsvold's study was followed up by Tinbergen (1987), also working with Great Tits. Tinbergen's population in Holland had a relatively high frequency of second (rather than replacement) broods. Again brood sizes were manipulated, but the birds were then allowed to rear the young until they were independent. Tinbergen found that parents given enlarged broods were less likely to start second broods than were parents given normal-sized broods, although parents given reduced broods were only slightly more likely to start second broods than were parents of normal broods. Smith et al. (1987), also working with manipulated broods of Great Tits, had similar results. All three of these studies again give clear evidence of the cost of reproduction.

Those interested in reproductive strategies are particularly concerned with whether the observed reproductive behavior serves to maximize the fitness of the individuals performing it. Do individuals actually manage to achieve the best possible balance be-

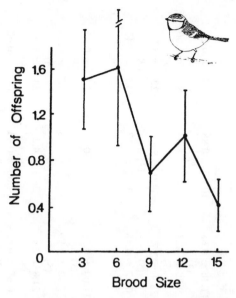

Fig. 6-16. Number of surviving Blue Tit offspring produced in relation to manipulated
brood size in the previous year. Only adults
that were manipulated during one year were
included. The figure depicts combined data
for males and females over three years.
Means (± SE) are depicted for each brood
size group. Sample sizes for brood sizes
along the horizontal axis are 10, 5, 6, 8, and
10, respectively. Note that the number of
surviving offspring (based on recapture at
least three months postfledging) produced
in year $n + 1$ declined significantly as the
parent's brood size in year $n$ increased (regression analysis, $P < 0.01$). (From Nur
1988, courtesy of *Evolution*.)

tween current reproduction (both results and costs) and future
productivity? Nur (1984a, 1984b, 1988) discussed this in detail for
the Blue Tit. Perhaps some of the most convincing data on this
question, however, are those of Ekman and Askenmo (1986) for
Willow and Crested Tits. As they pointed out, these two species
are remarkably similar both morphologically and ecologically.
Using a comparative approach, Ekman and Askenmo demonstrated that the Crested Tit has a more conservative reproductive
strategy than the Willow Tit, investing less energy per nest. This
strategy makes a great deal of sense, because Crested Tits suffer

Table 6-8. Indices of reproductive costs (mean plus or minus SE) in relation to manipulated Blue Tit brood sizes

| | Brood size in year $n$[a] | | | | |
|---|---|---|---|---|---|
| Trait in year $n + 1$ | 3 | 6 | 9 | 12 | 15 |
| **Males** | | | | | |
| Clutch size | 12.00 ± 1.00 (2) | 14.00 (1) | 11.40 ± 0.68 (5) | 10.67 ± 0.88 (3) | 11.11 ± 0.26 (9) |
| Brood size | 11.50 ± 1.50 (2) | 14.00 (1) | 9.40 ± 1.21 (5) | 9.67 ± 1.33 (3) | 9.33 ± 1.00 (9) |
| Hatching date of brood[b] | 25.5 ± 0.5 (2) | 22.0 (1) | 23.4 ± 2.7 (5) | 34.0 ± 5.8 (3) | 22.7 ± 5.8 (9) |
| Offspring surviving[c] | — (0) | 4.00 (1) | 0.67 ± 0.58 (3) | 1.00 ± 0.17 (3) | 0.17 ± 0.43 (6) |
| **Females** | | | | | |
| Clutch size | 11.45 ± 0.62 (11) | 10.80 ± 1.36 (5) | 11.00 ± 0.55 (5) | 12.00 ± 0.97 (6) | 12.25 ± 0.63 (4) |
| Brood size | 10.64 ± 0.83 (11) | 10.75 ± 1.03 (4) | 7.40 ± 1.99 (5) | 11.00 ± 1.26 (6) | 10.75 ± 0.25 (4) |
| Hatching date of brood[b] | 24.1 ± 1.8 (11) | 26.8 ± 1.0 (4) | 21.8 ± 2.9 (4) | 26.3 ± 4.2 (6) | 21.8 ± 1.9 (4) |
| Offspring surviving[c] | 1.50 ± 0.43 (10) | 1.00 ± 0.41 (4) | 0.67 ± 0.67 (3) | 1.00 ± 0.63 (5) | 0.75 ± 0.48 (4) |

Source: Nur 1988, courtesy of Evolution.
[a]Numbers in parentheses are sample sizes.
[b]Calibrated to 1 = May 1.
[c]Number of offspring recaptured in following winter or spring.

Table 6-9. Age-specific survival rates of Willow and Crested Tits, expressed as means of annual rates ± 1 SE

|  | Willow Tit | Crested Tit | Significance (P) |
|---|---|---|---|
| Juveniles[a] | 0.030 ± 0.0072 | 0.026 ± 0.0114 | <0.05[a] |
| Adults[b] | 0.53 ± 0.12 | 0.67 ± 0.26 | <0.01 (t test) |

Source: Ekman and Askenmo 1986, courtesy of Evolution.
[a]Significant interspecific difference in juvenile survival rates for nest survival component; other components similar for the two species. Data from five years.
[b]Data from seven years.

more nest predation. On the other hand, adult Crested Tits actually survive somewhat better than do adult Willow Tits (Table 6-9). Ekman and Askenmo suggested that the lower survivorship of adult Willow Tits may be a consequence of their higher reproductive effort. They further suggested that the reproductive strategy of each species may be optimal for its own particular situation.

## Breeder Mortality and the Presence of Summer Floaters

Not all breeding chickadees survive the summer. It is not uncommon for one parent to disappear, leaving the other parent to care for the offspring as best it can.

Sometimes the missing birds are not replaced, and often nests with only one parent will fail. If the death of one of the pair occurs fairly well into the nestling stage, when the nestlings no longer need much brooding, a single parent can support an entire brood, although it sometimes so exhausts itself in the effort that it lowers its chances of surviving through postbreeding molt (pers. observ.). If the death occurs early in the nest cycle and there is no replacement, the widowed bird usually remains on its territory but does not attempt any further breeding that summer.

Sometimes, however, replacements appear and take the place of the breeding chickadee that disappeared. At this point, the newly formed pair has two options: they can start a new nest right away, or they can continue with the old one. The latter option could involve the newly inserted bird's giving parental care to offspring that are not its own. Yet records show that this does in fact occur.

Odum (1941a) reported a case in which a female Black-capped Chickadee lost her mate soon after her brood had hatched. A male that had lost his own mate joined her and helped to raise her brood; the newly formed pair then started a new nest, so the female raised two broods that summer, one by each of two mates. The advantage to the new male of raising another male's offspring is clear in this case: by inserting and forming a pair bond, he managed to raise his own brood later that summer. Howitz (1986a) related an incident in which an inserting male Black-capped Chickadee helped his new mate raise her original brood (that is, young birds fathered by another bird). Again the replacement occurred during the nestling stage. Howitz (1986a) reported that the new male behaved just as a normal male parent would toward these adopted offspring. In this case, however, the newly formed pair did not attempt a second brood, so the adopting male did not get to breed that season. Nevertheless, Howitz argues that, by inserting, the male very likely did increase his own expected re- productive output. Because older females are in general more efficient breeders, and pair bonds, once formed, are often main- tained for the life of the individuals involved, the formation of a pair bond with an older female would increase the male's chances of a highly successful breeding season the following year.

Both of the replacements discussed so far involved breeders that had lost their mates (Odum 1941a, Howitz 1986a). Occasionally, however, the inserting adult may be a summer floater.

Floaters during the breeding season can be defined fairly simply as individuals that are capable of breeding but are prevented from doing so by some factor such as the territorial behavior of others (Brown 1975). Odum (1942b) reported the existence of unmated Black-capped Chickadees of unknown sex in his New York popu- lation, and he noted that they were far more common in one year than they had been in the previous year. In my two-year study of chickadees in British Columbia, I found one summer floater each summer: both were females. Each ranged over several breeding territories, mostly avoiding the territory owners, but, if dis- covered, giving what I called begging notes (Smith 1967c); these were almost certainly broken dees. One of these females survived the following winter and nested in a territory within her last sum- mer's home range. Similarly, Weise and Meyer (1979) reported six yearling Black-capped Chickadees that were nonterritorial during their first breeding season but had restricted home ranges. All six apparently succeeded in obtaining breeding territories within these home ranges in their second year. Ficken et al. (1981) described a female summer floater in their Wisconsin study area: this bird associated closely with a breeding pair during the summer, but evidently did not ever help raise the offspring. And Desrochers et al. (1988) did summer removal experiments, removing seven birds: three females and two pairs. All seven were replaced, the fastest replacement being only one day after the resident adult had been removed. Three of the seven replacements were banded, and all were yearlings that had remained on the study area in the spring.

It is important to note the difference between these nonbreeding chickadees and the nonbreeding male Willow Tits studied by Ekman and Askenmo (1986; see Reproductive Success and Strategies, above). The Willow Tits lived in an area of such severe climate that no potential recruits were available to replace mates lost over the winter. By contrast, chickadee populations in the study areas mentioned all typically have dispersal phases in the spring (see, for example, Weise and Meyer 1979, Desrochers et al.

Table 6-10. Observed summer floater Black-capped Chickadees

| Year | Male | Female |
|------|------|--------|
| 1980 | — | — |
| 1981 | — | — |
| 1982 | — | AG RK |
| 1983 | AY RO | — |
| 1984 | AY RO | |
| | AR BG | |
| | AK RO | — |
| | AY RR | |
| | AY RG | |
| 1985 | AY RG | AR BO[a] |
| 1986 | AO KK[a] | AO OO[b] |
| | | AO BB[a] |
| 1987 | — | — |
| 1988 | AK OY[b] | — |
| TOTAL | 7 (2 repeats) | 4 (no repeats) |

Source: Smith 1989, courtesy of Wilson Bulletin.
[a] A summer floater that replaced a breeder during the summer.
[b] A former flock switcher.

1988) during which available mates (typically young birds) move about in search of places to settle. In fact, what the nonbreeding chickadees mentioned above lacked was not mates, but rather breeding territories.

Between 1980 and 1988 I observed a total of 11 summer floater Black-capped Chickadees: 7 males and 4 females (Table 6-10). All 11 were color-banded. As Odum (1942b) noted, summer floater density can vary markedly from year to year. When you see floaters, you know they are present; it is harder to document absence. The conclusion that no floaters of a certain sex were present in some summers is based on the fact that, in several years, territory owners that had died were not replaced, even when the death was early in the breeding season (S. M. Smith 1989).

Male floaters are relatively easy to find. Some even sing (fee-bees), usually in areas well removed from the nest sites of the resident pairs. Female summer floaters are, in my experience, much harder to detect. Curiously enough, I have not heard them giving broken dees as did the West Coast birds in response to meeting local territory owners. I do not know if this observation is a population difference or simply a result of some change in my own field methods.

Chickadee summer floaters of either sex typically range over several breeding territories, often as many as five. Most such birds, if they survive their "floating" summer and the subsequent winter, manage to obtain breeding territories the following summer within their former floater range (Weise and Meyer 1979, S. M. Smith 1989). Some actually wait two full years (spending two consecutive summers as floaters) before finally obtaining a local breeding territory (Table 6-10). A very few, however, actually have a chance to breed right away—the floaters that replace breeding birds that died during the summer. I have three such records: one male and two females. The one inserting male joined a female whose brood was just about to fledge; he helped her raise this brood, even though they were (presumably) fathered by another male. Although this new pair did not nest together that summer, both members survived the following winter and bred together the following spring. Each of the two female replacements came early in the breeding season, before the eggs had hatched. In both cases, the newly formed pairs deserted the old nests and began new ones, each some distance from the former site (S. M. Smith 1989).

### Postbreeding Molt

The postbreeding molt is the last big energy drain on adult chickadees before the onset of winter. The molt begins in July or early August, and generally lasts two to three months. In this molt, every feather, including those of the wing and tail (by far the largest feathers a chickadee has), is replaced. Chickadees with late or second broods may be forced to delay the onset of postbreeding molt, as is the case with several European titmice. Indeed, some of the latter with very late nests have actually been observed beginning their molt before the young leave the nest (Perrins 1979). Dhondt (1981) showed that Great Tits in southern Sweden that had the greatest delay in the onset of this molt grew shorter wings than did earlier molting Great Tits; such short wings once again reflect the price of delayed or second broods.

Molting chickadees are often hard to find. They tend to be exceptionally silent and move about as little as possible, especially in the mornings. At other times of day they are a bit more active and can occasionally be seen interacting with newly arrived young birds that have dispersed from nests some distance away. These newly arrived young chickadees eventually join with the local adults to form the nonbreeding flocks, which are the subject of the next chapter.

# 7

# The Nonbreeding Season

## Flock Formation

Toward the end of the breeding season, "foreign" juvenile chickadees will sometimes associate with local family groups and even beg for food from the adults. Such birds are typically ignored or even attacked (Glase 1973). Late-breeding adults, or those with replacement or second broods, may have to deal with the presence of several unrelated juveniles associating with their family groups.

Newly dispersing young chickadees may occasionally band together, at least temporarily. Such aggregations of unrelated young chickadees are particularly prevalent in July and early August (Odum 1941b). Hinde (1952) found similar groups of unrelated juveniles among Great Tits (*Parus major*). They show little integration, and their composition changes frequently. Newcomers may associate briefly with such groups, then leave either to settle locally or in some more distant spot. In my experience, these aggregations are not formed every summer; whether or not they do form may depend in part on the success and synchrony of breeding in the general area over the past few months. In any case, such groups usually do not last long, and dissolve as the young chickadees settle into true winter flocks. Most of these groups have disbanded by mid-August; however, in unusual years a few may persist as late as the third week in September (pers. observ.).

After the dispersal of locally produced young, the chickadees that remain in an area will be the adults that survived the breeding season along with a number of dispersing young birds, most of which are from natal areas some distance away. With the adults acting as a kind of nucleus, the juveniles choose where to settle, and thus the true flocks begin to form.

Just what is meant by a true flock? Some investigators (e.g., Desrochers and Hannon 1989) define Black-capped Chickadee winter flocks in terms of foraging associations, stating that a chickadee winter flock consists of birds that invariably forage together throughout the winter. I would modify this somewhat, since foraging chickadees may often wander (see Cohesion and Mobile Elements, below). Perhaps it would be more useful to define a flock as those chickadees that typically roost relatively close together throughout the winter (see also Saitou 1982, 1988). Regardless of which definition is used, the stress here is on constant and stable membership.

Data on the roosting behavior of Black-capped Chickadee flocks can be difficult to get for several reasons. For one thing, chickadees typically do not go to roost until it is too dark for investigators to read color bands. Also, roosting itself often occurs rather suddenly: a flock will arrive, feed normally—then suddenly all will be silent, movement will stop, and the birds will be roosting. However, if one starts following a flock a good half hour before normal roosting time, there is usually enough light to see which birds are around, and then the number of silhouettes can be counted as the group enters the roosting trees. On relatively mild winter nights even a large flock, say 8 or 10 members, may roost within a few meters of each other (Odum 1942a). Admittedly, on very cold nights chickadees often roost in cavities, and thus their spacing is necessarily more spread out, depending on the local distribution of suitable roost chambers. Even then, I suspect that the vast majority of chickadees will roost closer to their flockmates than to members of any other flock.

Desrochers and Hannon (1989) and others (Saitou 1982) have referred to winter flocks as having constant and stable membership. I also have seen stable winter flocks, both in West Coast and in eastern populations—within certain time constraints. For my current population, winter chickadee flocks are stable for a four to five-month period: from mid-September or early October through about mid-February. Before mid-September, not all flocks are fully formed, so some flux is possible; after mid-February, certain low-ranked birds may start to wander widely and may settle into other flocks if suitable openings exist (see Flock Breakup, below).

The process of flock formation is complicated because it almost certainly involves some pair formation as well. Not only may adults that have been widowed over the summer form pairs at this time, but apparently juveniles only a few months out of the nest may also. Indeed, Hafton (1990) found evidence that juvenile Willow Tits (*Parus montanus*) can form pairs in late summer before joining flocks. (As mentioned in Chapter 5, the fact that some parids form pairs in late summer and early fall is well established [Carolina Chickadees, *Parus carolinensis*: Dixon 1963; Willow Tits: Hogstad 1987a].) Probably pairs involving adults are formed first, after which juveniles come in and fill out the rest of the flock. Some pairs are formed when two adults, each of which has lost a mate over the summer, pair together at flock formation. During the first seven years of my current study, seven such new alliances between widowed adults were made this way. Four of these alliances were between widowed birds from the same former flock. The other three were between widowed birds from adjacent former flocks. Of these three, one new pair joined the male's flock, one joined the female's flock, and the third started its own new flock. Fourteen other widowed adults paired with juveniles during the autumn period of flock formation. Any juvenile able to join a flock paired with an adult is lucky indeed, because it will automatically obtain a high position in the flock's dominance hierarchy. Such openings are typically snapped up by the first juveniles to arrive via dispersal, that is, they are filled by young from the earliest successful broods in the general area.

Chickadees that live at or near the edge of their geographical range are likely to exist in conditions that are in some way suboptimal. Hence it is not too surprising if chickadee flocks at the edge of their range are at least somewhat atypical. For example, Minock (1972) described a Black-capped Chickadee flock from a peripheral population in Utah that consisted of just three individuals: an old mated pair and an adult female, unpaired the previous breeding season—and no yearling chickadees at all. I suspect that such a flock would be unlikely to form over most of this species' geographical range.

Similarly, Haftorn (1990), working in a subalpine area in northern Norway, frequently found Willow Tit flocks that contained an "extra" individual of either sex, unlike those in less severe habitat in Norway (e.g. Hogstad 1987a) or Sweden (Ekman 1979a). Moreover, Haftorn found no evidence of any individual's being excluded from joining the flocks in the study area, although Hogstad (1989c) showed that certain individuals were excluded from joining his Willow Tit flocks by the aggressive behavior of others. Hogstad's observations strongly suggest that the flocks Haftorn was working with were incomplete, possibly because of the severity of the local conditions.

Just how long it takes to complete the flock formation process under more normal circumstances varies markedly from year to year. Glase (1973) reported that the flocks in his three-year study in New York were fully formed by late August. In 1980, 1981, 1982, and 1984 of my current study in Massachusetts, the winter flocks were essentially complete by the first week of September; however, in 1983 and again in 1985 and 1986, new birds continued to join my study flocks until mid-October (Smith 1988a).

In each of these three late years, I noticed unbanded juvenile chickadees giving begging dees to other chickadees (both adult and juvenile) in my study area as late as mid-September. These were almost certainly newly arrived birds whose family groups had only just broken up, that is, birds from very late nests. Clearly years of late or prolonged breeding will of necessity also be years of late winter flock formation.

### Flock Composition

I contend that Black-capped Chickadee flocks, at least over most of the species' geographic range, are made up of mated pairs. Two major sorts of evidence support this contention: sex ratios immediately after flock formation and behavior of flock members (specifically who associates most closely with whom within a flock) throughout the winter.

Sex ratios of 1:1 are widespread in winter Black-capped Chickadee flocks (see, for example, Smith 1967c for flocks on the West Coast [British Columbia], Desrochers et al. 1988 for flocks in the northern interior [Alberta], and Glase 1973 for flocks in the East [New York State]). In my own current study area, all 51 central flocks over a total of nine winters have had an even number of members at initial completion, and every flock contained equal numbers of males and females. Obviously a key phrase here is "at initial completion": winter mortality can change these numbers, because birds that die over the winter are typically not replaced (especially flock members less than a year old).

Naturally, exceptions can occur, although documentation of these is rare. The only published exceptions I know of are for flocks living in suboptimal habitat at the edge of the Black-capped Chickadee's geographic range (e.g., Minock 1972, mentioned above). At suboptimal edge habitats, during flock formation, recruits of the appropriate sex are simply not available (or perhaps are unwilling to settle). The lack of suitable recruits results in essentially incomplete flocks. Black-capped Chickadee winter flocks with unbalanced sex ratios should be examined to see whether these skewed ratios are simply the result of overwinter mortality or whether they are present, as in Minock's flocks, at flock formation. If the latter, the skewed ratios would be particularly interesting, because they may suggest that such populations, like those of Minock (1972), are inhabiting areas that are in some way suboptimal (see also Population Dynamics, Chapter 9).

Why do even sex ratios support the idea that pairing occurs during flock formation? Consider the case of a hypothetical flock that, when fully formed, will contain six members: an old pair that bred in the area and four young chickadees hatched a couple of months ago. If the sex of the young birds entering the flock made no difference, then it should be possible to find flocks of one male and five females, or one female and five males: yet chickadee flocks of such uneven composition rarely, if ever, occur (at least in most areas). The conclusion seems inescapable that the gender of the settling birds does matter—and that something is acting to assure that the fully formed flock will contain equal numbers of males and females. The most obvious candidate for this "something" seems to be pair formation.

Investigators working on other parids have come to the same conclusion. Sex ratios of approximately 1:1 have also been reported for winter flocks of Carolina Chickadees (Brewer 1961, Dixon 1963) and Mountain Chickadees (*Parus gambeli*) (Dixon 1965) in North America, and many European titmice including the Willow Tit (Hogstad 1987a) as well. Dixon (1963) concluded that Carolina Chickadees pair in the autumn of their first year or even earlier (that is, during flock formation), and Hogstad (1987a) and others have reached a similar conclusion for Willow Tits. Indeed, Nakamura (1975), in a review of social organization of members of the genus *Parus,* suggested that nonbreeding flocks of ,all chickadees and titmice are simply stable groups of pairs. And while Saitou (1978) challenged the generality of Nakamura's claim, it remains true that winter flocks in many populations of chickadees and titmice do fit very well with Nakamura's model. (See Matthysen 1990 for a recent review of parid winter social organization.)

In addition to sex ratios, there is also strong behavioral evidence that newly formed chickadee flocks contain actual pairs (Fig. 7-1). Ficken et al. (1981), analyzing associations between individual members of a winter Black-capped Chickadee flock in Wisconsin, demonstrated that, even in midwinter, the strongest attachments were between males and females who subsequently bred together. However, Ficken et al. (1981) did not begin their observations until January. I conducted a similar study, begun in late August, and found that association indices, even in pairs of chickadees only a few months old, can also be remarkably strong in early fall (Table 7-1; Smith 1990).

The data necessary for calculating association indices are not easy to obtain. One has to wait until more than two birds are seen feeding within 3 meters (about 10 feet) of each other; the two closest can then be recorded as "nearest associates." The association index for two chickadees (A and B) can be calculated by taking two times the total number of observations when these two birds were nearest associates with each other, and dividing this by the sum of the total nearest-associate observations for bird A plus the total nearest-associate observations for bird B (Table 7-1).

Association indices do not invariably reveal chickadee pairs. I still remember the first year of my current study, when the top two birds in one flock always seemed to be together. I actually wondered if the flock's second-ranked bird was a very high ranking female—until the spring, when it became clear that both high-ranked birds were males. Yet the following winter, the two males again associated strongly together (pers. observ.). Such nonmated "buddies" within a flock are nevertheless infrequent. It is probably safe to say that, for the vast majority of chickadee flocks, data on association indices can provide reliable information about which birds are mated together.

Another aspect of flock composition concerns the age makeup

Fig. 7-1. Even within winter flocks, members of pairs typically forage closely together.

within flocks. This can be looked at in several ways. One way involves determining how many adult pairs are contained in a typical flock. Evidently this number varies considerably from place to place. For example, Glase (1973) found that approximately two-thirds of the flocks in his New York study area contained just one

Table 7-1. Association indices in Black-capped Chickadee flock 1, August 31–November 15, 1987

| Bird[a] | ABRR | AROO | ARGR | ARYR | ARRG | ARYY | ARYB | ARKB | AROY | ARGK | Age/sex |
|---|---|---|---|---|---|---|---|---|---|---|---|
| ABRR (13) | | .19(3) | .08(1) | .10(1) | .08(1) | **.50(6)** | .07(1) | — | — | — | Old male |
| AROO (21) | | | .06(1) | .15(2) | .12(2) | .06(1) | **.69(12)** | — | — | — | Old male |
| ARGR (13) | | | | .09(1) | — | .16(2) | .07(1) | **.52(6)** | .11(1) | — | Young male |
| ARYR (9) | | | | | .10(1) | .10(1) | — | .11(1) | **.29(2)** | — | Young male |
| ARRG (11) | | | | | | .08(1) | .07(1) | .10(1) | .11(1) | **.40(3)** | Young male |
| ARYY (13) | | | | | | | .07(1) | — | .10(1) | — | Old female |
| ARYB (17) | | | | | | | | — | .08(1) | — | Old female |
| ARKB (10) | | | | | | | | | .13(1) | .14(1) | Young female |
| AROY (7) | | | | | | | | | | — | Young female |
| ARGK[b] (4) | | | | | | | | | | | Young female |

*Source*: Smith 1990, courtesy of Springer Verlag.

*Note*: Five pairs (boldface numbers) emerge, even with data taken so early in the season. Numbers in parentheses in columns 3–11 indicate number of nearest-associate observations involving both birds (read horizontally and vertically).

[a]Number in parentheses indicates total number of times bird was counted as a nearest associate.

[b]This young female vanished from the area approximately September 15, 1987.

adult pair, and only 32 percent contained more than one. By contrast, 73 percent of the flocks in my current Massachusetts study area have contained at least two adult pairs (Smith 1988a).

Part of this difference may be due to the abundance of feeders in my study area. In this context, it is suggestive that Desrochers et al. (1988), in a two-year study involving supplemental food provision, found that in the first year most flocks had only one adult pair, whereas in the second year most flocks contained two adult pairs. Hence perhaps under strictly natural conditions, most winter flocks of Black-capped Chickadees will contain only one adult pair, with only about a third containing two or more.

Another approach is simply to look at a collection of flocks and determine the percent adults and juveniles present. Glase (1973) reported that his average flock, based on 23 autumn Black-capped Chickadee flocks, contained 45.4 percent adults and 54.6 percent juveniles. In my current study, 43.8 percent of my flock members have been adults and 56.2 percent juveniles (Smith 1988a)—remarkably similar figures. Yet, as mentioned above, almost three-quarters of my flocks contained more than one adult pair, whereas most of Glase's flocks contained only one adult pair. How is it possible that both Glase's flocks and my own had similar proportions of older birds, yet mine had so many more flocks with two adult pairs than his?

### Flock Size

This apparent discrepancy is due in part to the fact that my flocks are somewhat bigger than Glase's. Over an eight-year period, my flocks contained anywhere from 2 to 12 members at initial flock formation, with an average size of just over 8 members (Table 7-2); the most common flock sizes during this period were 8 and 10 members (Fig. 7-2). By contrast, Glase (1973) reported a mean flock size of just 6.35 members. Odum (1942a) reported that the average-sized natural flock in his study area was apparently 7–8 members, and Wallace (1941) stated that the "standard" chickadee flock in Massachusetts was 6–8 individuals. It is particularly interesting to note that Brewer (1961) found that a more southern Black-capped Chickadee population, in southern Illinois, had winter flocks averaging only 3.3 members. This finding suggests a

Table 7-2. Size of Black-capped Chickadee flocks in a study area in
western Massachusetts

| Year | No. of flocks | No. of regular members | Range (no. of regulars) | Mean no. of regular members |
|---|---|---|---|---|
| 1979–80 | 4 | 42 | 10–12 | 10.5 |
| 1980–81 | 5 | 42 | 6–10 | 8.4 |
| 1981–82 | 4 | 40 | 8–12 | 10.0 |
| 1982–83 | 5 | 44 | 6–12 | 8.8 |
| 1983–84 | 6 | 52 | 4–12 | 8.7 |
| 1984–85 | 6 | 30 | 2–8 | 5.0 |
| 1985–86 | 7 | 48 | 4–10 | 6.9 |
| TOTAL | 37 | 298 | | 8.05 |

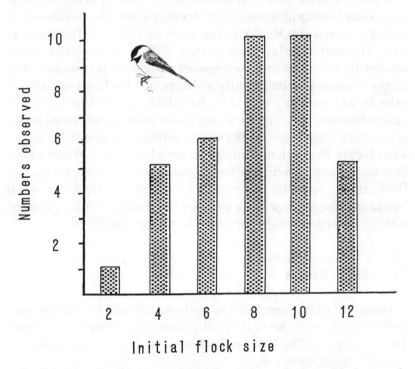

Fig. 7-2. Size distribution, at initial formation, of winter Black-capped
Chickadee flocks (flock regulars only). (From S. M. Smith, "Social Dynamics in Wintering Black-capped Chickadees," *Acta XIX Congressus Internationalis Ornithologici* (1988), pp. 2382–2390. Courtesy of University of Ottawa Press.)

possible latitudinal gradient in flock size, with more northern flocks being somewhat larger than those farther south. A similar latitudinal gradient in flock size may also occur in Willow Tit populations in Scandinavia (Hogstad 1987a).

Factors that affect flock size can include latitude, age and history of the adults in the flock, and local food supply—studies have shown that supplemental food (such as that provided by feeders) can increase chickadee flock size (e.g., Samson and Lewis 1979). Recently, Ekman (1989a, 1989b) suggested that flocks may be larger in areas with strong local variability in habitat quality. According to his argument, joining a flock with dominants may be a poor option for subordinates, so in more-or-less uniform habitats, there will be many, relatively small flocks. In areas with steep gradients in habitat quality, however, the benefits of joining a flock that lives in a rich area may outweigh the costs of being subordinate, thus birds will form larger flocks. Finally, the likelihood of forming mixed-species flocks can have an effect on flock size as well. Hogstad (1987a) showed that Willow Tit numbers were smaller in areas where mixed-species flocking was common, and larger in areas that had mostly monospecific flocks. Hogstad's results fit well with my own data for Black-capped Chickadees in Massachusetts: my current study population, which inhabits an area where mixed-species flocking is infrequent, does have somewhat bigger flocks than those in an area less than 100 miles (160 km) to the east, where chickadee participation in mixed-species flocks is very common. There, the most common flock size was 6 birds, and the average flock size was 6.6 (Smith 1976), compared with an average of eight members in my current flocks.

### Flock Ranges

Winter Black-capped Chickadee flocks typically inhabit distinct, well-defined areas. Several investigators (e.g., Butts 1931, Odum 1942a, Glase 1973) have commented on how "remarkably restricted" these areas are.

Odum (1942a) measured nine flock ranges and found that they were anywhere from 8.8 to 22.6 ha (22 to 56 acres), with an average of 14.6 ha (just over 36 acres). Butts (1931), also in New York, estimated one flock range to be about 16 ha (40 acres), and Hartzler (1970) described a flock range of just over 14 ha (35 acres) in Minnesota. Glase (1973) reported seven flock ranges of 8–11 ha, with an average of 9.5 ha (23.5 acres). Finally, Dixon (1963) found that the ranges of winter Carolina Chickadee flocks in Texas seldom exceed 8 ha (20 acres).

Not all flock members necessarily use all of their flock's range. For example, Brewer (1978) found that individual Black-capped Chickadee winter home ranges varied from 5.7 to 38.9 ha (14 to 96 acres). I have a few records of similar variation in my current study area. While most individuals do use their entire flock range, some, within a very few flocks, regularly restrict their movements to just a portion of that range—although even these birds will on occasion travel to more outlying portions with the rest of their flock. I suspect that these individuals, even with their restricted movements, typically maintain vocal contact with the rest of their flock.

Dixon (1963, 1965) found that both Carolina and Mountain Chickadee winter flocks occupy circumscribed ranges that overlap the ranges of other, conspecific flocks only very slightly, if at all. Odum (1942a) and others have found similarly restricted ranges for Black-capped Chickadee flocks. Indeed, Glase (1973) stated that the ranges occupied by winter chickadee flocks are functionally territories, at least in his study area, since each of his flocks defended its range from encroachment by other chickadee flocks (Fig. 7-3). Glase (1973) studied flock-flock aggressive encounters in detail during one of the winters of his study. During that winter, he observed some 76 interflock territorial disputes. In most of these disputes, the most aggressive birds were the two alpha males. However, at least 19 times, Glase also saw lower-ranking males from the home flock chasing intruding birds away. Evidently, at least in some areas, flock ranges can properly be called flock territories.

Nevertheless, not all chickadee flocks maintain exclusive winter flock territories. Overlap of flock ranges has been reported for winter Black-capped Chickadee flocks by Butts (1931), Odum (1942a), and Hartzler (1970), among others. Even Glase (1973) reported that unusually rich food sources, such as deer carcasses, attracted more than one flock. This fits nicely with my own experience: in relatively undisturbed, feederless areas, flock-flock aggressive interactions are fairly common, and each flock tends to occupy a largely exclusive area defended against all neighboring chickadee flocks throughout the winter. By contrast, in areas with

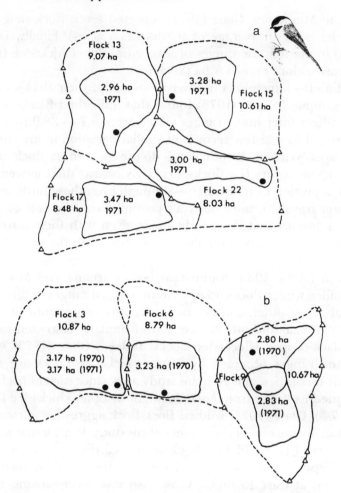

Fig. 7-3. A comparison of the foraging area (in hectares) of the alpha pair of Black-capped Chickadees during the breeding season (smaller areas) with the territory of the flock dominated by each alpha pair during the following winter (larger areas). (a) and (b) refer to two different study sites. Triangles = sites of territorial encounters between flocks during fall and winter. Dark circles = nest sites. (From Glase 1973, courtesy of *The Living Bird*, 12, Cornell University Laboratory of Ornithology.)

rich food sources (such as dead mammals or bird feeders), the defense gradually breaks down over time. In my current study area, with its many feeders, the nonbreeding flocks start out with essentially exclusive flock territories each fall, and flock-flock aggressive encounters at mutual boundaries are both common and, being quite noisy, easy to detect. However, as more and more of the area's feeders get stocked, there occurs more and more encroachment, and progressively less defense, until by about the end of October, considerable overlap results. Such a high degree of overlap is probably an artifact, resulting from the abnormally high level of rich food sources (the feeders). Hence, the fact that overlap is common may in part reflect the how widespread bird feeders are within the geographic range of Black-capped Chickadees. Recently, however, Desrochers and Hannon (1989) showed that some feederless, undisturbed areas can be inhabited by Black-capped Chickadee flocks that show considerable range overlap. Working with two large study areas in northern Alberta, one supplied with several feeders, and the other left unsupplemented, they found that, in both areas, the resident chickadee flocks' ranges overlapped; indeed, when flocks met, flock-flock aggressive interactions were actually less likely than were aggressive interactions between members of the same flock, even in the feederless area. Given that "territory" is often defined as a defended area, the rarity of flock-flock aggressive interactions suggests that Desrochers and Hannon's flocks were not defending territories. However, their chickadees were evidently well aware of the location of the boundaries of local flock home ranges. When chickadee flocks do meet, the relative dominance of the interacting birds depends on the location of the encounter, with residents being dominant over birds from adjacent flocks (e.g., Hartzler 1970, Glase 1973, Desrochers and Hannon 1989). Desrochers and Hannon found that this dominance of the resident flock extended almost to the edge of its home range, and that there were apparently narrow zones between adjacent range centers in which relative dominance of the neighboring flocks changed rapidly (Fig. 7-4). As Desrochers and Hannon pointed out, these narrow range interfaces could easily become true territory borders under ecological conditions that favor territoriality.

Wherever flock ranges overlap, data on actual flock sizes and composition become considerably more difficult to obtain, for two reasons. One reason is simply that when two flocks meet at a feeder they may mingle, so one must make observations in areas well away from the feeders in order to tell which bird belongs to which flock. An additional factor can complicate flock identification even more: some parids may form compound flocks. The group of 18 Black-capped Chickadees that Hartzler (1970) re-

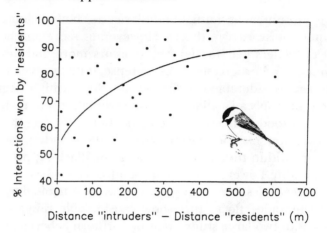

Fig. 7-4. Percentage of agonistic interactions won by members of resident Black-capped Chickadee flocks in relation to the difference between the distance of intruders and residents from their respective home-range centers. The residents became rapidly more dominant over intruders as they got closer to the center of their own home range. Curve fitted by hand. Each point represents a percentage of wins generated from at least 10 interactions. (From Descrochers and Hannon 1989, courtesy of *Condor*.)

ported in Minnesota may have been such a compound flock. Saitou (1982, 1988) studied compound flocks of Great Tits in Japan in considerable detail. These were typically combinations of two neighboring flocks whose ranges partially overlapped. Saitou (1982) even found one case where two basic flocks whose ranges did not overlap became associated with each other through the intermediary of a third flock whose range overlapped the ranges of the other two. Each basic flock typically retired to roost in its own flock range at night; the compound flocks then re-formed when the two basic flocks next met. Saitou also found that relative dominance between members of different flocks was site-dependent, with members of the "home" basic flock dominating members of the other flock; site-related interflock dominance of Black-capped Chickadees was also found by Hartzler (1970), Glase (1973), and Desrochers and Hannon (1989).

In my own study area, compound flocks of Black-capped Chickadees do occur, but not every flock-flock encounter results in the formation of a compound flock. Many of my flocks never form compound flocks at all, and most of the rest form compound flocks with just one of their neighboring flocks, even though they may share boundaries with three or four others. Evidence of a compound flock includes foraging together for extended periods of time in areas well away from artificial or unusually rich food sources such as feeders (Saitou 1982).

What happens if a Black-capped Chickadee is displaced from its winter flock range for some reason, such as being caught up in a strong windstorm? Will it be able to make its way back—and if it can, will it always choose to do so? Odum (1941c) did some removal experiments designed to answer some of these questions.

Odum was careful to use only color-banded chickadees whose previous residency was well established. In late February or March, he moved 21 chickadees. Each had been caught in late morning, kept in a dark cage, and then released in early afternoon of the same day at a site between 2.4 and 2.8 km (1.5 to 1.75 miles) away from the place where it had been caught. Of the 21 releases, 5 (19 percent) returned to their home range within 24 hours, and 3 more returned the following day. Two more made it back within a week of release, and another 2, for a total of 12 (57 percent), managed to return to their original home range before flock breakup in mid-April. Of the remainder, 2 settled into local flocks at the release point, and the other 7 disappeared, although whether they died trying to get back (as I suspect) or simply settled elsewhere is not known. About equal proportions of high- and low-ranked birds returned before flock breakup. Interestingly enough, one of the birds that did home successfully subsequently moved away at flock breakup and actually paired with a member of the local flock at the release site, some 2.8 km (1.75 miles) away (Odum 1941c). I might add that the first two chickadees that I placed into my aviaries for my removal experiments (Smith 1987) each escaped almost immediately (much to my disgust at the time). Both birds (an alpha male and a top-ranked female from different flocks) returned to their home flocks, about 1.5 km (almost 1 mile) away, within three hours of escape.

## Behavior of Natural Flocks

Odum (1942a) gathered considerable data on the movements of his Black-capped Chickadee flocks. One thing he measured was their rate of movement within their flock ranges. He determined that their overall average rate of movement was approximately one-quarter mile (about 0.4 km) per hour. This figure is perhaps misleading, however, in that it suggests that flock movement is more or less constant. Instead, the movements of chickadee flocks are much more rhythmic, with periods of fairly rapid movement (up to 8 km, or 5 miles, per hour) accompanied by virtually no feeding, alternating with periods of active feeding and little or no flock movement.

Odum (1942a) managed to identify several factors that affect the rate of progression by chickadee flocks. One was time of day: flocks tended to move faster in the morning than in the middle of the day. Although Odum did not provide data for later in the day, my own impression (without precise measurement) is that the speed with which flocks move picks up again toward the end of the afternoon.

Another important influence on how fast flocks travel is exerted by the weather. Odum (1942a) recorded the fastest flock movements on warm cloudy days, and the slowest on cold and especially very windy days. Kessel (1976), working in Fairbanks, Alaska, where the mean January temperature was −24° C (−11° F) found similar results, with overall movement curtailed both by cold and by wind; she also found that aggressive behavior was repressed during extreme cold—and believe me she had extreme cold: during her study the coldest temperature recorded in her study area was −52° C, or an incredible −62° F.

The third factor Odum reported that affected rate of flock movement was time of year. Oddly, Odum (1942a) recorded faster flock movements in late fall than in either early fall or in midwinter. (One wonders if Odum encountered a fall with a period of unusually cold or windy weather, followed by somewhat warmer conditions). Clearly more work needs to be done on winter flocks to unravel how time of year, independently of either time of day or weather, actually affects chickadee flock movements.

Some early workers suggested that flocks might follow regular routes through their flock ranges, always arriving at, say, a particular hemlock tree at a particular time of day. Butts (1931) spent some time demonstrating that his flocks did not show any evidence of regular routes, and Odum (1942a) reported the same. Certainly my study flocks show no evidence of such regular routes; I wish they did, because it would make banding them much easier. I suspect that people who have the impression that chickadee flocks always visit their feeders at a certain time of day may actually be marking some regularity of their own behavior, rather than of the chickadees. If a flock is usually somewhere close to a feeder, and if people always look for the birds at a certain time (right after lunch, for instance), then their presence might be taken to indicate a regular route, even though this is not the case.

Although they follow no regular routes, chickadee flocks do typically have certain areas within their flock range that they use far more frequently than others. Naturally, areas that contain particularly rich food resources or effective cover or both will be used more than poorer, more exposed areas. For example, Odum (1942a) found that some of his chickadee flocks spent much of their time in clumps of hemlock trees that had a particularly good cone crop. Glase (1973) also recorded differential use of areas with flock ranges. He further noted that a given flock's preferred foraging areas differed with the season: a flock might spend much of its autumn days foraging on weed seeds in an open part of the flock range, then shift to spending more of its time in conifers later in the season.

## Dominance Hierarchies

Wherever one finds the fairly stable groupings characteristic of chickadee winter flocks, one can expect to find stable dominance hierarchies, or peck orders, within these flocks. To measure dominance, most investigators use some or all of the five criteria for dominance used by Dixon (1965). These are (1) supplanting attacks, in which the dominant individual flies at and takes over the place of a more subordinate bird; (2) chasing; (3) retention of position by a bird despite an attempted supplanting (here the bird that retains its position ranks above the one that failed to supplant it); (4) obvious waiting by one individual until another, higher ranked individual has completed its feeding and left; and (5) withdrawal upon detection of a higher ranked individual approaching from some distance away. In my own research, I generally use the first four of these criteria.

At one point I wondered if dominance data taken at feeders would be the same as those taken in more natural circumstances, so I spent a lot of time generating dominance hierarchies at and away from feeders. I was excited about the project because Dunham (1966) had found food-related dominance to be different from perch-related dominance in captive Rose-breasted Grosbeaks (*Pheucticus ludovicianus*).

I was initially quite disappointed when I found there was no difference between peck orders generated at and away from feeders (Smith 1976). Now, however, I am glad there is no difference, because dominance data are much more easily obtained at feeders.

Within true winter flocks, Black-capped Chickadees form stable, linear peck-right dominance hierarchies (Hartzler 1970, Glase 1973, Ficken et al. 1981). In such hierarchies, the top, or alpha, bird is able to chase or supplant all other flock members, the second bird is able to supplant all but the top bird, and so on down to the lowest-ranked bird, which cannot supplant or chase any other bird in the flock (Table 7-3). Within a single flock, the peck order is not site-related, but instead remains constant wherever the flock happens to be (Smith 1976, Desrochers and Hannon 1989). Mountain Chickadees exhibit similar linear peck-right hierarchies (Dixon 1965, Minock 1971), as do some Eurasian titmice such as Great Tits (Hinde 1952) and Willow Tits (Ekman 1979a, Hogstad 1987a). By contrast, Carolina Chickadees apparently have a somewhat more flexible system. For example, Dixon (1963) reported that the rank of a given female seemed to vary with whether her mate was in the immediate vicinity or not. Mostrom (1988) also found considerable variation in apparent dominance within flocks of Carolina Chickadees. She reported several records

Table 7-3. Dominance-subordination relationships in a winter Black-capped Chickadee flock

|         | RRR | YTT | GC | BGT | RRF | BRF | RC | Total wins | % wins |
|---------|-----|-----|----|-----|-----|-----|----|-----------|--------|
| ♂ RRR   | —   | 5   | 18 | 8   | 15  | 11  | 7  | 64        | 96     |
| YTT     | 0   | —   | 4  | 0   | 9   | 6   | 9  | 28        | 85     |
| GC      | 0   | 0   | —  | 2   | 2   | 6   | 1  | 11        | 31     |
| ♀ BGT   | 3   | 0   | 0  | —   | 0   | 3   | 2  | 8         | 44     |
| ♂ RRF   | 0   | 0   | 0  | 0   | —   | 12  | 6  | 18        | 40     |
| BRF     | 0   | 0   | 2  | 0   | 1   | —   | 6  | 9         | 20     |
| ♀ RC    | 0   | 0   | 0  | 0   | 0   | 0   | —  | 0         | 0      |

*Source:* Hartzler 1970, courtesy of *Wilson Bulletin.*
*Note:* Data from five feeders, January 2 to February 29, 35 days of observation. Winners read horizontally. — indicates no possible interaction.

of "ambiguous relationships" within her flocks, and stated that they can occur anywhere within the hierarchy, but are more common among the lower-ranked chickadees. These ambiguities in rank may last from a few days to several months (Mostrom 1988). The winter social organization of this species is clearly different from the constant, stable peck orders of Black-capped Chickadee flocks.

One interesting aspect of these hierarchies is that for them to be functional, at least some degree of individual recognition is essential. Chickadees can clearly tell the relative rank of an approaching bird while that bird is still some distance away. Whether the amount of individual recognition is restricted to a bird's immediate rivals, as has been suggested by Glase (1973), or whether each chickadee can recognize the identity of each other flock member, is a fascinating and important question that awaits further investigation.

Four important factors that can affect an individual chickadee's rank within its winter hierarchy are age, sex, size, and seniority. Within each sex, old birds are typically dominant over younger birds. This pattern is virtually always true for males, and, with few exceptions, true for females as well. Rarely, a young female can pair with the alpha male of a flock, while an older female maintains her pair bond with the beta (second-ranked) male. Under these circumstances, since the rank of a female often reflects the rank of her mate, the young female may actually be dominant over the older, beta female. I have only one record of such an occurrence in eight winters; Glase (1973) also had one record in his three-year study. By contrast, Ficken et al. (1990) reported two such records in one flock during a single winter.

By the time of flock formation, males have typically become dominant over their mates, and in winter flocks, most males rank above most females. Occasionally, however, some females may be dominant over some males within a flock (Table 7-3). This is often because of the influence of age: it is not uncommon for older females to rank above young males (e.g., Hartzler 1970, Ficken et al. 1981, 1990), although Glase (1973) apparently had no records of such dominance. Hogstad (1987a), working with Willow Tits, reported that the number of males that an older female outranked depended on the individuals involved; my Black-capped Chickadee data show the same variability. Most of my females that ranked above males were at least two years old, but I have one record of a female just over one year old that was dominant over two juvenile males in an eight-bird flock (pers. observ.)

The third factor affecting rank is the size of the bird in question. Two ways in which one can measure a chickadee's size are by weighing it and by measuring its wing length. Some caution has to be taken in using either one of these measures—wing length is best compared between chickadees of the same age, and weights can vary considerably with such factors as season and time of day (e.g., Lawrence 1958; Haftorn 1988b, 1989). Neither Glase (1973) nor I (Smith 1976) reported finding any correlation between the weight of a chickadee and its rank, but we both used weights taken throughout the day. More recently, Hogstad (1987a) showed that body weight of Willow Tits explained 77 percent of the recorded variation in dominance rank of his birds. This result is almost certainly because Hogstad was careful to consider only weights taken between 11:00 A.M. and 1:00 P.M., thus minimizing the effects of daily weight fluctuations. Although Hogstad (1987a) also felt that wing length, as it reflects size, was correlated with dominance in both sexes in his population of Willow Tits, the same correlation does not seem to be present in populations of Black-capped Chickadees (Glase 1973).

The fourth factor affecting dominance is seniority, which is probably best described as the "first come, first served" principle— or, the early bird gets to rank higher. Arrival dates of dispersing young chickadees are not easily obtained: it is difficult to prove that a bird that was banded late has not simply been avoiding capture for several weeks. Glase (1973) solved this problem by using the degree of skull pneumatization of his birds. If we assume that all chickadees disperse and settle by the time they have reached approximately the same age posthatching, at any given date, birds with the greatest amount of pneumatization are likely to have arrived earlier than those with less pneumatization. Glase was able to show a positive correlation between the relative amount of cranial pneumatization and the number of other juvenile flockmates dominated, meaning that young chickadees arriving earliest in late summer obtain higher rank in the developing hierarchies than do later arrivals. My own data support this conclusion: young birds banded in July and August typically have relatively high rank with respect to their immediate peers (pers. observ.). Seniority also affects rank in other parids. Nilsson and

Smith (1985, 1988) and Nilsson (1989a, 1989b) showed that even small differences in hatching date of Marsh Tits (*Parus palustris*) greatly influence starting rank after dispersal, and, in fact, could even influence the probability of becoming established in a winter flock at all. Braun and Samson (1983) found that three juvenile male Tufted Titmice (*Parus bicolor*) were dominant over other juvenile males that joined the same flock later, and Hogstad (1987a) reported that in 14 cases for which he knew the order that two juvenile male Willow Tits joined a flock, the one that joined first got the higher rank every time.

Rather surprisingly, once rank has been established, the physical condition of an individual does not have as much effect on its position in the peck order as one might expect. Hamerstrom (1942) noted that a crippled male Black-capped Chickadee, having recently broken its leg, had no difficulty in maintaining a high position in the local hierarchy (his leg was broken sometime around midwinter). I have a similar record, also for a male Black-capped Chickadee. The bird, formerly the alpha male of his flock, broke his leg sometime during the summer, and the healed leg was noticeably crooked, affecting the bird's ability to perch. Nevertheless, when the flocks re-formed in the fall, this male once again became the alpha male of an eight-bird flock and had no difficulty in maintaining his rank throughout that winter.

If one works out the peck order of a chickadee winter flock, one will arrive at some linear arrangement of the members (Table 7-3). Yet it may actually be more accurate to think of dominance in a winter flock as being a hierarchy of pairs, not of individuals. As we have seen, in many areas pair bonds are established early, and members of pairs associate relatively closely all winter. In many chickadee populations, rank matching within pairs is quite common: the top-ranked male is paired with the top-ranked female, the beta male with the beta female, and so on throughout the flock. Hogstad (1987a) reported similar rank matching in Willow Tits. I have found that both members of a flock's top-ranked pair survive the winter considerably better than do the members of the lowest-ranked pairs (Table 7-4). Hence an eight-bird flock can be viewed not only as having a hierarchy of eight individuals, but also as being a hierarchy of four pairs.

If this is so, then within-sex rank should be far more important to any flock member than between-sex rank. The data of Glase (1973) support this contention: he found significantly more ag-

Table 7-4. Winter survival of Black-capped Chickadees and success in obtaining breeding territories

| Winter | | Old regulars | | Young regulars | | Switchers | | Members of high-ranked pairs | Members of low-ranked pairs |
|---|---|---|---|---|---|---|---|---|---|
| | | Males | Females | Males | Females | Males | Females | | |
| 1979–80 | N | 8 | 8 | 11 | 9 | 3 | 3 | 19 | 17 |
| | WS[a] | 75.0 | 87.5 | 36.4 | 33.3 | 33.3 | 66.7 | 84.2 | 23.5 |
| | BT[b] | 75.0 | 62.5 | 18.2 | 22.2 | — | 33.3 | 73.7 | 11.7 |
| 1980–81 | N | 6 | 4 | 14 | 16 | 6 | 8 | 24 | 16 |
| | WS | 83.3 | 75.0 | 50.0 | 56.3 | 33.3 | 50.0 | 79.2 | 31.3 |
| | BT | 83.3 | 75.0 | 35.7 | 31.2 | 16.7 | 25.0 | 66.7 | 12.5 |
| 1981–82 | N | 10 | 8 | 10 | 11 | 7 | 8 | 23 | 16 |
| | WS | 50.0 | 50.0 | 80.0 | 72.7 | 71.4 | 62.5 | 56.5 | 75.0 |
| | BT | 50.0 | 50.0 | 40.0 | 54.5 | 28.6 | 25.0 | 56.5 | 37.5 |
| 1982–83 | N | 10 | 7 | 11 | 12 | 4 | 8 | 29 | 11 |
| | WS | 80.0 | 71.4 | 81.8 | 66.7 | 75.0 | 62.5 | 75.9 | 54.5 |
| | BT | 80.0 | 71.4 | 18.2 | 25.0 | 50.0 | 50.0 | 62.1 | — |

Source: Smith 1984, courtesy of American Naturalist, © 1984 by the University of Chicago.
[a]WS = % of that age and sex class that survived the winter.
[b]BT = % of that age and sex class that succeeded in obtaining a breeding territory.

gressive encounters that were intrasexual (78 percent) than inter-
sexual (only 22 percent).

Withiam et al. (1988) looked at within-flock aggression in a
slightly different light. They predicted that high-ranking male
Black-capped Chickadees should show less aggression to their own
mates than they do toward other lower-ranking chickadees. Their
data support this prediction. Thus pair-bonded females were less
often interrupted by their own mates than were other low-ranked
members of a flock. Moreover, at least for the top-ranked pair,
females experienced less aggression from other males when their
own mate was nearby. Interestingly enough, Leak (1986) found
that old females engaged in significantly fewer aggressive interactions with males than predicted by chance alone (on the basis of
proportions of old to young females), while young females engaged in more interactions with males than predicted by chance.
Whether this is related to protection by the old females' high-
ranking mates, to greater experience of older females, or to some
combination of the two is not known (Leak was working "blind" at
the time, not knowing age, sex, or mate of her birds). Withiam and
his colleagues found that females that were pair-bonded to dominant males could maintain higher feeding rates than could other
low-ranked chickadees, at least in part because they had to spend
less time scanning to detect aggressors. Ekman (1990) found that
virtually the same dominance relationships were true for Willow
Tits in Sweden: females that were paired with dominant males
were subject to aggression less often than expected. Both Withiam
et al. (1988) and Ekman (1990) concluded that the pair-bond status of a female chickadee may have a greater effect on her winter
survival than does her absolute dominance rank—a conclusion
with which I certainly agree. Thus there are actually two behavioral features of chickadee winter flocks that give clear evidence of
the existence of pair bonds between flock members: association
indices and differential protection of high-ranking females by
their mates. With this kind of protection, it is no wonder that
females in winter flocks tend to associate preferentially with their
mates.

Dominant chickadee pairs potentially gain a great deal because
of their high rank. One long-term advantage is a far better chance
of obtaining a local breeding territory in the spring. In many areas
the number of pairs in a winter flock is often considerably greater
than the number of breeding territories the flock's winter home

range will hold. If the dominant pairs survive the winter, they will get these territories, and more subordinate pairs will be forced to move elsewhere to try to find breeding space. It is the forced departure of such low-ranked chickadees that accounts for the sharp drop in numbers at flock breakup (early March) seen in Figure 7-5 (see also Desrochers et al. 1988).

Dominant birds also get more immediate returns throughout the winter, because their ability to supplant subordinates results in priority access to the richest food sources and the safest foraging spots (Ficken et al. 1990). Both Glase (1973) and Desrochers (1989) showed that there are measurable differences in foraging positions between high-ranked and lower-ranked Black-capped Chickadees (Foraging Niche, Chapter 3). Willow Tits also exhibit such differences, and work in Sweden by Ekman and Askenmo (1984) showed that subordinate Willow Tits, given the chance to forage in the absence of the flock's dominant members, changed their behavior to be like that of the former dominants (Fig. 7-6).

If dominant birds gain both short-term advantages (priority access to necessary resources such food) and longer-term advantages (assurances of getting local breeding territories) that are denied to subordinates, one can very reasonably ask why any subordinate birds join flocks at all. One possible answer is that every flock member, simply by joining a flock, may share in the two advantages traditionally ascribed to flocking: increased efficiency in finding food (Krebs et al. 1972, Morse 1978, Ekman and Hake 1988) and greater safety from predators because of increased chances of predators' being detected (Powell 1974, Caraco 1979, Barnard 1980). The basic argument for each is that more pairs of eyes can detect food and predators more efficiently.

Some people have recently asked, however, whether subordinates really do get to share in either of these advantages. For example, Krebs et al. (1972) showed that subordinate captive Great Tits did find more food in groups than by themselves (Table 7-5); but in groups, these subordinates typically were supplanted by dominants, so although they found more food, they actually managed to eat less than when alone (Table 7-6). There is also some question about how much advantage subordinates gain in terms of increased predator protection. Ekman et al. (1981) found that the prediction rate on subordinate first-year Willow Tits was higher than on dominant members of the flock, and later Ekman (1987) showed that these subordinates are in fact excluded from

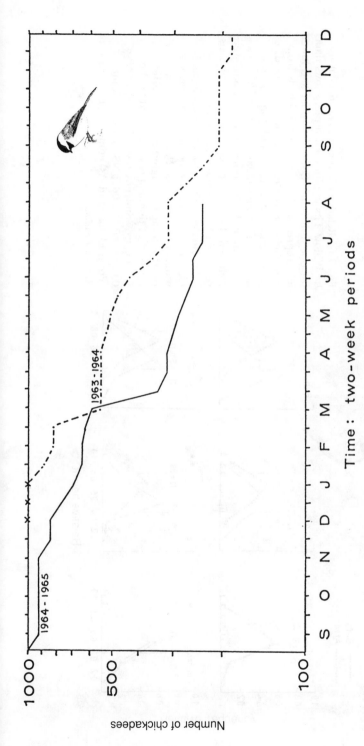

Fig. 7-5. Yearly survival of banded Black-capped Chickadees in a study area in Vancouver, British Columbia. Note the sudden sharp drop in numbers in early March (the time of flock breakup) of both years. Only high-ranked pairs remained after these decreases; each obtained a local breeding territory. (From Smith 1967c, courtesy of *Condor*.)

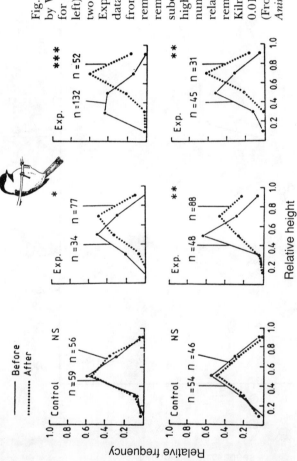

Fig. 7-6. Relative dominance and habitat use by Willow Tits in pines. Each plot shows data for one individual. Controls (upper and lower left) represent data for two individuals from two flocks where dominants were retained. Exp. (central and right-hand graphs) show data for four individuals (two of each sex) from three flocks from which dominants were removed. In all four experimental conditions, removal of dominants resulted in subordinates shifting to forage significantly higher than they had before removals. $n$ = number of observations. Differences in relative foraging height before and after removal of dominants were tested by the Kilmogorov-Smirnov test: $*P < 0.05$; $**P < 0.01$; $***P < 0.001$; NS: not significant. (From Ekman and Askenmo 1984, courtesy of *Animal Behaviour*.)

Table 7-5. Success of Great Tits at finding food when in a group of
four, in a pair, and alone

|  | Birds kept alone | Groups of four |
|---|---|---|
| Single birds vs. groups of four |  |  |
| Found food in 15-min test | 6 | 18 |
| Did not find food | 18 | 6 |
| $\chi^2 = 12.0$, $P < 0.1\%$ |  |  |
| Pairs vs. groups of four |  |  |
| Found food in 15-min test | 10 | 40 |
| Did not find food | 14 | 8 |
| $\chi^2 = 13.09$, $P < 0.1\%$ |  |  |

Source: Krebs et al. 1972, Ibis 114: 507–530, courtesy of the British
Ornithologists' Union.

the safer parts of the trees, and are forced to feed in more exposed
places, where they are more vulnerable to predation. Indeed,
some researchers (e.g., Gaston 1978) have actually suggested that
subordinates simply serve as food finders and sitting ducks for the
dominants.

Baker (1978) came to a similar conclusion. He suggested that
while dominants clearly gain advantages by having subordinates
around, the subordinates actually stand to lose by being close to
the dominants. Hence he felt the subordinates should always be
trying to escape, while the dominants should be busily hurrying
along after them.

Table 7-6. Effects of dominance and aggression in groups of Great Tits, showing (a) that after
food was found the rate of occurrence of dominance acts increased and (b) that birds low in the
hierarchy were more likely to be prevented from obtaining food after it had been found

| a) Increase in dominance acts after food found | No. of acts observed | Acts/min |
|---|---|---|
| Before | 31 | 0.24 |
| After | 45 | 0.7 |

| b) Birds that were prevented from feeding at the food source as a result of dominance behavior | Position in hierarchy | No. times prevented |
|---|---|---|
|  | 1 and 2 | 1 |
|  | 3 and 4 | 8 |

Source: Krebs et al. 1972, Ibis 114: 507–530, courtesy of the British Ornithologists' Union.

One prediction of this theory is that subordinate flock members should lead (in their attempts to escape), and more-dominant members should follow during flock movements. I tested this prediction for six chickadee flocks over a three-month period (mid-November through mid-February) in 1985–86, and my results showed no consistent relation between rank and leadership. In four of the six flocks, no single leader emerged—any flock member was just as likely as any other to initiate flock movements. In each of my other two flocks, one member initiated movements somewhat more than expected by chance: in one flock of six, the leader was the beta male; in the other, a flock of eight, the leader was the top-ranked female (pers. observ.). Odum (1942a) also remarked on the lack of consistent leadership in his chickadee flocks. Similarly, Ekman and Askenmo (1984) found no evidence that low-ranked Willow Tits avoided the company of dominants.

Actually, I suspect that under natural conditions, subordinates do gain some of the traditional advantages of flocking, even though such advantages are clearly far greater for dominants. Natural winter food for chickadees tends to be widely dispersed, unlike in the laboratory conditions of Krebs et al. (1972); thus even the lowest-ranked chickadee in a flock stands a good chance of eating the food it finds before being supplanted by a dominant. Glase (1973) and others have remarked on how very few aggressive interactions (like chases and supplantings) are to be seen within naturally foraging chickadee flocks. Along these lines, the findings of Witham and his colleagues (pers. comm.) are particularly interesting. They have found that whether or not a subordinate chickadee gets the traditional benefits of flocking (increased feeding rate; less time spent scanning) depends on social context. Working with Black-capped Chickadee flocks in the field, they showed that in the absence of nearby dominants, the feeding rate of subordinate chickadees did increase with increasing group size, although when the subordinates were feeding with the alpha birds, their feeding rate actually went down with group size. Similarly, vigilance, as measured by scanning time, also went down with group size for subordinate chickadees in the absence of dominants, but went up for subordinates in the presence of dominants. This is because scanning can actually serve two functions: detection of predators, and detection of potentially aggressive rivals. All chickadees must scan for predators, but only subordinate chickadees must also scan for higher-ranked aggressive rivals. Hence subordinate chickadees can get the same kinds of benefits from flocking as the alpha birds do, provided they spend at least some time feeding some distance from the flock's top-ranked birds (M. L. Withiam, D. Lemon, and C. P. L. Barkan, pers. comm.). Recently Hogstad (1989a) published one of the few studies to test directly what benefits, if any, subordinates gain through association with dominants. Working with free-living Willow Tits, Hogstad removed the adult pair from 13 flocks in early January, leaving 11 other flocks intact as controls. Amazingly, the survival of the subordinate birds in the experimental flocks (with the dominant pair removed) was significantly *lower* than the subordinate survival in the intact, control flocks (Table 7-7). In these Willow Tit flocks, the dominant pair is typically older and more experienced than the subordinate birds. Hogstad concluded that the presence of experienced birds in the control flocks gave all members both improved predator evasion and better food-finding efficiency, resulting in better survival for all. Hogstad's study area was in Norway, where winter conditions are relatively severe. It will be interesting to see how general a pattern these results actually are.

There is another reason why subordinate chickadees should associate with other, higher-ranking birds as part of stable flocks. West-Eberhard (1975) pointed out that subordinates of flocking species may become dominants later on in their lives; low-ranked individuals can join flocks as "hopeful dominants." If most or all individuals must be a subordinate before having a chance to become a dominant, then this paying of one's dues, as it were, is

Table 7-7. Numbers of juvenile Willow Tits that survived from January to April in experimental flocks with and without adults present

| | With adults | | | Without adults | | |
|---|---|---|---|---|---|---|
| Year | No. of flocks | Jan. | April | Proportion of survivors | No. of flocks | Jan. | April | Proportion of survivors |
| 1981 | 4 | 8 | 4 | 0.50 | 4 | 16 | 3 | 0.19 |
| 1982 | 4 | 8 | 5 | 0.63 | 4 | 16 | 3 | 0.19 |
| 1983 | 3 | 6 | 2 | 0.33 | 5 | 20 | 2 | 0.10 |
| TOTAL | 11 | 22 | 11 | 0.50 | 13 | 52 | 8 | 0.15 |

*Source:* Hogstad 1989a, *Ibis* 131: 128–134, courtesy of the British Ornithologists' Union.

simply an early and transient fitness loss through which many birds must pass. In most years, a few fortunate young chickadees manage to join flocks as dominants (replacing breeders that have died over the summer), but most young chickadees do not have this option. At least in my study area, however, even very low-ranked chickadees do have at least some chance of becoming dominants some day (Smith 1988a). Ekman and Askenmo (1984) concluded that West-Eberhard's hopeful dominant theory is one of the most plausible explanations for why subordinate Willow Tits associate with dominants in their study flocks in Sweden (see also Hogstad 1989b, and Flock Size, above).

With a somewhat different slant, Rohwer and Ewald (1981) suggested that perhaps dominant members of a flock incur certain costs not imposed on more subordinate flock members and that these additional costs may to some extent balance the benefits dominants gain through resource priority. If true, then the short-term fitness would be more-or-less similar for all birds, regardless of rank. Even though this theory was originally proposed for birds in which plumage differences serve as status signals in large, unstable flocks, some of the ideas have considerable relevance for chickadee and titmouse flocks. There are indeed certain costs associated with being a dominant bird in a flock. For example, the fact that dominant birds are more aggressive than lower-ranked birds has been shown not only for Black-capped Chickadees (e.g., Glase 1973), but also Mountain Chickadees (Dixon 1972), Great Tits (Järvi and Bakken 1984), and Willow Tits (Hogstad 1987a). This relationship between dominance and aggression holds true not only for within-flock encounters but also for between-flock skirmishes, where typically the highest ranked males from the two flocks engage in most of the actual aggressive encounters (Dixon 1963, 1965; Glase 1973, Hogstad 1987a). All such encounters carry some risk of injury, and time spent in these activities is time not available for foraging. Orr (1985) found that in groups of captive Black-capped Chickadees, the dominant males spent considerably more time searching for invaders than did subordinates. This activity both lowered their foraging time and also took them away from rich food patches that had poor visibility in preference for somewhat poorer food patches with better scanning possibilities. Orr's results are strongly reminiscent of what Ydenberg (1987) found with captive male Great Tits (see Breeding Territories, Chapter 5). Similarly, Hogstad (1988a) found that, at any given

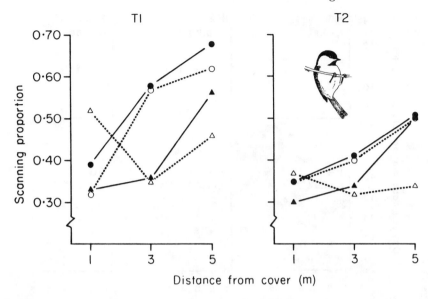

Fig. 7-7.  Mean proportion of time spent scanning by the members of two winter flocks of Willow Tits when visiting feeders placed 1, 3, and 5 meters from cover, under relatively mild temperatures (T1, left, from −6 to −1° C); and under colder temperatures (T2, right, from −15 to −10° C). Filled circles denote adult males; open circles, adult females; filled triangles, juvenile males; and open triangles, juvenile females. Overall scanning level increased with distance from cover, and even under the cold conditions, the older birds spent more time scanning that did younger, less-experienced flock members. (From Hogstad 1988a, *Ibis* 130: 45–56, courtesy of the British Ornithologists' Union.)

feeder, members of the dominant pair of free-living Willow Tits scanned relatively more than did subordinates (Fig. 7-7).

Recent studies on European titmice have shown that such costs have a measurable effect on the birds' metabolic rates: dominant birds must maintain higher daytime metabolic rates than do lower-ranked members of flocks of both Great Tits (Røskaft et al. 1986) and Willow Tits (Hogstad 1987b; see Fig. 7-8). Dominant Black-capped Chickadees probably pay a similar metabolic price for their high winter rank. As Hogstad has said, it is expensive to be dominant. The data indicate that the price dominant birds pay for their high status lowers their net gain over subordinates and provide some support for the Rohwer and Ewald's (1981) proposal that dominant birds incur additional costs that balance the advantages of dominance.

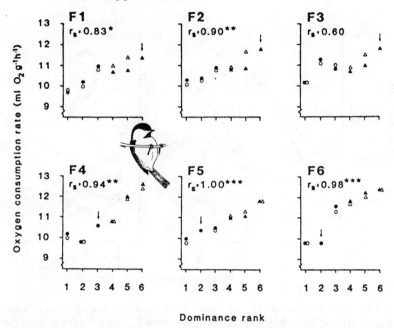

Fig. 7-8. Oxygen-consumption rates of male (triangles) and female (circles) Willow Tits in six winter flocks (F1–F6) relative to their respective dominance rankings. Symbols denote the oxygen-consumption rate before (closed) and after (open) removal of one individual from each flock (arrow). Along the horizontal axis, 1 indicates least dominant, and 6, most dominant. The highest-ranked birds consistently had the highest oxygen consumption, suggesting that there is a measurable metabolic cost associated with high rank. (From Hogstad 1987b, courtesy of *Auk*.)

## Mixed-Species Flocks

Many species have been recorded associating and moving with Black-capped Chickadee flocks (Odum 1942a, Brewer 1961, Morse 1970). Such associations may last a matter of minutes, hours, days, or even longer (Odum 1942a, Morse 1970). Odum listed 19 species that commonly formed stable, if transient, associations with Black-capped Chickadees in his New York study area. These included 10 arboreal wood warblers; Red-eyed Vireo (*Vireo olivaceus*) and Solitary Vireo (*V. solitarius*); Golden-crowned Kinglet (*Regulus satrapa*) and Ruby-crowned Kinglet (*R. calendula*); Red-breasted Nuthatch (*Sitta canadensis*) and White-breasted Nuthatch (*S. carolinensis*) (Fig. 7-9); Downy Woodpecker (*Picoides pubsecens*) and Hairy Woodpecker (*P. villosus*); and Brown Creeper (*Certhia americana*). He also pointed out that in most such assemblages, the chickadees were definitely the leaders (except in associations with the Golden-crowned Kinglets, which moved about in their own

Fig. 7-9. The White-breasted Nuthatch (right) frequently associates with Black-capped Chickadees in mixed-species flocks. (Photograph by Arthur A. Allen, courtesy of Bird Photographs, Inc.)

flocks). Odum also observed that other species associating with chickadees kept in vocal contact and responded quickly to any chickadee alarm call (see also Sullivan 1985, and Predators and Antipredator Behavior, Chapter 9).

Naturally, the species associating with Black-capped Chickadee flocks varies with such factors as season and location. Brewer (1961), working in Illinois, found Black-capped Chickadees in 24 mixed-species feeding parties. Of these, 83 percent included Tufted Titmice; 71 percent, White-breasted Nuthatches; 46 percent, Downy Woodpeckers; 33 percent, Red-bellied Woodpeckers (*Centurus carolinus*); 29 percent, Brown Creepers; and 21 percent, Hairy Woodpeckers; he also noted three other species that associated only rarely. In West Coast areas, associations can include Hutton's Vireos (*V. huttoni*) and Chestnut-backed Chickadees (*Parus rufescens*), among others; and mixed flocks combining Black-capped Chickadees with Mountain Chickadees, Carolina Chickadees, or Boreal Chickadees (*Parus hudsonicus*) are also known (Morse 1980).

Species that are regularly involved in mixed-species flocks generally include both leader and follower species. Chickadees and titmice are leader species, while most others, such as woodpeckers, nuthatches, warblers, and creepers, are follower species (Morse 1970).

Typically there is an interspecific peck order based on species rather than on individual recognition. For the most part, bigger species stand higher in such orders than do smaller species, although some exceptions can occur (Morse 1980). Tufted Titmice, with their much greater weight, rank above chickadees in mixed-species flocks, just as chickadees rank above kinglets. Morse (1970) found that various species in mixed-species feeding flocks may modify their foraging behavior, depending on how high they rank with respect to other associating species. Generally the highest-ranked species will not change its behavior at all, whereas lower-ranked species will tend to modify their foraging such that overlap with more dominant species is minimized.

One thing I find particularly interesting is the fact that chickadees are seldom involved with mixed-species flocks in some areas and are commonly involved in others. Thomas C. Grubb, Jr., and his colleagues investigated this problem in some detail and found a definite effect of food level on degree of participation in mixed-species flocks. In effect, where feeders make it relatively easy to find food, chickadees and titmice are not likely to be in mixed-species flocks, but in unsupplemented areas, where extra eyes might be useful, chickadees and titmice more often engage in mixed-species flocking. Thus Berner and Grubb (1985) found that Carolina Chickadees, Tufted Titmice, White-breasted Nut-hatches, Brown Creepers, and Downy Woodpeckers (Fig. 7-10) all

Fig. 7-10. Another species that often associates with Black-capped Chickadees in mixed-species flocks is the Downy Woodpecker. Chick-adees are seldom intimidated, even by species such as woodpeckers, which weigh far more and rank higher in such flocks.

showed significant decreases in mixed-species flocking in an area with added food, compared with mixed-species flocking in an unsupplemented study area. Grubb (1987) also found that Great Tits and Blue Tits (*Parus caeruleus*) form mixed feeding flocks significantly less often in the presence of supplemental food than in feederless areas. These findings fit very well with my own observations on Black-capped Chickadees: my current study population, which lives in an area that has many feeders, is involved far less in mixed flocking than was a former study population in an essentially feederless area less than 100 miles (160 km) away. Grubb (1987) reported that certain weather conditions can also affect the likelihood of forming mixed flocks. Similarly, Klein (1988) showed that the degree of participation in mixed-species flocks was greater in periods of increased energy demand, such as severe weather.

In many places in Europe, four or more species of parids may occasionally join in mixed-species flocks (Hogstad 1987a). Where such mixed flocks occur regularly, each species is often represented by only a few individuals (Morse 1980, Hogstad 1987a). Having a number of species in a flock means that there can still be many eyes looking for predators, but with less severe competition for food than in monospecific flocks. This is so because two individuals of one species will have essentially identical needs, but two members of different species will have at most just partial niche overlap. Many species associating together but foraging in somewhat different parts of the habitat may be better at detecting predators than a similar-sized flock of just one species (Morse 1980). Hogstad (1988b) documented that the vigilance time of Willow Tits does, in fact, decrease with flock size, regardless of the composition of the flock (Fig. 7-11). Hogstad (1987a) suggested that Willow Tits prefer feeding in mixed-species flocks and will tolerate many other conspecifics only in areas where there are no other parids with which to associate. If that is true, then Willow Tits should form larger monospecific flocks in areas where they are the only parid than in areas where other *Parus* species are available. Certainly his Willow Tit flocks, living in areas with no other tit species, were consistently larger than those studied by Ekman (1979a), which regularly formed mixed flocks with Crested Tits. In most of North America, no more than two parid species occur in any one area (Morse 1970), and there are large areas in which only one species occurs. It would be interesting to see if, in areas of range overlap,

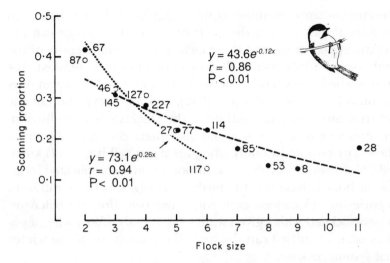

Fig. 7-11. Mean scanning proportion of Willow Tits in relation to size of single-species flocks (open circles) in one area and mixed-species flocks (closed circles) in another area. Numbers denote sample sizes. Vigilance (as measured by proportion of time spent scanning) decreased with flock size, regardless of whether the flock was monospecific or mixed-species. (From Hogstad 1988b, *Ibis* 130: 275–283, courtesy of the British Ornithologists' Union.)

chickadees, like Willow Tits, show smaller numbers in mixed-parid flocks than they do in monospecific flocks at similar latitudes.

### Cohesion and Mobile Elements

Although some investigators have found cohesive winter chickadee flocks of constant membership (e.g., Wallace 1941, Glase 1973, Desrochers and Hannon 1989), many others have remarked on the apparent lack of cohesion in groups of wintering Black-capped Chickadees (e.g., Hamerstrom 1942, Odum 1942a, Smith and Van Buskirk 1988). Indeed, Robins and Raim (1970) actually suggested that Black-caped Chickadees do not form real flocks at all, but instead individuals and mated pairs exist as independent entitities, with flocks simply apparently occurring where ranges overlap. However, such an extreme view seems unwarranted, at least over most of the Black-caped Chickadee's geographic range.

Many factors—such as weather, food, predators, and individual differences—can contribute to the apparent lack of cohesion in chickadee flocks, even in the heart of winter. Unless one can unravel the effects of each of these factors, the actual identity of the membership in true winter flocks can be effectively masked. For instance, chickadees tend to be far more dispersed on warm days than on colder ones (Johnston 1942), and the distribution of the food they are eating can influence the chickadees' own distribution. Presence of a predator can also affect cohesion: dispersed Willow Tits reunite instantly when an alarm call is given (Ekman 1988). However, by far the most important and complicated influence on flock cohesion is the birds themselves, because different categories of chickadees, each with their own flocking behavior, can be associated with a given winter flock. Only after each category has been identified can the basic flock structure of the winter social system be seen.

Soon after I began my current research project, I realized that my study population contained two kinds of chickadees: those that behaved the way I expected them to, and those that didn't. The predictable ones, which I now call sedentary flock regulars, could always be found in the same flock where I had originally caught them. But then there were the other ones—birds that ranged among three or four flocks, so that I could never be sure where I would find them next.

Having discovered that these more mobile chickadees existed, even in the middle of winter, I set about trying to figure out who they were and how they fitted into the overall social structure of my chickadee population. This turned out to be far harder than I had thought, because, to begin with, nothing I found seemed to make any sense. My mobile birds were either high-ranked or very low-ranked; some had bred in the study area, others had not; some moved singly and were very hard to locate when not associating with a flock, others typically moved in pairs, called frequently, and were easy to find when between flocks. The mystery seemed unsolvable, until at last it occurred to me that my mobile birds themselves belonged to several different categories of chickadees, with just about the only feature in common being their expanded home range. Once I had realized this, things fell rapidly into place. Up to three categories of wide-ranging chickadees can be associated with the sedentary flock regulars in my chickadee flocks. The most common of these, at least for the first eight years in my own study area, have been what I termed the winter floaters, or flock switchers. Always young birds, these low-ranked, un-paired birds' home ranges encompass the ranges of three to five flocks, although they may settle down and join one of the flocks as a sedentary regular if a suitable opportunity appears (see below). The second most common category in my area consists of certain high-ranked former breeders, which may move around singly or in pairs. Unlike flock switchers, these birds, which I call dominant wanderers, do have one home flock, and thus are just unusually mobile flock regulars with expanded home ranges. These ranges can include up to five flock territories. The last category of wide-ranging chickadees in my study area are visiting migrants. These chickadees, like flock switchers (but unlike dominant wanderers), are all young birds (less than a year old). Yet unlike switchers, migrants are easily found away from flocks—perhaps even more so than dominant wanderers. The migrants in my study area ap-parently pay little attention to the boundaries between flock ranges; each migrant seems to have its own home range, within which it may form temporary associations with any resident chick-adees it encounters. Both flock switchers and dominant wanderers have occurred in my study area in each of the first eleven winters. By contrast, visiting migrants are considerably rarer, having stayed in the study area in only one of these winters. Figure 7-12 shows the relative proportion of sedentary regulars, dominant wan-derers, flock switchers, and visiting (overwintering) migrants in my study area for seven winters.

Migrant chickadees are not uncommon in the fall, at least in certain years, but the vast majority keep on going, and very few settle in my study area. In the first eight years of the study, I banded a total of 69 migrant chickadees. Of these, 62 left the study area within a few days of being banded. The other seven, all banded in October and November of 1983, stayed all winter. All seven (three males, four females) were young birds when I banded them. They were unique in several ways. Their home ranges par-tially overlapped several flock ranges, but they seemed to pay relatively little attention to the local flocks, spending much time by themselves. They showed no evidence of any pair bonding. They all had unexpectedly high rank, each being able to supplant at least some local regulars of their sex. Finally, no migrant ever attempted to settle into local flocks when suitable openings oc-

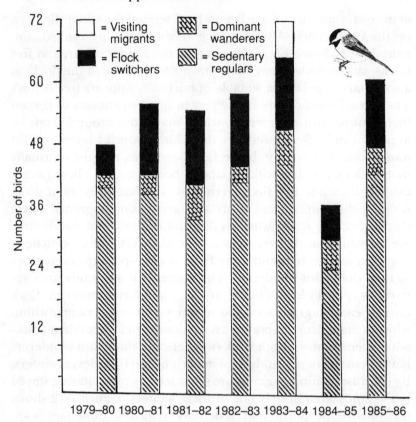

Fig. 7-12. Local wintering Black-capped Chickadees, over seven years in a study area in western Massachusetts. Most were flock regulars, either sedentary or wandering (dominant wanderers). There were always some flock switchers and, in one year, visiting migrants as well. (From S. M. Smith, "Social Dynamics in Wintering Black-capped Chickadees," *Acta XIX Congressus Internationalis Ornithologici* (1988), pp. 2382–2390. Courtesy of University of Ottawa Press.)

curred (see below). All seven survived the winter, and every one left the study area within a 10-day period in late March and early April of 1984 (Smith 1988a).

Although I call such birds migrants, I have no direct evidence of where they came from. Their relatively high rank, however, is suggestive: if they came from more northerly populations, they might well weigh somewhat more on the average than the members of my study population (unfortunately, I did not weigh these birds when I banded them). In addition, they consistently held themselves aloof from the local chickadees, and never attempted to integrate themselves in any way with local flocks. This aloofness, plus the fact that they all left in a very short time period in the spring, suggests that they had somewhere else to go for breeding.

Smith and Van Buskirk (1988) also had a winter population of Black-capped Chickadees in which migrants occurred, but in their case, the migrants evidently outnumbered the residents. This may have been due largely to the topography of their study area: it was located at the bottom of an extensive and exposed ridge, from which chickadees evidently moved in the colder months. Hence most of their migrants were apparently altitudinal, rather than birds that had moved south for the winter. Nevertheless, their migrants behaved in a remarkably similar manner to mine, with large numbers of birds moving independently over their study area, effectively masking any local flock structure (Fig. 7-13). I suspect that the actual resident chickadees in the area did, in fact, form true flocks, although it would require more than one-half of one winter's data to be sure. (It is an interesting point that the two papers most strongly questioning the existence of winter flocks of Black-capped Chickadees—Robins and Raim 1970 and Smith and Van Buskirk 1988—are both based on less than one full winter's data).

As mentioned above, dominant wanderers are actually just un-usually wide-ranging flock regulars, and, like the more sedentary regulars, they clearly belong to just one home flock. What data I have suggest that no matter where they have been during the day, they typically return to roost with the other regulars in their own flock range at night. It is the flock regulars, both wandering and sedentary, whose pair bonds are formed during flock formation and whose dominance relations result in each flock being a hier-archy of pairs. In most winters in my study area, at least 80 percent of the flock regulars are sedentary; thus actual dominant wan-derers make up just a small fraction of the total local regulars, and many flocks seem to contain no dominant wanderers at all.

Dominant wanderers are always old, high-ranked former local breeders. Earlier, I had thought that only intact pairs wandered, especially since in two cases when a wandering pair lost a member, the surviving chickadee became sedentary. However, both lone males and lone females can be dominant wanderers, and members of beta as well as alpha pairs may wander (Smith 1988a). Birds that

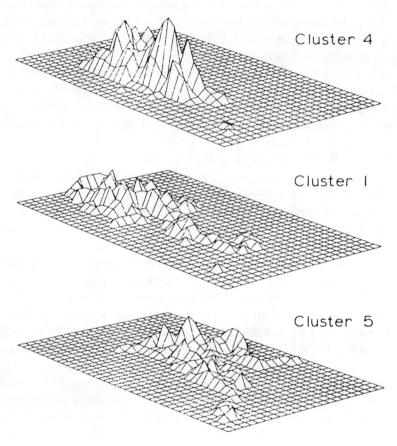

Fig. 7-13. Utilization distributions of three Black-capped Chickadee co-herence clusters. Adjacent ranges overlap extensively. Each grid square is 25 meters on a side. Evidently with the large number of migrants in this winter population, local flock structure was effectively masked. (From Smith and Van Buskirk 1988, courtesy of *Animal Behaviour.*)

wander in one winter are very likely to do so again in subsequent years. Of 22 known wanderers, 8 were of unknown background, 8 were former flock switchers, and 6 entered the system as seden-tary flock regulars. With such diverse origins, it seems unlikely that any single thing in their background induces these birds to expand their winter ranges. While not knowing what causes these birds to wander, I can nevertheless suggest a possible function for their movements. By exploring neighboring areas, such birds could keep watch for any unusually rich food sources such as dead mammals or (more recently) feeders, which, in times of severe winter food shortage, might save the lives of both the wanderers themselves and the other members of their flock. The large aggregations of chickadees at deer carcasses reported by Glase (1973) are a case in point: Glase's study flocks kept within such exclusive ranges that he referred to these as flock territories, yet he found three or more flocks feeding together at deer carcasses. The two invading flocks could learn of such food sources only if at least some of their members had moved well over the territory boundaries. Quite probably these flock members were dominant wanderers.

The third category of wide-ranging chickadees is the flock switchers, or winter floaters. For the first eight year of my current study, these were the most common sort of highly mobile chickadee in my study area, and were thus the group I have spent most time following. Quite clearly my study area, with its many, long-established feeders and consequently elevated winter food supply, has for some time supported an unusually high density of flock switchers (Table 7-8). Nevertheless, flock switchers also occur in feederless areas, though often at far lower densities. For example, Desrochers et al. (1988) found that flock switchers made up only 0.6 percent of their study population in northern Alberta. Stephen Nowicki (pers. comm.) found probable flock switchers in unsupplemented areas in New York. It was probably flock switchers that I observed in a mostly feederless area in eastern

Table 7-8. Number of banded Black-capped Chickadee flock switchers in a study population in western Massachusetts

| Year | No. of flock regulars | No. of banded switchers | Percent of total population |
|---|---|---|---|
| 1979–80 | 42 | 6[a] | 12.5 |
| 1980–81 | 42 | 14 | 25.0 |
| 1981–82 | 40 | 15 | 27.3 |
| 1982–83 | 44 | 14 | 24.1 |
| 1983–84 | 52 | 14 | 21.2 |
| 1984–85 | 30 | 7 | 18.9 |
| 1985–86 | 48 | 13 | 21.3 |
| 1986–87 | 48 | 15 | 23.8 |
| 1987–88 | 54 | 6 | 10.0 |

*Source:* Smith 1990, courtesy of Springer-Verlag.
[a]The only year in which there were several unbanded flock switchers in the study area all winter.

Massachusetts (Smith 1976), and flock switching could explain both the lone chickadees reported by Barash (1974) and the wide-ranging bird noted by Samson and Lewis (1979). Flock switchers have been found in Willow Tit (Ekman 1979b, Hogstad 1990) and Great Tit flocks (Hinde 1952, Drent 1984) as well.

Flock switchers are typically young birds less than a year old. They rank below all regulars of their sex and typically range among three to five flocks, with an established position in the dominance hierarchy of each. Like regulars, switchers have linear dominance relations. Thus wherever two or more switchers are members together of more than one flock, their relative ranking always remains the same—that is, if switcher A ranks above switcher B in one flock, it remains higher in any other flock where both occur. Very rarely, small groups of switchers can be found moving as a unit, but the more usual pattern is to find switchers either with a flock, or, when between flocks, moving singly, silently, and quickly straight to the next flock. Significantly, as long as they remain switchers, they never show any evidence of pair bonding.

Why have I been so interested in these odd low-ranked chickadees that don't even have pair bonds? At first glance they certainly appear to be unsuccessful, and even irrelevant, in the chickadee winter social system. I would argue, however, that they are never irrelevant, although it is true that their impact seems to vary considerably, apparently depending on their relative abundance. When they are sufficiently abundant, their impact can be enormous. Suppose the top-ranked male of a flock disappears—maybe he was picked off by the local cat or an overwintering hawk. Will the beta male take over? Not if there is a male switcher associated with the flock and a high overall density of local flock switchers. When these conditions are met, this male switcher will settle down into the flock and assume the rank of the bird that vanished. Similarly, if a high-ranked female vanishes, her place in the flock hierarchy may rapidly be taken by a female switcher who settles down immediately and starts acting like the regular she has, in fact, become.

This jump in rank is startling. Consider the first case above, in which a male switcher settles into a flock after the alpha male has disappeared. Why doesn't the beta male simply move up and become the alpha bird? Regulars always rank above switchers, so in a flock of eight, the three surviving male regulars must all be higher in the peck order than any switcher. How, then, can a switcher suddenly jump up four notches and become higher ranked than birds that, just days before, were dominant over him? One might imagine a domino effect to be more likely, with each flock regular of the sex that died moving up one notch, so that the dominant switcher of that sex would, if anything, form a pair with the lowest-ranked regular of the other sex. Yet this doesn't happen. I suspect that the reason it doesn't is, at least in part, because the regulars of the flock are already paired. For a domino effect to occur, almost every pair bond in the whole flock would have to be broken and new ones formed. What actually happens (at least when switcher density is sufficiently high) is far simpler. The highest-ranked local flock switcher, being unpaired, is free to pair with the widowed regular, permitting all intact pair bonds among the surviving regulars to remain unchanged. This behavior suggests that most regulars may actually be more or less locked into their rank by their pair bonds, whereas switchers, being unpaired, are far freer to move in right away and take over when a suitable opening occurs. Over the first nine winters of my current study, I had records of 27 banded switchers—11 males and 16 females—that managed not only to insert into a flock in this manner, but also to breed within that flock's territory the following summer (Smith 1990).

A switcher can settle into a vacancy in one of two ways. By far the most common sort of substitution (24 of my 27 records) is a simple process involving just three birds: the regular that died, its mate, and the switcher that takes over the dead bird's rank. In three other cases, however, the process was more complicated. If a flock contains at least two intact pairs of old, high-ranked birds, and if a member of the higher-ranked pair vanishes, its slot may be taken, not by a flock switcher (although one will try at first), but instead by a member of the second-ranked old pair. Then the switcher will settle into the newly vacant second-ranked slot. In one of my three records of this, it was the top-ranked male that vanished; in the other two, the top-ranked female. Such complex substitution is clearly rare, and I suspect it could occur only when all four regulars involved have been closely associated for some time.

Even at high switcher densities flock switchers do not settle into a flock every time a regular disappears. First of all, switcher-switcher pairs are seldom, if ever, formed: if the mate of a newly inserted switcher dies, a second switcher will not settle in and pair with the first; instead, the first will give up its newly won rank, resume its former status, and start switching again. Second, switchers will move in only when a member of a high-ranked pair disappears—widowed members of low-ranked pairs remain mateless for the rest of the winter. High-ranked pairs comprise a flock's most-dominant males and their mates. A four-bird flock has one high-ranked pair; a six-bird flock, two; an eight-bird flock, generally three, and so on. Significantly, only the high-ranked pairs are assured of getting local breeding territories the following spring, at least in most years. In some years, however, winter chickadee numbers are far lower than usual, as was the case in my study area in 1984–95 (see Fig. 7-12). At the end of that winter, every flock regular that survived, including eight low-ranked regulars, obtained a local breeding territory. Yet even in that peculiar year, no low-ranked regular was replaced (during the winter) by any switcher (Smith 1988a).

In the first eight years of my current study, just over 40 high-ranked regulars disappeared during the winter. Several of these were intact pairs, which (since switcher-switcher pairs are not formed) could not provide permanent openings for switchers. Yet of the more than two dozen other openings in this eight-year period, all but one were filled rapidly by switchers. The exception was a third-ranked female of a 10-bird flock, whose mate went unpaired for four months after she had vanished; he finally obtained a new mate right after flock breakup. Oddly, at least one female flock switcher had been locally available during those four months; perhaps the intermediate rank of the opening had something to do with its not being filled right away (Smith 1987). By contrast, of 66 low-ranked birds that vanished over the same eight winters, none was replaced by any switcher.

In order to study the replacement process more closely, I did a series of removal experiments. I caught chickadees of known rank from my flocks, held them for a maximum of four days in an outdoor aviary, and then released them back into their flocks. All six members of the high-ranked pairs that I removed (three males, three females) were replaced rapidly by switchers—one by complex substitution. By contrast, none of the four members of low-ranked pairs was replaced (Table 7-9). Where replacement occurred, the settling switcher was seen to supplant regulars of its sex in a matter of hours (Table 7-10). All 10 birds that had been removed had no trouble regaining their former rank within the flock as soon as they were released, after which the six switchers

Table 7-9. Removal experiments on wintering Black-capped Chickadees

| Removed bird | | | | | Replacement absence |
| Rank | Sex | Flock size | Dates in captivity | Replacement switcher | after return of regular (d) |
|---|---|---|---|---|---|
| 1 | Female | 8 | Nov. 29–Dec. 2, 1984 | A1R KY | 21 |
| 2 | Female | 6 | Jan. 3–Jan. 7, 1985 | A1R KG | 23 |
| 1 | Female | 4 | Feb. 14–Feb. 18, 1985 | Unbanded | ? |
| 2 | Male | 8 | Dec. 2–Dec. 6, 1984 | A1R GR | 7 |
| 1 | Male | 4 | Dec. 13–Dec. 17, 1984 | A1R BY | 24 |
| 1 | Male | 8 | Jan. 10–Jan. 14, 1986 | A1G OR[a] | 1 |
| 3 | Male | 6 | Nov. 24–Nov. 28, 1985 | — | — |
| 4 | Male | 8 | Feb. 26–Mar. 2, 1985 | — | — |
| 2 | Male | 4 | Nov. 18–Nov. 22, 1985 | — | — |
| 3 | Male | 6 | Jan. 18–Jan. 22, 1986 | — | — |

Source: Smith 1987, courtesy of Behavioral Ecology and Sociobiology.
[a]Replacement via complex substitution; all five other replacements were by simple substitution.

that had replaced them all reverted to switching once again (Smith 1987).

As mentioned above, the impact that switchers have on a winter population seems to depend on what proportion of the total population they represent. Evidently, switchers can (or at least do) insert

Table 7-10. Removal experiments on wintering Black-capped Chickadees, showing some details of replacement and interactions between switchers and other flock members

| Removed bird | | | Time to first observed supplanting by switcher[a] (h) | No. of interactions with nearest rival | |
| Rank | Sex | Flock size | | Switcher supplants rival | Rival supplants switcher |
|---|---|---|---|---|---|
| 1 | Female | 8 | 26 | 5 | 0 |
| 2 | Female | 6 | 27 | 3 | 0 |
| 1 | Female | 4 | 5.5 | 2 | 0 |
| 2 | Male | 8 | 23 | 11 | 1 |
| 1 | Male | 4 | 30.25 | 7 | 0 |
| 1 | Male | 8 | 22 | 9 | 0 |
| AVERAGE | | | 22.3 | | |

Source: Smith 1987, courtesy of Behavioral Ecology and Sociobiology.
[a]Rounded to the nearest quarter hour.

and replace high-ranked regulars during the central part of the winter only if the local switcher density is greater than some critical level. During the past few winters of my study, the switcher level dropped greatly, and high-ranked vacancies, which in previous years would have been snapped up within hours, have gone unfilled for months. In the first eight years of my study, the switcher density was remarkably high—from 1980 through 1987, the average proportion of switchers in my total population was just over 23 percent (see Table 7-8). Suddenly, in the winter of 1987–88, the proportion of switchers in my population dropped to 10 percent. Exactly what caused such a drop is as yet unknown, although the apparent density of Tufted Titmice in the area increased dramatically that same winter (Smith 1990). With only six switchers in my entire study area, there were plenty of areas in which high-ranked openings occurred with no switcher available to fill them. Rather unexpectedly, no domino effect occurred. In fact, two of my study flocks went for several months without an alpha male, yet each beta pair remained intact (as measured by association indices like those used by Ficken et al. 1981). High-ranked birds that had been widowed during the winter finally obtained new mates during the period of flock breakup in the spring, and a few of these new mates were former low-ranked regulars, rather than switchers (Smith 1990).

Some people might assume that because of flock switchers' low rank and lack of pair bonds, they must be birds that arrived too late to get a position within any flock and thus were forced to become winter floaters. This is apparently true in a Norwegian population of Willow Tits (Hogstad 1990a), but it is not always the case for Black-capped Chickadees. For example, one of the four successful switchers in the winter of 1986–87 was a female I had banded in late August. Although that fall my study flocks were not fully formed until late October, this particular female maintained her four-flock home range until mid-November, when she inserted and become the top-ranked female in a six-bird flock. I have similar records of switchers banded well before the end of flock formation in other years as well (Smith 1984). Such data suggest that during the period of flock formation, top-ranked switchers may actually settle in an area well before all the low-ranked regulars do, at least in years of high switcher density.

A lot more work needs to be done in this area. For example, my experiments have shown that high-ranked birds of either sex have no difficulty in regaining their former status after being held out of their flocks for just four days. However, data from studies on other species suggest that birds kept out for much longer periods might be unable to regain their former positions (e.g., Beletsky and Orians 1987). It would be interesting to see how long a chickadee could be kept out of its flock and still manage to regain its former rank within that flock.

Another interesting area concerns what happens when high-ranked openings occur in flocks where there are no switchers available to fill them. Dixon (1965:293) removed an alpha male Mountain Chickadee from its winter flock in late February and reported that the beta male assumed "the bold, direct approach . . . and confident manner" of the alpha male within a few minutes—but then dropped this attitude when the alpha male was released and returned some unspecified time later. Hogstad (1987b) also reported beta males becoming dominant members of a flock, this time of Willow Tits, after the alpha male had been removed. Unfortunately, neither Dixon nor Hogstad reported on what happened to the beta male's pair bonds after the alpha male was removed—that is, did the beta male form a bond with the widowed alpha female, and if not, did the widowed female continue to rank above the beta male's mate? Naturally, if the alpha bird is removed, and there is no floater available to replace him, then the beta male will, by default, now be the flock's top-ranked bird. However, if the beta male still associates primarily with his original mate, and that mate still ranks below the original (and now widowed) alpha female, then I think it is fair to say that the beta male has *not* replaced the removed bird. This lack of replacement seems to be the norm recently in my study area, now that the density of flock switchers has dropped so low (Smith 1990).

Finally, what happens to high-ranked birds whose mates vanish during the winter and are not replaced until spring? The work of Withiam et al. (1988) and Ekman (1990) has shown that high-ranked females derive considerable protection from their mates. How do they fare if their mate dies and is not replaced for weeks or even months?

The answer may vary with a number of factors, including the age and experience of the widowed bird in question. To date I have rather few examples of widowed high-ranked females, since up to a very few years ago, all such high-ranked openings were filled immediately. However, one example is particularly interesting. An alpha male, who was mated to the top-ranked female in a 10-bird flock, died in mid-November, and association indices clearly showed that he was not replaced until the flock broke up the following spring (Smith 1990). Yet his mate maintained her position as top-ranked female in the flock all winter, even without the protection of a high-ranked mate. This case may be exceptional, however, because the female happened to be the oldest bird in my entire study area. Perhaps a younger, less experienced female would not have been so successful at maintaining rank after losing her mate.

## Fate of Each Class of Chickadees after Flock Breakup

As mentioned above, any high-ranked regular that survives the winter is virtually assured of obtaining a breeding territory encompassing at least part of its former flock range. By contrast, in most years low-ranked regulars do not have such assurances. In my own study area, from 1979 to 1988, of 72 low-ranked birds that survived the winter, more than half were driven away from the area, and less than a third actually succeeded in obtaining a breeding territory immediately after flock breakup (Table 7-11); Desrochers et al. (1988) have similar data from their Alberta study population. Nevertheless, low-ranked regulars can become breeders in a variety of ways. A few (ironically, especially those that have lost their mate over the winter) are able to replace high-ranked regulars during flock breakup, if there are no flock switchers locally available. Especially in years with unusually low winter populations, up to 100 percent of surviving low-ranked regulars may obtain territories and breed locally (see 1984–85 in Table 7-11). Moreover, at least in some years, a few may stay on as summer floaters (S. M. Smith 1989). And finally, those that do get driven away in the spring also have a chance to settle close by if a suitable opening exists.

The two other classes, migrants and flock switchers, both typically vanish from my study area as soon as the flocks break up in the spring. A coordinated and persistent banding program may eventually result in recoveries that will help us understand where these birds go after the winter flocks dissolve.

Table 7-11. Fate of low-ranked (L-R) regular members of Black-capped Chickadee winter flocks in a western Massachusetts study area

| Year | No. of L-R birds in fall | No. of L-R birds that passively attained a higher rank[a] | L-R slots not replaced | Total L-R birds alive at end of March | No. of L-R birds that bred locally | No. of L-R birds that became summer floaters | No. of L-R birds driven away |
|---|---|---|---|---|---|---|---|
| 1979–80 | 18 | 2 | 12 | 4 | 0 | 0 | 4 |
| 1980–81 | 18 | 2 | 14 | 2 | 1 | 0 | 1 |
| 1981–82 | 16 | 6 | 6 | 4 | 0 | 1 | 3 |
| 1982–83 | 18 | 0 | 8 | 10 | 0 | 1 | 9 |
| 1983–84 | 18 | 2 | 7 | 9 | 3 | 5 | 1 |
| 1984–85 | 10 | 0 | 2 | 8 | 8 | 0 | 0 |
| 1985–86 | 20 | 0 | 9 | 11 | 2 | 3 | 6 |
| 1986–87 | 18 | 0 | 8 | 10 | 2 | 0 | 8 |
| 1987–88 | 20 | 0 | 6 | 14 | 4 | 1 | 9 |
| TOTAL | 156 | 12 | 72 | 72 | 20 | 11 | 41 |

Source: S. M. Smith, "Social Dynamics in Wintering Black-capped Chickadees," Acta XIX Congressus Internationalis Ornithologici (1988), pp. 2382–2390. Courtesy of University of Ottawa Press.
[a]Both members of a higher ranked pair in the flock had vanished over winter.

## Mate Fidelity and Divorce

As the days get warmer in late winter and early spring, the pairs become more and more obvious (Fig. 7-14) until at last all traces of the winter flocks disappear. Pair bonds in chickadees and titmice often last for years (Black-capped Chickadees: Odum 1942b, Glase 1973; other chickadee species: Brewer 1961; Dixon 1963, 1965), as they do in most European parids (e.g., Perrins 1979). Occasionally, however, divorces do occur—that is, one member of an intact pair will leave to form a new alliance with another individual. I have already mentioned the case of a high-ranked male who insisted on nesting in a metal signpost (see Nest Site, Chapter 5) and who was deserted at the end of every summer (Smith 1974b). Over the past nine years of my current study, I have observed 11 more instances of divorce (Table 7-12). All occurred in

Fig. 7-14. As the spring days get warmer, Black-capped Chickadee flocks begin to split up into their component pairs.

Table 7-12. Divorces in Black-capped Chickadee flocks in a western Massachusetts study area

| Season of divorce | Sex of deserter | Former rank of deserter | New rank of deserter | Deserter moved within (W) or between (B) flocks | Newly formed pair joined flock of: | Fate of deserted mate |
|---|---|---|---|---|---|---|
| Winter | F | 2 | 1 | W | | Formed pair with a switcher |
| Winter | F | 2 | 1 | W | | Formed pair with a switcher |
| Winter | M | 2 | 1 | W | | Formed pair with a switcher |
| Late spring | F | 2 | 1 | W | | Paired with a widowed female from a neighboring flock |
| Late spring | F | 2 | 1 | W | | Paired with a widowed female from own flock |
| Late spring | F | 1 | 1 | B | | Paired with unbanded female |
| Late spring | M | 2 | 1 | W | Deserter died oversummer | Paired with a widowed male from a neighboring flock |
| Summer | F | 2 | 1 | W | Female | Did not breed |
| Summer | F | 2 | 1 | B | | Did not breed |
| Summer | F | 2 | 1 | W | Female | Did not breed |
| Summer | M | 2 | 1 | B | Female | Did not breed |

response to the death of a member of an alpha pair. In 8 cases, females deserted their mates to move into an alpha alliance; in other three, it was the male that did so. Before the divorces, 10 of the 11 birds had been members of beta pairs; all thus moved up in rank via the divorce. The exception was a female paired with the alpha male of a 4-bird flock, who deserted her mate to pair with the alpha male of a neighboring 10-bird flock. Three divorces occurred in the winter during the process of complex substitution (see Cohesion and Mobile Elements, above); the other 8 occurred either at flock breakup in the spring or over the summer. During this same time period, 53 other intact pairs remained together without breaking pair bonds.

Clearly, much has been learned about the Black-capped Chickadee annual cycle since the pioneering work of Odum (1941a, 1941b, 1942a) was first published. Nevertheless, as I hope I have shown, a large number of important and fascinating questions still await further investigation.

# 8

# Surviving the Winter

Even though chickadees and their relatives are very small, they manage to spend the winter in areas that typically experience severe weather—areas that most chickadee-sized birds leave during the winter. This chapter explores some of the adaptations of parids that help such small birds withstand the rigors of a northern winter.

## Environmental Problems

Wintering chickadees encounter two major environmental problems. One is severe weather: cold temperatures that may be exacerbated by high winds and/or precipitation (Fig. 8-1). The second is the length of the winter nights, especially at high latitudes. Unlike certain arctic birds, such as some ptarmigan (*Lagopus* sp.), that can forage even after dark (Dawson et al. 1983), chickadees apparently forage only during daylight (Kessel 1976). Periods suitable for foraging can therefore be remarkably short. Near Fairbanks, Alaska (64° north latitude), for example, wintering Black-capped Chickadees experience a period between sunrise and sunset of only 3 hours and 38 minutes at winter solstice (Kessel 1976; Fig. 8-2). Consequently, they must endure periods of

Fig. 8-1. Chickadees curtail their activity in adverse conditions such as snowstorms and tend to forage where the food is most concentrated.

nocturnal fasting of 21 hours or even longer during the cold temperatures of midwinter.

Added to these two environmental problems is the tiny size of chickadees, which poses problems concerning heat loss. Birds, being warm-blooded, must maintain body temperatures that, in cold winter conditions, are considerably higher than the surrounding air temperature. Because the smaller the bird, the larger its surface-area to volume ratio, chickadee-sized birds have partic-

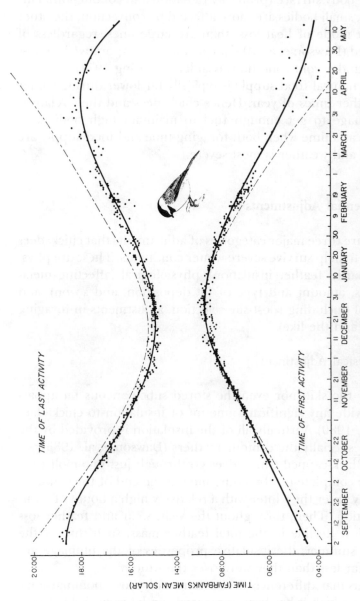

Fig. 8-2. Times of first and last activity of Black-capped Chickadees recorded from 1960 through 1967 near Fairbanks, Alaska. Times have been adjusted for longitude and are true solar times. The dotted lines represent the times of the beginning of morning Civil Twilight and ending of evening Civil Twilight, respectively; the solid lines are best-fit polynomial curves, adjusted somewhat by eye. (From Kessel 1976, courtesy of *Wilson Bulletin*.)

ularly severe problems with those modes of heat loss that occur across the body surface (primarily radiation and conduction). Furthermore, small bodies are more affected by convection, the other important mode of heat loss, than are large ones, regardless of wind speed (Dawson et al. 1983). Fortunately, evaporative heat loss is minor under cold conditions (Calder and King 1974).

Finally, natural food supply is typically far lower during winter than at other times of year. Hence chickadees and their relatives must manage to get enough fuel to maintain high body temperatures at a time when both foraging time and food supply are restricted and weather is most severe.

## Potential Adjustments

There are three major categories of adjustments that chickadees can make to help survive severe winter conditions. These are physical (primarily, feather insulation), physiological (affecting metabolic rates, amount and type of fat deposition, and so on), and behavioral (including roost-site selection, adjustments in foraging behavior, and the like).

### Physical Adjustments

Neither the skin nor even the stored subcutaneous fat apparently provide any significant amount of insulation to chickadees (Hill et al. 1980). Virtually all of the insulation is provided by the feathers, especially the contour feathers (Dawson et al. 1983).

Adult Black-capped Chickadees go through just one molt each year—the complete postbreeding molt at the end of the summer. Thus, they enter the winter with a relatively high amount of natural insulation. Then, throughout the year, wear and feather loss cause a slow decline in the total feather mass, such that by the following summer, the insulative properties of the plumage are typically far less than they were over the winter.

The seasonal difference in insulation of those nonmigratory species for which it has been measured can be remarkably large. Differences between the weight of worn summer plumage and fresh fall plumage in Steller's Jays (*Cyanocitta stelleri*) were estimated to be about 45 percent (total plumage) by Pitelka (1958); similarly, for the Eurasian Bullfinch (*Pyrrhula pyrrhula*), the body plumage weight was estimated to increase over molt by about 53 percent (Newton 1968). No corresponding data are available for chickadees, although Rising and Hudson (1974) found that Black-capped Chickadees do have measurably less effective insulation in summer than they do in winter.

The timing of the annual molt therefore ensures that chick-adees have thicker, less worn plumage when they need insulation the most. In addition, they can control to some extent the position of each contour feather. Such ptilomotor control permits the birds, when cold, to fluff their feathers, thereby increasing the thickness of their insulative layer (Fig. 8-3). Hill et al. (1980)

Fig. 8-3. On cold winter days, chickadees fluff their feathers, thus increasing their layer of insulation so that they can stay warm. The bent tail feathers, a common sight in cold weather, are usually the result of being wedged into the cramped quarters of a typical winter roost site. (Photograph by David G. Allen, courtesy of Bird Photographs, Inc.)

showed that captive Black-capped Chickadees exhibit large increases in feather fluffing, or ptiloerection, over broad ranges of subthermoneutral temperatures (Table 8-1). Such fluffing works remarkably well. When captive chickadees experienced a drop in air temperature from 10° C down to −16° C, they responded by increased ptiloerection such that the thermal conductance of their breast plumage actually decreased by 12–17 percent (Hill et al. 1980).

Apparently most small birds are not as well insulated as large ones (Calder and King 1974). This difference has been related to aerodynamic constraints (Dawson et al. 1983). An early study by Veghte and Herreid (1965) suggested that Black-capped Chickadees fitted into this general pattern. When Hill et al. (1980) repeated Veghte and Herreid's comparisons, using more sophisticated equipment, however, they found remarkably small differences between the outer surface temperature of most parts of the bodies (in response to various ambient temperatures) of Black-capped Chickadees and Common Ravens (*Corvus corax*), even though, as they pointed out, these species represent the virtual extremes of passerine body size. Chaplin (1982) found that Black-capped Chickadees actually have much denser plumage than other birds of similar size, and Hissa and Palokangas (1970) reported similar data for Great Tits (*Parus major*) as well. This denser plumage may represent a trade-off: species such as chickadees, which are mostly nonmigratory and live year-round at high latitudes, may have given up some aerodynamic efficiency in favor of having thicker, more insulative plumage. Certainly chickadees are notoriously poor flyers, especially over long distances (e.g., Hussell and Stamp 1965).

Some interesting data have been gathered on the insulation efficiency of captive Black-capped Chickadees by measuring their body surface temperatures (the temperature at the outer surface of the feathers) at various ambient temperatures (Hill et al. 1980). Using infrared radiography on unencumbered birds, Hill and his colleagues obtained accurate information on temperatures over the entire body surface of their birds (Fig. 8-4). They found that the head region, especially around the eye, typically has the highest surface temperatures, and thus can be expected to show the highest rate of heat loss per unit area when the chickadee is in low air temperatures. Other differences between body regions also exist; for example, the breast is typically warmer than the sides

Table 8-1. Lateral profile area and body diameter of Black-capped Chickadees as functions of ambient temperature

| Animal no. | Approximate ambient temperature | | | | Results of linear regression | |
|---|---|---|---|---|---|---|
| | $+10°$ C | $0°$ C | $-10°$ C | $-16°$ C | Slope (SD)[a] | Coefficient of determination, $r^2$ |
| Profile area (cm²) | | | | | | |
| 1 | 21.2 (3) | 23.5 (3) | 29.0 (4) | 29.0 (6) | −.34 (.03) | .90 |
| 2 | 21.7 (3) | 22.6 (4) | 22.6 (5) | 23.9 (5) | −.07 (.02) | .49 |
| 3 | 21.7 (3) | 26.2 (4) | 27.0 (4) | 29.7 (5) | −.26 (.03) | .87 |
| Body diameter (cm) | | | | | | |
| 1 | 3.50 (3) | 3.86 (3) | 4.77 (3) | 4.85 (6) | −.057 (.004) | .94 |
| 2 | 3.81 (3) | 4.27 (4) | 4.50 (5) | 4.64 (5) | −.029 (.004) | .74 |
| 3 | 3.62 (3) | 4.40 (4) | 4.79 (5) | 5.20 (5) | −.054 (.005) | .87 |

Source: Hill et al. 1980, courtesy of *Physiological Zoology*, © 1980 by the University of Chicago.
Note: Profile area excludes the tail, feet, legs, and beak. Diameter was measured on an axis perpendicular to the longitudinal axis and passing through the midback. Actual ambient temperature was typically within 1.5° C of approximate temperature. Number of measurements is in parentheses.
[a] Units are cubic centimeters per degree centigrade for profile area and centimeters per degree centigrade for body diameter.

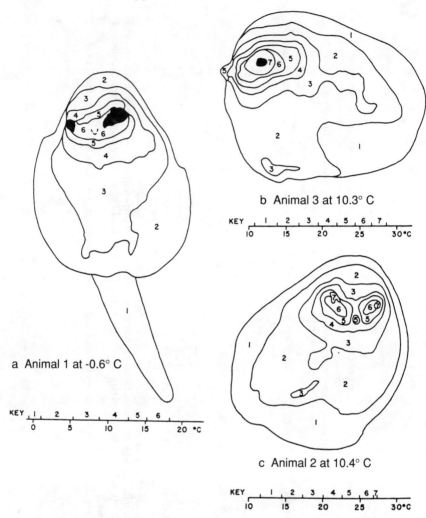

a  Animal 1 at -0.6° C

KEY

b  Animal 3 at 10.3° C

KEY

c  Animal 2 at 10.4° C

KEY

Fig. 8-4. Drawings of three infrared radiographs of freely moving, active Black-capped Chickadees. Numbered isotherms indicate surface temperatures shown on the scale below each drawing. Blackened regions were outside the range of instrument calibration. The dashed V-shaped line in the left-hand radiograph indicates the position of the beak. Note that the head region, particularly around the eye, typically has the highest surface temperatures. (From Hill et al. 1980, courtesy of *Physiological Zoology,* © 1980 by the University of Chicago.)

(Fig. 8-4). Overall, however, the surface temperatures they recorded for every feathered region were linearly related to the ambient temperature. So while the body temperature of the chickadee remains warm, the temperature at the outer surface of its feathers drops with the air temperature. This finding certainly suggests that a remarkably efficient insulation is working here. Indeed, as Hill et al. (1980:316) stated: "It is hard not to be impressed by the fact that temperature can fall over 40° C through the plumage, over a distance of perhaps 1.5 cm [just over half an inch]." Clearly, the feather insulation of Black-capped Chickadees can be remarkably effective.

Physiological Adjustments

One way in which chickadees can adapt to winter conditions is by adjusting their fat deposition. Not surprisingly, the kinds of food a bird eats can have a marked effect on how much fat it can store. Work on granivorous species that overwinter at high latitudes has shown that the amounts of stored subcutaneous fat (that is, fat stored just below the skin) typically increases markedly in winter, and in some species, this fat may actually almost ensheath the body (King and Farner 1965, King 1972). However, it is not quite so easy for chickadees to increase their subcutaneous fat deposition because their diet contains much animal matter, which is far less fat-rich than are most seeds. Hence, while wintering granivorous birds typically store as subcutaneous fat many more calories than they need to meet their overnight metabolic expenditures, chickadees seldom have the luxury of such surpluses. In fact, virtually all of the subcutaneous fat a chickadee has as it goes to roost at the end of a winter day will typically be used up overnight (Chaplin 1974).

Figure 8-5 shows some of Chaplin's (1974) data on stored fat in free-living Black-capped Chickadees from the vicinity of Ithaca, New York. Two important points can be seen from this graph. One is that, throughout the winter, morning fat levels were relatively low, but by late afternoon the chickadees had managed essentially to double their stored fat reserves. The second point is that overall fat levels, both in percentage of total body weight and in number of grams added over a day's foraging, peaked in midwinter and were lower both in fall and in spring. At first glance this might not seem surprising. But remember, daylength is shortest in mid-

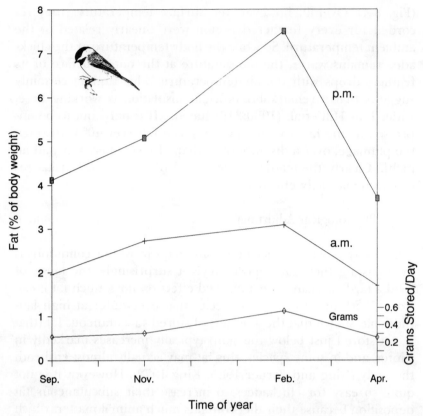

Fig. 8-5. Seasonal changes in amount of stored fat in Black-capped Chickadees. Afternoon fat levels (upper line) were essentially double the morning fat levels (central line) and amount of fat stored per day (bottom line) was actually higher in the short days of February than it was during the longer days of September or April. (data from Chaplin 1974: table 1, courtesy of *Journal of Comparative Physiology.*)

winter. Hence the chickadees managed to store over twice as many grams of fat in the shortest foraging days of midwinter than they stored in the longer photoperiods of either spring or fall. Chickadees must make some very strong seasonal physiological adjustments in order to accomplish this.

A few years ago Oliphant (1983) examined subcutaneous fat from Black-capped Chickadees wintering in Saskatchewan and in New York. He found fat that was pinkish to brownish, rather than the typical bright yellow of most avian fat. On examining this fat more closely, Oliphant discovered various features, such as high capillary densities and a complex multilocular cell form complete with relatively high densities of mitochondria: all characteristics of mammalian brown adipose tissue (BAT), something not known to occur in birds. In another species, the Ruffed Grouse (*Bonasa umbellus*), Oliphant found both typical yellow or white fat and fat that resembled brown fat. In mammals, brown fat is the primary site of nonshivering thermogenesis, a process in which intense catabolic activity in the brown fat results in a major increase in heat production. Oliphant (1983) reasoned that at least some birds, including Black-capped Chickadees, may also be able to produce heat in this manner. More recent work has challenged this view, however. Olson et al. (1988) showed that catabolic enzyme activities, such as are necessary for nonshivering thermogenesis in mammalian brown fat, are far lower in chickadee stored fat than they are in the true BAT of a comparably sized mammal, the white-footed mouse (*Peromyscus leucopus*) (Table 8-2). Moreover, the histological similarities between chickadee fat and true BAT varied with time of day, being greatest in chickadees collected early in the morning when their fat stores were depleted. These data suggest that the fat stores of chickadees serve simply as a depot for fat rather than as a site for intense thermogenesis. Olsen et al. therefore concluded that there is no real evidence for the existence of true BAT in chickadees and that, if nonshivering thermogenesis occurs in birds at all, its mechanism and site remain to be identified.

Regardless of whether chickadees produce any heat by nonshivering thermogenesis, it is well established that they generate a considerable amount by shivering. Chaplin (1976) studied in detail the production of heat by shivering Black-capped Chickadees in winter. She found that shivering activity, as measured by duration and amplitude of bursts, increased markedly as the ambient temperature went down (Fig. 8-6). Most of the shivering measured occurs in the large pectoral (flight) muscles. It is this shivering, used to provide body heat, that consumes so much of a bird's stored fat reserves.

Chickadees must respond to severe daytime conditions by adjusting their heat production, and consequently their metabolic rates. Any drop in air temperature (which increases radiative and conductive heat loss) or increase in wind speed (which increases convective heat loss) must be met by higher metabolic rates if the chickadee is to maintain its warm body temperature.

Cold temperatures during the night constitute a still more se-

Table 8-2. Tissue mass, protein concentration, and catabolic enzyme activities for Black-capped Chickadee (*Parus atricapillus*) and white-footed mouse (*Peromyscus leucopus*) tissues

| Tissue | Time of assay | Temperature (° C) | Mass (g) | Protein (mg/g tissue) | Citrate synthase μmol (min/mg prot) | HOAD μmol (min/mg prot) |
|---|---|---|---|---|---|---|
| *Parus atricapillus* | | | | | | |
| Furcular fat | Jan. | 25 | 0.044 ± 0.010 (9) | 78.118 ± 8.758 (9) | 0.338 ± 0.028 (9) | 0.056 ± 0.008 (9) |
| | | 35 | 0.044 ± 0.010 (9) | 78.118 ± 8.758 (9) | 0.589 ± 0.041 (9) | 0.250 ± 0.047 (9) |
| Furcular fat | Feb.–Mar. | 25 | 0.050 ± 0.005 (15) | 44.219 ± 6.762 (15) | 0.134 ± 0.018 (15) | 0.026 ± 0.004 (15) |
| *Peromyscus leucopus* | | | | | | |
| BAT | Winter | 25 | 0.139 ± 0.012 (17) | 121.9 ± 13.3 (12) | 2.30 ± 0.12 (7) | 8.11 ± 0.52 (10) |
| BAT | Summer | 25 | 0.068 ± 0.012 (15) | 136.0 ± 12.1 (15) | 0.732 ± 0.043 (11) | 0.767 ± 0.091 (7) |
| *Parus atricapillus* | | | | | | |
| Pectoralis muscle | Jan. | 25 | | 207.01 ± 4.23 (9) | 1.379 ± 0.103 (9) | 0.146 ± 0.008 (9) |
| | | 35 | | 207.01 ± 4.23 (9) | 2.299 ± 0.169 (9) | 0.658 ± 0.052 (9) |
| Pectoralis muscle | Feb.–Mar. | 25 | | 208.06 ± 2.31 (8) | 0.808 ± 0.030 (8) | 0.116 ± 0.014 (7) |

*Source:* Olson et al. 1988, courtesy of *Condor.*
*Note:* Values are means ± 1 SE, and numbers in parentheses are sample sizes.

Fig. 8-6. Amplitude of shivering (mV/s) of six Black-capped Chickadees following exposure to a particular temperature for at least 2 hours. Each data point represents the mean of 10 bursts of shivering for a particular bird at that temperature. Shivering activity was highest at the coldest temperature, and the birds shivered progressively less with warmer temperatures. (From Chaplin 1976, courtesy of *Journal of Comparative Physiology B*.)

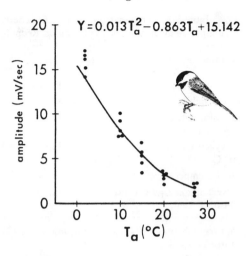

$$Y = 0.013T_a^2 - 0.863T_a + 15.142$$

vere problem for chickadees, since they must be withstood during a period of fasting. As the air temperature drops, it becomes more and more costly to maintain a high internal temperature. Granivorous birds such as the Common Redpoll (*Carduelis flammea*), with their large reserves of stored fat, manage nicely to maintain body temperature overnight (Chaplin 1974, Reinertsen and Haftorn 1986). Chickadees, however, must make do with considerably less fat reserves.

What chickadees do on cold winter nights is one of the most amazing adaptations they possess. Instead of spending all the energy necessary to maintain high body temperature overnight, with the risk of using up all of their reserves before morning, chickadees go into a regulated hypothermia—that is, they actually drop their body temperature, in a controlled manner, to 10–12° C below their normal daytime body temperature of 42° C (Budd 1972; Chaplin 1974, 1976). Thus their overnight energy expenditure is considerably less than that of birds that do not undergo hypothermia (Table 8-3). Chaplin (1974) calculated that when chickadees, during winter, are exposed to 0° C overnight, their resulting hypothermia reduces their hourly metabolic expenditure by 23 percent.

Black-capped Chickadees achieve hypothermia by decreasing, but not stopping, shivering in the pectoral muscles during exposure to decreasing air temperatures (Chaplin 1976). The birds

Table 8-3. A comparison of the daily energetics in winter of two northern
temperate avian species, the Common Redpoll and the Black-capped Chickadee

| Parameter | Common Redpoll | Black-capped Chickadee |
|---|---|---|
| Weight: winter | 13–15 g[a] | 11–12 g |
| Food habits | 80–90% seeds[a] | 60–70% animals[b] |
| Evening fat reserve (% body weight) | 11.8[a] | 7.5 |
| Oxygen consumption: 0° C | 13.0 cm³/g/h[c] | 6.8cm³/g/h |
| Body temperature: 0° C | 39–40° C[d] | 31–34° C |
| Overnight energy expenditure: 14 h, 0° C | 12.23 kcal/bird | 5.48 kcal/bird |

Source: Chaplin 1974, courtesy of *Journal of Comparative Physiology.*
[a]Brooks 1968.
[b]Tyler 1946.
[c]West 1965.
[d]West 1962.

can actually moderate the rate of decline in body temperature by
performing intermittent and reduced bursts of shivering during
the cooling period, after which they maintain their new, lower
body temperature by regulating the rate of intense shivering
bursts (Table 8-4).

A few other species of *Parus* are also capable of achieving hypothermia on cold winter nights: the Siberian Tit, *Parus cinctus*
(Haftorn 1972); the Carolina Chickadee, *P. carolinensis* (Mayer et
al. 1982); and the Willow Tit, *P. montanus* (Reinertsen and Haftorn
1983). Because Reinertsen and Haftorn (1983) measured the
Willow Tits' body temperatures by radio telemetry, they could get
temperatures from undisturbed birds. In a subsequent paper,
Reinertsen and Haftorn (1986) reported that, when given normal
food levels, Willow Tits underwent nocturnal hypothermia,
whereas neither Common Redpolls nor Great Tits (*P. major*) did
(Fig. 8-7). However, they also found that subjecting these species
to severe food shortage was sufficient to cause both the Great Tits
and the redpolls to enter nocturnal hypothermia as well. Future
studies may well show that some other parids, such as Boreal (*P.
hudsonicus*) and Mountain (*P. gambeli*) Chickadees, also have the
capacity to achieve nocturnal hypothermia.

Table 8-4. Frequency, duration, and amplitude of shivering bursts of six Black-capped Chickadees during exposure to stable and declining temperatures

| Ambient temp. (°C) | No. of bursts | Frequency of bursts (1 SE) ($\bar{x}$ no. bursts/ min exposed) (a) | Duration of bursts (1 SE) ($\bar{x}$ s/burst) (b) | Shivering time (1 SE) ($\bar{x}$ s of shivering/ min exposure) (a × b) | $\bar{x}$ amplitude of burst (1 SE) (mV/s) (c) | Relative heat production (mV/min) (a × b × c) |
|---|---|---|---|---|---|---|
| Stable temperatures | | | | | | |
| 27 | 5 | 0.58 (0.55) | 9.27 (7.29) | 5.36 | 1.72 (0.56) | 9.22 |
| 20 | 5 | 1.49 (0.25) | 10.68 (12.84) | 15.91 | 3.06 (0.59) | 48.68 |
| 15 | 5 | 1.11 (0.80) | 17.84 (33.50) | 19.80 | 5.12 (1.21) | 101.39 |
| 10 | 5 | 1.90 (0.68) | 19.86 (22.38) | 37.73 | 8.48 (1.07) | 319.95 |
| 2 | 5 | 1.94 (0.85) | 19.74 (27.96) | 38.30 | 15.74 (1.17) | 602.84 |
| Declining temperatures | | | | | | |
| 27–20 | 4 | 0.15 (0.45) | 4.33 (2.31) | 0.65 | 1.92 (24° C) | 1.25 |
| 25–15 | 4 | 0.15 (0.50) | 10.33 (11.06) | 1.55 | 3.08 (20° C) | 4.77 |
| 20–10 | 5 | 0.60 (0.37) | 6.00 (5.43) | 3.60 | 5.12 (15° C) | 18.43 |
| 15–2 | 3 | 1.03 (0.43) | 7.94 (6.05) | 8.18 | 8.42 (9° C) | 68.88 |

Source: Chaplin 1976, courtesy of Journal of Comparative Physiology B.

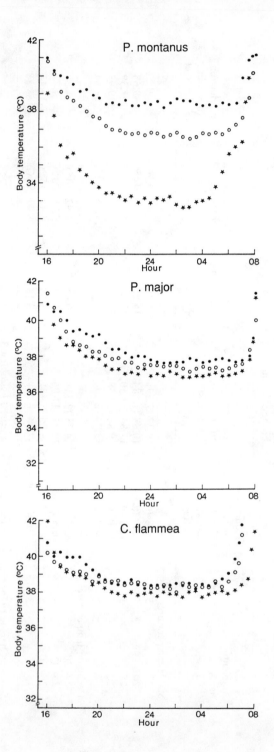

In light of all this, it is surprising that Grossman and West (1977), working on Black-capped Chickadees wintering in Fairbanks, Alaska, found only small nocturnal reductions in body temperature of approximately 3° C below normal daytime temperatures. It certainly seems odd that Chaplin's chickadees, from New York State (about 44° N) undergo true nocturnal hypothermia, whereas the more northern ones of Grossman and West do not. One possible explanation for this discrepancy is that subspecific differences are involved. This hypothesis could easily be tested by bringing wintering chickadees from each population together and testing them under identical conditions; to the best of my knowledge, this has not yet been done. Another possibility is that, in handling the chickadees to measure their body temperatures, Grossman and West may have caused the birds to warm up, thus masking the true extent of their hypothermia. It would certainly seem worthwhile to repeat the tests on Alaskan chickadees using the telemetry techniques of Reinertsen and Haftorn (1983, 1986). Clearly, further tests are needed to resolve this apparent paradox.

Actually the extent of temperature drop recorded by Grossman and West (1977) of 3° C is within the normal range of circadian (daily) fluctuations in body temperature of many bird species, regardless of season (Calder and King 1974, Reinertsen and Haftorn 1983). During warm summer nights, the body temperature of most birds, including titmice, and, presumably, chickadees, falls at

Fig. 8-7. Nocturnal body temperature changes of Willow Tit (*Parus montanus*), Great Tit (*P. major*), and Common Redpoll (*Carduelis flammea*) when entering, during, and while emerging from the deep sleep phase, acclimatized to winter photoperiod (8L-16D) and ambient temperature conditions. All three species were kept at three different, but constant, ambient temperatures (closed circles = 20° C; open circles = 0° C; stars = −20° C) with food ad libitum. The birds were in normal condition in terms of body weight. The three curves on each diagram are from the same bird. Only the Willow Tit (top graph) underwent nocturnal hypothermia, as shown by the marked drop in body temperature under colder conditions; neither the Great Tit (middle graph) nor the Redpoll (lower graph) showed any such nocturnal drop in body temperature, even under very cold conditions. (From Reinertsen and Haftorn 1986, courtesy of *Journal of Comparative Physiology B*.)

roosting time until it levels off two to three hours before midnight. The temperature is then held constant until two to three hours before sunrise, when it begins to rise once again (Fig. 8-8). Therefore the true hypothermia achieved by wintering chickadees and titmice is a controlled exaggeration of a basic circadian rhythm characteristic of avian body temperatures.

As Reinertsen and Haftorn (1983) pointed out, the degree of nocturnal hypothermia any bird attains must represent a compromise between two conflicting interests—the need to save as much energy as possible (which would tend to drive the temperature downward) and the need to maintain a fairly high state of alertness (which would tend to pull up the temperature). Significantly, Black-capped Chickadees, Carolina Chickadees, and Willow Tits are all capable of flight while still in hypothermia (Chaplin 1976, Mayer et al. 1982, Reinertsen and Haftorn 1983).

Affecting all of these physiological adjustments is the complex and apparently still not fully understood process of winter acclimatization. It is beyond the scope of this chapter to discuss this process in detail (but see, for example, Calder and King 1974 and Dawson et al. 1983). However, several of the results of the process are well documented. Winter-acclimatized Black-capped Chickadees, for example, will store more fat in fewer daylight hours than will chickadees in the longer photoperiods of other seasons (see Fig. 8-5). Similarly, chickadees' resistance to cold varies with the season, being greatest in midwinter (Odum 1943, Chaplin 1976). Particularly pronounced are seasonal differences in when and how deeply chickadees and titmice enter into hypothermia. For example, Willow Tits achieve the greatest depth of hypothermia under a given set of cold conditions at midwinter, while summer-acclimatized birds show almost no response when exposed to the same conditions (Fig. 8-9). Moreover, in between these two extremes a steady gradient of response exists (Reinertsen and Haftorn 1983). Similar results have also been found for Black-capped Chickadees (Chaplin 1974, 1976).

Finally, dominant individuals of both Willow Tits (Hogstad 1987b) and Great Tits (Røskaft et al. 1986) maintain higher daytime metabolic rates than do lower-ranked birds under the same conditions. It would be interesting to see whether such birds can and do achieve the same depth of nocturnal hypothermia as do lower-ranked birds on cold winter nights.

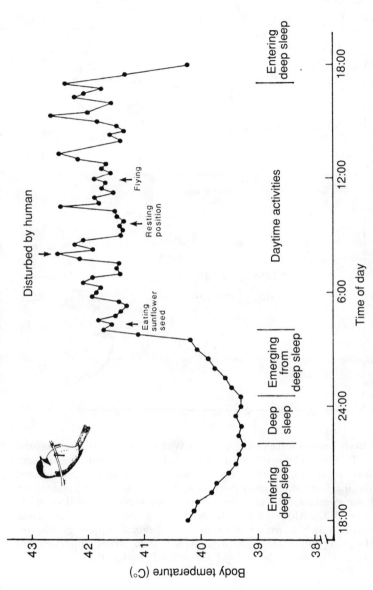

Fig. 8-8. Circadian body temperature rhythm of a summer-acclimatized Willow Tit. Even on warm summer nights, a small nocturnal drop of 2–3° C can be found. (From Reinertsen and Haftorn 1983, courtesy of *Journal of Comparative Physiology B*.)

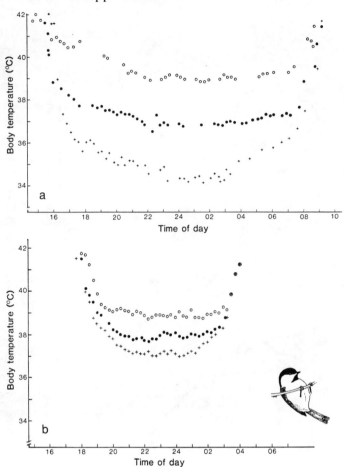

Fig. 8-9. Body temperature changes of two Willow Tits, one (a) acclimatized to winter (8L-16D), and one (b) to summer (>12L) photoperiods and ambient temperature conditions. Graphs show responses when entering, during, and while emerging from the nightly deep sleep phase, when kept under three different, but constant, temperatures (open circles = 20° C; closed circles = 0° C; + = −30° C). Although both birds were exposed to exactly the same temperatures, only the winter-acclimatized individual (upper graph) responded by going into marked nocturnal hypothermia. (From Reinertsen and Haftorn 1983, courtesy of *Journal of Comparative Physiology B*.)

Behavioral Adjustments

One of the most important behavioral adjustments is the selection of winter roost sites. Most members of the genus *Parus*, both in North America (Bent 1946) and in Europe (Perrins 1979), typically roost in holes of some sort. Almost any nook or cranny can be used (Perrins 1979). Certainly most chickadee species for which there are any data show great flexibility in their choice of roost sites. Thus both Black-capped Chickadees (Odum 1942a) and Carolina Chickadees (Brewer 1963) may roost either in cavities in trees or in dense vegetation such as vines (Carolina Chickadees) or conifers (Black-capped Chickadees).

If cavities are used, they tend to be smaller than those used for nesting. This is true for Great Tits (Perrins 1979) and also for Carolina Chickadees, which can sometimes be found roosting in holes that are barely large enough for a chickadee to fit into (Pitts 1976). What little air is contained in such small cavities may be very efficiently warmed by heat lost through radiation from the bird roosting inside. Although I have found no data on the size of roost sites of Black-capped Chickadees, it is suggestive that none of the hole-roosting chickadees observed by Odum (1942a) subsequently bred in their roost cavity. Perhaps the roost cavities were simply too small for nesting purposes.

In areas where suitable cavities are in short supply, dominant individuals may exclude more subordinate birds from favored roost sites, as Kluyver (1957) found for Great Tits. All members of flocks in species that form winter flocks, such as chickadees, typically roost within the flock's home range (Odum 1942a, Pitts 1976).

A few Old World titmice, including both Willow Tits (Zonov 1967, quoted in Calder and King 1974) and Siberian Tits (Korhonen 1981), regularly roost in holes in the snow. Willow Tits in Siberia can burrow a 20-cm (almost 8-inch) tunnel in 10–15 seconds, using movements of the head, wings, and feet (Zonov 1967). Apparently these birds use the same burrow for extended periods in a winter. Naturally, such birds must dig their way into and out of such burrows after any snowfall, but, given the speed of excavation, this clearly does not present any major problem to the birds. Because undisturbed snow contains a considerable amount of trapped air, it can act as fairly efficient insulation. Snow burrows also give protection from wind and from radiation to the cold winter sky (Calder and King 1974). It is entirely conceivable that North American species such as Boreal Chickadees or indeed Black-capped Chickadees living in areas of deep winter snow may also use snow burrows for winter roosts.

Occasionally, chickadees may roost in abandoned nests of other species; both Black-capped Chickadees (Bent 1946) and Mountain Chickadees (Williams 1941) are known to do this. However, apparently no member of the genus *Parus* actually builds a nest of its own for roosting purposes, although other small passerines, such as House Sparrows (*Passer domesticus*) (Perrins 1979) and Verdins (*Auriparus flaviceps*) (Buttemer et al. 1987), do. At first glance, it does seem curious that parids do not build roosting nests, since soft nesting material would surely help to keep them warm at night. Perrins (1979) concluded that there must be some disadvantage, as yet unknown, associated with parids' building such winter nests. I am not convinced there is much of a disadvantage for parids; rather, I suspect that, given their ability to achieve nocturnal hypothermia in cold winter nights and their unusually thick plumage, they simply may not need to spend the time and energy to build winter roosting nests.

Actual benefits of cavity roosting have been measured for Carolina Chickadees by Mayer et al. (1982). They found that roosting in an enclosed cavity, as opposed to roosting in the open air, reduced net radiant heat loss from a chickadee by 60–100 percent and reduced heat loss by convection to zero, since there was no wind in the roost cavities (Table 8-5). Roosting within thick vegetation evidently provides similar benefits. Thus Walsberg (1986), working on Phainopeplas (*Phainopepla nitens*), which roost in dense vegetation, showed that such roosts can provide nearly complete (88 percent) reduction of radiation heat loss and even greater reduction of convective heat loss. Any enclosed roost site, then, whether in dense foliage or in a tree or snow cavity, provides a major reduction in heat loss, thus lowering the nightly metabolic expenditures of the roosting bird.

Roosting posture is also important. In cooler temperatures, roosting chickadees fluff into a ball and turn their head such that their beak and part of their face are covered by their scapular (shoulder) feathers (sometimes misinterpreted as "putting the head under the wing"). Since the beak, face, and uncovered legs all have relatively high surface temperatures (Hill et al. 1980), this roosting posture serves to reduce heat loss, although some still escapes, particularly from the face region (Fig. 8-10).

Table 8-5. Parameters affecting the heat balance of four Carolina Chickadees roosting in a cavity and in the open

| Date | Sky cover | $T_a$ °C | $T_{sky}$ °C | $T_g$ °C | $T_t$ °C | $T_s$ °C | Wind in open (m/s) | Wind in cavity (m/s) | $R$ in open (watts/m$^2$) | $R$ in cavity (watts/m$^2$) |
|---|---|---|---|---|---|---|---|---|---|---|
| Feb. 2 | Clear | −12 | −34 | −9 | −12 | −6 | 4.06 | 0.01 | 57.48 | 14.70 |
| Feb. 3 | Cloudy | −10 | −10 | −10 | −9 | −7 | 0.51 | 0 | 12.82 | 6.22 |
| Feb. 4 | Clear | −9 | −33.5 | −8 | −9 | −8 | 1.01 | 0.025 | 46.55 | 2.02 |
| Feb. 5 | Cloudy | −5 | −10 | −5 | −2 | −2 | 0.25–0.5 | 0 | 23.93 | 0.0 |
| Feb. 8 | Clear | −6 | −33 | −6 | −6 | −2 | 0.5–1.52 | 0 | 66.90 | 8.23 |
| Feb. 25 | Clear | 0 | −26 | 3 | 0 | 0–3 | 0.1 | 0.01 | 63.70 | 12.06 |
| Feb. 25 | Clear | 0 | −26 | 3 | 0 | 0–3 | 0.1 | 0.01 | 63.70 | 4.11 |
| Feb. 26 | Cloudy | 0 | −4.5 | 0 | 0 | 6 | 0.25 | 0.0 | 37.69 | 8.25 |
| March 3 | Clear | −3 | −28 | −3 | −3 | +3 | 0.48 | 0.0 | 76.70 | 47.49 |
| March 3 | Clear | −3 | −28 | −3 | −3 | +3 | 0.48 | 0.0 | 76.70 | 33.0 |

*Source:* Mayer et al. 1982, courtesy of *International Journal of Biometeorology*.
*Note:* $T_a$ = air temperature; $T_{sky}$ = sky temperature; $T_g$ = ground temperature; $T_t$ = tree temperature inside cavity; $T_s$ = bird surface temperature in open; $R$ = rate of heat loss by radiation.

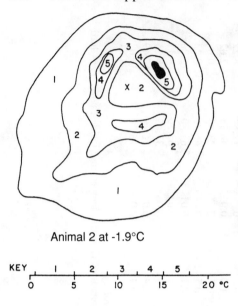

Animal 2 at -1.9°C

KEY

| 1 | 2 | 3 | 4 | 5 |

0    5    10    15    20 °C

Fig. 8-10. Black-capped Chickadee roosting posture: drawing of a radiograph of a sleeping chickadee with its head tucked into its scapular feathers. The view is of the right side, and the top of the head is marked X. This roosting posture reduces heat loss to some extent (compare with Fig. 8-4), although some heat still escapes from near the more exposed eye of the sleeping bird. (From Hill et al. 1980, courtesy of *Physiological Zoology*, © 1980 by The University of Chicago.)

Over much of the year, both chickadees and Old World titmice roost singly (Bent 1946, Odum 1942a, Perrins 1979). One published report suggests that on very cold nights, Black-capped Chickadees may roost in huddled groups (Loery and Nichols 1985). However, the authors were just describing what someone else had seen. Given how many field studies have been conducted on chickadees and European tits, it is safe to conclude that huddled roosting by these species, if it occurs at all, is rare. And that seems rather curious, especially since several small related species, including both Long-tailed Tits (*Aegithalos caudatus*) (Perrins 1979) and Common Bushtits (*Psaltriparus minimus*) (S.M. Smith 1972, Chaplin 1982), roost in huddles. In such groups, all members benefit, especially if they are in a relatively confined space. The advantages of huddled roosting are well documented: Brenner (1965) showed that groups of four European Starlings (*Sturnus vulgaris*) that roosted together could withstand cold and fasting far better than could birds that roosted alone. This advantage should be even greater for smaller species such as chickadees. Further observation, especially in higher latitudes, may show that Black-capped Chickadees, and possibly other chickadee species as well, occasionally roost clumped together during the coldest nights of winter.

Besides adjusting their roosting behavior, chickadees are also known to modify several aspects of their foraging behavior in response to weather conditions. For example, Odum (1942a) reported that winter Black-capped Chickadee flocks moved most slowly on cold days and especially on very windy days: down to less than a quarter of the fastest speed recorded on warmer days. Similarly, Kessel (1976) found that Black-capped Chickadees wintering in Alaska were less "lively" and markedly reduced their feeding radius on extremely cold days.

Grubb (1978) studied this behavior using several small birds including Tufted Titmice (*Parus bicolor*) and Carolina Chickadees. He found that for both chickadees and titmice, higher wind (Fig. 8-11) and lower air temperatures (Fig. 8-12) both resulted in increased time spent stationary and increased number of stops per minute, for an overall decrease in distance traveled.

This makes a great deal of sense. Flight under even the best of conditions is costly: heat transfer in flight is increased to about

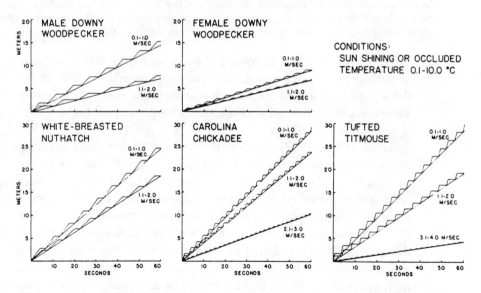

Fig. 8-11. Wind-dependent foraging curves for four bird species wintering in a deciduous woodlot. Each line on the graphs represents data taken at a particular wind velocity (shown in the figure). Each "sawtooth" consists of a sloped component representing the rate of an average individual movement and a flat component denoting the time span of an average stop. The diagonal common to all sawteeth marks the average foraging speed over 1 min. For every species shown, increased wind velocity resulted in slower average foraging speed and more time spent stationary. (From Grubb 1978, courtesy of *Auk*.)

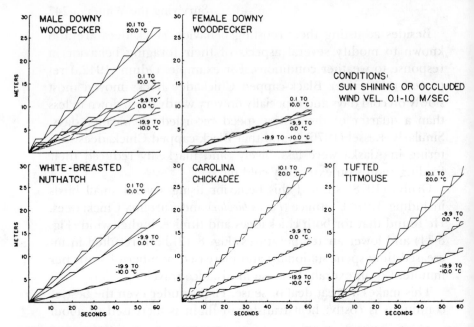

Fig. 8-12. Temperature-dependent foraging curves for four species wintering in a deciduous woodlot. Temperatures are shown in the figure. The "sawteeth" are as in the previous figure. Lower air temperature invariably resulted in slower average foraging speed and more time spent stationary. (From Grubb 1978, courtesy of *Auk*.)

three to six times that at resting (Calder and King 1974), because of both exposure of less insulated parts of the bird (such as under the wings) and forced convection due to flight speed. It is hardly surprising, therefore, that chickadees sharply curtail flight under severe winter conditions.

Grubb (1975, 1977) also documented significant shifts in foraging location associated with certain weather conditions. He found that for both Black-capped Chickadees and Tufted Titmice, either increased wind speed or lowered temperatures caused significant decreases in foraging heights. He attributed this shift to the fact that, because of increased friction, wind speed is slower closer to the ground. Thus as a bird moves lower within the vegetation, it will encounter correspondingly less thermal stress. On cold days, he frequently saw both chickadees and titmice plunging down into the shrub layer at each wind gust, then moving back up as the wind died down again (Grubb 1975).

Apparently, degree of cloud cover can also affect some aspects of foraging behavior, particularly on cold, windy days. Grubb (1977) found that Tufted Titmice kept to the leeward side of their foraging substrate significantly more under cloud than when the sun was shining. Also, in cold and windy conditions, Carolina Chickadees spent significantly more time foraging in sheltered areas (a stream valley) when it was cloudy than they did in full sunshine. Laboratory studies on other bird species have suggested that artificial insolation can moderate the metabolic cost of low temperature (Lustick 1969, Lustick et al. 1970). Evidently natural

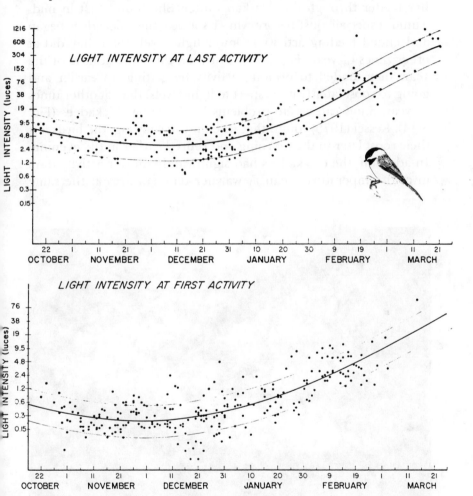

Fig. 8-13.  Light intensity at the time of first and last Black-capped Chickadee activity near Fairbanks, Alaska, 1960–67. The center lines are the best-fit polynomial curves for first and last activity, and the lines on either side are the distance of one standard deviation from the best-fit lines. At midwinter, the chickadees began and ended their activity at lower light intensities than at any other time of year. (from Kessel 1976, courtesy of *Wilson Bulletin*.)

insolation (sunshine) can have a somewhat similar effect. However, this effect may be rather small: a subsequent field study (Grubb 1978) failed to find any significant difference in the foraging speed of either Tufted Titmice or Carolina Chickadees in sunny versus cloudy conditions.

Kessel (1976) studied how various meteorological conditions affected the length of Black-capped Chickadees' "activity days" at her feeder through the Alaskan winter. She found that in midwinter, especially just before winter solstice, the chickadees began and ended feeding activity at lower light levels than they did at other times of year (Fig. 8-13). Thus, on the shortest days of the year, they tended to prolong activity by getting up earlier and going to roost later (with respect to light levels) than at other times of year. Snow can create problems for foraging chickadees (Fig. 8-14). Kessel (1976) found that when it was snowing, the birds left their roost later in the morning and retired earlier in the evening. In addition, the chickadees had significantly shorter activity days in cold temperatures than at warmer temperatures at the same

Fig. 8-14. Snowy conditions can pose some difficulties, especially for bark foragers such as chickadees.

photoperiod, but the intensity of their feeder use, measured as total number of bird-minutes per unit time spent at the feeder, was greater in colder temperatures (Fig. 8-15). This fits nicely with Grubb's (1978) finding that chickadees travel less in cold conditions. When cold induces restricted movement, it is surely adaptive to center activity around a rich food source such as a feeder.

Another behavioral modification that may help chickadees survive winter conditions is their habit of storing food (see Food Storage and Memory, Chapter 3). Food storage can occur in any month, but is most common in fall and early winter; for example,

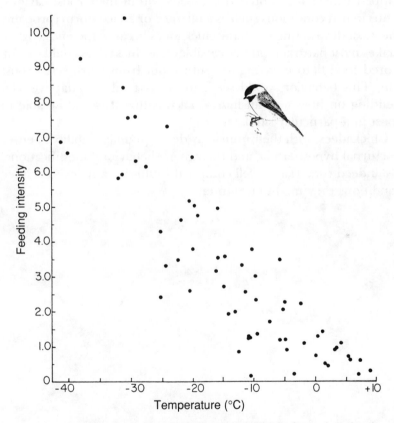

Fig. 8-15. Feeding intensity of Black-capped Chickadees wintering in Alaska, relative to daily mean temperatures, 1964–67. Feeding intensity was derived by dividing the total bird-minutes spent at the feeder per day by the total number of minutes in that activity day. The colder the temperature, the greater the feeding intensity. (From Kessel 1976, courtesy of *Wilson Bulletin*.)

Kessel (1976) recorded a November peak in food storage by her Black-capped Chickadees in Alaska. Haftorn (1956) concluded that food hoarding by certain Scandinavian tits, particularly Willow, Coal (*Parus ater*) and Crested (*P. cristatus*) Tits, plays a significant role in their overwinter survival. Rather amazingly, about 70 percent of the winter food consumed by a Japanese population of Willow Tits was seeds stored during the autumn (Nakamura and Wako 1988). Certainly any bird whose movements were restricted by severe weather would benefit greatly from moving directly from one stored food item to another.

Grossman and West (1977) found that their captive Black-capped Chickadees would store seeds within their roost cavities. Thus in bad conditions such as a blizzard or an ice storm (probably the most devastating of all for chickadees because the encasing ice makes most natural food inaccessible), the chickadees could eat the stored food before having to venture out from a protected roost site. This behavior would seem to be particularly adaptive (depending on how sure an individual was that it would be able to roost in a particular site later on).

Chickadees, with their unusually dense plumage, ability to enter nocturnal hypothermia, and their many behavioral modifications, are indeed remarkably well equipped to survive any severe winter conditions they might encounter.

# 9

# Survivorship and Population Dynamics

## Survivorship

### Longevity

Potentially, Black-capped Chickadees can live for an amazingly long time. So far, the oldest known chickadee was a bird of unknown sex that was banded in New Hampshire by John Kennard. The bird, when last recovered, was at least 12 years and 5 months old (Kennard 1975, Clapp et al. 1983). Table 9-1 presents some additional published age records for Black-capped Chickadees.

The age records of other parids are quite similar (Table 9-2). Very likely at least some of the shorter age records, such as that of the Chestnut-backed Chickadee (*Parus rufescens*), reflect not so much that the species is less long-lived, but rather that it is simply less well studied than the Black-capped Chickadee.

The ages shown in Tables 9-1 and 9-2 are, in fact, exceptional—the vast majority of chickadees and titmice live much shorter lives. And, while the fact that Black-capped Chickadees can live to be almost 13 years old is interesting, it really does not tell us much, because, in typical populations, old age is simply not a common source of mortality. If it were, as Perrins (1979) pointed out, then it would be possible to find data showing a sharp increase in the death rate past a certain critical age. So far, no such data have been

Table 9-1. Maximum longevity of Black-capped Chickadees

| Authority | Area | Sample size | Age of oldest bird |
|---|---|---|---|
| Butts 1931 | N.Y. | 50 | 7 yr |
| Harding 1932 | Mass. | Not given | 7 yr 6 mo |
| Baldwin 1935b | Mass. | Not given | 8 yr |
| Wallace 1941 | Mass. | 3500 | 8 yr plus |
| Brewer 1963 | Kans. to N.J. | 1276 | 8 yr plus |
| Cooke 1950 | Manitoba | Not given | 8 yr 8 mo |
| Lawrence 1958 | Ontario | 340 | 9 yr |
| Elder and Zimmerman 1983 | Mo. | 253 | 9 yr |
| Smith 1964 | Mass. | Not given | 9 yr 3 mo |
| Wharton 1964 | Mass. | Not given | 9 yr 4 mo |
| Smiley 1964 | N.Y. | Not given | 9 yr 5 mo |
| Downs 1964 | Vt. | Not given | 10 yr 3 mo |
| Kennard 1964 | N.H. | Not given | 10 yr 8 mo |
| Loery and Nichols 1985 | Conn. | 1412 | 11 yr 10 mo |
| Kennard 1975 | N.H. | Not given | 12 yr 5 mo |

*Source:* Slightly expanded from Elder and Zimmerman 1983.

found (but see Loery et al. 1987, discussed in Age-Specific Survival Rates, below). Perhaps a more useful and informative figure than simple age records is average life span. Various estimates of average life span have been made, with techniques of varying degrees of sophistication, yet the results are remarkably uniform. There is general agreement that the average life span for Black-

Table 9-2. Age records of some parids from North America and Britain

| Species | Age of oldest bird |
|---|---|
| North America | |
| Black-capped Chickadee (*Parus atricapillus*) | 12 yr 5 mo |
| Carolina Chickadee (*P. carolinensis*) | 10 yr 11 mo |
| Mountain Chickadee (*P. gambeli*) | 10 yr 1 mo |
| Chestnut-backed Chickadee (*P. rufescens*) | 7 yr 9 mo |
| Tufted Titmouse (*P. bicolor*) | 13 yr 3 mo |
| Britain | |
| Great Tit (*P. major*) | 9 yr 4 mo |
| Blue Tit (*P. caeruleus*) | 11 yr 5 mo |
| Willow Tit (*P. montanus*) | 8 yr 11 mo |
| Marsh Tit (*P. palustris*) | 9 yr 0 mo |

*Source:* North American data from Clapp et al. 1983; British data from Perrins 1979.

Table 9-3. Estimates of average life span of Black-capped Chickadees

| Authority | State | Years of study | Average mortality rate (%) | Average life span (yr) |
|---|---|---|---|---|
| Odum 1942b | N.Y. | 4 | 38 | ≈ 2.5 |
| Elder and Zimmerman 1983[a] | Mo. | 9 | 35 | 2.4 |
| Elder and Zimmerman 1983[b] | Mo. | 9 | 33 ± 3 | 2.6 ± 0.28 |
| Loery and Nichols 1985 | Conn. | 25 | 41 (range: 10–57) | ≈ 2.5 |

[a]Resighting data, life table method of calculation.
[b]Resighting data, stochastic method of calculation.

capped Chickadees is approximately 2½ years (Table 9-3). Even this can be misleading, however, because all such estimates very likely underestimate mortality during the first six months of life (see Age-Specific Survival Rates, below).

Hence chickadees can live to be almost 13 years old, or even older, yet their average life span is only 2½ years. Many sources of mortality can act to maintain the difference between these two figures.

### Human-related Mortality

Some of the better-known sources of mortality involve human-related causes, which include birds being hit by cars, flying into windows, dying of pesticide poisoning, or being killed by house cats or other introduced predators. Precisely because these causes are human-related, people are often more aware of them than of more natural sorts of mortality. Such deaths can often be mini-mized by restraint of pets, placing warning silhouettes (falcon shapes and the like) on windows, and taking care to place feeders such that they do not create or encourage flight paths that pass low over busy streets. However, given that these are unnatural sources of death, I will not consider them any further here.

### Predators and Antipredator Behavior

Evidently most predation on adult chickadees away from their nests is done by avian predators: hawks, owls, and shrikes. Among the hawks, the Sharp-shinned Hawk (*Accipiter striatus*) is probably the most frequent chickadee predator (Fig. 9-1). Its diet, which is

Fig. 9-1. The Sharp-shinned Hawk is one of the most effective predators on small birds such as chickadees. (© F. K. Schleicher / VIREO.)

mostly small birds, is known to include chickadees (Bent 1937, Reynolds and Meslow 1984). Yet the vast majority of their attempts at capture (like those of other predators) are probably failures. Gaddis (1980) reported seeing many attacks on his mixed-species flocks in Florida, none of which was successful. I have seen over 20 dashes at chickadees by this species, of which only one was successful. Other small, fast-moving hawks such as Cooper's Hawk

(*Accipiter cooperi*) (Gaddis 1980, Waite and Grubb 1987), American Kestrel (*Falco sparverius*) (Bent 1946), and Merlin (*F. columbarius*) (pers. observ.), may also attempt to catch a chickadee or titmouse on occasion.

A few owls, especially some of the smaller species, may also occasionally prey on chickadees. The Eastern Screech Owl (*Otus asio*) is known to do so (Bent 1938, Smith 1947). The only Saw-whet Owl (*Aegolius acadicus*) I have seen in my current study area was holding a dead chickadee when I found it. Boreal (*A. funereus*) and Northern Pygmy (*Glaucidium gnoma*) Owls may also take chickadees in areas where their ranges overlap. Chickadees are well known to mob owls (e.g., Shedd 1983, Sullivan 1985); even strictly nocturnal owls may reach out a foot and grab a mobbing chickadee if it comes too close.

Another avian predator that catches adult chickadees is the Northern Shrike (*Lanius excubitor*). This species, whose numbers seem to have decreased in recent years, may once have been at least the equivalent of the Sharp-shinned Hawk as a major predator on chickadees, especially during the winter (Cade 1962, Ficken and Witkin 1977). It evidently still is in certain areas (Desrochers 1989).

In Europe, as in North America, free-flying adult tits are preyed upon largely by avian predators. Apparently, European tit populations experience considerable predation, especially at certain times of year. In the boreal coniferous forests of northern Europe, European Pygmy Owls (*Glaucidium passerinum*) are a major predator of wintering passerines (Ekman 1986), preying upon at least five tit species.

In Britain, predation on Great (*Parus major*) and Blue (*P. caeruleus*) Tits by Eurasian Sparrowhawks (*Accipiter nisus*) is particularly severe (Geer 1978, 1982; Perrins and Geer 1980). This hawk is well known to attack winter tit flocks (Morse 1973), just as its close relative, the Sharp-shinned Hawk, attacks chickadee flocks in North America. Perhaps the most intense pressure exerted by Eurasian Sparrowhawks is during the breeding season, when they can reportedly take 20–25 percent of the local tit population (Geer 1978, Perrins and Geer 1980). Breeding adult tits tend to form habitual flight paths toward their nest, especially after the young have hatched. Sparrowhawks can learn where these are, then lie in wait and pick off adult tits as they return to their nest with food (Gibb 1960). Evidently Sparrowhawks time their breeding such that they have nestlings during the period when most young tits have just fledged—a time when there will be a large supply of young, inexperienced tits available as food for nestling Sparrowhawks. Along the same lines, Barnard et al. (1987) reported that the Northern Harrier (*Circus cyaneus*) in North America also apparently times its nesting to take advantage of young songbirds as potential food for their young. This raptor, which is usually considered to be a rodent specialist (Bent 1937), evidently switches from field mice to young passerines as soon as the latter become available (Barnard et al. 1987).

One interesting question that might be asked here is: do predators take only the weakest prey, or do they select more or less at random? Given the observed low success rate in hawk attacks on chickadees, for example, it is tempting to conclude that only the sick or weak are taken, but this is not necessarily the case. One study that addresses this question was done in Europe by Geer (1982), who found that the answer may vary from year to year, depending on ecological conditions. Geer made the assumption that juvenile tits, being inexperienced, were more vulnerable than adults. He then looked at the ratio of juveniles to adults taken by nesting Sparrowhawks in Britain. He found that in 1977, the hawks took significantly more juveniles than adults, yet both in the preceding and in the following years, the hawks showed essentially nonselective hunting. This variation in selectivity reflected the number of tits available to the hawks: the hawks concentrated on young tits only in the year of greatest tit abundance (Table 9-4). Geer reasoned that perhaps in years of lower prey availability, time spent searching for easier prey might result in the hawk's ending up catching less food overall—that is, when food is scarce, preda-

Table 9-4. Predation by nesting Eurasian Sparrowhawks on ringed tits in Wytham Woods, Great Britain

| Year | No. of pairs of Sparrowhawks | No. of banded tits | No. of banded tits/hawk pair | Did hawks select juveniles over adults? |
|------|------|------|------|------|
| 1976 | 6 | 578 | 96.3 | No |
| 1977 | 6 | 819 | 136.5 | Yes |
| 1978 | 9 | 602 | 66.8 | No |

*Source:* Data from Geer 1982.

tors cannot afford to be choosy. Some studies (e.g., Gibb 1950) have found evidence of selectivity for young prey, while others (e.g., Hamerstrom and Hamerstrom 1951) have not. The importance of Geer's study is that he found selectivity and nonselectivity and then came up with a reasonable explanation for why each occurred.

A rather different category of predators concerns those species that attack eggs or nestlings or both, as well as potentially catching incubating adults. In North America, the most persistent and successful destroyer of chickadee eggs is undoubtedly the House Wren (*Troglodytes aedon*). This species typically enters a chickadee nest, pierces the eggs, then removes egg shells and nesting material; it is also known to attack nestlings (Belles-Isles and Picman 1986). Recent evidence (Belles-Isles and Picman 1987) suggests that House Wrens may actually kill other adult wrens in nest cavities; the possibility exists that they might attempt to kill adult chickadees as well. Kluyver (1961) reported that House Wrens destroyed the eggs of 20 percent of his study broods of Black-capped Chickadees: by far the major source of nest mortality in his study area. Brewer (1963) also noted considerable destruction of both Carolina (*Parus carolinensis*) and Black-capped Chickadee nests by House Wrens, although he referred to such activity as nest-site competition. Given that such nest raiding involves piercing eggs and throwing out both eggs and young, the net result is still brood mortality. More rarely, other hole-nesting species may also evict chickadees from their nest site. For example, Walkinshaw (1941) reported that a Prothonotary Warbler (*Prothonotaria citrea*) briefly took over a nest cavity containing seven Black-capped Chickadee eggs, only to be evicted in turn by a House Wren that then proceeded to destroy and remove the chickadee eggs.

Odum (1941b) reported losses of Black-capped Chickadee nestlings to two mammalian predators: a raccoon (*Procyon lotor*) and a red squirrel (*Tamiasciurus hudsonicus*). Other mammals, including the eastern gray squirrel (*Sciurus carolinensis*), which is known to attack tit nests in Britain (Perrins 1979), various species of chipmunks (*Tamias* and *Eutamias* spp.), and opossums (*Didelphis marsupialis*) probably also attack chickadee and titmouse nests on occasion. Snakes are also known to eat eggs and nestlings. Gold and Dahlsten (1983) reported snake predation on their chickadee nests, but did not reveal which species of snakes were involved, and Howitz (1986b) reported predation on Black-capped Chickadee nests by bullsnakes (*Pituophis melanoleucus*).

Long (1982) made some interesting observations on the responses of breeding Black-capped Chickadees to various potential predators (live or stuffed) placed near their nest. He found that parent chickadees gave the full nest distraction display (see Visual Displays, Chapter 4) to a variety of stimuli, including stuffed gray and red squirrels, and even to a stuffed white-footed wood mouse (*Peromyscus leucopus*), as well as to a live fox snake (*Elaphe vulpina*). Unfortunately, Long did not present any clearly innocuous stimulus of approximately the same size to test whether the chickadees were giving distraction displays to any unfamiliar object near their nest (as I suspect) or were actually recognizing and responding to these species as true nest predators.

For European tits, the most serious avian nest predator is evidently the Great Spotted Woodpecker (*Dendrocopos major*), both in Britain (Perrins 1979) and on the Continent (Orell and Ojanen 1983). Woodpecker predation on chickadee nests can also occur in North America, although it is far more rare than in Europe (Fig. 9-2). For example, Red-bellied Woodpeckers (*Melanerpes carolinus*) have been seen entering Carolina Chickadee nests and carrying off their nestlings (Conner 1974).

More serious than nest predation on European tits by woodpeckers is predation by weasels and their relatives, both *Mustela nivalis,* the European weasel, and, to a lesser extent, *M. erminea,* the stoat, or short-tailed weasel (Perrins 1979). The latter is widespread in North America, overlapping much of the Black-capped Chickadee's geographic range. Weasels, being long, slender predators that climb readily and fit through the entrance of typical chickadee nests, should be able to raid such nests easily. Gold and Dahlsten (1983) reported weasel predation (probably either *M. erminea* or *M. frenata*) on Mountain (*Parus gambeli*) and Chestnut-backed Chickadee nests in California. Further studies may show that weasels are more serious nest predators on chickadees than was originally thought.

A wide variety of antipredator behavior has been described for chickadees and their relatives, some of which is remarkably subtle. For example, flock formation itself can be considered a sort of antipredator behavior. Many studies have shown that as flock size increases, the amount of vigilance by individual flock members

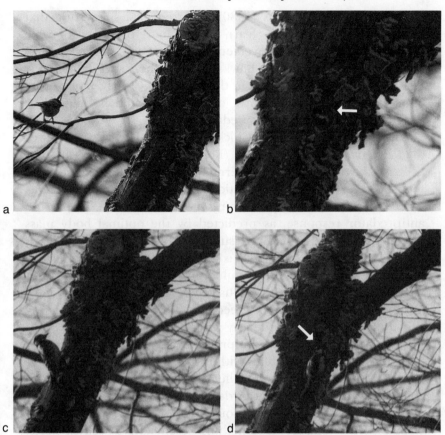

Fig. 9-2. Action at a chickadee nest site. A Black-capped Chickadee approaches (a) and removes wood chips (b) from a potential nest site in early spring. Later that morning, with the chickadees involved in a territory boundary dispute, a Downy Woodpecker approaches (c) and investigates the same site (d). While this Downy Woodpecker is probably not much of a threat, some of the larger woodpeckers can be serious nest predators on chickadees and titmice, especially in Europe.

decreases, and the amount of time available for foraging correspondingly increases (e.g., Waite 1987, Ekman 1988).

Gaddis (1980) proposed that the unpredictable nature of chickadee flock movements can also be considered a type of antipredator behavior. Hawks of the genus *Accipiter,* such as Eurasian Sparrowhawks or Sharp-shinned Hawks, are particularly good at learning regular routes taken by potential prey. Eurasian Sparrowhawks are known to do this during the breeding season (see above). Moreover, Gaddis (1980) reported data suggesting that Sharp-shinned Hawks may learn the one more-or-less predictable aspect of natural flock movements: that is, the location of their roosting sites. Evidently the hawks may visit these sites deliberately just before the birds emerge in the morning. Clearly, irregularity of movements during the rest of the day would be helpful in avoiding ambushes by such predators.

Wintering Black-capped Chickadees have lower fat reserves than do ground-feeding birds (Rogers 1987), doubtless in part because they undergo hypothermia in winter, thereby reducing their need for daily lipid deposition (see Physiological adjustments in Chapter 8). Their lower fat reserves may also be in part an antipredator response, as predicted by the optimal body mass model of Lima (1986). Lima suggested that leaner individuals would be more agile, and thus could escape predation better, yet the leaner a bird is, the more vulnerable it is to starvation. Chickadees, which forage almost exclusively in trees, can afford to have less fat reserves than ground feeders, whose food can frequently and unpredictably be hidden by winter snow.

Some of the most subtle antipredator behavior involves the interactions among individuals within the flocks. Essentially, dominant members tend to take for themselves the safest situations and behavior, with subdominant birds being forced, either directly or indirectly, into the more dangerous situations (Fig. 9-3). Dominant birds evidently engage in something resembling a "selfish herd" strategy (Hamilton 1971), forcing lower ranking birds to use riskier foraging sites, while selecting the safest spots for themselves. Such behavior has been reported for many European tit species (e.g., Ekman et al. 1981; Ekman and Askenmo 1984; Hogstad 1988c, 1988d, 1989b).

Somewhat less information is available on this kind of behavior in North American species, although Glase (1973) did report finding some consistent differences in foraging site associated with rank in Black-capped Chickadees. Recently Desrochers (1989) did an elegant field experiment, showing that higher-ranked Black-capped Chickadees do, in fact, feed preferentially in certain (presumably safer) sites, and that lower-ranked individuals, given the opportunity, also choose to feed there. Desrochers documented that male chickadees in his Alberta study area foraged lower and closer to trunks than females did. Then he removed all the males from three flocks, leaving three other, control, flocks intact. With

Fig. 9-3. Ground foraging is unusual for Black-capped Chickadees; often the individuals that feed on the ground have been excluded from safer, more productive foraging sites by higher ranking individuals.

the males gone, the females in the three experimental flocks foraged in areas formerly occupied by males; meanwhile, as expected, no change occurred in female foraging in the control flocks. However, as soon as the males were put back in the experimental flocks, the females resumed feeding as before (Fig. 9-4). Desrochers (1989) related this preference for lower foraging sites to predator risk. The main diurnal chickadee predator in northern Alberta is the Northern Shrike, which forages mainly in the upper canopy, that is, the area avoided by local males. In contrast, Glase (1973) reported that his males foraged higher, not lower, than females in his New York study site, where the prime diurnal predator is the Sharp-shinned Hawk, which, unlike shrikes, does not hunt primarily in the upper canopy. Hence preferred sites seem to vary with local predator pressure. It would be interesting to see if this behavior difference had any genetic basis.

The behavior or adaptations discussed so far are present even in the absence of predators—they are anticipatory antipredator responses, as it were. The kinds of antipredator behavior discussed

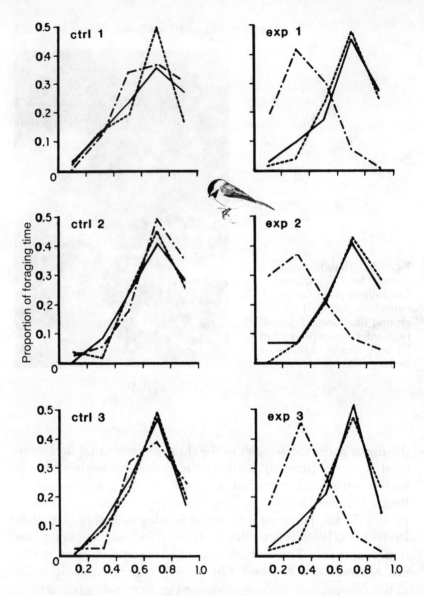

Relative height in trees

Fig. 9-4. Proportion of time spent by female Black-capped Chickadees foraging at different heights before males were removed (solid lines), when males were absent (dots and dashes), and after males had been returned to the flocks (dashed lines). Height 0 represents ground; height 1, tree top. The total number of observations for each curve is greater than 40. In each experiment (the right-hand graphs), females fed far lower in the trees with the males absent than they did in the presence of males. (From A. Desrochers, "Sex, Dominance and Microhabitat Use in Wintering Black-capped Chickadees: A Field Experiment," *Ecology* 70 (1989): 636–645. Copyright 1989 by the Ecological Society of America. Reprinted by permission.)

below are typically given only after a predator has actually been detected.

Evidently, the response may vary with the species of predator. For example, Ficken and Witkin (1977) observed winter flocks of Black-capped Chickadees responding to natural encounters with a variety of potential predators and found responses ranging from high-intensity alarm calls (high zees), given to Sharp-shinned Hawks, Northern Shrikes, and the like, through simple mobbing, to no response given to Red-shouldered Hawks (*Buteo lineatus*) and two species of squirrels (Table 9-5).

Some chickadee species can vary even a single kind of alarm call: the high zees. Evidently high zees often vary with predation risk to the calling bird. Thus high zees given by Black-capped Chickadees at the sight of a nearby mink (*Mustela vison*), which represents a relatively low risk, were lower pitched and of shorter duration than high zees given to a rapidly approaching Sharp-shinned Hawk (Ficken and Witkin 1977). Ficken (1990a) found that Mexican Chickadees (*Parus sclateri*) vary their responses in a similar manner; their high zees given in low-risk situations differ significantly in pitch from those given in high-risk situations.

Risk can also vary with how close a predator is. Alatalo and Helle (1990) presented captive Willow Tits with Hawk models at two simulated distances above their aviary. When the apparent predator passed within 10 meters (about 11 yards), no Willow Tit gave alarm calls, whereas over half of the Willow Tits tested gave alarm

Table 9-5. Responses of wintering Black-capped Chickadees to some potential predators

| Predator | Chickadee response |
| --- | --- |
| Sharp-shinned Hawk (*Accipiter striatus*) | High zees (high-intensity alarm) |
| Saw-whet Owl (*Aegolius acadicus*) | High zees |
| Northern Shrike (*Lanius excubitor*) | High zees |
| Mink (*Mustela vison*) | High zees |
| Goshawk (*Accipiter gentilis*) | Mob |
| Weasel (*Mustela* sp.) | Mob |
| Red-shouldered Hawk (*Buteo lineatus*) | No response |
| Red squirrel (*Tamiasciurus hudsonicus*) | No response |
| Gray squirrel (*Sciurus carolinensis*) | No response |

*Source:* Data from Ficken and Witkin 1977.

calls when the apparent predator passed by 40 meters away (about 44 yards).

The degree of risk a given predator species represents may also vary with season or context particularly in the case of potential nest predators. For example, although the European weasel is a well-known nest predator on various tit species (Perrins 1979), the data of Hogstad (1988a) suggest that during the winter, even older, dominant Willow Tits are not particularly alarmed by it. Similarly, Ficken and Witkin (Table 9-5) showed that wintering Black-capped Chickadees pay no attention to squirrels, although the data of Long (1982) suggest that chickadees respond to squirrels as potential predators when they get close to their nests in the breeding season.

The response may also vary with the individual and, in particular, with the experience of the individual. A growing body of evidence suggests that predator recognition—and perhaps the meaning of high zees themselves—must be learned.

Cade (1962, 1967) reported that several small passerines, including individuals of both House Sparrows (*Passer domesticus*) and Black-capped Chickadees, seemingly did not recognize Northern Shrikes as predators, thus permitting the shrikes to come dangerously close. By contrast, other, presumably more experienced, Black-capped Chickadees were clearly capable of recognizing and responding appropriately to this predator (Table 9-5). More recently, Hill (1986) reported that in fully 35.7 percent (5 out of 14) of his trials in which Tufted Titmice (*Parus bicolor*) were presented with a stuffed Merlin, the titmice did not appear to recognize it as a threat.

The necessity of learning features of predators has also been demonstrated in a variety of European small passerines. Shalter (1978b) reported data suggesting that Pied Flycatchers (*Ficedula hypoleuca*) must learn to recognize European Pygmy Owls. Working in an area in which these owls have been absent for decades, Shalter found that almost half of the breeding adult flycatchers failed to recognize stuffed Pygmy Owls close to their nests as a threat. Every nonresponder, however, when presented with a caged, live Pygmy Owl, instantly responded with strong mobbing, and subsequently mobbed the stuffed owl as well. In a remarkable series of experiments, Curio (1978) demonstrated that young European Blackbirds (*Turdus merula*) learn predator recognition by watching the behavior of adults. It is highly likely that most other passerines, including chickadees and titmice, learn in a similar fashion.

Apel and Ficken (1981) studied the alarm call behavior of very young, hand-reared Black-capped Chickadees. They found that high zees, along with the hiss, were the earliest adult calls to appear in their young birds, being first heard at approximately 18 days posthatching. At first, the young chickadees gave high zees to a wide variety of moving stimuli, including a human hand and flowers moving in a breeze; however, within a few days, the fledgling chickadees were giving high zees almost exclusively to flying birds. Interestingly enough, the young birds' responses to high zees, being immobility and sudden silence (also the usual adult response), evidently did not require any experience to appear.

Rydén (1978) showed that early experience can affect nestling Great Tits' responses to adult alarm calls. He set up three experimental groups of nestlings: one that heard alarm calls only in positive settings, one only in neutral settings, and one only in negative settings. The normal aversive response to the alarm calls was weakened in the first group, remained unchanged in the second group, and was strengthened in the third group. It would be interesting to see if similar learning could also occur in other parids.

Despite such possibilities for within-species variation, the fact remains that certain bird species (such as chickadees) are much more likely to give alarm calls than are others. For example, both Black-capped Chickadees and Tufted Titmice gave alarm calls to a given stimulus far more readily than did Downy Woodpeckers (*Picoides pubescens*) (Sullivan 1985). The chickadees were quicker to respond not only to hawk models, but also to free-flying hawks. In natural encounters with live raptors, 100 percent of both parids gave high zees or their equivalent, while only 27 percent of the woodpeckers gave alarm responses. A more graded response was given to the hawk model: most chickadees gave high zees, only half of the titmice gave equivalent calls, and less than 10 percent of the woodpeckers gave alarm calls (Table 9-6).

Sullivan (1985) proposed three possible explanations for this difference between parids and woodpeckers. By far the most likely, at least to my mind, is that both Black-capped Chickadees and (perhaps to a lesser extent) Tufted Titmice typically associate in pairs and maintain long-term pair bonds. Hence an alarm call warns an actual or potential mate (Witkin and Ficken 1979, Ficken

Table 9-6. High-intensity alarm calls given by birds to encounters with either live
raptors or hawk models

| Species | Live raptors | | Hawk models | |
|---|---|---|---|---|
| | No. of encounters | % responding | No. of encounters | % responding |
| Downy Woodpecker | 11 | 27 | 50 | 6 |
| Tufted Titmouse | 2 | 100 | 6 | 50 |
| Black-capped Chickadee | 7 | 100 | 16 | 88 |

*Source:* Data from Sullivan 1985.

et al. 1981). By contrast, Downy Woodpeckers spend only about 32
percent of their foraging time with their (presumed) mates (82 of
250 sightings: Sullivan 1985).

Another possibility proposed by Sullivan is that the alarm call of
chickadees may actually be safer to give. It is much higher in pitch
than that of woodpeckers, and might be too high for some predators to hear (see also Perrins 1968). At least two avian predators,
however, the Goshawk (*Accipiter gentilis*) and the European Pygmy
Owl, are able to perceive and localize very high alarm calls (Shalter
1978a). Other predator species such as the Sharp-shinned Hawk
may be able to as well.

Sullivan's third proposed explanation is on still less sure ground.
It is based on two equally doubtful claims: first, that chickadees
typically dive for cover in response to alarm calls, rather than
simply freezing in place (as woodpeckers typically do); and second,
that diving is actually a safer response than freezing. Sullivan argues that because chickadees dive more, and diving is safer, chickadees can more safely give alarm calls than can woodpeckers.
However, diving for cover may well be more dangerous than simply not moving (Charnov and Krebs 1975; see below); moreover,
many studies indicate that chickadees that hear alarm calls typically freeze rather than dive for cover (e.g., Witkin and Ficken
1979, Gaddis 1980).

The period of immobility after an alarm call has been studied
both in chickadees and in European tits. Gaddis (1980), looking at
the length of time Carolina Chickadees remained immobile,
searched for any correlation with such factors as flock size, time of

day, cloud cover, number of species in the flock, or habitat density; he found no significant correlation with any of them. There was not even a significant difference in period of immobility between actual attacks and simple overflights, although oddly enough Morse (1973) found that tit flocks began to forage sooner after attacks by Eurasian Sparrowhawks than after overflights.

There is a definite correlation between relative rank and the order in which birds risk approaching a feeder after a predator has appeared and then (apparently) left. For example, when Hegner (1985) flew a model Eurasian Sparrowhawk over his captive groups of Blue Tits, he found a significant negative correlation between sequence of return to the feeder and relative rank: the lowest-ranked birds consistently returned before the more dominant ones. De Laet (1985) did a similar study on free-living Great Tits, and again showed that the lowest-ranked Great Tits were the first to return to the feeders after encounters with predators, with the dominant birds coming in somewhat later (Fig. 9-5). Obviously, if the predator had still been around, those returning first would have been at greatest risk of being eaten. Duryea (1989) found that when presented with a lifelike stuffed Eastern Screech Owl, yearling Black-capped Chickadees tended to return to a feeder sooner than did adults, although there was no age-related difference in response to the control stimulus, a roll of

Fig. 9-5. Relationship between the average dominance relationship and the sequence of return to feeding by Great Tits. Rank (dominance relationship) was calculated as the proportion of the observed active and passive interactions that resulted in victories. The sequence of return was related to relative dominance, with lower-ranked birds returning earlier than more dominant individuals. $r_s = 0.659$, $n = 17$, $P < 0.05$. (From De Laet 1985, *Ibis* 127: 372–377, courtesy of the British Ornithologists' Union.)

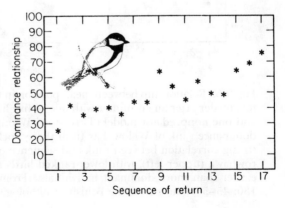

paper towels about the same height as the owl model (see also Smith et al. 1990). Hogstad (1988a) did a similar study on free-living flocks of Willow Tits. Using stuffed models of potential predators, Hogstad showed that, like Great and Blue Tits, Willow Tits also exhibit a strong negative correlation between rank and sequence of return after encountering a Eurasian Sparrowhawk. Hogstad also found similar strong, but not necessarily significant, correlations in response to three other potential predators: Siberian Jay (*Perisoreus infaustus*), Hooded Crow (*Corvus corone*), and Pygmy Owl; by contrast, there was no correlation between rank and order of return after the Willow Tits had encountered either a model of a harmless woodpecker or of a weasel (Fig. 9-6). This

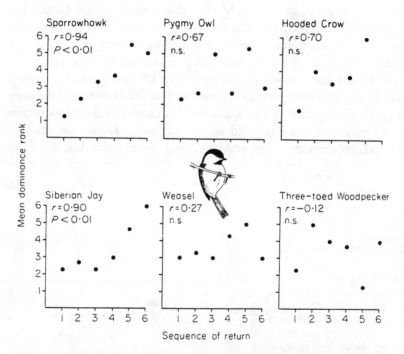

Fig. 9-6. Relationship between mean position in the sequence of return to a feeder after an encounter with one of five lifelike predator models and one nonpredator model (Three-toed Woodpecker) and the mean dominance rank of Willow Tits from three flocks. Note especially the strong correlation between rank and sequence of return for the Sparrowhawk (upper left), with lower-ranked birds returning significantly earlier than more dominant individuals. (From Hogstad 1988a, *Ibis*, 130: 45–56, courtesy of the British Ornithologists' Union.)

weasel is a known nest predator on tits (Perrins 1979), but is evidently not likely to attack full-grown tits in the nonbreeding season.

Why do subordinate parids risk moving or returning to a feeder before dominants? Part of the explanation might be that they are inexperienced: most subordinates are young, relatively naive birds. Another, possibly more important, factor may be relative hunger levels. If high rank conveys any advantage at finding or obtaining food, then dominants could well afford to wait a bit longer than hungrier, lower-ranked birds before returning to a feeder. In this context, the findings of Waite and Grubb (1987) are particularly interesting. They studied the reactions of captive groups of Tufted Titmice to a taped alarm call, and found that although subordinates resumed activity significantly sooner than did dominants, there was no correlation between rank and sequence of return to the feeders. They attributed the lack of correlation, at least in part, to the unnatural abundance of food in the aviaries—even their lowest ranked captive titmouse was probably not much hungrier than the dominant birds.

What is the real function of alarm calls? Researchers have argued convincingly that, at least for chickadees, a major function may be warning a mate (Witkin and Ficken 1979, Sullivan 1985). It is well known that parids maintain pair bonds for years, and pairs typically forage close together within winter flocks (Ficken et al. 1981). Given that older mates are often more productive than younger ones (Howitz 1986a, Ekman 1990), saving one's mate may benefit the caller as well as the mate.

A radically different function of alarm calls was proposed in 1975 by Charnov and Krebs. Essentially what they said is that the calling bird knows two things: there is a predator, and the predator is over *there*. However, the alarm call conveys only one of these: it discloses the presence of a predator, but not its location. Birds that move in response to these calls may be considerably more at risk than the caller itself, which is why Charnov and Krebs suggested that alarm calls may, at least sometimes, be more accurately called manipulation of others than any form of altruism. Witkin and Ficken (1979) argued that, since most chickadees freeze on hearing high zees, it is probably not manipulation in chickadees. On a within-species basis, I agree—other chickadees are probably seldom put in greater danger by hearing a flockmate's high zees. At the interspecific level, however, some manipulation may be occurring. Some species that form mixed-species flocks with chickadees are known to scatter on hearing high zees (Gaddis 1980). According to Charnov and Krebs's line of reasoning, any manipulation of nonchickadees would still further increase the selective advantage of the calling chickadees' giving high zees.

A third potential use of alarm calls was demonstrated by Møller (1988). Working with free-flying Great Tits in Denmark in an area where sparrows of the genus *Passer* were effective competitors for food with Great Tits, especially at concentrated food sources, he noticed that local wintering Great Tits regularly gave false alarm calls—that is, they gave alarm calls even when no actual or potential predator was around. He showed that the responses of birds hearing taped false alarm calls was indistinguishable from their response to tapes of real (predator-generated) alarm calls. What is fascinating is that the Great Tits were selective in when they gave false alarm calls. They gave them significantly more at concentrated than at dispersed food sources, and, at concentrated food sources, significantly more in the presence of competing sparrows than when foraging alone (Table 9-7). Moreover, the use of false alarm calls varied with rank. Dominant Great Tits used false alarm calls when another dominant was present, but not when only subordinates were present; by contrast, lower-ranked Great Tits gave false alarm calls both if dominant and if subordinate Great Tits were present (Table 9-8). Finally, false alarm calls were used particularly at times of increased feeding rates, that is, during snowstorms and in the early morning and late afternoon (Møller 1988). Interestingly, Gaddis (1980) reported that, of 55 instances of ob-

Table 9-7. Number of Great Tits giving false alarm calls during 30 min of observation in response to the presence of sparrows and food dispersion

| Food dispersion | Presence of sparrows | Giving alarm calls | Not giving alarm calls | $P$[a] |
|---|---|---|---|---|
| Concentrated | Present | 10 | 2 | 0.00032 |
| Concentrated | Absent | 1 | 11 | |
| Dispersed | Present | 2 | 10 | 0.24 |
| Dispersed | Absent | 0 | 12 | |

Source: Møller 1988, courtesy of *Ethology*.
[a]According to Fisher exact probability test.

Table 9-8. Number of Great Tits giving false alarm calls during 30 min of observation in relation to the dominance rank of the bird giving alarm calls and that of the Great Tit present at the feeder

| Dominance rank of bird giving alarm call | Dominance rank of bird at food | No. of Great Tits | | $P$[a] |
|---|---|---|---|---|
| | | Giving alarm call | Not giving alarm call | |
| Dominant | Dominant | 5 | 1 | 0.0076 |
| Dominant | Subdominant | 0 | 6 | |
| Subdominant | Dominant | 6 | 0 | 0.23 |
| Subdominant | Subdominant | 4 | 2 | |

*Source:* Møller 1988, courtesy of *Ethology.*
[a]According to Fisher exact probability test.

served alarm responses in mixed Carolina Chickadee and Tufted Titmouse flocks, fully 26 occurred when he could see no likely cause for alarm. It may well be that North American parids, like Møller's Great Tits, also use alarm calls deceptively as a means of gaining unchallenged access to food. This seems a particularly interesting area for future research.

High zees are most often given when the caller spots a rapidly approaching predator. By contrast, when chickadees encounter stationary predators, such as perched hawks or owls, they often respond by mobbing. Mobbing is usually performed by two or more birds that assemble around a predator, often within a meter of it. The mobbing birds typically change positions frequently and often perform relatively stereotyped wing and tail movements while giving loud calls, usually with a broad frequency spectrum (Curio 1978). The Black-capped Chickadee's mobbing call typically includes versions of the chick-a-dee call complex (Ficken, Ficken and Witkin 1978). A mobbing assembly generally builds up within less than a minute after the first individual has begun mobbing. A prey bird in the grasp of, or close to, a predator will enhance the level of mobbing elicited (Curio 1978).

Shedd (1983) studied mobbing by Black-capped Chickadees, looking in particular at how mobbing intensity varied with time of year. He found that chickadees mob all year, with the greatest intensity occurring in July, August, and September (Fig. 9-7). Shedd seemed to suggest that the late summer peak primarily reflects mobbing done by recently fledged chickadees. I would think, however, that much of the mobbing done at this time would

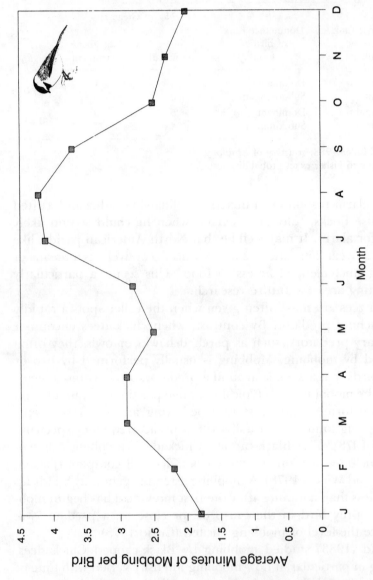

Fig. 9-7. Seasonal variation in mobbing responses of free-living Black-capped Chickadees to a stuffed Eastern Screech Owl. The peak intensity occurred in July and August and there was no season in which mobbing intensity fell to zero. (Data from Shedd 1983, courtesy of *Wilson Bulletin*.)

be by parents still accompanied by dependent offspring, especially since one of the best-documented functions of mobbing is cultural transmission of predator recognition from one generation to the next (Curio et al. 1978). The fact that chickadees mob all year is apparently rather unusual; several passerines, such as American Robins (*Turdus migratorius*) mob only during and immediately after the breeding season (Shedd 1983). Two factors may contribute to this difference. One is that chickadees have a long-term association with, and investment in, their mates, something American Robins are not known to have. A second factor is that chickadees are sedentary, while robins are migratory. The "move-on" hypothesis (Curio 1978) states that sedentary species should mob more persistently than migrant species because, unlike migrants, sedentary species can escape completely only if they can drive local predators away.

So far I have considered antipredator behavior by only fully grown birds away from the nest. Much work has also been done on various aspects of the nest defense behavior of chickadees and titmice.

Bill sweeping (Kilham 1968) is a kind of behavior, generally interpreted as nest defense, that until recently only White-breasted Nuthatches (*Sitta carolinensis*) were known to do. Ficken and Ficken (1987) recently discovered that at least one parid, the Mexican Chickadee, also performs bill-sweeping behavior. This behavior evidently makes use of defensive secretions by certain insects, primarily beetles. The bird holds such insects in its bill, then sweeps or dabs the insects onto the area just below the nest hole. The scent is thought to help repel climbing species trying to enter the nest, especially those with well-developed senses of smell such as mammals or reptiles. Meanwhile, because birds generally have a very poorly developed sense of smell, the scent would not bother them at all. Ficken and Ficken (1987) pointed out that their area contained large numbers of potential mammalian and reptilian predators, which might well be repelled by these defensive secretions. Perhaps other chickadees living in similar circumstances may have developed similar behavior.

Incubating or brooding adults, as well as nestlings, can give the snake display (see Vocalizations, Visual Displays, Chapter 4) if cornered in the nest cavity. If nothing else, this tactic may permit the adult to escape and breed again (Perrins 1979). Once out, she and/or her mate can then give the nest distraction display, which, together with mobbing behavior, may drive the predator away. There even exists one report (which I confess I find hard to believe) suggesting that a pair of adult Carolina Chickadees may have carried their nestlings away, presumably to a new site, after the original nest had been disturbed (Goertz and Rutherford 1972).

Studies done by Eberhard Curio and his colleagues in West Germany focused on just how much risk an adult Great Tit will undertake to defend its nest (e.g., Curio et al. 1983, 1984, 1985; Regelmann and Curio 1983; Regelmann and Curio 1986). This team found many interesting things concerning Great Tit nest defense levels. For example, Great Tits apparently have no difficulty in distinguishing among various predator species and tend to give response levels correlated with the particular predator's degree of specialization on Great Tits (Curio et al. 1983). The level of defense generally increases with advanced time in the breeding season, as well as with the age of young being defended, and (for a population in which second broods are common) also with the number of young in second broods (Curio et al. 1984), but not with the weight of the offspring (Curio and Regelmann 1987).

How closely a male will approach a predator depends in part on whether his mate is nearby: when she is present, he will approach much closer. This behavior suggests an additional, social role of male defense behavior (Curio et al. 1985). Moreover, male Great Tits typically spend more energy and take bigger risks in predator defense than do females (Curio et al. 1983). This may be, at least in part, because of the male's greater interest in protecting his mate or his territory or both (Regelmann and Curio 1986). To date, no comparable study has been done on any North American parid. This is clearly another very interesting area for future research.

### Effects of Winter Starvation

Once productivity ends in the autumn, the amount of available natural food in an area is generally not replenished until spring; hence food supplies go steadily down throughout the winter. The diminishing food supply coupled with the increased energy demands imposed by cold temperatures and the shorter photoperiods available for foraging make winter starvation seem to be a very real possibility.

Some of these adverse effects can be alleviated to a certain extent by such adaptations as hypothermia and food hoarding (Jansson et al. 1981; see Chapter 8). Nevertheless, some winter energy stress must still be experienced. How well such conditions will be tolerated must depend, among other things, on the species, the latitude, and the relative severity of the local winter.

Jansson et al. (1981) did a fine study of food supply and its effects on autumn and winter mortality of Willow and Crested (*Parus cristatus*) Tits in Scandinavia. They used two well-separated study areas, only one of which was given extra food. Supplemental food induced increased immigration and settling during flock formation; moreover, it greatly increased overwinter survival of both species (Fig. 9-8). Earlier European studies, mostly on yearly variations in natural food supply, produced similar results (e.g., Gibb 1960, van Balen 1980).

Other studies have looked at how winter food levels affect the survival of Black-capped Chickadees. In a relatively early one, Samson and Lewis (1979) reported finding no difference in overwinter survival between supplemented and unsupplemented chickadee flocks. Unfortunately, it is rather difficult to interpret these results. For one thing, the number of birds studied was very small: there were only eight chickadees living in the unsupplemented area. Even worse, however, is the fact that the two areas (one being supplemented and the other being the so-called control) bordered on one another. Because chickadees are known to move into adjacent home ranges when food is scarce (e.g., Mueller 1973, Desrochers et al. 1988), it is highly likely that the control flock did visit the feeder occasionally. Given these sources of error, it is not surprising that no difference in survival was found between the two groups.

Desrochers et al. (1988) worked on two well-separated sites (one supplemented, the other as a control) in northern Alberta. They found that overwinter survival was greater in their supplemented area than it was in the control area for both years of their study. Hence food abundance in the natural site could have been limiting winter survival of their chickadees.

Brittingham and Temple (1988) did a three-year study in Wisconsin on the effects of supplemental food on winter chickadee survival. This carefully designed experiment involved replicate sites, with control (unsupplemented) areas each at least 2 km (1¼ miles) from the nearest feeder. Brittingham and Temple found significantly better winter survival in supplemented areas, calcu-

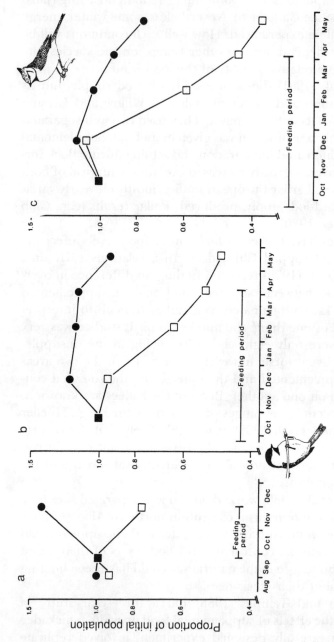

Fig. 9-8. Population changes in control (open squares) and experimental, food-supplemented (filled dots) populations of Willow Tits (a, b) and Crested Tits (c), autumn 1977 (a) and winter 1976–77 (b, c). Population size is expressed in proportions of the number present at the start of supplemental feeding (a) or at the first population estimate (b, c). For technical reasons, no population estimates were obtained at the very start of feeding in winter (b, c). For both species, populations in areas with feeders survived much better than those in unsupplemented, control areas. (From Jansson et al. 1981, courtesy of *Oikos*.)

Table 9-9. Monthly and seasonal Black-capped Chickadee survival rates on control and experimental (food-supplemented) sites

| | Control sites | | Experimental sites | | | |
|---|---|---|---|---|---|---|
| Measurement interval | $\bar{X} \pm$ SD | No. of estimates | $\bar{X} \pm$ SD | No. of estimates | $t$ | $P$ |
| Monthly (Oct–Apr) | 0.87 ± 0.14 | 27 | 0.95 ± 0.06 | 48 | 3.49 | <.01 |
| Overwinter (Oct–Apr) | 0.37 ± 0.12 | 6 | 0.69 ± 0.20 | 9 | 3.48 | <.01 |
| Oversummer (May–Sep) | 0.86 ± 0.09 | 4 | 0.90 ± 0.10 | 6 | 0.64 | >.25 |

*Source:* M. C. Brittingham and S. A. Temple, "Impacts of Supplemental Feeding on Survival Rates f Black-capped Chickadees," *Ecology* 69 (1988): 581–589. Copyright 1989 by the Ecological ociety of America. Reprinted by permission.

lated both by month and for the winter as a whole (Table 9-9). Moreover, the survival differences between the two site types were apparently restricted to months having relatively prolonged periods of severe weather and were essentially nonexistent in milder months (Table 9-10). Brittingham and Temple concluded that natural winter food supply may be sufficient to support chickadees during mild or even average winter weather, but in winters where temperatures become extremely cold, especially for extended periods, starvation is likely to result. Given that Wisconsin is fairly far south in the overall geographic range of Black-capped Chickadees, winter starvation is likely a regular, and potentially major, source of mortality for this species.

Table 9-10. Monthly survival rates of Black-capped Chickadees on control and experimental (food-supplemented) sites during months with moderate or severe winter weather

| | Control sites | | Experimental sites | |
|---|---|---|---|---|
| Weather during month | $\bar{X} \pm$ SD | No. of estimates | $\bar{X} \pm$ SD | No. of estimates |
| Moderate (≤ 5 d below −18° C) | 0.92 ± 0.08 | 21 | 0.96 ± 0.06 | 36 |
| Severe (> 5 d below −18° C) | 0.67 ± 0.13 | 6 | 0.93 ± 0.08 | 12 |

*Source:* M. C. Brittingham and S. A. Temple, "Impacts of Supplemental Feeding on Survival Rate of Black-capped Chickadees," *Ecology* 69 (1988): 581–589. Copyright 1989 by the Ecological Society of America. Reprinted by permission.

Parasites and Diseases

I have come across rather few reports of diseases in chickadees or titmice. Nonetheless, where chickadees join other species at crowded feeders, several diseases could be picked up from other species. For example, chickadees and titmice may occasionally become infected with *Salmonella,* bacteria known to infect various seed-eating birds (Fichtel 1978). While species such as House Sparrows (*Passer domesticus*) get salmonellosis more commonly, it may occur in various passerine species congregating at feeders in the winter (Locke et al. 1973, Brittingham and Temple 1986). Individuals that take seeds from the ground below feeders (as chickadees sometimes do) are particularly susceptible, because the disease is passed through infected birds' droppings. Infection with *Salmonella* can cause acute illness in passerines and often results in death within a short period (Brittingham et al. 1988). Another disease, more commonly known in waterfowl but also known to infect both House and White-crowned Sparrows (*Zonotrichia leucophrys*) as well as other passerines (Snipes et al. 1988), is avian cholera (*Pasteurella multocida*). Again, chickadees and titmice that gather at feeders might be susceptible, especially where droppings can mix with the food. Crowded conditions at such food sources and poor body conditions due to cold weather are likely to contribute to outbreaks. Regular disposal of litter from below feeders can help to slow the spread of such diseases.

Brittingham et al. (1988) examined the prevalence of several bacterial species in Black-capped Chickadees. Surprisingly, they found that the prevalence of at least two genera of bacteria was significantly less in birds using feeders than it was in birds from feederless areas. This result, however, is almost certainly due to the fact that one of their feederless areas contained a horse farm, where chickadees often fed by picking seeds out of horse manure: a most effective way to increase their load of bacteria. The prevalence of bacteria did not differ between male and female chickadees. As might be expected, the cumulative mortality rates of infected birds were consistently higher than the rates of noninfected birds, although the differences were not significant. Brittingham and her colleagues remarked that, although the infections (at the levels observed) may cause slight reductions in survival rates, more data would be needed before any further conclusions could be made.

Recently, Lyme disease has been discovered in several species of wild birds (Anderson et al. 1990, Burgess 1990). It is a bacterial infection caused by the spirochete *Borrelia burgdorferi*, and although it is generally transmitted through the bites of ticks, Burgess (1990) recently found that at least sometimes it can be transmitted directly from bird to bird through simple contact. To date, I know of no reports of Lyme disease in any parid, but it seems entirely possible that some chickadees or titmice could be infected. How infection would affect chickadee survival is not yet known. Meanwhile, banders should take appropriate precautions when handling wild birds (see Banding, Chapter 2).

Both Carolina Chickadees and Tufted Titmice are known to be susceptible to infection by eastern encephalitis, an arthropod-borne viral disease (Herman 1962). Other parids, including Black-capped Chickadees, are likely to be equally susceptible to this disease.

Most of the studies that contain data on the ectoparasites found on chickadees and titmice (e.g., Peters 1936, Bequaert 1955, Wheeler and Threlfall 1986, Spicer 1987) have remarked on the relatively light intensity of infection on these parids, as compared with many other bird species. For example, Peters (1936) found just three kinds of ectoparasites on Black-capped Chickadees: a louse (*Ricinus* sp.), a hippoboscid fly, or "louse-fly" (*Ornithoica confluenta*), and a mite (*Analgopsis passerinus*). Bequaert (1955), working only with hippoboscid flies, reported two kinds known to occur (rarely) on Black-capped Chickadees: *Ornithoica vicinia* and *Ornithomyia fringillina*; the latter is known to occur on Boreal (*Parus hudsonicus*) and Chestnut-backed Chickadees (Bequaert 1955) and on Tufted Titmice (Brackbill 1970) as well. Wheeler and Threlfall (1986) examined both Black-capped and Boreal Chickadees in Newfoundland, searching for fleas, lice, louse-flies, and mites. They found only low levels of lice on both chickadee species and failed to find any other kind of ectoparasite.

By contrast, many European tits are evidently affected by large numbers of fleas (Perrins 1979, DuFeu 1987). Flea infestations are especially prevalent in species that use nest boxes. The Black-capped Chickadees' habit of excavating a new cavity every time they nest serves to avoid the buildup of such parasites that can occur in more regularly used cavities. Certain other chickadee species, especially those that live primarily in coniferous forests, such as Mountain and Chestnut-backed Chickadees, do reuse nest sites (Gold and Dahlsten 1983, Hill and Lein 1988); such species may be more vulnerable to ectoparasite buildup than are Black-capped Chickadees. Gold and Dahlsten (1983), working in both interior and coastal California, managed to get good numbers of both Chestnut-backed and Mountain Chickadees to breed in nest boxes. These nest boxes were frequently reused year after year. Gold and Dahlsten found that many of the nests became infested with the blood-sucking larvae of flies of the genus *Protocalliphora*. Rather surprisingly, virtually none of the coastal nests were infested, and the fly larvae that did occur there showed very poor development. Gold and Dahlsten suggest that possibly some environmental factor exists in the coastal area that is unsuitable for these flies. By contrast, the interior sites clearly lack this factor: more than 90 percent of the chickadee nests were infested with *Protocalliphora* larvae. Infestation levels varied, but one nest had more than 45 fly larvae per fledgling. There was no significant difference in infestation level between the two chickadee species. Incredibly, nestling mortality, even in the heavily infested interior sites, was low and did not seem to be affected by the parasites. Even the brood with 45 *Protocalliphora* per nestling managed to fledge normally. However, Gold and Dahlsten (1983) suggest that fledglings stressed by blood losses resulting from heavy fly infestations are likely to have reduced postfledging survival.

The most detailed information I have been able to find for internal parasites in chickadees and titmice concerns species found in the blood. Evidently, the most prevalent kind, at least in Black-capped and Boreal Chickadees, is a protozoan of the genus *Leucocytozoon* (Bennett et al. 1975; Greiner et al. 1975). A recent paper (Bennett and Pierce 1989) has just described a new blood parasite, *Hepatozoon parus*, for which the Black-capped Chickadee is the type host. Very low levels of other blood parasites, including *Haemoproteus*, *Plasmodium* (malaria), and *Trypanosoma*, have also been recorded in various chickadees and titmice (Greiner et al. 1975). Evidently little is known about helminth (worm) parasites in chickadees and titmice; nevertheless, tapeworms are known from at least some parid species (Gaikwad and Shinde 1984).

One other kind of parasite should be mentioned here: the social parasite, namely Brown-headed Cowbirds (*Molothrus ater*). Chickadees are protected from cowbird parasitism by two factors: their small size and the fact that they nest in holes. Very few chickadee nest cavities have entrances big enough for a female cowbird to enter; hence records of cowbird eggs in chickadee nests are rare. Indeed, Friedmann et al. (1977) reported a total of only six records for Black-capped Chickadees. An additional, very unusual case was reported by Lowther (1983), who found a Black-capped Chickadee nest containing three cowbird eggs. Incredibly, the pair managed to raise all three cowbirds to at least 20 days of age. One wonders if either member of the chickadee pair survived to breed again.

### Interspecific Competition

Competition can occur both between members of the same species (intraspecific competition) and between members of two different species (interspecific competition). Within-species competition has been discussed in several places already (especially throughout Chapters 3 and 7); this section focuses on competition with other species. Moreover, it deals primarily with competition between parids. It is often assumed that the more closely related two species are, the more intense the competition between them will be, because usually the degree of relatedness reflects to some extent the amount of overlap of needed resources.

Recently the importance of interspecific competition in field conditions has been challenged, and its very existence has been claimed to be unproven (e.g., Simberloff 1983, Strong 1983; see also Schoener 1982, 1983). What Simberloff and others have contended is that rigorous field experiments that provide undeniable evidence of the existence of interspecific competition are rare. Indeed, even among ecologists who are convinced of the importance of interspecific competition, estimates on how many rigorous field demonstrations actually exist can vary (see, for example, Schoener 1983; Connell 1983 and also Ferson et al. 1986).

By definition, if competition is actually occurring, then the fitness of individuals exposed to it should be reduced (Roughgarden 1983, Gustafsson 1987). Yet fitness of organisms living in the field is often extremely difficult to measure. Several sorts of evidence have been sought, especially in studies on parids. First, ecologists have tried to find whether manipulation of the numbers of one species affects either the population density (e.g., Dhondt and Eyckerman 1980b) or foraging-site selection (e.g., Alatalo et al. 1985) of the other species. Another approach involves studies in the breeding season, seeking to find whether increases in the density of one species have any effect on the breeding productivity of the other species (e.g., Minot 1981, Perrins 1990). Other effects of competition to look for are increased population turnover and reduced adult survival (Dhondt 1989b).

Many of the studies on parid competition are related to foraging—competition either for food or for particular foraging locations—by winter flocks of three or more species of European tits (e.g., Alatalo 1982, Alatalo et al. 1987). Such flocks are not uncommon, and there is abundant evidence that competition exists among these tit species. Some of this evidence is nonexperimental, essentially studying foraging behavior of birds in areas where they forage alone and comparing solitary foraging with how tits forage when with other parids. In general, it is exactly this sort of "evidence" that Simberloff and others have argued is inconclusive. Nevertheless, Alatalo et al. (1986) continue to contend that at least some of these nonexperimental studies can provide valid evidence for the existence of competition among tit species. In addition, there are several excellent experimental studies, involving removals (e.g., Alatalo 1982; Alatalo et al. 1985, 1987), to support conclusions drawn from the nonexperimental studies. For example, Willow Tit flocks foraging in spruce trees will change what parts of the tree they forage in, depending on which (if any) species they are foraging with (Fig. 9-9). Such competition can affect survivorship in two ways: first by affecting quality and quantity of food available to a bird, and second, by affecting a bird's access to the foraging sites that are most protected from predators.

Obviously, competition will be most severe when resources are in shortest supply. One such time is in late winter; another is potentially during the breeding season, especially after the young have hatched. Minot (1981) studied competition for food between breeding Great and Blue Tits in England. He found that Great Tit breeding success, as measured by the mean fledging weight of chicks, was negatively correlated with the density of breeding Blue Tits, although, interestingly, Blue Tit breeding success was not affected by the density of Great Tits. Dhondt and Eyckerman (1980a) found similar results in their study area in Belgium. Indeed, recent evidence suggests interspecific effects occur even earlier in the breeding season. Perrins (1990) reported that clutch size of both Blue and Great Tits in Wytham Wood varied not only with their own population density, but also, remarkably, with the population density of the other species.

Fig. 9-9. The effects of competition on foraging location of Willow Tits in northern Finland during winter. The graphs show the average tree part score in spruce for each Willow Tit flock, in the presence of Crested Tits (above); while foraging alone (middle); and in the presence of Great Tits (below). Tree parts are scored from larger to smaller diameter (1 = trunk; 2 = branch diameter over 8 mm; 3 = twig; 4 = needled twig). Black arrows indicate the average tree part score for the Willow Tit flocks in each situation, and open arrows give the average tree part score of the putative competitor. The Willow Tits shifted their foraging to be more toward the larger, inner tree parts in the presence of Crested Tits, while in the presence of the much larger Great Tits, the Willow Tits shifted to forage much more on the thin, outer branches. (From Alatalo 1982, courtesy of Rauno Alatalo.)

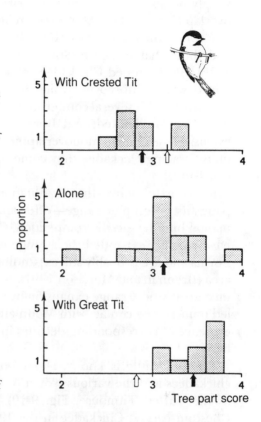

Competition among North American chickadees and titmice may be considerably less severe. Hill and Lein (1988, 1989a, 1989b) did studies, somewhat similar to Minot's, on breeding Black-capped and Mountain Chickadees living in the same area in southwestern Alberta. They found the two species had major differences in foraging behavior, and concluded that the two did not compete for food during the breeding season. Indeed, they found that in encounters between the two species territorial residents largely ignored heterospecific invaders (Hill and Lein 1989b). Unfortunately, Hill and Lein did not present data from areas that have only one chickadee species present, to confirm that the observed foraging differences were not, in fact, generated by competition. While Hill and Lein's conclusions may well be correct, further data are needed to confirm them.

Winter food competition among chickadees, if not less severe, is certainly far less complex than it often is among European parids, simply because North American parids have so much less range overlap (Dixon 1961). Some researchers speak of dividing parids into two distinct categories: those that forage primarily in conifers and those that forage mostly in deciduous woods (e.g., Perrins 1979). Black-capped Chickadees typically forage in deciduous or mixed woods. Moreover, while their geographic range overlaps extensively with several coniferous-dwelling species such as Mountain, Chestnut-backed, and Boreal Chickadees, they are almost exclusively allopatric (nonoverlapping) with the one other decid- uous-foraging chickadee they come in contact with: the Carolina Chickadee.

Range extensions—that is, situations in which one species ex- pands its geographic range—offer an interesting source of infor- mation on interspecific competition. Chestnut-backed Chickadees have recently expanded their range in the Sierra Nevada of Cal- ifornia and are probably still expanding it in the San Francisco Bay area (Brennan and Morrison 1991). Brennan and Morrison exam- ined areas where range expansion by Chestnut-backed Chickadees led to increased contact with Mountain Chickadees, and found no evidence of corresponding declines in Mountain Chickadee num- bers.

Relatively little is known about possible competition between chickadees and the various North American crested titmice (such as the Tufted Titmouse, Fig. 9-10). A range extension by the Chestnut-backed Chickadee in the 1950s and 1960s caused it to come in contact with the Plain Titmouse (*Parus inornatus*) in Cal- ifornia, but no evidence of severe interspecific competition be- tween the two was detected (Dixon 1954, Root 1964). Currently, still another range extension is taking place, this time by the Tufted Titmouse, which is expanding its range northward in east- ern North America (Kricher 1981), thus coming into ever greater contact with Black-capped Chickadees. Loery and Nichols (1985) and Loery et al. (1987) published data suggesting that Black- capped Chickadee populations are, at least to some extent, ad- versely affected by initial contact with the titmice. My own data seem to support this view (Smith 1990). This range extension is still going on; more studies are needed to determine the extent of the effect that invading Tufted Titmice actually have on resident chickadee numbers, foraging, and productivity.

Fig. 9-10. The Tufted Titmouse, a much larger species than the Black-capped Chickadee, is a potential competitor wherever the two species' ranges overlap. (© F. K. Schleicher / VIREO.)

Other resources, besides food and foraging sites, can also be in short supply. One such resource is nest sites. Evidently European tits compete fiercely for nest boxes (Perrins 1979), and, among some species, even for natural cavities. For example, apparently Blue Tits sometimes evict Willow Tits from the cavities they have just excavated (Perrins 1979). Among chickadees, nest-site competition is probably most severe among species that live primarily in coniferous habitats, where natural nest sites are relatively rare. For deciduous-woodland species such as Black-capped Chickadees, nest-site competition most frequently involves nonparids such as House Wrens, which typically occupy far more nest sites than they actually use for breeding (Kluyver 1961, Brewer 1963), rather than other chickadees or titmice.

### Age-specific Survival Rates

Before discussing age-specific survival rates, a few definitions are in order. A population is the total number of individuals of a given species living in a given area. Two commonly used attributes of populations are survival and mortality rates. These rates are inevitably bound together—in fact, survival is the converse of mortality. Thus if a population has a survival rate of 60 percent over a given period, then 40 percent disappeared during that time. It is therefore impossible to talk about survival in a population without also referring to mortality.

Earlier in this chapter, I referred briefly to various estimates of the average life span for Black-capped Chickadees (Table 9-3). Not all members of a population have an equal chance of reaching this age or beyond, however. It is generally accepted that in most avian populations, survivorship for individuals less than a year old tends to be considerably lower than it is for older birds (e.g., Lack 1946, von Haartman 1971). Among parids, this is true not only for Black-capped Chickadees (e.g., Speirs 1963, Loery et al. 1987) but for many European titmice (Dhondt 1979; Perrins 1979; Ekman 1984a) as well.

Exactly when these young birds disappear is not always well known. The most thorough and detailed studies on juvenile mortality have, for the most part, been done in Europe. The first period of lowered survival is between fledging and the end of juvenile dispersal in many species, including Great Tits (e.g., Geer 1978; Perrins 1979) and Willow Tits (Ekman 1984a). Ekman noted a sharp late-summer (period between fledging and the end of juvenile dispersal) decrease in overall juvenile Willow Tit numbers in all six years of his study; moreover, yearlings overall experienced far steeper mortality than did adults (Fig. 9-11). Indeed, some investigators (e.g., Perrins 1965) have suggested that postfledging survival may have a major impact on the level of breeding numbers the following spring, at least in some Great Tit populations (see Population Dynamics, below).

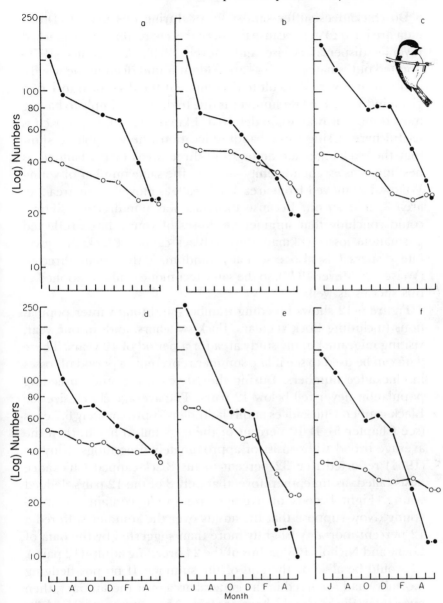

Fig. 9-11. Seasonal changes in Willow Tit numbers, showing both adults (open circles) and yearlings (closed circles), for different seasons and for six consecutive years, from 1974–75 (a) to 1979–80 (f). Numbers are given on a log scale so that the line slope is proportional to the mortality rate. (From Ekman 1984a, courtesy of *Journal of Animal Ecology*.)

Do chickadees suffer similar losses during this period? Direct data are hard to get because the period is characterized by marked juvenile dispersal (Weise and Meyer 1979). As Perrins (1979) pointed out, small songbirds are seldom found dead in the woods, and thus it is very difficult to determine if the disappearance of a given individual in late summer is due to death or simply to having moved too far away to be detected. Ekman's (1984a) approach is useful here. Using three banding locations, he was able to show that the exchange rate among the three areas of tits banded as nestlings was essentially unity—that is, the same number of young Willow Tits moved from area 1 to area 2 as moved from area 2 to area 1, and so on. Because dispersal was nondirected, Ekman could conclude that summer net losses of young birds reflected permanent losses (Ekman 1984a). Black-capped Chickadee juvenile dispersal is also essentially random, rather than directed (Weise and Meyer 1979), so the same technique could be applied to this species as well.

Figure 9-12 shows breeding numbers and total winter populations (including flock regulars, flock switchers, and, in one year, visiting migrants) in my study area for a period of 10 years. These data can be used to see if late summer represents a period of losses in chickadee numbers. During the 10 years, the study breeding population never fell below 12 pairs. The average clutch size for Black-capped Chickadees at this latitude is approximately 6.7 eggs (see Chapter 5). If 10 percent of the eggs fail to hatch, then the average brood will consist of approximately 6 nestlings. Kluyver (1961) reported that 32 percent of his Black-capped Chickadee nests failed; assume, therefore, that only 8 of the 12 pairs fledged young. Eight broods of average size would contain about 48 young. Now suppose that the adults over the summer suffered a 12 percent mortality (slightly more than suggested by the data of Loery and Nichols 1985): thus of the 24 breeding adults (12 pairs), 21 would be alive by the end of the summer. If no postfledging mortality had occurred in the general area over the summer, then my winter flocks should have contained an average of 21 adults plus 48 young, for a total of 69 birds (or more, in years when the breeding density was higher). In only one year of the study did the winter population even approach this number—and that year, 7 of the wintering birds were migrants. In fact, the average winter

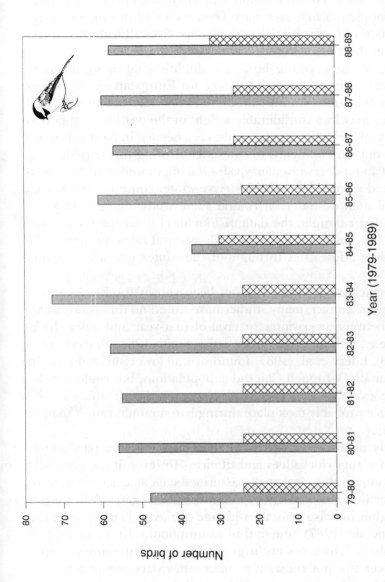

Fig. 9-12. Winter (shaded bars) and breeding (cross-hatched bars) densities in a western Massachusetts Black-capped Chickadee population over a 10-year period. The breeding density remained remarkably stable, and any fluctuations in breeding numbers were evidently not correlated with fluctuations in winter densities.

population in my study area over the 10-year period was only about 57 birds. Thus the summer postfledging losses in my chickadee population may well have been about 12 out of 48, or approximately 25 percent. This percentage fits well with the figures found in the European studies.

Some of these young birds are doubtless taken by breeding predators, as has been shown so well for European tits (e.g., Geer 1982). Others may simply starve; there is evidence that Great Tit juveniles may lose considerable weight in the postfledging period (Perrins 1965, 1979). Similar studies are needed in North America to find out what happens to chickadees during this period.

What about overwinter survival? One might well think that inexperienced young birds would survive winter conditions somewhat less well than do older birds, and some studies suggest that this is true. For example, the data of Ekman (1984a) for Willow Tits (Fig. 9-11) clearly show that juvenile survival rates continue to be lower than adult rates throughout the winter (see also Hogstad 1988d).

Nevertheless, the same has not been shown for Black-capped Chickadees. In fact, many studies have found no difference whatsoever between overwinter survival of first-year and older chickadees (e.g., Odum 1942a; Glase 1973; Smith 1984; Desrochers et al. 1988). Loery et al. (1987) found overall lower survival rates in first-year Black-capped Chickadee populations, but could not determine exactly when these differences occurred; much of the difference probably took place during late summer, rather than in the winter.

Clearly at least some parts of their first year are particularly hard on young chickadees and titmice. However, it has generally been assumed that, for small passerines such as chickadees, once past that first year, adults experience survival rates that are not only higher but also constant with age (e.g., von Haartman 1971). Loery et al. (1987) tested this assumption with Black-capped Chickadees. Their results showed that survival rates of adult chickadees are not constant—rather, they decrease at a rate of about 3.5 percent per year. This is still a relatively slow decline; even six-year-old chickadees have better average survival rates than do yearling chickadees (Loery et al. 1987). Future studies may show that such declines in adult survivorship are common for many other bird species as well.

**Population Dynamics**

Population Stability

If a population is stable, then, on average, birth plus immigration must equal death plus emigration. Even if a population can be shown to be stable, however, there will always be some fluctuations in numbers from year to year.

Brennan and Morrison (1991) analyzed 41 years of Christmas bird counts for Black-capped, Mountain, and Chestnut-backed Chickadees, and reported that most locations (76–83 percent) showed no long-term increases or decreases in number of chickadees detected per observer hour for any of the three species. This certainly suggests widespread stability, although as McCallum (1990) pointed out, local population crashes can be obscured by immigration.

By far the best long-term series of population estimates for Black-capped Chickadees from one place is that of Loery and Nichols (1985), which reports estimates for the period from 1959 through 1982 (Fig. 9-13). While considerable fluctuations in numbers occurred, there were no obvious trends in overall numbers—that is, there were no sustained increases or declines in their chickadee population.

Unfortunately, Loery and Nichols did not identify the time within the annual cycle at which their estimates were made. Because the study involved mark-recapture techniques, I suspect that the estimates were for the maximum numbers of chickadees present each year—that is, late summer or early fall numbers. Such numbers typically show considerably more year-to-year variation than do breeding numbers, and they do not necessarily reflect breeding densities. For example, in my current study, the lowest winter population was actually followed by the highest breeding density in the first nine years of the study (see Fig. 9-12). Nevertheless, if even late-summer numbers have shown no obvious trends, it is very likely that breeding densities would show none either. Other studies (e.g., Blake 1952) have also shown Black-capped Chickadee breeding densities to be remarkably stable.

Most population studies on European tits have concentrated primarily on breeding densities. Again, over the long run, numbers tend to be stable; any long-term trends tend to reflect gradual

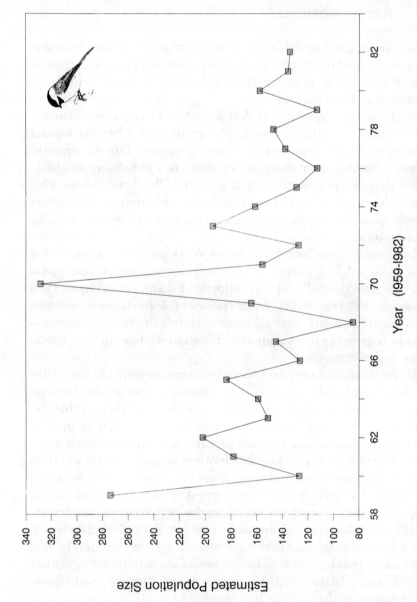

Fig. 9-13. Changes in estimated population size over a 24-year period for Black-capped Chickadees. (Data from Loery and Nichols 1985.)

changes in the habitat, such as the maturing of deciduous forests (Kluijver 1951, Perrins 1979). Ekman (1984b) also reported that Willow Tit numbers best fit mathematical models with feedback mechanisms that keep fluctuations within relatively narrow limits.

## Fluctuations in Population Density

Many ecologists believe that the factors that cause fluctuations in population density can be divided into two major groups: density-independent and density-dependent. The density-independent factors, such as weather or food supply, are not influenced by the density of the birds. The severity of a storm, for example, is not influenced by how many chickadees lie in its path. By contrast, density-dependent factors, as the name implies, are strongly influenced by population density. For some parids, one such factor is clutch size. Great Tits, for example, typically lay more eggs when population density is low than when it is high (Perrins 1979).

Many studies show clear evidence of density-dependent responses in parid populations. Some of the most frequent ways in which density-dependent factors may work is by changes in clutch size, the proportion of second broods, postfledging summer survival, and annual survival of both juveniles and adults.

For example, Kluyver (1966) performed a remarkable experiment on an isolated Great Tit population in Holland. First he determined the normal survival rates in the population. Only about 27 percent of the adult Great Tits survived from year to year, and about 6 percent of the locally produced young bred there the following year. Then for the next four years, Kluyver proceeded to remove about 60 percent of the young produced locally. Incredibly, the Great Tit population continued to fluctuate about the same mean as it had before the removal experiment began. Moreover, immigration from outside continued to be negligible. What happened was that the survival rates of both adults and young rose dramatically—the adults' to about 56 percent, and the young birds' to almost 22 percent. Thus at high population densities, survivorship of both adults and yearlings was quite low, but when population numbers were reduced, both age groups survived far better. Clearly this population had an amazing ability to recover, in a density-dependent fashion, from fairly major disasters.

One interesting thing about Kluyver's data is that evidently adult Great Tits, as well as younger birds, show density-dependent mortality. Ekman (1984a) found a similar effect in Willow Tits; in his study, too, adult summer survival rates fell at high population densities and rose when numbers were lower. Ekman also found that his Willow Tits showed a positive density-dependent feedback on yearling survival both over the summer as well as in late winter.

As mentioned above, population studies on European tits have shown a density-dependent effect on reproductive output. For example, lowered reproductive output at higher population densities (and vice versa) have been found in many Great Tit populations (Kluijver 1951, Perrins 1965, Dhondt and Eyckerman 1980a, O'Connor 1980) and also in Willow Tit populations (Jansson et al. 1981, Ekman 1984a).

Unfortunately, comparable data are not yet available for Black-capped Chickadees. Although there are many papers on chickadee population dynamics (e.g., Blake 1952, Speirs 1963, Elder and Zimmerman 1983, Loery and Nichols 1985, Loery et al. 1987), virtually none gives any information on long-term reproductive output. Such data are far more easily obtained for species that breed readily in nest boxes. Hence there is currently no way of knowing if chickadees, like European tits, show density-dependent responses in clutch size or the frequency of second broods.

Density-independent factors can also have considerable impact on population numbers. In Europe, where many population studies are often conducted concurrently, some interesting results have been obtained concerning fluctuations in population numbers. For example, Great Tit populations in different areas frequently fluctuate in parallel with one another (Perrins 1979). This finding suggests that these populations are responding to events (an early spring, for example) that affect large land areas, such as much of western Europe. Sometimes populations of two or more tit species may also fluctuate in parallel, as is particularly true for Blue and Great Tits (Perrins 1979). Similar fluctuations in parallel may occur across wide areas of North America as well—both among populations of one species, and even involving two or more species. In general, the factors causing such widespread effects are density-independent.

On a more local level, severe winter storms could cause massive starvation, which could be worsened by widespread failure of the food supply (Ekman 1984a, 1984b, McCallum 1990). Minot (1981) claimed that, in England, Great Tit winter mortality is mostly caused by density-independent factors; the same appears to be true for my current study population of Black-capped Chickadees (Fig. 9-14). Natural disasters at other times of year could prevent birds from breeding or destroy nests already begun, thus lowering or even eliminating local productivity. Severe rainstorms can kill entire broods of newly fledged Black-capped Chickadees (pers. observ.). The consequences of density-independent factors are not always negative. Unusually favorable weather or sudden surpluses of natural food may occasionally result in unusually high population densities. Yet at least in temperate zone climates, large effects, whether positive or negative, are unusual. And while they can have a major impact on local numbers, and the effects of that impact may be seen over wide geographical areas, these effects are usually only temporary.

Actually, density-dependent and density-independent factors can interact in complex ways. As Ekman (1984a) put it, phenomena such as weather can introduce a density-independent "noise" in observed mortality variations, which may effectively mask a functional but relatively weak density-dependent relationship. Thus even when such a relationship is occurring, it may be difficult to detect.

Moreover, it is not impossible for a given factor to affect a population in both density-dependent and density-independent ways. For example, Dunn (1977) showed that two major factors affect the intensity of predation by weasels on nestling tits. One of these is the availability of alternative prey, in particular certain rodents. Some of these rodents have more or less cyclic fluctuations in numbers, and clearly their availability to weasels will bear no relation to tit population densities. Hence to the extent that weasel predation levels on tits are affected by rodent availability, their influence on tits is density-independent. Nevertheless, there is a density-dependent relationship too, because weasels, once they discover and eat a brood of tits, will tend to hunt more diligently for other broods, at least for a short while. If the density of tit broods is sufficiently high, then the weasel will have a good chance of finding more broods, so the proportion of tit broods taken by weasels is actually higher in years of high tit population densities. Ekman (1984a) described a similar situation with predation on Willow Tits by European Pygmy Owls, whose major alternative prey is also cyclic rodents.

In general, density-independent factors tend to cause deviations

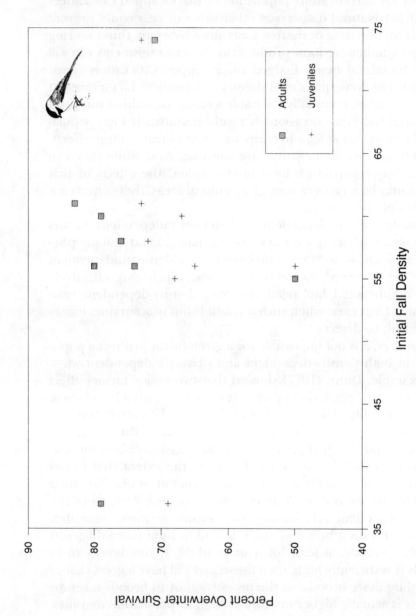

Fig. 9-14. Overwinter survival of adult and juvenile (yearling) Black-capped Chickadees in a western Massachusetts study area, plotted against initial fall density. If survival of either adults or yearlings had been density-dependent, then survival values at the left of the graph (low density) should have been higher than those at the right; however, no such trend can be seen for chickadees of either age group.

away from the mean (average population size), while density-dependent factors typically cause population changes toward the mean. Thus some ecologists (e.g., Perrins 1979, Perrins and Birkhead 1983) have argued that if one defines regulation as a compensatory process, involving feedback mechanisms that damp perturbations in population numbers, then only density-dependent factors, in the long run, can truly regulate population numbers. While for some other groups, in harsher climates, this may not always hold true, it does seem accurate for most avian populations (Perrins and Birkhead 1983).

### What Determines Local Population Size?

As mentioned above, most parid populations in both North America (e.g., Loery and Nichols 1985) and Europe (Perrins 1979; Ekman 1984a, 1984b) fluctuate about some mean density and seldom deviate very far from that mean. But how is the mean determined? What sorts of factors affect how many chickadees or titmice can live in a certain area? Because chickadees have a dual social system of winter flocks and territorial breeding pairs, this question actually has two parts: What determines breeding densities, and What regulates the number of chickadees that can settle in or associate with winter flocks?

#### Determinants of Breeding Densities

One obvious factor that affects breeding density is resources. The absolute amount of resources available must set outer limits on how many individuals can successfully breed in a given area. But which resources are critical? And is it always resources that limit population density, or can other factors (such as social behavior) also be involved?

Lack (1954) and others proposed that breeding numbers may often be regulated by the level of the preceding winter's food supply. Several studies suggest that such regulation may occur, at least in certain northern European tit populations (e.g., Gibb 1960, Orell and Ojanen 1983, Bejer and Rudemo 1985). One of the most impressive of those studies is that of Jansson et al. (1981) on Willow and Crested Tits in Sweden. They had two study areas, both in coniferous forest: one was given extra food, and the other (the control) was unsupplemented. The extra food was withdrawn two to four weeks before egg laying. The results were extraordinary: in the supplemented area, breeding numbers of both Willow and Crested Tits were roughly double those in the control area (Jansson et al. 1981). There at least, winter food supply did have a major impact on breeding numbers.

However, the same effect does not seem to occur very often in chickadee populations. For example, Brittingham and Temple (1988) reported that even though food supplementation greatly increased overwinter survival of Black-capped Chickadees, they could find no difference in breeding densities between their control (unsupplemented) and experimental study sites. Desrochers et al. (1988) found similar results in their study in northern Alberta. Therefore, at least over most of their range, Black-capped Chickadee breeding densities seem to be controlled by factors other than winter food supply.

What about food supply at other times of year? Another possible critical period is in late summer. Can food supply in late summer affect breeding densities the following spring? Perrins (1965) believed it could, claiming that many of the young Great Tits that died soon after fledging actually starved to death (but see Kluyver 1971). Dhondt (1979) reported data suggesting that at least in some years, suitable food may be in short supply in late summer; hence high summer mortality of young Great Tits could thus be related, in those years, to competition for food.

But can this regulate subsequent breeding numbers? Yes, if breeding densities are affected by the amount of fall recruits. In populations where every individual left alive at the end of the winter stays on to breed, the total number of fall recruits could well affect the number later breeding in that area. There are conflicting reports on whether this actually happens in European tit populations (Perrins 1965, Kluyver 1971, Dhondt 1979). It certainly does not appear to be the usual case in most Black-capped Chickadee populations, where late summer/early fall numbers bear little relationship to subsequent breeding levels (see Fig. 9-11 and below).

Another resource that could be in short supply is available nest sites (van Balen et al. 1982, Nilsson 1984). Over most of Black-capped Chickadees' natural habitat (primarily deciduous or mixed woodland), nest sites should be plentiful. (An exception is more built-up areas, where suitable nest sites may well be in short supply). Chickadee species that live mostly in coniferous forests are apparently not so fortunate, however. Mountain Chickadees, for example, in certain sites in California (Dahlsten and Copper 1979) and perhaps elsewhere (Brawn and Balda 1988) are evidently limited by the number of available nest cavities; the same may be true for certain populations of other coniferous-dwelling chickadees such as Boreal and Chestnut-backed Chickadees (Dixon 1961) as well.

Dhondt and Eyckerman (1980b) found that, in their study area in Belgium, competition between Great Tits and Blue Tits for winter roost sites can actually regulate local Blue Tit breeding densities, if the larger Great Tit is allowed to exclude Blue Tits from roost boxes. After Great Tits had been experimentally excluded from nest boxes, Blue Tit breeding numbers almost doubled in the two experimental areas and remained at that level afterward, in contrast to the essentially constant level observed in the control areas. The same boxes could be used for both roosting and nesting, but evidently the crunch in these populations came in competition for safe winter roosting locations. Again, given the superabundance of natural cavities over much of Black-capped Chickadees' geographic range, roost site abundance seems unlikely to be a major factor affecting breeding numbers in most Black-capped Chickadee populations.

Local habitat quality might theoretically limit breeding densities, but if it does, it probably operates in a roundabout way. That is, breeding density in particularly poor-quality habitats may be regulated not so much by what happens locally as by what happens in better quality habitats nearby. Kluyver and Tinbergen (1953) found this to be true for Great Tit populations in pine woods in Holland, and Krebs (1971) obtained similar data for certain Great Tit populations in England. Optimal habitat fills up quickly, and breeding numbers there are more or less stable year after year, whereas poorer-quality habitat is occupied only when there are more birds than can fit into the better areas. Where this relationship occurs, the poorer habitat, which takes up the slack, so to speak, has been called buffer habitat. Kluyver (1961) did search briefly for evidence of such buffer habitats for Black-capped Chickadees, but failed to find any in his study area. Nevertheless, I suspect that residential areas, with their reduced canopy and relatively rare nest sites, may well serve a rather similar function for Black-capped Chickadees: perhaps chickadee populations in residential areas, like Great Tit populations in the pine woods of Holland, are regulated, at least to some extent, by events in better quality habitat nearby.

Over much of their range, therefore, nest sites and safe winter roosting places for chickadees are abundant. Winter food supply, even in supplemented areas, seems to have little effect on breeding numbers, even in quite northern populations. Late-summer juvenile starvation, while possibly affecting breeding numbers in some populations, seems to have very little effect on many others. There remains one last factor, however, whose effect on chickadee populations is both great and widespread: social behavior in general, and, more particularly, territorial behavior.

Interestingly, in Europe, the question of whether spring territoriality can regulate breeding numbers is still a matter of some controversy. Unfortunately, many of the available data are circumstantial and, therefore, difficult to interpret.

If territoriality really regulates breeding density, then it should be possible, at least in years of good overwinter survival, to show that some individuals have been prevented from breeding. To this end, several removal experiments have been performed, with remarkably mixed results. For example, when several pairs of Coal Tits were removed in the early breeding season, they were not replaced; similarly, a small number of Great Tits taken from their territories right after the start of breeding were also unreplaced (Perrins 1979). Yet by contrast, Krebs (1971) did removal experiments using Great Tits, and did get replacements. And, although the replacements in his early experiments were evidently from territories in suboptimal habitat nearby, those that he found in later removals (Krebs 1977) apparently were nonterritorial birds that may well have been excluded from breeding through the territorial behavior of others. Similarly, removal experiments on Great Tits in Poland have also resulted in immediate replacement of both sexes (Wesolowski et al. 1987).

Where territoriality regulates breeding numbers, there should be, in most years, a sudden spring drop in local numbers. Dhondt (1971b) reported a sudden spring loss of young male Great Tits after high-density winters, but not after lower-density winters. Slagsvold (1975) stated that spring losses of young Great and Blue Tits likely represented losses through territorial behavior of others, and that the breeding numbers in his British study area may well have been regulated by this territorial behavior.

Even more interesting is what happens in areas where experimental manipulations have been made. For example, when Jansson et al. (1981) artificially raised the winter density of Willow Tits by adding extra food, they found sudden spring losses in the experimental, but not in the control (unsupplemented) area, where the late winter density was much lower. Similarly, Dhondt et al. (1982) increased Blue Tit winter density in certain plots by adding Great Tit–proof roosting boxes. They found that territorial skirmishes were far more frequent in the experimental plot than in the control area and that intruders (which they suspected were excluded from breeding) were found only on the experimental, high-density site. They concluded that, where protected roost boxes were plentiful, Blue Tit breeding numbers were limited by spring territorial behavior.

Hence, in many European tit populations, other factors, such as low winter food supply or lack of suitable winter roost sites, may hold the populations down below the level at which spring territoriality has any effect on breeding numbers. When these factors are removed or alleviated, then territoriality can and does have a regulating effect.

The regulating effect of territoriality on Black-capped Chickadee populations seems to be far more widespread. For example, studies on the West Coast (Smith 1967c), the northern interior (Desrochers et al. 1988), and in the East (Butts 1931, Glase 1973, Samson and Lewis 1979, Smith 1984) have shown that the onset of spring territorial behavior is typically a time of sudden drops in local population numbers.

Brittingham and Temple (1988), studying Black-capped Chickadees in Wisconsin, found no evidence of spring losses, and therefore suggested that territoriality may not have much effect on chickadee breeding numbers in their study area. While it may not have as much effect as it does elsewhere, I would argue that it has more than they claim. They showed that winter survival was lower in unsupplemented areas; hence one can assume that late-winter densities would be lower on control than on experimental (food-supplemented) areas. If territoriality had no effect, then breeding densities should also have been higher in the experimental sites— but this apparently was not the case. Indeed, they stated that they could not detect any difference in breeding densities between control and experimental sites, and concluded that "a seasonal movement" of chickadees caused more even dispersal over the available habitat. I suggest that this seasonal movement was actually caused, in large part, by territoriality. If so, then the birds that moved away from the higher density sites would be those so low-ranked that they could not manage to defend a territory themselves. Unfortunately, the census methods used by Brittingham and Temple, while excellent for the main objectives of their study, do not permit learning the relative age or rank of those chickadees that moved away from their experimental sites.

Desrochers et al. (1988) studied the spring movements of Black-capped Chickadees in detail. They demonstrated that the bulk of the spring losses were young, low-ranked individuals; by contrast, dominant chickadees stayed put (Fig. 9-15). Dixon (1965) reported

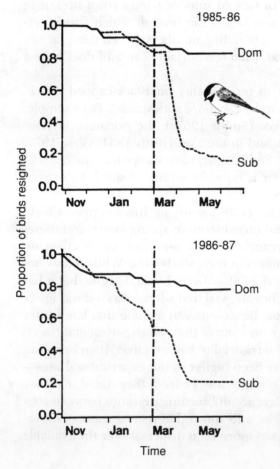

Fig. 9-15. Proportion of dominant (DOM) and subordinate (SUB) yearling Black-capped Chickadees that survived or stayed in a study area in Alberta. The effect occurred in both supplemented and feederless areas, so the results presented here are pooled. Vertical lines indicate onset of breeding territoriality. Numbers of birds on November 1 were: 72 dominants and 68 subordinates (1985–86); 79 dominants and 95 subordinates (1986–87). Only dominant birds had a good chance of obtaining a local breeding territory. (From Desrochers et al. 1988, courtesy of *Auk*.)

similar rank-related spring dispersal by both Carolina and Mountain Chickadees as well.

One criticism of the studies showing such spring drops in numbers is that several were done only in food-supplemented areas (e.g., Smith 1967c; Glase 1973; Smith 1984). It might therefore be argued that Black-capped Chickadees, like the Willow Tits studied by Jansson et al. (1981), are normally regulated by winter starvation and will be affected by territoriality only in areas where extra food is provided. The data of Desrochers et al. (1988) strongly argue against this, however. As did Brittingham and Temple, Desrochers et al. worked both in natural and supplemented areas. Desrochers et al. (1988) found a marked spring drop in numbers, not only in the supplemented area, but also in the natural, unsupplemented area. Furthermore, later removal experiments clearly demonstrated a nonbreeding, floating population in both areas. That is, both had birds living there that were prevented from breeding by the territorial behavior of others. If territoriality regulates breeding numbers even in feederless areas in northern Alberta, it seems likely that it is a major factor in the population regulation of Black-capped Chickadees over much of their range.

The fact remains, however, that the regulatory effect of territoriality, if it existed (as I claim) in the Wisconsin study area of Brittingham and Temple, occurred only in the supplemented areas. Their data show no indication of any spring dispersal away from their control (natural) sites. They have, moreover, essentially eliminated winter starvation as the likely regulatory agent. So what does regulate population numbers in that area? Perhaps the most likely candidate is late-summer starvation of juveniles, before winter flock formation. Further research is needed to test whether late-summer juvenile survival really does have a regulatory impact on subsequent breeding levels in this area. If so, this brings up another very important question: What makes this area so different? Why are populations in this particular area regulated by factors different from those that regulate so many other Black-capped Chickadee populations? There could, for example, be some important difference in what insects make up the late-summer food of local chickadees. Clearly, much exciting research remains to be done on these and related problems.

In any event, it seems as though a sort of hierarchy of factors can affect, and govern, breeding numbers. In certain areas, necessary resources such as winter food or safe roosting sites or nest holes may be in short supply. Elsewhere, factors such as low mid-to late-summer food supply may keep overall juvenile recruits at a very low level. In such areas, numbers may well be held down below the level at which territoriality has any effect. However, wherever sufficient resources are available, then social behavior (that is, territoriality) comes into play and probably sets the upper limit on local breeding numbers. From the data available, it appears that a fairly large proportion of Black-capped Chickadee populations are relatively unaffected by the other factors and hence are largely regulated by territoriality. By contrast, considerably fewer European tit populations seemingly manage to have enough members in late winter for territoriality to have much of an effect, although both Kluyver and Tinbergen (1953) and Krebs (1971) concluded that territoriality can regulate breeding numbers of Great Tit populations living in optimal habitats.

Chickadee territories do tend to be smaller in richer areas, even in populations where territoriality regulates breeding density (e.g., Smith 1976). However, even the smallest breeding territories often seem to contain superabundant resources. Exactly what determines how many breeding territories can fit into a given area is still unknown.

## Regulation of Winter Flock Size

So far, the discussion about population limitation has focused on breeding densities. The other equally important question is: What regulates the number of chickadees that can settle in an area after breeding is over and join locally forming winter flocks?

Some European tits, including the Great Tit, show peaks of territoriality both in the spring and in the fall (Hinde 1952, Kluyver 1971). Some investigators (e.g., Kluyver 1971) have argued that autumn territoriality is largely responsible for regulating winter numbers.

Although a few North American titmice, such as the Plain Titmouse, do evidently hold and defend territories year-round (Dixon 1949), to the best of my knowledge no chickadee species does so. Instead, one or more pairs of adults are joined by settling juveniles, and the whole group forms a winter flock. Moreover, even though adjacent flocks may start out defending mutual boundaries from each other, these boundaries often break down so quickly that it is probably more accurate to talk about flock ranges, rather than flock territories. It is highly unlikely, therefore, that fall territoriality has any effect on autumn levels of

Black-capped Chickadee populations. In an apparent effort to test this relationship, Samson and Lewis (1979) removed an entire Black-capped Chickadee flock from its winter range one September and reported that no other chickadees settled to replace it. It is unclear what they expected to find—but at least no hidden population of chickadees, prevented from settling by the territorial behavior of others, was available to replace that removed flock. Actually, it would be interesting to do a similar experiment in an area where there was normally a high number of winter floaters. I suspect that the results might be very strongly affected by exactly when in the fall the resident birds were removed.

If not fall territoriality, then what? Late-summer juvenile survivorship, discussed above, can of course affect how many potential recruits are available to settle in an area. But do they all stay put, or does some fraction arrive, then move on? And if so, what factors affect how many actually stay?

An obvious candidate is local food supply. That food supply may be a major factor is suggested by several studies. For example, Hamerstrom (1942) reported that if one begins adding winter food to an area, the chickadee population builds up across winters, usually not peaking until at least the third winter. Mueller (1973) reported a similar buildup in winter Black-capped Chickadee populations after three years of local feeding. Samson and Lewis (1979) observed natural flock sizes of Black-capped Chickadees one year, then started providing extra food in mid-July of the next year, and found substantial increases in local flock size. A similar effect evidently occurs in some European tit populations as well. Jansson et al. (1981), for example, found that provision of extra food, even when not begun until September, induced increased autumn immigration and settling of both Willow and Crested Tits.

Hence supplemental food can induce increases in local flock size. There are three ways in which this effect could occur. First, the extra food could prevent late-summer starvation, so that more individuals are alive to settle at flock formation. Second, dispersing young birds may perceive that the area has an exceptionally rich food supply and settle there preferentially. Finally, other flock members, such as adults or early-settling juveniles (Hogstad 1989c), could perceive the food increase and therefore allow more juveniles to join their flocks. More work is needed to see which of these possibilities are actually working here.

Some researchers claim that in certain areas, winter numbers of

Black-capped Chickadees do not peak until December or January. Many of these studies involved banding, and the authors recorded the timing of arrivals at their feeder-based traps (e.g., Butts 1931; Lawrence 1958; Elder and Zimmerman 1983). Butts (1931) stated that many Black-capped Chickadees did not appear in his study area until December, and Elder and Zimmerman (1983) reported that the peak of arrivals into their area was in January. Is this phenomenon real, and, if so, how general is it?

Actually there are two major sources of such apparent new-comers to the food sources associated with the traps. I would argue that by far the most common source is from outlying flocks living in feederless areas nearby. Perhaps by means of their dominant wanderers, such flocks would detect these feeders and come to them during particularly severe weather (such as occurs in December and January). I have seen this behavior regularly at outlying feeders in my own study area; color-banded flocks will sometimes travel almost 2 km (just over 1 mile) beyond their normal flock range to get to a feeder if the weather is particularly severe. Once having visited these feeders, moreover, a flock is very likely to keep coming even after the weather becomes more moderate, although, at least in my experience, these flocks still return to their own flock range each night to roost. The point is that these flocks were in the general area all winter, and they simply extended the range of their normal flock movements to include the feeder; hence they were not really new arrivals at all.

Alternatively, the observed increases may represent actual new-comers to the area: so-called migrants. These could either be from higher elevations relatively nearby (Butts 1931; Smith and Van Buskirk 1988) or possibly from more northern areas. The latter is conceivably the explanation for at least some of the late arrivals reported by Elder and Zimmerman (1983) in their study area in Missouri, and may, in some years, explain late arrivals in other areas as well.

### Migration and Irruptions

Unfortunately, the terms *migration* and *irruption* (or *eruption*) have been used rather loosely by many people working on parids, myself included. Migration is often defined as more-or-less regular movements that occur on a yearly basis. Irruptions, by contrast, are more likely to occur at greater intervals, with periods of one or more years of nonmovement separating irruption years (Perrins 1979). By such definitions, the vast majority of documented long-distance movements by Black-capped Chickadees are actually irruptions; indeed, it may well be that Black-capped Chickadees do not migrate, by the strict definition of the term, at all (with the exception of vertical migrations, which are generally not long-distance movements). Nevertheless, the term *migrant* is often used to denote a bird that is passing through or one that stays only for the winter (e.g., Smith 1988a); it is shorter than the more accurate "individual participating in an irruption," so I continue to use it. Irruptions are common and well documented in several northern parid populations (Bagg 1969; Bock and Lepthien 1976; Perrins 1979); by contrast, relatively few parids are known to migrate, although at least some populations of European tits may be partially migratory (Perrins 1979; Smith and Nilsson 1987).

Information from northern populations clearly indicates that Black-capped Chickadees are resident year-round, even in areas with no supplementary food (e.g., in Alaska: Kron 1975; in northern Alberta: Desrochers and Hannon 1989). It is also well known that Black-capped Chickadees can be found south of their normal breeding range in winter (e.g., Butts 1931, Elder and Zimmerman 1983). One might argue that the appearance of some chickadees south of the range every year might indicate at least partial migration. It does not necessarily do so, however, because such individuals might simply have wandered south during normal juvenile dispersal. At least over most of the range, the direction of juvenile dispersal is known to be random (Weise and Meyer 1979). Hence some young chickadees, from the very southern edge of the breeding range, would be expected to disperse southward after every breeding season.

There is abundant evidence that Black-capped Chickadees, particularly in eastern North America, can undergo irruptions (Lawrence 1958; Hussell and Stamp 1965; Bagg 1969; Bock and Lepthien 1976; Yunick 1981; Loery and Nichols 1985). In irruption years, the numbers can vary markedly, not only from one irruption year to the next, but also from location to location. In exceptional years, the numbers can be extraordinarily enormous. For example, Bagg (1969) reported approximately 31,000 Black-capped Chickadees flying along the lakeshore near Rochester, New York, in October and November of 1954 and over 36,000 moving along the same shore in October 1961. Such high numbers are most often seen where chickadees encounter natural barriers such as large bodies of open water. Interestingly, chickadees (Bagg 1969), like European tits (Perrins 1979), make their long-distance movements during the day, especially in the morning, and thus are easily seen. By contrast, most migrating passerines move primarily at night.

The vast majority of birds involved in irruptive movements are young; that is, they hatched only a few months before the southward movement began. This is so not only for Black-capped Chickadees (Lawrence 1958, Hussell and Stamp 1965), but for European parids as well (Perrins 1979). However, at least in years of major irruptions, some adults can also be involved, in both Black-capped Chickadee (e.g. Bagg 1969; Yunick 1981) and European tit irruptions (Perrins 1979). Given the often intense competition for nesting territories, it is hard to imagine why any adult chickadee, having once obtained a territory, would leave the area, thus giving up the "inside track" to regaining it the following spring. One possible cause is habitat destruction, such as clearing of former nesting habitat by humans, which forces both young and older birds to leave the area. Another possibility is the threat of starvation.

The single most important factor affecting irruptions is reduction of food supply. Although Kimberly Smith (1986) showed that many southern populations of chickadees living in built-up areas may not depend strongly on local seed (mast) production, many more northern chickadee populations evidently do (Lawrence 1958; Bagg 1969; Bock and Lepthien 1976). At least in northeastern North America, irruption years are strongly correlated with years of low seed crops from boreal forest trees (Fig. 9-16a). Even more interesting, perhaps, are the findings that chickadee numbers fluctuate in synchrony with those of many other boreal seed-eating birds and that boreal tree species, from both sides of the Atlantic, also seem to produce high and low seed crops in unison, thus generating synchronous fluctuations in populations of a number of seed-eating bird species over a remarkably wide area (Bock and Lepthien 1976, see Fig. 9-16b).

Besides food supply, several other factors have also been proposed as possible causes of irruptions. For example, Odum (1942b) suggested that Black-capped Chickadees may be more likely to undergo irruptions following summers of particularly

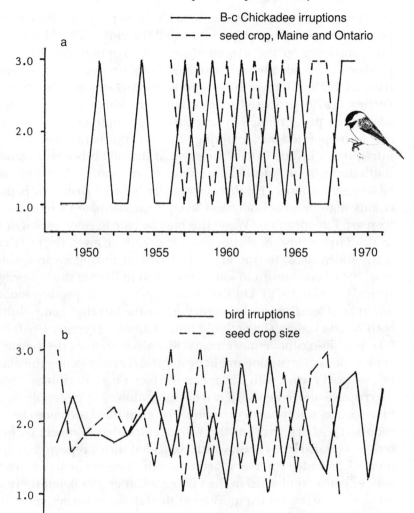

Fig. 9-16. Pattern of seed crop size and bird irruptions, 1948–71. (a) Black-capped Chickadee irruptions (solid lines) vs. seed crop size in Maine and Ontario (dashed lines); (b) combined irruptions of 10 species of boreal seed-eating birds (solid lines) vs. seed crop size (dashed lines). The data in (b) are from North American and European sites. Both for seed-eating birds in general and for chickadees in particular, the birds were far more likely to undergo an irruption in years of poor northern seed crops than they were in years when seeds were plentiful. (Data from Bock and Lepthien 1976, courtesy of *American Naturalist,* © 1976 by the University of Chicago.)

high reproductive success; the same has been proposed for certain populations of European parids as well (Perrins 1979). This factor can contribute to the magnitude of an irruption, but high reproduction is not always correlated with irruptions themselves (Perrins 1979). Another factor affecting irruptions may be genetic. Perrins (1979) proposed that certain individuals may be genetically more programmed to participate in irruptions than are others. As he pointed out, irrupting tits from continental Europe not infrequently invade Britain; however, if British birds were to move south and east, they would encounter mostly water: clearly not an advantageous move. He therefore suggested that British tit populations may be genetically less likely to participate in irruptions than are European tits. While this may be true to some extent, it is difficult to see how the distinction is maintained, given the fact that many individuals, having arrived in Britain during an irruption year, have been known to settle and breed in Britain the following spring (Perrins 1979). On the other hand, genetic predisposition might be at least a partial explanation for the fact that some adults, both of chickadees (Bagg 1969) and of titmice (Perrins 1979) do take part in irruptive movements. More research on the possible genetic basis of irruption might be helpful (perhaps along the lines of Berthold's work with European warblers; e.g., Berthold 1988).

Irruptive movements, like true migration, are generally in a more or less south-north direction. For example, Lawrence (1958) reported a sharp drop in the winter chickadee numbers of her central Ontario study area, which coincided with a reported irruption in chickadee numbers farther south. The major movements are generally southward in the fall (e.g., Cutler 1933), but there is also at least some return movement the following spring, more or less northward (Brooks 1987). The return movement can sometimes be rather aimless (Hussell and Stamp 1965), and indeed much of the movement seems to be so late that the individuals involved may not have time to breed. It is not known what proportion of chickadees begin a northward movement in the spring following an irruption, or what fraction of these actually manage to obtain territories and breed in that or subsequent years. Coordinated banding efforts by a network of researchers over a wide area would be necessary to obtain such data.

# 10

# Future Research

Although there is much left to discover about Black-capped Chickadees, I mention only a few of the potential research projects here. First, I briefly discuss the numerous possibilities that were raised in the preceding chapters. Second, I mention a few of the research possibilities that appeal especially to my own particular interests.

It would be especially interesting to see whether individual Black-capped Chickadees differ in their preferred mode of foraging, as Partridge (1976) discovered for Great Tits (*Parus major*) (see Foraging Niche, Chapter 3). Further studies on long-term cache recovery (discussed in the last section of Chapter 3) would also be welcome.

In the first section of Chapter 4, I mentioned several possibilities for research on chickadee vocalizations: Is there any correlation between the length of the dee note (in the chick-a-dee call complex) and future social behavior, as Kelly (1988) found for Carolina Chickadees (*P. carolinensis*)? Might the meaning of complex calls such as gargles vary with degree of harshness, as Smith (1977) demonstrated for Eastern Kingbirds (*Tyrannus tyrannus*)? Is there any evidence that any chickadee vocalization shows geographical variation based on optimal sound propagation, as Hunter and Krebs (1979) found for Great Tits? Also, from a more developmental perspective, can early experience affect how nestling Black-capped Chickadees respond to adult alarm calls (see Predators and Antipredator Behavior, Chapter 9)?

Many of the topics for future research that I mentioned in previous chapters pertain to chickadee reproduction. For example, do female chickadees need to modify their foraging behavior in order to obtain sufficient calcium for egg shell production in the spring (see Diet, Chapter 3)? Do female chickadees ever engage in intraspecific nest parasitism—that is, lay eggs in another chickadee's nest (see Clutch Size, Chapter 5)? If presented with a choice of a rich but hidden (poor vigilance) food source and a poorer but exposed (good vigilance) food source, how will both male and female chickadees respond, and how will the stage within the breeding cycle affect the choices of each gender (see Breeding Territories, Chapter 5)? Is there any genetic basis for length of juvenile dispersal in Black-capped Chickadees (see Family Group Breakup and Onset of Juvenile Dispersal, Chapter 6)? Does local population density have any effect on such parameters as clutch size, juvenile dispersal, and likelihood of second broods in Black-capped Chickadees (see the sections on juvenile dispersal and replacement and second broods in Chapter 6)? Do older chickadees ever forego breeding, as Dhondt (1985) found for Great Tits (see Reproductive Rates and Strategies, Chapter 6)? Finally, what factors affect how much risk each parent chickadee is willing to take in nest defense (see Predators and Antipredator Behavior, Chapter 9)?

With regard to winter flocks, how much individual recognition is necessary for dominance hierarchies to function properly? And on what is this recognition based? Moreover, if all the adult chickadees are removed from a winter flock, how is juvenile survival affected, and will the effect be the same in both severe and more moderate winters (see Dominance Hierarchies, Chapter 7)? A related question is raised in the section on cohesion and mobile elements in Chapter 7: given the fact that adult female Willow Tits (*Parus montanus*) (Ekman 1990) and Black-capped Chickadees (Witham et al. 1988) in winter flocks derive considerable protection from the presence of their mates, how does the loss of a mate, and thus his protection, affect the rank of a widowed female? And will the result vary with such factors as the age of the widowed bird and the month of disappearance? If chickadees are removed from winter flocks, how long can they be kept out and still manage to regain their former rank upon release? And what are the effects of age, sex, and date on this length of time (see Cohesion and Mobile Elements, Chapter 7)? Finally, how is flock size determined? That is, what factors influence how many juvenile chickadees settle into a particular flock each fall (see Population Dynamics, Chapter 9)?

It would be helpful if we could resolve the question of whether Black-capped Chickadees ever roost huddled together under very cold conditions, as Loery and Nichols have suggested (1985; see Behavioral Adjustments, Chapter 8). It would also be interesting to explore the effect of dominance rank on metabolism to see if dominant Black-capped Chickadees, like Willow Tits (Hogstad 1987b), really have measurably higher metabolic rates (see Dominance Hierarchies, Chapter 7), and, if so, whether this means that higher-ranked chickadees actually take longer to enter hypothermia than do lower-ranked birds (see Physiological Adjustments, Chapter 8).

Currently, Tufted Titmice (*Parus bicolor*) are extending their range northward, thus coming into ever greater contact with Black-capped Chickadees (see, for example, Kricher 1981). The opportunity exists for us to study chickadee populations just ahead of this range extension to get base data on chickadee levels in the absence of titmice, so that we can compare these levels with those after the titmice arrive. Such studies, particularly if carried out over several years, should yield enormously important information on the effects of interspecific competition between chickadees and titmice (see Interspecific Competition, Chapter 9). Another pressing question concerns the fate of juvenile chickadees in late summer, since evidence suggests that many disappear during this period (see Age-Specific Survival Rates, Chapter 9). Last, are all irruptions correlated with low food supply? Is there any genetic predisposition for irruption in Black-capped Chickadees? Where do irrupting individuals come from? Where do they go? (See Migration and Irruptions, Chapter 9.)

It seems to me that there is a particularly pressing need for a well-designed study of the visual displays of Black-capped Chickadees—or of any other chickadee species, for that matter. We have excellent information on vocalizations, but what information there is on visual communication consists primarily of incidental observations scattered piecemeal throughout the literature. I drew the line diagrams in Chapter 4 from my own field sketches; undoubtedly some details are inaccurate. It would fill a great need if someone would undertake a thorough study of these displays, perhaps on captive birds in large aviaries, but also, if possible, on free-living birds, so that we could get a grasp of the range of visual displays, as well as some idea of how each is used. Such a study would necessarily involve some method of filming the displays, preferably in slow motion: chickadees move so quickly that often an observer has no time to catch any details of their displays at all. This study might involve presenting the birds with video images as social stimuli, as Evans and Marler (1991) have recently done with chickens (*Gallus domesticus*). The study need not be simply descriptive; there is plenty of room for experimentation. It will be important to discover for every given display not only what elicits the display, but also as much as possible what the display conveys within various contexts.

Another area where interesting research can be done concerns the effect of band colors on the bird that bears them. Some pertinent questions stem from Burley's (1981, 1986) work, mentioned in the first section of Chapter 2. One such question is whether the color of an individual's bands has any effect on the bird's chances of finding and being accepted by a mate. While I doubt that band colors affect chickadees' mating success, for reasons discussed in Chapter 2, the possibility still remains to be tested. Another question is whether the colors of an individual's bands might affect its vulnerability to predation. Avian predators such as hawks and shrikes have excellent color vision; it is entirely possible that a bird wearing two or more red bands may be more vulnerable to such predators than are birds wearing green or black bands. (Those of us who are studying long-term survivorship hope they are not.) As far as I know, no study of the effect or color banding on predation rates has yet been conducted on any small passerine.

Considerable work has been done in Europe on the effects of brood size on both reproductive costs and offspring survival. This work has been done primarily by manipulating existing broods (that is, moving very young nestlings from one nest to another such that some broods are enlarged and others reduced, while control broods remain unchanged). While a few studies of a similar nature have been done in North America (see, for example, Grundel's [1987] work on Mountain Chickadees, *Parus gambeli*), nothing of the kind has so far been done with Black-capped Chickadees. Admittedly it is much more convenient to have a population that is partially or wholly nesting in boxes for this kind of experiment; however, while more difficult, it is not impossible to do such manipulations on a population nesting in natural cavities. Such a study could give a great deal of insight into factors affecting the clutch size and overall reproductive success of this species.

Recently Møller (1988) reported that Great Tits may give false alarm calls, thus manipulating the location of higher-ranked competitors and gaining easier access to food resources. Low-ranked Great Tits gave such calls when dominant Great Tits were nearby, and tits of any rank gave false alarm calls in the presence of larger competitors, such as House Sparrows (*Passer domesticus*). Some published field data suggest that at least one chickadee species, the Carolina Chickadee, may also give false alarm calls (Gaddis 1980; see Predators and Antipredator Behavior, Chapter 9). If any chickadee species actually does give such false alarm calls, it would be interesting to vary conditions in order to discover what is necessary to elicit them; one could also find out whether there was a necessary encounter rate with actual predators for such false alarms to continue being effective, and, if so, what that critical rate actually is.

One question I find especially fascinating is how and when chickadees develop their ability to recognize predators. Hand-rearing experiments could show whether naive young chickadees have any ability to recognize certain types of potential predators innately. The effects of mobbing by older birds are doubtless of considerable importance here; further tests in the presence of mobbing adults, as well as just with a tape recording of mobbing vocalizations, would help to clarify exactly what is needed for chickadees to acquire this information. I suspect that each chickadee has the capacity to learn to recognize and avoid new kinds of predators throughout its life; it would be nice to see actual data on this.

The scope for within-species comparisons is particularly great in a species as wide-ranging as Black-capped Chickadees. Occasionally two people, each studying the same species, may come up with differing results. When this happens, they should not feel uncomfortable or threatened (although I have sometimes suspected they do). Undoubtedly both are right. It is these very differences that are exciting, because they lead to an examination of how the conditions of the two studies differ, resulting in an increased understanding of exactly which factor(s) generated the difference in the first place. Recently, Frank Gill and Millicent Ficken organized a superb symposium on current research on various members of the genus *Parus* (*Wilson Bulletin* 101[2], 1989). Perhaps sometime in the future we will have a similar symposium focusing entirely on within-species variation in such wide-ranging species as Black-capped Chickadees and Great Tits.

Along these lines, I find it most interesting that Brittingham and Temple (1988) apparently worked in an area where breeding territoriality did not regulate local Black-capped Chickadee breeding numbers—something very different from what occurs in many other chickadee populations elsewhere in North America. This difference cannot simply be a matter of presence or absence of feeders, because I found breeding territoriality to be regulating in a feederless area in eastern Massachusetts for four consecutive years (Smith 1976). Future work to determine the critical difference between the Wisconsin site and others should yield important results.

In two separate studies on winter flocks of Black-capped Chickadees, one in New York (Glase 1973) and the other in Alberta (Desrochers 1989), dominant chickadees were observed to exclude more subordinate flock members from preferred feeding sites. While the New York chickadees fed preferentially in the higher branches, those in Alberta fed primarily in the lower parts of trees, forcing subordinates up into the higher branches. Desrochers (1989) suggested that this difference was related to differing hunting techniques of the major avian predators of the two areas (see Predators and Antipredator Behavior, Chapter 9). Hand-rearing experiments could easily show whether there is any genetic basis for the two preferences (the two populations do, after all, represent different subspecies). If not, perhaps personal experience with predator attacks was necessary for learning the safer sites, or perhaps younger, more subordinate birds can learn simply by observing where the more experienced, higher-ranked chickadees choose to feed.

Although Chaplin (1974, 1976) demonstrated that Black-capped Chickadees wintering in upstate New York typically undergo nocturnal hypothermia on cold winter nights, Grossman and West (1977) found no evidence that Black-capped Chickadees in their Alaskan study area did the same. I suspect that this discrepancy is actually a result of different experimental techniques (see Physiological Adjustments, Chapter 8). Nevertheless, the two populations are from quite distinct subspecies, and the possibility, even if unlikely, exists that the two populations actually do differ in their propensity to undergo hypothermia. It would be worthwhile to obtain individuals from each population and present them with conditions simulating cold winter nights to see if eastern birds enter hypothermia more readily or at higher temperatures than do Alaskan chickadees. If so, breeding experiments could be done to explore the genetic basis of this difference.

For some years now I have been intrigued by the problem of how to sex Black-capped Chickadees in the field. The chickadees themselves seem to be able to do this instantly. For example, the process of joining a flock seems to be very rapid, and even young birds apparently form pairs when they join their first nonbreeding flock, only a few weeks after hatching. Yet researchers must go through the complex process of laparotomy, laparoscopy, flow cytometry, or, more commonly, the even more convoluted process of taking various measurements such as wing length and body weight, and then following the birds for several weeks to confirm sex through subsequent behavior. I wonder what cues the birds themselves use. One possibility is that there are sex-related differences in vocalizations, although so far our studies have failed to detect any such differences that can be picked up instantly (it seems unlikely that how often a particular call is given would be sufficient). Another possibility is that there are plumage differences; this is the idea at the root of the attempt by Mosher and Lane (1972) to distinguish the sexes of Black-capped Chickadees on the basis of the shape of the throat patch and cap (see Aging and Sexing Techniques, Chapter 2). It is certainly possible that the chickadees can distinguish each other's gender on the basis of a combination of small plumage and voice differences, features too subtle for most researchers to use with confidence.

There is, however, another, perhaps more far-fetched possibility. Data show that Black-capped Chickadees possess certain cone cells in their retinas whose peak sensitivity is at wavelengths of 370 nm (Chen et al. 1984). By contrast, the normal range of sensitivity for human eyes is usually given as being from wavelengths of 400 nm, at the violet end of the spectrum, up to 750 nm, at the red end of the visible spectrum (Gould 1982). Theoretically at least, chickadees can see wavelengths that are shorter than those visible to humans—in other words, chickadees may actually be able to see ultraviolet light. It has long been known that certain insects can see ultraviolet light, and the careful work of Eisner and his colleagues (e.g., Eisner et al. 1969) demonstrated that some flowers that appear to be unpatterned white to human eyes actually bear distinctive patterns of ultraviolet readily seen by insect pollinators. To our eyes chickadees seem to have a relatively simple color pattern, consisting largely of black, white, and gray. But, because chickadees may see wavelengths that are invisible to us (Chen et al. 1984), it is conceivable that they may have a distinctive sex difference in ultraviolet patterns, analogous to the ultraviolet guidelines in flowers, which permit them to distinguish each other's sex as easily as, say, Downy Woodpeckers (*Picoides pubescens*) can. Two obvious white patches where such patterns could be located are the cheek patches and the area immediately below the throat patch.

Research on chickadee biology is virtually endless, and is to a large extent limited only by a researcher's imagination. Important projects needing to be done range from those that require sophisticated technology to those that require simply patience and a good pair of binoculars. Every reader can contribute to our overall knowledge of chickadee biology. I look forward to reading about the results of those discoveries in the years to come.

# Glossary

Agonistic behavior   Originally, a complex of behavior, including attack, threat, defense, appeasement, and escape. Now often used to mean aggression only.

Altricial   Young hatched at an early stage of development; being, at hatching, naked, blind, and totally dependent on parents for food and warmth.

Ambient temperature   Surrounding air temperature.

Brood   (n.) A group of nestlings. (v.) To cover a group of nestlings, thus keeping them warm.

Brood (social) parasite   A species or individual that lays its eggs in other birds' nests.

Brood patch   An area of the belly region that normally comes in contact with the eggs during incubation. Down feathers are shed and the area receives increased blood supply, thus allowing more efficient heat transfer to the eggs.

Brown fat (brown adipose tissue, BAT)   Specialized fatty tissue containing many large mitochondria and a particularly rich blood supply. This tissue can be broken down such that heat can be produced without shivering.

Call   Any of numerous vocalizations, often relatively short and unmusical, that birds use for specific functions, such as warning, location, threat, and the like. Usually innate.

Capillary   A small, thin-walled blood vessel, very narrow in diameter.

**Catabolic reaction**  A metabolic pathway in which large molecules are broken down into smaller ones, often with the release of considerable heat.

**Circadian rhythm**  A rhythm that has a period of approximately 24 hours between successive peaks.

**Clutch**  The total number of eggs a female lays in a given nesting attempt.

**Conductance, thermal**  The ease with which heat can move between the body core and the environment. The better the insulation around the body, the lower the thermal conductance.

**Conduction**  The transfer of heat between objects and substances that are in contact with each other.

**Conspecific**  Member of the same species.

**Contour feathers**  Complex feathers whose interlocking structure makes a strong, flexible blade. Although restricted to feather tracts, they serve to cover the entire body of the bird. Includes both wing and tail feathers. Normally contour feathers are the only feathers visible to the observer.

**Convection**  The transfer of heat via currents (such as wind).

**Crissum**  Undertail coverts—a triangle of feathers just under the base of the tail.

**DNA**  A complex molecule, usually double stranded, that contains encoded genetic information. DNA in birds can occur both in the nucleus of cells and in the mitochondria.

**Dominance hierarchy**  Peck order.

**Dominant wanderer**  A high-ranked wintering chickadee (flock regular) that frequently leaves its own flock home range and moves into areas occupied by other flocks. Typically returns to its own flock range each night to roost.

**Ectoparasite**  An external parasite, such as a flea, louse, or tick.

**Enzyme**  A protein that permits or speeds up the rate of a specific biochemical reaction.

**Fitness**  Relative evolutionary success, often measured by the proportion of an individual's genes in the next generation.

**Flank**  An area along a bird's side, just below the wing.

**Fledge**  To leave the nest. Once a bird fledges, it typically does not re-enter the nest.

**Fledgling**  A young bird that has recently left its nest.

**Flock regular**  A wintering chickadee that is a regular member of a single flock. Most are sedentary, but a few (dominant wanderers) can have expanded ranges.

**Flock switcher**  A winter floater—a wintering chickadee, young, low-ranked and unpaired, that typically has an established position in the dominance hierarchies of three to four flocks, and often spends some time each day with each of these flocks. Has no single home flock.

Flow cytometry   A sexing technique that involves the examination of DNA content from tissue samples.

Granivorous   Seed-eating.

Heterospecific   A member of another species.

Histology   The biological study of the tissues that make up living organisms.

Hypothermia   Controlled lowering of internal body temperature under cold external conditions. In birds, this is achieved by reducing the amount of shivering.

Insolation   The amount of solar radiation arriving per unit area.

Irruption   A more or less sporadic, long-distance movement of a bird species that typically occurs at intervals of two or more years. Distinguished from true migration by the fact that irruptions do not occur every year.

Juvenal plumage   The first plumage a young bird grows that includes contour feathers.

Laparotomy   A sexing technique that entails anesthetizing a bird, then opening it up to examine its gonads directly.

Laparoscopy   A sexing technique that uses fiber optics to examine a bird's gonads.

Metabolic rate   The rate at which an organism uses the energy stored within its body, via the oxidation of carbohydrates, fats, and proteins. Measured by the organism's rate of oxygen consumption or carbon dioxide production.

Mist net   A soft mesh net, usually of black nylon, that is used to catch birds. It is fine enough that, when placed correctly, it is essentially invisible to flying birds.

Mitochondria (singular: mitochondrion)   Structures found within the cells of higher plants and animals that are involved in the production and storage of energy-containing molecules. Mitochondria contain their own DNA.

Mobbing   Two or more birds moving rapidly around a predator, usually within one meter of it. Typically involves loud calls and exaggerated, stereotyped wing and tail movements. A frequent response to a stationary predator.

Nape   Back of the neck.

Natal down   Soft fluffy feathers that cover a newly hatched bird. In altricial birds, such as chickadees, can be sparse and wispy.

Nestling   A young bird that has not yet left the nest.

Niche   An organism's position within the ecosystem, including its relation to food and to enemies.

Nucleotides   Units that can be linked together to form long complex molecules that are vital to the operation and reproduction of cells. DNA and RNA are both made up of long strings of nucleotides.

**Parid**   A member of the family Paridae (includes all chickadees and titmice).

**Passerine**   A member of the order Passeriformes, or perching birds.

**Photoperiod**   The number of hours of daylight within a 24-hour period.

**Pneumatization (of skulls)**   The gradual development of very small pockets of gas in the bones of a bird's skull. This normal part of a young bird's development has been used to distinguish between young and older birds in the hand.

**Proximate factors**   Actual factors an organism encounters that can trigger some response. For example, experience with increasing photoperiod in the spring (a proximate factor) can cause many bird species to come into reproductive condition.

**Ptiloerection**   Fluffing of feathers.

**Radiation**   Heat emitted by means of electromagnetic waves. Takes place without direct contact between objects.

**Raptor**   A bird of prey, such as a hawk or an owl.

**Roost**   Location where a diurnal (day-active) bird will spend the night.

**Song**   A vocalization type, often long, complex, and including a number of fairly pure tones, that typically functions in repelling rivals and attracting mates.

**Subcutaneous fat**   Fatty tissue deposited just under the skin.

**Subspecies**   Recognizably different populations, often with fairly small geographical overlap. According to some, each subspecies should have 75 percent of its members distinguishable from other members of the species, usually by size or plumage. Probably not too useful a distinction for most migratory species, but still worth considering for species as sedentary as chickadees.

**Subthermoneutral temperature**   Air temperature sufficiently low that a bird must raise its resting metabolic rate to maintain its internal temperature.

**Territory**   A defended area, fixed in space.

**Thermoneutral temperature**   A range of ambient temperature over which resting metabolic rate is lowest. Within this range, no physiological work is needed to maintain a stable internal temperature, which is why the resting metabolic rate is so low.

**Thermoregulate**   In birds, to achieve and maintain a high and constant internal temperature. Young birds must grow contour and other feathers before being able to thermoregulate.

**Type host**   The host species on (or in) which the type specimen of a parasite was found.

**Type specimen**    The specimen that formed the basis for the original description of a species.

**Ultimate factors**    Factors that directly affect the evolution of a characteristic or response. For example, the availability of a certain kind and/or quantity of food for the developing young is an ultimate factor affecting the timing of breeding.

**Uropygial gland**    A gland located on the rump at the base of the tail of a bird. Its waxy, oily secretion, spread on feathers by preening, cleans, waterproofs, and maintains the feathers' flexibility.

**Visiting migrant**    Among chickadees, usually a bird that has moved to a lower elevation (in vertical migration) or has moved south (in an irruption) to a new area for the winter; such birds generally move away just before local breeding begins.

**Wing coverts**    Feathers that lie over the bases of the primaries and secondaries (that is, the long wing feathers).

**Winter floater**    *See* Flock switcher.

# References

Alatalo, R.V. 1982. Evidence for interspecific competition among European tits *Parus* spp.: a review. Ann. Zool. Fenn. 19: 309–317.

Alatalo, R.V., A. Carlson, A. Lundberg, and S. Ulfstrand. 1981. The conflict between male polygamy and female monogamy: the case of the Pied Flycatcher, *Ficedula hypoleuca*. Am. Nat. 117: 738–753.

Alatalo, R.V., D. Eriksson, L. Gustafsson, and K. Larsson. 1987. Exploitation competition influences the use of foraging sites by tits: experimental evidence. Ecology 68: 284–290.

Alatalo, R.V., L. Gustafsson, M. Lindén, and A. Lundberg. 1985. Interspecific competition and niche shifts in tits and the Goldcrest: an experiment. J. Anim. Ecol. 54: 977–984.

Alatalo, R.V., L. Gustafsson, and A. Lundberg. 1986. Interspecific competition and niche changes in tits (*Parus* spp.): evaluation of nonexperimental data. Am. Nat. 127: 819–834.

Alatalo, R.V., and P. Helle. 1990. Alarm calling by individual Willow Tits, *Parus montanus*. Anim. Behav. 40: 437–442.

Alcock, J. 1970. Punishment levels and the response of Black-capped Chickadees (*Parus atricapillus*) to three kinds of artificial seeds. Anim. Behav. 18: 592–599.

Allen, A.A. 1929. Autobiography of the chickadee. Bird-lore 31: 69–78.

American Ornithologists' Union. 1983. The AOU Check-list of North American Birds, 6th ed. Washington, D.C.

Amlaner, C.J., and D.W. MacDonald (eds.) 1980. A Handbook on Biotelemetry and Radiotracking. Pergamon, Oxford.

Anderson, J.F., L.A. Magnarelli, and K.C. Stafford III. 1990. Bird-feeding ticks transstadially transmit *Borrelia burgdorferi* that infect Syrian hamsters. J. Wildl. Dis. 26: 1–10.

Apel, K.M., and M.S. Ficken. 1981. Predator alarm calls of young Black-capped Chickadees. Auk 98: 624.

Apel, K.M., and C.M. Weise. 1986. The hiss-display of nestling Black-capped Chickadees in captivity. Wilson Bull. 98: 320–321.

Bagg, A.M. 1969. The changing seasons: a summary of the fall migration season 1968 with special attention to the movements of Black-capped Chickadees. Audubon Field Notes 23: 4–12.

Baird, J.W. 1980. The selection and use of fruit by birds in an eastern forest. Wilson Bull. 92: 63–73.

Baker, M.C. 1978. Flocking and feeding in the Great Tit, *Parus major*—an important consideration. Am. Nat. 112: 779–781.

Baker, M.C., J.T. Boylan, and D.A. Goulart. 1991. Effect of gargle vocalizations on behavior of Black-capped Chickadees. Condor 93: 62–70.

Baker, M.C., M.D. Mantych, and R.J. Shelden. 1990. Social dominance, food caching and recovery by Black-capped Chickadees, *Parus atricapillus*: is there a cheater strategy? Ornis Scand. 21: 293–295.

Baker, M.C., E. Stone, A.E.M. Baker, R.J. Shelden, P. Skillicorn, and M.D. Mantych. 1988. Evidence against observational learning in storage and recovery of seeds by Black-capped Chickadees. Auk 105: 492–497.

Balda, R.P., A.C. Kamil, and K. Grim. 1986. Revisits to emptied cache sites by Clark's Nutcrackers (*Nucifraga columbiana*). Anim. Behav. 34: 1289–1298.

Baldwin, D.A. 1934. Three returning mated pairs of chickadees. Bird-Banding 5: 47–48.

Baldwin, D.A. 1935a. Returning chickadee mates. Bird-Banding 6: 35.

Baldwin, D.A. 1935b. Percentages of surviving chickadees of different ages. Bird-Banding 6: 69–70.

Balen, J.H. van. 1973. A comparative study of the breeding ecology of the Great Tit, *Parus major,* in different habitats. Ardea 61: 1–93.

Balen, J.H. van. 1980. Population fluctuations in the Great Tit and feeding conditions in winter. Ardea 68: 143–164.

Balen, J.H. van, C.J.H. Booy, J.A. van Franeker, and E.R. Osieck. 1982. Studies on hole-nesting birds in natural nest sites. I. Availability and occupation of natural nest sites. Ardea 70: 1–24.

Balen, J.H. van, A.J. van Noordwijk, and J. Visser. 1987. Lifetime reproductive success and recruitment in two Great Tit populations. Ardea 75: 1–11.

Banks, R.C. 1970. Re-evaluation of two supposed hybrid birds. Wilson Bull. 82: 331–332.

Barash, D.P. 1974. An advantage of winter flocking in the Black-capped Chickadee, *Parus atricapillus*. Ecology 55: 674–676.

Barkan, C.P.L. 1990. A field test of risk-sensitive foraging in Black-capped Chickadees (*Parus atricapillus*). Ecology 71: 391–400.

Barkan, C.P.L., and M.L. Withiam. 1989. Profitability, rate maximization, and reward delay: a test of the simultaneous encounter model of prey choice with Black-capped Chickadees, *Parus atricapillus*. Am. Nat. 134: 254–272.

Barnard, C.J. 1980. Flock feeding and time budgets in the House Sparrow (*Passer domesticus* L.) Anim. Behav. 28: 295–309.

Barnard, P., B. MacWhirter, R. Simmons, G.L. Hansen, and P.C. Smith. 1987. Timing of breeding and the seasonal importance of passerine prey to Northern Harriers (*Circus cyaneus*). Can. J. Zool. 65: 1942–1946.

Barrowclough, G.F., N.K. Johnson, and R.M. Zink. 1985. On the nature of genic variation in birds. Pp. 135–154 *in* R.F. Johnston, ed., Current Ornithology, vol. 2. Plenum, New York.

Behle, W.H. 1951. A new race of the Black-capped Chickadee from the Rocky Mountain region. Auk 68: 75–79.

Bejer, B., and M. Rudemo. 1985. Fluctuations of tits (Paridae) in Denmark and their relations to winter food and climate. Ornis Scand. 16: 29–37.

Beletsky, L.D., and G.H. Orians. 1987. Territoriality among male Red-winged Blackbirds. Behav. Ecol. Sociobiol. 20:21–34.

Belles-Isles, J.-C., and J. Picman. 1986. House Wren nest-destroying behavior. Condor 88: 190–193.

Belles-Isles, J.-C., and J. Picman. 1987. Suspected adult intraspecific killing by House Wrens. Wilson Bull. 99: 497–498.

Bennett, G.F., M. Cameron, and E. White. 1975. Hematozoa of the passeriformes of the Tantramar Marshes, New Brunswick. Can. J. Zool. 53: 1432–1442.

Bennett, G.F., and M.A. Pierce. 1989. *Hepatozoon parus* n. sp. from the Paridae and redescription of *H. atticorae* (de Beaurepaire Aragao, 1911) Hoare, 1924 from the Hirundinidae. Can. J. Zool. 67: 2859–2863.

Bent, A.C. 1937. Life histories of North American birds of prey, part 1. U.S. Natl. Mus. Bull. 167.

Bent, A.C. 1938. Life histories of North American birds of prey, part 2. U.S. Natl. Mus. Bull. 170.

Bent, A.C. 1946. Life histories of North American jays, crows, and titmice. U.S. Natl. Mus. Bull. 191.

Bequaert, J.C. 1955. The hippoboscidae or louse-flies (Diptera) of mammals and birds. Part II. Taxonomy, evolution and revision of American genera and species. Entomol. Am. 34/35: 1–232.

Berner, T.O., and T.C. Grubb, Jr. 1985. An experimental analysis of mixed-species flocking in birds of deciduous woodland. Ecology 66: 1229–1236.

Berthold, P. 1988. The control of migration in European warblers. Acta XIX Congr. Int. Ornithol.: 215–249.

Björklund, M., and B. Westman. 1986a. Mate-guarding in the Great Tit: tactics of a territorial forest-living species. Ornis Scand. 17: 99–105.

Björklund, M., and B. Westman. 1986b. Adaptive advantages of monogamy in the Great Tit (*Parus major*): an experimental test of the polygamy threshold model. Anim. Behav. 34: 1436–1440.

Blake, C.H. 1952. A population balance for the Black-capped Chickadee. Bird-Banding 23: 165–168.

Blake, C.H. 1956. Wing length in the Black-capped Chickadee. Bird-Banding 27: 32.

Blem, C.R. 1989. Review of "On Watching Birds," by Lawrence Kilham. Wilson Bull. 101: 151–152.

Bock, C.E., and L.W. Lepthien. 1976. Synchronous eruptions of boreal seed-eating birds. Am. Nat. 110: 559–571.

Bowles, J.H. 1909. Notes on *Parus rufescens* in western Washington. Condor 11: 55–57.

Brackbill, H. 1970. Tufted Titmouse breeding behavior. Auk 87: 522–536.

Brander, R.B., and W.W. Cochran. 1969. Radio-location telemetry. Pp. 95–103 *in* R.H. Giles, ed., Wildlife Management Techniques. Wildlife Society, Washington D.C.

Braun, M.J., and M.B. Robbins. 1986. Extensive protein similarity of the hybridizing chickadees *Parus atricapillus* and *P. carolinensis*. Auk 103: 667–675.

Brawn, J.D., and R.P. Balda. 1988. Population biology of cavity nesters in northern Arizona: do nest sites limit breeding densities? Condor 90: 61–71.

Brawn, J.D., and F.B. Samson. 1983. Winter behavior of Tufted Titmice. Wilson Bull. 95:222–232.

Bray, O.F., J.J. Kennelly, and J.L. Gaurino. 1975. Fertility of eggs produced on territories of vasectomized Red-winged Blackbirds. Wilson Bull. 87: 187–195.

Brennan, L.A., and M.L. Morrison. 1991. Long-term trends of chickadee populations in western North America. Condor 93:130–137.

Brenner, F.J. 1965. Metabolism and survival time of grouped Starlings at various temperatures. Wilson Bull. 77: 388–395.

Brewer, R. 1961. Comparative notes on the life history of the Carolina Chickadee. Wilson Bull. 73: 348–373.

Brewer, R. 1963. Ecological and reproductive relationships of Black-capped and Carolina Chickadees. Auk 80: 9–47.

Brewer, R. 1978. Winter home ranges of Black-capped Chickadees in southern Michigan oak forest. Jack-Pine Warbler 56: 96–98.

Brewer, R., and K.G. Harrison. 1975. The time of habitat selection by birds. Ibis 117: 521–522.

Brittingham, M.C., and S.A. Temple. 1986. A survey of avian mortality at winter feeders. Wildl. Soc. Bull. 4: 445–450.

Brittingham, M.C., and S.A. Temple. 1988. Impacts of supplemental feeding on survival rates of Black-capped Chickadees. Ecology 69: 581–589.

Brittingham, M.C., S.A. Temple, and R.M. Duncan. 1988. A survey of the prevalence of selected bacteria in wild birds. J. Wildl. Dis. 24: 299–307.

Bromssen, A. von, and C. Jansson. 1980. Effects of food addition to Willow Tit *Parus montanus* and Crested Tit *P. cristatus* at the time of breeding. Ornis Scand. 11: 173–178.

Brooks, E.W. 1987. A summary of Black-capped Chickadee recoveries during spring migration. N. Am. Bird Bander 12: 19–20.

Brown, C.R. 1984. Light-breasted Purple Martins dominate dark-breasted birds in a roost: implications for female mimicry. Auk 101: 162–164.

Brown, J.L. 1975. The Evolution of Behavior. W.W. Norton, New York.

Budd, S.M. 1972. Thermoregulation in Black-capped Chickadees. Am. Zool. 12: 33.

Burgess, E.C. 1990. The role of wild birds in the transmission of *Borrelia burgdorferi*: Lyme disease. Acta XX Congr. Int. Ornithol. (Suppl.): 325.

Burley, N. 1981. Sex ratio manipulation and selection for attractiveness. Science 211: 721–722.

Burley, N., G. Krantzberg, and P. Radman. 1982. Influence of colour-banding on the conspecific preferences of Zebra Finches. Anim. Behav. 30: 444–455.

Buttemer, W.A., L.B. Astheimer, W.W. Weathers, and A.H. Hayworth. 1987. Energy savings attending winter-nest use by Verdins (*Auriparus flaviceps*). Auk 104: 531–535.

Butts, W.K. 1931. A study of the Chickadee and White-breasted Nuthatch by means of marked individuals. Part II. The Chickadee (*Penthestes atricapillus atricapillus*). Bird-Banding 2: 1–26.

Cade, T.J. 1962. Wing movements, hunting and displays in the Northern Shrike. Wilson Bull. 74: 386–408.

Cade, T.J. 1967. Ecological and behavioral aspects of predation by the Northern Shrike. Living Bird 6: 43–86.

Calder, W.A., and J.R. King. 1974. Thermal and caloric relations of birds. Pp. 259–413 *in* D.S. Farner and J.R. King, eds., Avian Biology, vol. 4. Academic Press, New York.

Caraco, T. 1979. Time budgeting and group size: a test of theory. Ecology 60: 618–627.

Censky, E.J., and M.S. Ficken. 1982. Responses of Black-capped Chickadees to mirrors. Wilson Bull. 94: 590–593.

Chaplin, S.B. 1974. Daily energetics of the Black-capped Chickadee, *Parus atricapillus*, in winter. J. Comp. Physiol. B 89: 321–330.

Chaplin, S.B. 1976. The physiology of hypothermia in the Black-capped Chickadee, *Parus atricapillus*. J. Comp. Physiol. B 112: 335–344.

Chaplin, S.B. 1982. The energetic significance of huddling behavior in Common Bushtits (*Psaltriparus minimus*). Auk 99: 424–430.

Charnov, E., and J. Krebs. 1975. The evolution of alarm calls: altruism or manipulation? Am. Nat. 109: 107–112.

Chen, D.-M., J.S. Collins, and T.H. Goldsmith. 1984. The ultraviolet receptor of bird retinas. Science 225: 337–340.

Clapp, R.B., M.K. Klimkiewicz, and A.G. Futcher. 1983. Longevity records of North American birds: Columbidae through Paridae. J. Field Ornithol. 54: 123–137.

Clemmons, J., and J.L. Howitz. 1990. Development of early vocalizations and the chick-a-dee call in the Black-capped Chickadee, *Parus atricapillus*. Ethology 86: 203–223.

Connell, J.H. 1983. On the prevalence and relative importance of interspecific competition: evidence from field experiments. Am. Nat. 122: 661–696.

Conner, R.N. 1974. Red-bellied Woodpecker predation on nestling Carolina Chickadees. Auk 91: 836.

Cooke, M.T. 1950. Returns from banded birds. Bird-Banding 21: 11–18.

Curio, E. 1978. The adaptive significance of avian mobbing. I. Teleonomic hypotheses and predictions. Z. Tierpsychol. 48: 175–183.

Curio, E., U. Ernst, and W. Vieth. 1978. The adaptive significance of avian mobbing. II. Cultural transmission of enemy recognition in Blackbirds: effectiveness and some conclusions. Z. Tierpsychol. 48: 184–202.

Curio, E., G. Klump, and K. Regelmann. 1983. An antipredator response in the Great Tit (*Parus major*): is it tuned to predator risk? Oecologia 60: 83–88.

Curio, E., and K. Regelmann. 1987. Do Great Tit *Parus major* parents gear their brood defence to the quality of their young? Ibis 129: 344–352.

Curio, E., K. Regelmann, and U. Zimmermann. 1984. The defence of first and second broods by Great Tit (*Parus major*) parents: a test of predictive sociobiology. Z. Tierpsychol. 66: 101–127.

Curio, E., K. Regelmann, and U. Zimmermann. 1985. Brood defence in the Great Tit (*Parus major*): the influence of life-history and habitat. Behav. Ecol. Sociobiol. 16: 273–283.

Cutler, M.F.M. 1933. A chickadee recovery. Bird-Banding 4: 115.

Dahlsten, D.C., and W.A. Copper. 1979. The use of nesting boxes to study the biology of the Mountain Chickadee (*Parus gambeli*) and the impact on selected forest insects. Pp. 217–260 *in* J.G. Dickson, R.N. Conner, R.R. Fleet, J.C. Kroll, and J.A. Jackson, eds., The Role of Insectivorous Birds in Forest Ecosystems. Academic Press, New York.

Davies, N.B. 1978. Parental meanness and offspring independence: an experiment with hand-reared Great Tits, *Parus major*. Ibis 120: 509–514.

Davis, M.F. 1978. A helper at a Tufted Titmouse nest. Auk 95: 767.

Dawson, W.R., R.L. Marsh, and M.E. Yacoe. 1983. Metabolic adjustments of small passerine birds for migration and cold. Am. J. Physiol. 245: R755–R767.

De Laet, J.F. 1985. Dominance and anti-predator behaviour of Great Tits: a field study. Ibis 127: 372–377.

De Laet, J.F., and A.A. Dhondt. 1989. Weight loss of the female during the first brood as a factor influencing second brood initiation in Great Tits, *Parus major,* and Blue Tits, *P. caeruleus*. Ibis 131: 281–289.

Den Boer-Hazewinkel, J. 1987. On the costs of reproduction: parental survival and production of second clutches in the Great Tit. Ardea 75: 99–110.

Desfayes, M. 1964. An observation on the song of the Black-capped Chickadee. Condor 66: 438–439.

Desrochers, A. 1989. Sex, dominance and microhabitat use in wintering Black-capped Chickadees: a field experiment. Ecology 70: 636–645.

Desrochers, A. 1990. Sex determination of Black-capped Chickadees with a discriminant analysis. J. Field Ornithol. 61: 79–84.

Desrochers, A., and S.J. Hannon. 1989. Site-related dominance and spacing among winter flocks of Black-capped Chickadees. Condor 91: 317–323.

Desrochers, A., S.J. Hannon, and K.E. Nordin. 1988. Winter survival and territory acquisition in a northern population of Black-capped Chickadees. Auk 105: 727–736.

Dhondt, A.A. 1971a. Some factors influencing territory in the Great Tit, *Parus major*. Gerfaut 61: 125–135.

Dhondt, A.A. 1971b. The regulation of numbers in Belgian populations of Great Tits. Pp. 532–544 *in* P.J. den Boer and G.R. Gradwell, eds., Dynamics of Populations. Pudoc, Wageningen.

Dhondt, A.A. 1979. Summer dispersal and survival of juvenile Great Tits in southern Sweden. Oecologia 42: 139–157.

Dhondt, A.A. 1981. Postnuptial moult of the Great Tit in southern Sweden. Ornis Scand. 12: 127–133.

Dhondt, A.A. 1985. Do old Great Tits forego breeding? Auk 102: 870–872.

Dhondt, A.A. 1987a. Polygynous Blue Tits and monogamous Great Tits: does the polygyny-threshold model hold? Am. Nat. 129: 213–220.

Dhondt, A.A. 1987b. Reproduction and survival of polygynous and monogamous Blue Tits, *Parus caeruleus*. Ibis 129: 327–334.

Dhondt, A.A. 1989a. The effect of old age on the reproduction of Great Tits, *Parus major,* and Blue Tits, *P. caeruleus.* Ibis 131: 268–280.

Dhondt, A.A. 1989b. Ecological and evolutionary effects of interspecific competition in tits. Wilson Bull. 101: 198–216.

Dhondt, A.A., and R. Eyckerman. 1980a. Competition and the regulation of numbers in Great and Blue Tits. Ardea 68: 121–132.

Dhondt, A.A., and R. Eyckerman. 1980b. Competition between the Great Tit and the Blue Tit outside the breeding season in field experiments. Ecology 61: 1291–1296.

Dhondt, A.A., and J. Hublé. 1968. Fledging date and sex in relation to dispersal in young Great Tits. Bird Study 15: 127–134.

Dhondt, A.A., and G. Olaerts. 1981. Variations in survival and dispersal with ringing date as shown by recoveries of Belgian Great Tits, *Parus major.* Ibis 123: 96–98.

Dhondt, A.A., and J. Schillemans. 1983. Reproductive success of the Great Tit in relation to its territorial status. Anim. Behav. 31: 902–912.

Dhondt, A.A., J. Schillemans, and J. De Laet. 1982. Blue Tit territories in populations at different density levels. Ardea 70: 185–188.

Dixon, K.L. 1949. Behavior of the Plain Titmouse. Condor 51: 110–136.

Dixon, K.L. 1954. Some ecological relations of chickadees and titmice in central California. Condor 56: 113–124.

Dixon, K.L. 1961. Habitat distribution and niche relationships in North American species of *Parus.* Pp. 179–216 *in* W.F. Blair, ed., Vertebrate Speciation. Univ. of Texas Press, Austin.

Dixon, K.L. 1962. Notes on the molt schedule of the Plain Titmouse. Condor 64: 134–139.

Dixon, K.L. 1963. Some aspects of social organization in the Carolina Chickadee. Proc. 13th Int. Ornithol. Congr., pp. 240–258.

Dixon, K.L. 1965. Dominance-subordination relationships in Mountain Chickadees. Condor 67: 291–299.

Dixon, K.L. 1972. Attack calls and territorial behavior of the Mountain Chickadee. Proc. 15th Int. Ornithol. Congr., pp. 640–641.

Dixon, K.L. 1983. Black-capped Chickadee performs "hiss-display" while in wire-mesh trap. Wilson Bull. 95: 313–314.

Dixon, K.L. 1987. Reversal of dominance in a pair of Song Sparrows. J. Field Ornithol. 58: 4–5.

Dixon, K.L., and J.D. Gilbert. 1964. Altitudinal migration in the Mountain Chickadee. Condor 66: 61–64.

Dixon, K.L., and D.J. Martin. 1979. Notes on the vocalizations of the Mexican Chickadee. Condor 81: 421–423.

Dixon, K.L., and R.A. Stefanski. 1970. An appraisal of the song of the Black-capped Chickadee. Wilson Bull. 82: 53–62.

Dixon, K.L., R.A. Stefanski, and F.N. Folks. 1970. Acoustic signals in the mating of the Mountain and Black-capped Chickadees. Auk 87: 322–328.

Downs, J.R. 1964. Old chickadee. Bird-Banding 35: 124.

Drent, P.J. 1984. Mortality and dispersal in summer and its consequences for the density of Great Tits, *Parus major*, at the onset of autumn. Ardea 72: 127–162.

du Feu, C.R. 1987. Some observations of fleas emerging from tit nestboxes. Ringing & Migr. 8: 123–128.

Dunham, D.W. 1966. Agonistic behavior in captive Rose-breasted Grosbeaks, *Pheucticus ludovicianus* (L.). Behaviour 27: 160–173.

Dunn, E.K. 1977. Predation by weasels (*Mustela nivalis*) on breeding tits (*Parus* spp.) in relation to the density of tits and rodents. J. Anim. Ecol. 46: 633–652.

Duryea, M. 1989. Some effects of predation risk on the foraging behavior of Black-capped Chickadees, *Parus atricapillus*. Honors thesis, Dept. of Biological Sciences, Mount Holyoke College.

Duvall, A.J. 1945. Distribution and taxonomy of the Black-capped Chickadees of North America. Auk 62: 49–69.

Dwight, J., Jr. 1897. The whistled call of *Parus atricapillus* common to both sexes. Auk 14: 99.

Dwight, J., Jr. 1900. The sequence of plumages and moults of the passerine birds of New York. Ann. N.Y. Acad. Sci. 13: 73–360.

East, M.L., and H. Hofer. 1986. The use of radio-tracking for monitoring Great Tit, *Parus major*, behaviour: a pilot study. Ibis 128: 103–114.

Eisner, T., R.E. Silberglied, D. Aneshansley, J.E. Carrel, and H.C. Howland. 1969. Ultraviolet video-viewing: the television camera as an insect eye. Science 166: 1172–1174.

Ekman, J. 1979a. Coherence, composition and territories of winter social groups of the Willow Tit, *Parus montanus* de Selys-Longchamp, and the Crested Tit, *P. cristatus* L. Ornis Scand. 10: 56–68.

Ekman, J. 1979b. Non-territorial Willow Tits, *Parus montanus* de Selys-Longchamp, in late summer and early autumn. Ornis Scand. 10: 262–267.

Ekman, J. 1984a. Density-dependent seasonal mortality and population fluctuations of the temperate-zone Willow Tit (*Parus montanus*). J. Anim. Ecol. 53: 119–134.

Ekman, J. 1984b. Stability and persistence of an age-structured avian population in a season environment. J. Anim. Ecol. 53: 135–146.

Ekman, J. 1986. Tree use and predator vulnerability in wintering passerines. Ornis Scand. 17: 261–267.

Ekman, J. 1987. Exposure and time use in Willow Tit flocks. Anim. Behav. 35: 445–452.

Ekman, J. 1988. Dominance, exposure and time use in Willow Tit flocks: the cost of subordination. Acta XIX Congr. Int. Ornithol.: 2373–2381.

Ekman, J. 1989a. Group size in dominance-structured populations. Ornis Scand. 20: 86–88.

Ekman, J. 1989b. Ecology of non-breeding social systems of *Parus*. Wilson Bull. 101: 263–288.

Ekman, J. 1990. Alliances in winter flocks of Willow Tits: effects of rank on survival and reproductive success in male-female associations. Behav. Ecol. Sociobiol. 26: 239–245.

Ekman, J., and C. Askenmo. 1984. Social rank and habitat use in Willow Tit groups. Anim. Behav. 32: 508–514.

Ekman, J., and C. Askenmo. 1986. Reproductive cost, age-specific survival and a comparison of the reproductive strategy in two European tits (genus *Parus*). Evolution 40: 159–168.

Ekman, J., G. Cederholm, and C. Askenmo. 1981. Spacing and survival in winter groups of Willow Tit, *Parus montanus*, and Crested Tit, *P. cristatus*—a removal study. J. Anim. Ecol. 50: 1–9.

Ekman, J., and M. Hake. 1988. Avian flocking reduces starvation risk: an experimental demonstration. Behav. Ecol. Sociobiol. 22: 91–94.

Elder, W. H., and D. Zimmerman. 1983. A comparison of recapture versus resighting data in a 15-year study of survivorship in the Black-capped Chickadee. J. Field Ornithol. 54: 138–145.

Emlen, S.T., and L.W. Oring. 1977. Ecology, sexual selection, and the evolution of mating systems. Science 197: 215–223.

Evans, C.S., and P. Marler. 1991. On the use of video images as social stimuli in birds: audience effects on alarm calling. Anim. Behav. 41:17–26.

Ferson, S., P. Downey, P. Klerks, M. Weissburg, I. Kroot, S. Stewart, G. Jacquez, J. Ssemakula, R. Malenky, and K. Anderson. 1986. Competing reviews, or why do Connell and Schoener disagree? Am. Nat. 127: 571–576.

Fichtel, C.C. 1978. A *Salmonella* outbreak in wild songbirds. N. Am. Bird Bander 3: 146–148.

Ficken, M.S. 1981a. Food finding in Black-capped Chickadees: altruistic communication? Wilson Bull. 93: 393–394.

Ficken, M.S. 1981b. What is the song of the Black-capped Chickadee? Condor 83: 384–386.

Ficken, M.S. 1989. Boreal Chickadees eat ash high in calcium. Wilson Bull. 101: 349–351.

Ficken, M.S. 1990a. Acoustic characteristics of alarm calls associated with predation risk in chickadees. Anim. Behav. 39: 400–401.

Ficken, M.S. 1990b. Vocal repertoire of the Mexican Chickadee. I. Calls. J. Field Ornithol. 61: 380–387.

Ficken, M.S. 1990c. Vocal repertoire of the Mexican Chickadee. II. Song and song-like vocalizations. J. Field Ornithol. 61: 388–395.

Ficken, M.S., and R.W. Ficken. 1987. Bill-sweeping behavior of a Mexican Chickadee. Condor 89: 901–902.

Ficken, M.S., R.W. Ficken, and K.M. Apel. 1985. Dialects in a call associated with pair interactions in the Black-capped Chickadee. Auk 102: 145–151.

Ficken, M.S., R.W. Ficken, and S.R. Witkin. 1978. Vocal repertoire of the Black-capped Chickadee. Auk 95: 34–48.

Ficken, M.S., J.P. Hailman, and R.W. Ficken. 1978. A model of repetitive behaviour illustrated by chick-a-dee calling. Anim. Behav. 26: 630–631.

Ficken, M.S., and C.M. Weise. 1984. A complex call of the Black-capped Chickadee (*Parus atricapillus*). I. Microgeographic variation. Auk 101: 349–360.

Ficken, M.S., and C.M. Weise. 1990. Long-term stability of culturally transmitted calls of chickadees. Acta XX Congr. Int. Ornithol. (Suppl.): 478.

Ficken, M.S., C.M. Weise, and J.W. Popp. 1990. Dominance rank and resource access in winter flocks of Black-capped Chickadees. Wilson Bull. 102: 623–633.

Ficken, M.S., C.M. Weise, and J.A. Reinartz. 1987. A complex vocalization of the Black-capped Chickadee. II. Repertoire, dominance and dialects. Condor 89: 500–509.

Ficken, M.S., and S.R. Witkin. 1977. Responses of Black-capped Chickadee flocks to predators. Auk 94: 156–157.

Ficken, M.S., S.R. Witkin, and C.M. Weise. 1981. Associations among members of a Black-capped Chickadee flock. Behav. Ecol. Sociobiol. 8: 245–249.

Forbush, E.H. 1929. Birds of Massachusetts and Other New England States, vol. 3. Norwood Press, Norwood, Mass.

Freidmann, H., L.F. Kiff, and S.I. Rothstein. 1977. A further contribution to knowledge of the host relations of the parasitic cowbirds. Smithson. Contrib. Zool. 235: 1–75.

Gaddis, P. 1980. Mixed flocks, accipiters and antipredator behavior. Condor 82: 348–349.

Gaddis, P.K. 1985. Structure and variability in the vocal repertoire of the Mountain Chickadee. Wilson Bull. 97: 30–46.

Gaikwad, P.M., and G.B. Shinde. 1984. *Shindeia aurangabadensis* gen. et sp. nov. (Cestoda: Anoplocephalidae) from *Parus major mahrattarum*. Riv. Parassitol. 45: 93–97.

Gaston, A.J. 1978. The evolution of group territorial behaviour and cooperative breeding. Am. Nat. 112: 1091–1100.

Gavin, T.A., and E.K. Bollinger. 1985. Multiple paternity in a territorial passerine: the Bobolink. Auk 102: 550–555.

Geer, T.A. 1978. Effects of nesting sparrowhawks on nesting tits. Condor 80: 419–422.

Geer, T.A. 1982. The selection of tits *Parus* spp. by Sparrowhawks, *Accipiter nisus*. Ibis 124: 159–167.

Getty, T., and J.R. Krebs. 1985. Lagging partial preferences for cryptic prey: a signal detection analysis of Great Tit foraging. Am. Nat. 125: 39–60.

Gibb, J.A. 1950. The breeding biology of Great and Blue Titmice. Ibis 92: 507–539.

Gibb, J.A. 1960. Populations of tits and Goldcrests and their food supply in pine plantations. Ibis 102: 163–208.

Gill, F.B., and M.S. Ficken. 1989. Comparative biology and evolution of titmice. Wilson Bull. 101: 180–181.

Gill, F.B., D.H. Funk, and B. Silverin. 1989. Protein relationships among titmice (*Parus*). Wilson Bull. 101: 182–197.

Glase, J.C. 1973. Ecology of social organization in the Black-capped Chickadee. Living Bird 12: 235–267. [The 1973 issue of *Living Bird* was not actually published until 1974.]

Gochfeld, M. 1977. Plumage variation in Black-capped Chickadees: is there sexual dimorphism? Bird-Banding 48: 62–66.

Goertz, J.W., and K. Rutherford. 1972. Adult Carolina Chickadee carries young. Wilson Bull. 84: 205–206.

Gold, C.S., and D.L. Dahlsten. 1983. Effects of parasitic flies (*Protocalliphora* spp.) on nestlings of Mountain and Chestnut-backed Chickadees. Wilson Bull. 95: 560–572.

Gompertz, T. 1967. The hiss-display of the Great Tit (*Parus major*). Vogelwelt 88: 165–169.

Goodbody, I.M. 1952. The post-fledging dispersal of juvenile titmice. Br. Birds 45: 279–285.

Goodpasture, K.A. 1955. Recovery of a chickadee population from the 1951 ice storm. Migrant 26: 21–23.

Gosler, A.G., and J.R. King 1989. A sexually dimorphic plumage character in the Coal Tit, *Parus ater*, with notes on the Marsh Tit, *Parus palustris*. Ringing & Migr. 10: 53–57.

Gould, J.L. 1982, Ethology: The Mechanisms and Evolution of Behavior. W.W. Norton, New York.

Gowaty, P.A., and A.A. Karlin. 1984. Multiple maternity and paternity in single broods of apparently monogamous Eastern Bluebirds (*Sialia sialis*). Behav. Ecol. Sociobiol. 15: 91–95.

Greenewalt, C.H. 1955. The flight of the Black-capped Chickadee and the White-breasted Nuthatch. Auk 72: 1–5.

Greenwood, P.J., P.H. Harvey, and C.M. Perrins. 1979. The role of dispersal in the Great Tit (*Parus major*): the causes, consequences, and heritability of natal dispersal. J. Anim. Ecol. 48: 123–142.

Greiner, E.C., G.F. Bennett, E.M. White, and R.F. Coombs. 1975. Distribution of the avian hematozoa in North America. Can. J. Zool. 53: 1762–1787.

Griffee, W.E. 1961. Mountain Chickadee nesting in a dirt bank. Murrelet 42: 9.

Gross, M. 1972. Mathematical Models in Linguistics. Prentice Hall, Englewood Cliffs, N.J.

Grossman, A.F., and G.C. West. 1977. Metabolic rate and temperature regulation of winter acclimatized Black-capped Chickadees, *Parus atricapillus*, of interior Alaska. Ornis Scand. 8: 127–138.

Grubb, T.C., Jr. 1975. Weather-dependent foraging behavior of some birds wintering in a deciduous woodland. Condor 77: 175–182.

Grubb, T.C., Jr. 1977. Weather-dependent foraging behavior of some birds wintering in a deciduous woodland: horizontal adjustments. Condor 79: 271–274.

Grubb, T.C., Jr. 1978. Weather-dependent foraging rates of wintering woodland birds. Auk 95: 370–376.

Grubb, T.C., Jr. 1979. Factors controlling foraging strategies of insectivorous birds. Pp. 119–135 *in* J.G. Dickson, R.N. Connor, R.R. Fleet, J.C. Kroll, and J.A. Jackson, eds., The Role of Insectivorous Birds in Forest Ecosystems. Academic Press, New York.

Grubb, T.C., Jr. 1987. Changes in the flocking behaviour of wintering English titmice with time, weather and supplementary food. Anim. Behav. 35: 794–806.

Grubb, T.C., Jr. 1989. Ptilochronology: feather growth bars as indicators of nutritional status. Auk 106: 314–320.

Grubb, T.C., Jr., and D.A. Cimprich. 1990a. Supplementary food improves the nutritional condition of wintering woodland birds: evidence from ptilochronology. Ornis Scand. 21: 277–281.

Grubb, T.C., Jr., and D.A. Cimprich 1990b. Interspecific competition between parids: a ptilochronology approach. Acta XX Congr. Int. Ornithol. (Suppl.): 291.

Grundel, R. 1987. Determinants of nestling feeding rates and parental investment in the Mountain Chickadee. Condor 89: 319–328.

Grundel, R. 1990. The role of dietary diversity, prey capture sequence and individuality in prey selection by parent Mountain Chickadees (*Parus gambeli*). J. Anim. Ecol. 59: 959–976.

Gustafsson, L. 1987. Interspecific competition lowers fitness in Collared Flycatchers, *Ficedula albicollis*: an experimental demonstration. Ecology 68: 291–296.

Gustafsson, L. 1988. Foraging behaviour of individual Coal Tits, *Parus ater*, in relation to their age, sex and morphology. Anim. Behav. 36: 696–704.

Haartman, L. von. 1971. Population dynamics. Pp. 391–459 in D.S. Farner and J.R. King, eds., Avian Biology, vol. 1. Academic Press, New York.

Haftorn, S. 1956. Contribution to the food biology of tits, especially about storing of surplus food. Part IV. A comparative analysis of *Parus atricapillus* L., *P. cristatus* L., and *P. ater* L. Det Kgl. Norske Vidensk. Selsk. Forh. 1956 Nr 4: 1–54.

Haftorn, S. 1959. The proportion of spruce seeds removed by the tits in a Norwegian spruce forest in 1954–55. Det Kgl. Norske Vidensk. Selsk. Forh. 32: 121–125.

Haftorn, S. 1972. Hypothermia of tits in the arctic winter. Ornis Scand. 3: 153–166.

Haftorn, S. 1974. Storage of surplus food by the Boreal Chickadee, *Parus hudsonicus*, in Alaska, with some records on the Mountain Chickadee, *Parus gambeli*, in Colorado. Ornis Scand. 5: 145–161.

Haftorn, S. 1988a. Incubating female passerines do not let the egg temperature fall below the "physiological zero temperature" during their absences from the nest. Ornis Scand. 19: 97–110.

Haftorn, S. 1988b. Survival strategies of small birds during winter. Acta XIX Congr. Int. Ornithol.: 1973–1980.

Haftorn, S. 1989. Seasonal and diurnal body weight variations in titmice, based on analyses of individual birds. Wilson Bull. 101: 217–235.

Haftorn, S. 1990. Social organization of winter flocks of Willow Tits, *Parus montanus*, in a Norwegian subalpine birch forest. Pp. 401–413 in J. Blondel, A. Gosler, J.-D. Lebreton, and R. McCleery, eds., Population Biology of Passerine Birds, an Integrated Approach. NATO ASI Series, vol. G-24. Springer-Verlag, Heidelberg.

Haftorn, S., and R.E. Reinertsen. 1985. The effect of temperature and clutch size on the energetic cost of incubation in a free-living Blue Tit (*Parus caeruleus*). Auk 102: 470–478.

Hailman, J.P. 1989. The organization of major vocalizations in the Paridae. Wilson Bull. 101: 305–343.

Hailman, J.P., and M.S. Ficken. 1986. Combinatorial animal communication with computable syntax: chick-a-dee calling qualifies as "language" by structural linguistics. Anim. Behav. 34: 1899–1901.

Hailman, J.P., M.S. Ficken, and R.W. Ficken. 1985. The "chick-a-dee" calls of *Parus atricapillus*: a recombinant system of animal communication compared with written English. Semiotica 56: 191–224.

Hailman, J.P., M.S. Ficken, and R.W. Ficken. 1987. Constraints on the structure of combinatorial "chick-a-dee" calls. Ethology 75: 62–80.

Hamerstrom, F. 1942. Dominance in winter flocks of chickadees. Wilson Bull. 54: 32–42.

Hamerstrom, F.N., and F. Hamerstrom. 1951. Food of young raptors on the Edwin S. George reserve. Wilson Bull. 63: 16–25.

Hamilton, W.D. 1971. Geometry for the selfish herd. J. Theoret. Biol. 31: 295–311.

Harding, K.C. 1932. Age record of Black-capped Chickadee. Bird-Banding 3: 118.

Hartzler, J.E. 1970. Winter dominance relationship in Black-capped Chickadees. Wilson Bull. 82: 427–434.

Hawks, C.E. 1983. Food quality discrimination by Black-capped Chickadees (*Parus atricapillus*) using color cues. Honors thesis, Dept. of Biological Sciences, Mount Holyoke College.

Hegner, R.E. 1985. Dominance and antipredator behaviour in Blue Tits (*Parus caeruleus*). Anim. Behav. 33: 762–768.

Heinrich, B., and S.L. Collins. 1983. Caterpillar leaf damage and the game of hide-and-seek with birds. Ecology 64: 592–602.

Herman, C.M. 1962. The role of birds in the epizootiology of eastern encephalitis. Auk 79: 99–103.

Hickey, M.B. 1952. Display of Black-capped Chickadee, *Parus atricapillus*. Auk 69: 88.

Hill, B.G., and M.R. Lein. 1987. Function of frequency-shifted songs of Black-capped Chickadees. Condor 89: 914–915.

Hill, B.G., and M.R. Lein. 1988. Ecological relations of sympatric Black-capped and Mountain Chickadees in southwestern Alberta. Condor 90: 875–884.

Hill, B.G., and M.R. Lein. 1989a. Territory overlap and habitat use of sympatric chickadees. Auk 106: 259–268.

Hill, B.G., and M.R. Lein. 1989b. Natural and simulated encounters between sympatric Black-capped Chickadees and Mountain Chickadees. Auk 106: 645–652.

Hill, G.E. 1986. The distress calls given by Tufted Titmice (*Parus bicolor*): an experimental approach. Anim. Behav. 34: 590–598.

Hill, R.W., D.L. Beaver, and J.H. Veghte. 1980. Body surface temperatures and thermoregulation in the Black-capped Chickadee (*Parus atricapillus*). Physiol. Zool. 53: 305–321.

Hinde, R.A. 1952. The behaviour of the Great Tit (*Parus major*) and some other related species. Behaviour Suppl. 2: 1–201.

Hinde, R.A., and J. Fisher. 1952. Further observations on the opening of milk bottles by birds. Brit. Birds 44: 393–396.

Hissa, R., and R. Palokangas. 1970. Thermoregulation in the titmouse (*Parus major* L.). Comp. Biochem. Physiol. 33: 941–953.

Hitchcock, C.L., and D.F. Sherry. 1990. Long-term memory for cache sites in the Black-capped Chickadee. Anim. Behav. 40: 701–712.

Hogstad, O. 1987a. Social rank in winter flocks of Willow Tits, *Parus montanus*. Ibis 129: 1–9.

Hogstad, O. 1987b. It is expensive to be dominant. Auk 104: 333–336.

Hogstad, O. 1988a. Social rank and antipredatory behaviour of Willow Tits, *Parus montanus*, in winter flocks. Ibis 130: 45–56.

Hogstad, O. 1988b. Advantages of social foraging in Willow Tits, *Parus montanus*. Ibis 130: 275–283.

Hogstad, O. 1988c. Rank-related resource access in winter flocks of Willow Tit, *Parus montanus*. Ornis Scand. 19: 169–174.

Hogstad, O. 1988d. The influence of energy stress on social organization and behaviour of Willow Tits, *Parus montanus*. Fauna Norv. Ser. C, Cinclus 11: 89–94.

Hogstad, O. 1989a. Subordination in mixed-age bird flocks—a removal study. Ibis 131: 128–134.

Hogstad, O. 1989b. Social organization and dominance behavior in some *Parus* species. Wilson Bull. 101: 254–262.

Hogstad, O. 1989c. The role of juvenile Willow Tits, *Parus montanus*, in the regulation of winter flock size: an experimental study. Anim. Behav. 38: 920–925.

Hogstad, O. 1990a. Winter floaters in Willow Tits (*Parus montanus*)—a matter of choice or making the best of a bad situation? Pp. 415–421 *in* J. Blondel, A. Gosler, J.-D. Lebreton, and R. McCleery, eds., Population Biology of Passerine Birds, an Integrated Approach, NATO ASI Series, vol. G-24. Springer-Verlag, Heidelberg.

Hogstad, O. 1990b. Food constraints and age-related mortality in wintering Willow Tits. Acta XX Congr. Int. Ornithol. (Suppl.): 375.

Högstedt, G. 1980. Evolution of clutch size in birds: adaptive variation in relation to territory. Science 210: 1148–1150.

Holleback, M. 1974. Behavioral interactions and the dispersal of the family in Black-capped Chickadees. Wilson Bull. 86: 466–468.

Horn, A.G., M.L. Leonard, L.M.R. Ratcliffe, and R. Weisman. 1989. Variability in the whistled song of Black-capped Chickadees. Abstract from the Northeast Animal Behavior Society Conference, 1989.

Howitz, J.L. 1986a. Brood adoption by a male Black-capped Chickadee. Wilson Bull. 98: 312–313.

Howitz, J.L. 1986b. Bull snake predation on a Black-capped Chickadee nest. Loon 58: 132.

Hunter, M.L., Jr., and J.R. Krebs. 1979. Geographical variation in the song of the Great Tit (*Parus major*) in relation to ecological factors. J. Anim. Ecol. 48: 759–786.

Hussell, D.J.T., and R.W. Stamp. 1965. Movements of Black-capped Chickadees at Long Point, Ontario during the spring of 1962. Bird-Banding 36: 71–80.

Hutchins, N.E. 1989. Individual rates of learning of food quality discrimination by Black-capped Chickadees (*Parus atricapillus*). Honors thesis, Dept. of Biological Sciences, Mount Holyoke College.

Immelmann, K., J.P. Hailman, and J.R. Baylis. 1982. Reputed band attractiveness and sex manipulation in Zebra Finches. Science 215: 422.

Jansson, C., J. Ekman, and A. von Brömssen. 1981. Winter mortality and food supply in tits *Parus* spp. Oikos 37: 313–322.

Järvi, T., and M. Bakken. 1984. The function of the variation in the breast stripe of the Great Tit (*Parus major*). Anim. Behav. 32: 590–596.

Järvi, T., Ø. Walsø, and M. Bakken. 1987. Status signalling by *Parus major*: an experiment in deception. Ethology 76: 334–342.

Johnston, D.W. 1971. Ecological aspects of hybridizing chickadees (*Parus*) in Virginia. Am. Midl. Nat. 85: 124–134.

Johnston, V.R. 1942. Factors influencing local movements of woodland birds in winter. Wilson Bull. 54: 192–198.

Joste, N., D.J. Ligon, and P.B. Stacey. 1985. Shared paternity in the Acorn Woodpecker (*Melanerpes formicivorus*). Behav. Ecol. Sociobiol. 17: 39–41.

Kacelnik, A., A.I. Houston, and J.R. Krebs. 1981. Optimal foraging and territorial defence in the Great Tit (*Parus major*). Behav. Ecol. Sociobiol. 8: 35–40.

Källander, H. 1974. Advancement of laying of Great Tits by the provision of food. Ibis 116: 365–367.

Kamil, A.C., S.I. Yoerg, and K.C. Clements. 1988. Rules to leave by: patch departure in foraging Blue Jays. Anim. Behav. 36: 843–853.

Kelly, K.C. 1988. Duration of the dee component of the "chickadee" call and associated behavior in Carolina Chickadees (*Parus carolinensis*). Abstract No. 62, Wilson Ornithological Society Centennial Meeting, June 8–12, 1988, Rosemont, Penn. Wilson Ornithological Society, Ann Arbor.

Kendra, P.E., R.R. Roth, and D.W. Tallamy. 1988. Conspecific brood parasitism in the House Sparrow. Wilson Bull. 100: 80–90.

Kennard, J.H. 1975. Longevity records of North American birds. Bird-Banding 46: 55–73.

Kessel, B. 1976. Winter activity patterns of Black-capped Chickadees in interior Alaska. Wilson Bull. 88: 36–61.

Ketterson, E.D., and V. Nolan Jr. 1986. Effect of laparotomy of Tree Sparrows and Dark-eyed Juncos during winter on subsequent survival in the field. J. Field Ornithol. 57: 239–240.

Keyes, B.E., and C.E. Grue. 1982. Capturing birds with mist nets: a review. N. Am. Bird Bander 7: 1–14.

Kilham, L. 1968. Reproductive behavior of White-breasted Nuthatches. I. Distraction display, bill-sweeping and nest-hole defense. Auk 85: 477–492.

King, J.R. 1972. Adaptive periodic fat storage by birds. Proc. 15th Int. Ornithol. Congr.: 200–217.

King, J.R., and D.S. Farner. 1965. Studies of fat deposition in migratory birds. Ann. N.Y. Acad. Sci. 131: 422–440.

Klein, B.C. 1988. Weather-dependent mixed-species flocking during the winter. Auk 105: 583–584.

Kluijver, H.N. 1951. The population ecology of the Great Tit, *Parus m. major* L. Ardea 39: 1–135.

Kluyver, H.N. 1957. Roosting habits, sexual dominance and survival in the Great Tit. Cold Spring Harbor Symp. Quant. Biol. 22: 281–285.

Kluyver, H.N. 1961. Food consumption in relation to habitat in breeding chickadees. Auk 78: 532–550.

Kluyver, H.N. 1966. Regulation of a bird population. Ostrich Suppl. 6: 389–396.

Kluyver, H.N. 1971. Regulation of numbers in populations of Great Tits (*Parus major major*). Pp. 507–523 *in* P.J. den Boer and G.R. Gradwell, eds., Dynamics of Populations. Pudoc, Wageningen.

Kluyver, H.N., and L. Tinbergen. 1953. Territory and the regulation of density in titmice. Arch. Neerl. Zool. 10: 265–289.

Korhonen, K. 1981. Temperature in the nocturnal shelters of the Redpoll

(*Acanthis flammea* L.) and the Siberian Tit (*Parus cinctus* Budd.) in winter. Ann. Zool. Fenn. 18: 165–168.

Krebs, J.R. 1970. The efficiency of courtship feeding in the Blue Tit, *Parus caeruleus*. Ibis 112: 108–110.

Krebs, J.R. 1971. Territory and breeding density in the Great Tit, *Parus major* L. Ecology 52: 1–22.

Krebs, J.R. 1973. Social learning and the significance of mixed-species flocks of chickadees (*Parus* spp.). Can. J. Zool. 51: 1275–1288.

Krebs, J.R. 1977. Song and territory in the Great Tit, *Parus major*. Pp. 47–62 *in* B. Stonehouse and C. Perrins, eds., Evolutionary Ecology. Macmillan, London.

Krebs, J.R. 1980. Optimal foraging, predation risk and territory defence. Ardea 68: 83–90.

Krebs, J.R., A. Kacelnik, and P. Taylor. 1978. Test of optimal sampling by foraging Great Tits. Nature (London) 275: 27–31.

Krebs, J.R., M.H. MacRoberts, and J.M. Cullen. 1972. Flocking and feeding in the Great Tit, *Parus major*—an experimental study. Ibis 114: 507–530.

Krebs, J.R., J.C. Ryan, and E.L. Charnov. 1975. Hunting by expectation or optimal foraging? A study of patch use by chickadees. Anim. Behav. 22: 953–964.

Krebs, J.R., D.F. Sherry, S.D. Healy, V.H. Perry, and A.L. Vaccarino. 1989. Hippocampal specialization of food-storing in birds. Proc. Nat. Acad. Sci. 86: 1388–1392.

Kricher, J.C. 1981. Range expansion of the Tufted Titmouse (*Parus bicolor*) in Massachusetts. Am. Birds 35: 750–753.

Kron, T.M. 1975. Late winter bird populations in subarctic taiga forest near Fairbanks, Alaska. Auk 92: 390–393.

Kroodsma, D.E. 1982. Learning and the ontogeny of sound signals in birds. Pp. 1–23 *in* D.E. Kroodsma and E.H. Miller, eds., Acoustic Communication in Birds, vol. 2. Academic Press, New York.

Lack, D. 1946. Do juvenile birds survive less well than adults? Br. Birds 39: 258–264.

Lack, D. 1954. The Natural Regulation of Animal Numbers. Clarendon, Oxford.

LaGory, K.E., M.K. LaGory, D.M. Meyers, and S.G. Herman. 1984. Niche relationships in wintering mixed-species flocks in western Washington. Wilson Bull. 96: 108–116.

Lawrence, E.S. 1986. Can Great Tits (*Parus major*) acquire search images? Oikos 47: 3–12.

Lawrence, L. de K. 1958. On regional movements and body weight of Black-capped Chickadees in winter. Auk 75: 415–443.

Leak, J.A. 1986. How do female Black-capped Chickadees avoid winter subordination costs? Honors thesis, Dept. of Biological Sciences, Mount Holyoke College.

Leighton, F.A. 1988. Some observations of diseases occurring in Saskatchewan wildlife. Blue Jay 46: 121–125.

Lendrem, D.W. 1983. Predation risk and vigilance in the Blue Tit (*Parus caeruleus*). Behav. Ecol. Sociobiol. 14: 9–13.

Lima, S.L. 1985. Maximizing feeding efficiency and minimizing time exposed to predators: a trade-off in the Black-capped Chickadee. Oecologia 66: 60–67.

Lima, S.L. 1986. Predation risk and unpredictable feeding conditions: determinants of body mass in birds. Ecology 67: 377–385.

Locke, L.N., R.B. Shillinger, and T. Jareed. 1973. Salmonellosis in passerine birds in Maryland and West Virginia. J. Wildl. Dis. 9: 144–145.

Loery, G., and J.D. Nichols. 1985. Dynamics of a Black-capped Chickadee population, 1958–1983. Ecology 66: 1195–1203.

Loery, G., K.H. Pollock, J.D. Nichols, and J.E. Hines, 1987. Age-specificity of Black-capped Chickadee survival rates: analysis of capture-recapture data. Ecology 68: 1038–1044.

Lohr, B., S. Nowicki, and R. Weisman. 1991. Pitch production in Carolina Chickadee songs. Condor 93: 197–199.

Long, C.A. 1982, Comparison of the nest-site distraction displays of Black-capped Chickadee and White-breasted Nuthatch. Wilson Bull. 94: 216–218.

Low, R.J. 1969. A Black-capped Chickadee variant. Auk 86: 354–355.

Lowther, P.E. 1983. Chickadee, thrasher, and other cowbird hosts from northwest Iowa. J. Field Ornithol. 54: 414–417.

Lucas, J.R. 1987. The influence of time constraints on diet choice of the Great Tit, *Parus major*. Anim. Behav. 35: 1538–1548.

Lustick, S. 1969. Bird energetics: effects of artificial radiation. Science 163: 387–390.

Lustick, S., S. Talbot, and E.L. Fox. 1970. Absorption of radiant energy in Red-winged Blackbirds (*Agelaius phoeniceus*). Condor 72: 471–473.

Mace, R.H. 1988. Diurnal patterns of mate guarding in Great Tits. Acta XIX Congr. Int. Ornithol.: 435–441.

Mace, R.H. 1989. Great tits choose between food and proximity to a mate. The effect of time of day. Behav. Ecol. Sociobiol. 24: 285–290.

Mack, A.L., F.B. Gill, R. Colburn, and C. Spolsky. 1986. Mitochondrial DNA: a source of genetic markers for studies of similar passerine bird species. Auk 103: 676–681.

MacWhirter, R.B. 1989. On the rarity of intraspecific brood parasitism. Condor 91: 485–492.

Malcomson, R.O. 1960. Mallophaga from birds of North America. Wilson Bull. 72: 182–197.

Mammen, D.L., and S. Nowicki. 1981. Individual differences and within-flock convergence in chickadee calls. Behav. Ecol. Sociobiol. 9: 179–186.

Martin, A.C., H.S. Zim, and A.L. Nelson. 1951. American Wildlife and Plants. McGraw-Hill, New York.

Matthysen, E. 1990. Nonbreeding social organization in *Parus*. Pp. 209–249 in D.M. Power, ed., Current Ornithology, vol. 7. Plenum Press, New York.

Mayer, L., S. Lustick, and B. Battersby. 1982. The importance of cavity roosting and hypothermia to energy balance of the winter acclimatized Carolina Chickadee. Int. J. Biometeorol. 26: 231–238.

Mayer, L., S. Lustick, and T.C. Grubb, Jr. 1979. Energetic control of behavior: foraging in Carolina Chickadees. Comp. Biochem. Physiol. 63A: 577–579.

Mayr, E. 1946. History of the North American bird fauna. Wilson Bull. 58: 1–68.

Mayr, E., and L.L. Short. 1970. Species taxa of North American birds. Publ. Nuttall Ornithol. Club, No. 9.

McCallum, D.A. 1988. Alternative emigration strategies and the adaptive significance of natal dispersal in a population of Mountain Chickadees (*Parus gambeli*). Ph.D. dissertation, Univ. of New Mexico, Albuquerque.

McCallum, D.A. 1990. Variable cone crops, migration, and dynamics of a population of Mountain Chickadees (*Parus gambeli*). Pp. 103–116 *in* J. Blondel, A. Gosler, J.-D. Lebreton, and R. McCleery, eds., Population Biology of Passerine Birds, an Integrated Approach. NATO ASI Series, vol. G-24. Springer-Verlag, Heidelberg.

McCamey, F. 1961. The chickadee trap. Bird-Banding 32: 51–55.

McClure, E. 1984. Bird Banding. Boxwood Press, Pacific Grove, CA.

McLaren, M.A. 1975. Breeding biology of the Boreal Chickadee. Wilson Bull. 87:344–354.

McLaren, M.A. 1976. Vocalizations of the Boreal Chickadee. Auk 93: 451–463.

McLaughlin, R.L., and R.D. Montgomerie. 1985. Brood division by Lapland Longspurs. Auk 102: 687–695.

Meigs, J.B., D.C. Smith, and J. Van Buskirk. 1983. Age determination of Black-capped Chickadees. J. Field Ornithol. 54: 283–286.

Merritt, P.G. 1978. Characteristics of Black-capped and Carolina Chickadees at the range interface in northern Indiana. Jack-Pine Warbler 56: 171–179.

Merritt, P.G. 1981. Narrowly disjunct allopatry between Black-capped and Carolina Chickadees in northern Indiana. Wilson Bull. 93: 54–66.

Metz, K.J., and P.J. Weatherhead. 1991. Color bands function as secondary sexual traits in male Red-winged Blackbirds. Behav. Ecol. Sociobiol. 28: 23–27.

Minock, M.E. 1971. Social relationships among Mountain Chickadees. Condor 73: 118–120.

Minock, M.E. 1972. Interspecific aggression between Black-capped and Mountain Chickadees at winter feeding stations. Condor 74: 454–461.

Minot, E.O. 1981. Effects of interspecific competition for food in breeding Blue and Great Tits. J. Anim. Ecol. 50: 375–385.

Mitchell, M.H. 1950. Unusual bathing techniques employed by birds. Wilson Bull. 62: 138.

Møller, A.P. 1988. False alarm calls as a means of resource usurpation in the Great Tit, *Parus major*. Ethology 79: 25–30.

Moreno, E. 1990. The musculi flexor perforatus digiti II and flexor digitorum longus in Paridae. Condor 92: 634–638.

Morrison, M.L. 1974. Influence of sample size and sampling design on analysis of avian foraging behavior. Condor 86: 146–150.

Morse, D.H. 1970. Ecological aspects of some mixed-species foraging flocks of birds. Ecol. Monogr. 40: 119–168.

Morse, D.H. 1973. Interactions between tit flocks and Sparrowhawks, *Accipiter nisus*. Ibis 115: 591–593.

Morse, D.H. 1978. Structure and foraging patterns of tit flocks in an English woodland. Ibis 120: 298–312.

344    References

Morse, D.H. 1980. Behavioral Mechanisms in Ecology. Harvard Univ. Press, Cambridge.

Morton, E. 1975. Ecological sources of selection on avian sounds. Am. Nat. 108: 17–34.

Mosher, J., and S. Lane. 1972. A method of determining the sex of captured Black-capped Chickadees. Bird-Banding 43: 139–140.

Mostrom, A.M. 1988. Carolina Chickadees (*Parus carolinensis*) exhibit ambiguous rank relationships. Abstract No. 96, Wilson Ornithological Society Centennial Meeting, June 8–12 1988, Rosemont, Penn. Wilson Ornithological Society, Ann Arbor.

Mueller, E. 1973. Chickadees at adjacent feeding sites: the effects of food deprivation. Auk 90: 520–532.

Murie, A. 1933. Chickadee occupies robin nest. Auk 50: 111.

Myton, B.A., and R.W. Ficken. 1967. Seed-size preference in chickadees and titmice in relation to ambient temperatures. Wilson Bull. 79: 319–321.

Nakamura, D., T.R. Tiersch, M. Douglass, and R.W. Chandler. 1990. Rapid identification of sex in birds by flow cytometry. Cytogenet. Cell Genet. 53: 201–205.

Nakamura, H., and Y. Wako. 1988. Food storing behaviour of Willow Tit, *Parus montanus*. J. Yamashina Inst. Ornith. 20: 21–36.

Nakamura, T. 1975. A study of Paridae community in Japan. III. Ecological separation in social structure and distribution. Misc. Rep. Yamashina Inst. Ornith. 7: 603–636.

Newton, I. 1968. The temperatures, weights, and body composition of molting Bullfinches. Condor 70: 323–332.

Nickell, W.P. 1956. Nesting of the Black-capped Chickadee in the southern peninsula of Michigan. Jack-Pine Warbler 34: 127–138.

Nilsson, J.-Å. 1989a. Causes and consequences of natal dispersal in the Marsh Tit, *Parus palustris*. J. Anim. Ecol. 58: 619–636.

Nilsson, J.-Å. 1989b. Establishment of juvenile marsh tits in winter flocks: an experimental study. Anim. Behav. 38: 586–595.

Nilsson, J.-Å., and H.G. Smith. 1985. Early fledgling mortality and the timing of juvenile dispersal in the Marsh Tit, *Parus palustris*. Ornis Scand. 16: 293–298.

Nilsson, J.-Å., and H.G. Smith. 1988. Effects of dispersal date on winter flock establishment and social dominance in Marsh Tits, *Parus palustris*. J. Anim. Ecol. 57: 917–928.

Nilsson, S.G. 1984. The evolution of nest-site selection among hole-nesting birds: the importance of nest predation and competition. Ornis Scand. 15: 167–175.

Norris, K.J., and J.K. Blakey. 1989. Evidence for cuckoldry in the Great Tit, *Parus major*. Ibis 131:436–442.

Nottebohm, F. 1975. Vocal behavior in birds. Pp. 287–332 *in* D.S. Farner and J.R. King, eds., Avian Biology, vol. 5. Academic Press, New York.

Nowicki, S. 1983. Flock-specific recognition of chickadee calls. Behav. Ecol. Sociobiol. 12: 317–320.

Nowicki, S. 1987. Vocal tract resonances in oscine bird sound production: evidence from birdsongs in a helium atmosphere. Nature (London) 325: 53–55.

Nowicki, S. 1989. Vocal plasticity in captive Black-capped Chickadees: the acoustic basis and rate of call convergence. Anim. Behav. 37: 64–73.

Nowicki, S., and R.R. Capranica. 1986a. Bilateral syringeal interaction in vocal production of an oscine bird sound. Science 231: 1297–1299.

Nowicki, S., and R.R. Capranica. 1986b. Bilateral syringeal coupling during phonation of a songbird. J. Neurosci. 6: 3595–3610.

Nowicki, S., and D.A. Nelson. 1990. Defining natural categories in acoustic signals: comparison of three methods applied to "chick-a-dee" call notes. Ethology 86: 89–101.

Nur, N. 1984a. The consequences of brood size for breeding Blue Tits. I. Adult survival, weight change and the cost of reproduction. J. Anim. Ecol. 53: 479–496.

Nur, N. 1984b. The consequences of brood size for breeding Blue Tits. II. Nestling weight, offspring survival and optimal brood size. J. Anim. Ecol. 53: 497–517.

Nur, N. 1986. Is clutch size variation in the Blue Tit (*Parus caeruleus*) adaptive? An experimental study. J. Anim. Ecol. 55: 983–999.

Nur, N. 1988. The consequences of brood size for breeding Blue Tits. III. Measuring the cost of reproduction: survival, future fecundity, and differential dispersal. Evolution 42: 351–362.

O'Connor, R.J. 1980. Pattern and process in Great Tit (*Parus major*) populations in Britain. Ardea 68: 165–183.

Odum, E.P. 1941a. Annual cycle of the Black-capped Chickadee—1. Auk 58: 314–333.

Odum, E.P. 1941b. Annual cycle of the Black-capped Chickadee—2. Auk 58: 518–534.

Odum, E.P. 1941c. Winter homing behavior of the chickadee. Bird-Banding 12: 113–119.

Odum, E.P. 1942a. Annual cycle of the Black-capped Chickadee—3. Auk 59: 499–531.

Odum, E.P. 1942b. A comparison of two chickadee seasons. Bird-Banding 13: 154–159.

Odum, E.P. 1943. Some physiological variations in the Black-capped Chickadee. Wilson Bull. 55: 178–191.

Oliphant, L.W. 1983. First observations of brown fat in birds. Condor 85: 350–354.

Olson, J.M., W.R. Dawson, and J.J. Camilliere. 1988. Fat from Black-capped Chickadees: avian brown adipose tissue? Condor 90: 529–537.

Orell, M. 1989. Population fluctuations and survival of Great Tits, *Parus major*, dependent on food supplied by man in winter. Ibis 131: 112–127.

Orell, M., and K. Koivula. 1988. Cost of reproduction: parental survival and production of recruits in the Willow Tit, *Parus montanus*. Oecologia 77: 423–432.

Orell, M., and K. Koivula. 1990. Effects of brood size manipulations on adult and juvenile survival and future fecundity in the Willow Tit, *Parus montanus*. Pp. 297–306 *in* J. Blondel, A. Gosler, J.-D. Lebreton, and R. McCleery, eds., Population Biology of Passerine Birds, an Integrated Approach. NATO ASI Series, vol. G-24. Springer-Verlag, Heidelberg.

Orell, M., and M. Ojanen. 1983. Breeding biology and population dynamics of the Willow Tit, *Parus montanus*. Ann. Zool. Fenn. 20: 99–114.

Orians, G.H. 1969. On the evolution of mating systems in birds and mammals. Am. Nat. 103: 589–603.

Orr, C.D. 1985. Some benefits and costs of living in flocks for male and female Black-capped Chickadees. Ph.D. dissertation, Simon Fraser Univ., Burnaby.

Orr, C.D., and N.A.M. Verbeek. 1984. Female demands: some fitness implications in chickadee flocks. Can. J. Zool. 62: 2550–2552.

Packard, F.M. 1936. A Black-capped Chickadee victimized by the Eastern Cowbird. Bird-Banding 7: 129–130.

Parkes, K.C. 1958. The palearctic element in the New World avifauna. Pp. 421–432 *in* C.L. Hubbs, ed., Zoogeography. Publ. No. 51. Amer. Assoc. Adv. Sci., Washington, D.C.

Partridge, L. 1976. Individual differences in feeding efficiencies and feeding preferences of captive Great Tits. Anim. Behav. 24: 230–240.

Peck, G.K., and R.D. James. 1987. Breeding Birds of Ontario: Nidology and Distribution. Vol. 2: Passerines. Royal Ontario Museum, Toronto.

Perrins, C.M. 1965. Population fluctuations and clutch size in the Great Tit, *Parus major*. J. Anim. Ecol. 34: 601–647.

Perrins, C.M. 1968. The purpose of the high-intensity alarm calls in small passerines. Ibis 110: 200–201.

Perrins, C.M. 1970. The timing of birds' breeding seasons. Ibis 112: 242–255.

Perrins, C.M. 1979. British Tits. William Collins and Co., Glasgow.

Perrins, C.M. 1988. Survival of young Great Tits: relationships with weight. Acta XIX Congr. Int. Ornithol.: 892–899.

Perrins, C.M. 1990. Factors affecting clutch-size in Great and Blue Tits. Pp. 121–130 *in* J. Blondel, A. Gosler, J.-D. Lebreton, and R. McCleery, eds., Population Biology of Passerine Birds, an Integrated Approach. NATO ASI Series, vol. G-24. Springer-Verlag, Heidelberg.

Perrins, C.M., and T.R. Birkhead. 1983. Avian Ecology. Blackie & Son, Glasgow.

Perrins, C.M., and T.A. Geer. 1980. The effect of Sparrowhawks on tit populations. Ardea 68: 133–142.

Perrins, C.M., and R.H. McCleery. 1989. Laying dates and clutch size in the Great Tit. Wilson Bull. 101: 236–253.

Perrins, C.M., and D. Moss. 1974. Survival of young Great Tits in relation to age of female parent. Ibis 116: 220–224.

Peters, H.S. 1936. A list of external parasites from birds of the eastern part of the United States. Bird-Banding 7: 9–27.

Petit, D.R., L.J. Petit, and K.E. Petit. 1989. Winter caching ecology of deciduous woodland birds and adaptations for protection of stored food. Condor 91: 766–776.

Piaskowski, V., C.M. Weise, and M.S. Ficken. 1988. Body ruffling display of the Black-capped Chickadee (*Parus atricapillus*). Abstract No. 99, Wilson Ornithological Society Centennial Meeting, June 8–12, 1988, Rosemont, Penn. Wilson Ornithological Society, Ann Arbor.

Pickens, A.L. 1928. Auditory protective mimicry of the chickadee. Auk 45: 302–304.

Picman, J., and J.-C. Belles-Isles. 1988. Interspecific egg pecking by the Black-capped Chickadee. Wilson Bull. 100: 664–665.

Pierce, V., and T.C. Grubb, Jr. 1981. Laboratory studies of foraging in four bird species in deciduous woodland. Auk 98: 307–320.

Pitelka, F.A. 1958. Timing of molt in Steller Jays of the Queen Charlotte Islands, British Columbia. Condor 60: 38–49.

Pitts, T.D. 1976. Fall and winter roosting habits of Carolina Chickadees. Wilson Bull. 88: 603–610.

Plowright, C.M.S., and R.C. Plowright. 1987. Oversampling by Great Tits? A critique of Krebs, Kacelnik, and Taylor's (1978) "Test of optimal sampling by great tits." Can. J. Zool. 65: 1282–1283.

Poor, H.H. 1946. The chickadee flight of 1941–42. Proc. Linn. Soc. New York 54–57: 16–27.

Popp, J.W., M.S. Ficken, and C.M. Weise. 1990. How are agonistic encounters among Black-capped Chickadees resolved? Anim. Behav. 39: 980–986.

Powell, G.V.N. 1974. Experimental analysis of the social value of flocking by Starlings (*Sturnus vulgaris*) in relation to predation and foraging. Anim. Behav. 22: 501–505.

Pyke, G.H., H.R. Pulliam, and E.L. Charnov. 1977. Optimal foraging: a selective review of theory and tests. Q. Rev. Biol. 52: 137–154.

Quinn, T.W., F. Cooke, and B.N. White. 1990. Molecular sexing of geese using a cloned Z chromosomal sequence with homology to the W chromosome. Auk 107: 199–202.

Quinn, T.W., J.S. Quinn, F. Cooke, and B.N. White. 1987. DNA marker analysis detects multiple maternity and paternity in single broods of the Lesser Snow Goose. Nature (London) 326: 392–394.

Ratcliffe, L.M. 1990. Neighbour-stranger discrimination of whistled songs in Black-capped Chickadees. Acta XX Congr. Int. Ornithol. (Suppl.): 423.

Ratcliffe, L.M., and P.T. Boag. 1987. Effects of colour bands on male competition and sexual attractiveness in Zebra Finches (*Poephile guttata*). Can. J. Zool. 65: 333–338.

Ratcliffe, L.M., and R.G. Weisman. 1985. Frequency shift in the *fee bee* song of the Black-capped Chickadee. Condor 87: 555–556.

Ratcliffe, L.M., and R.G. Weisman. 1986. Song sequence discrimination in the Black-capped Chickadee (*Parus atricapillus*). J. Comp. Psychol. 100: 361–367.

Rechten, C., M. Avery, and A. Stevens. 1983. Optimal prey selection: why do Great Tits show partial preferences? Anim. Behav. 31: 576–584.

Regelmann, K., and E. Curio. 1983. Determinants of brood defence in the Great Tit, *Parus major* L. Behav. Ecol. Sociobiol. 13: 131–145.

Regelmann, K., and E. Curio. 1986. Why do Great Tit (*Parus major*) males defend their brood more than females do? Anim. Behav. 34: 1206–1214.

Reinertsen, R.E. 1988. Behavioral thermoregulation in the cold: the energetic significance of microclimate selection. Acta XIX Congr. Int. Ornithol.: 2681–2689.

Reinertsen, R.E., and S. Haftorn. 1983. Nocturnal hypothermia and metabolism in the Willow Tit, *Parus montanus*, at 63 degrees north. J. Comp. Physiol. B 151: 109–118.

Reinertsen, R.E., and S. Haftorn. 1986. Different metabolic strategies of northern birds for nocturnal survival. J. Comp. Physiol. B 156: 655–663.

Reynolds, R.T., and E.C. Meslow. 1984. Partitioning of food and niche characteristics of coexisting *Accipiter* during breeding. Auk 101: 761–779.

Richner, H. 1989. Avian laparoscopy as a field technique for sexing birds and an assessment of its effects on wild birds. J. Field Ornithol. 60: 137–142.

Ricklefs, R.E. 1968. Patterns of growth in birds. Ibis 110: 419–451.

Rising, J.D. 1968. A multivariate assessment of interbreeding between the chickadees *Parus atricapillus* and *P. carolinensis*. Syst. Zool. 17: 160–169.

Rising, J.D., and J.W. Hudson. 1974. Seasonal variation in the metabolism and thyroid activity of the Black-capped Chickadee (*Parus atricapillus*). Condor 76: 198–203.

Risser, A.C., Jr. 1971. A technique for performing laparotomy on small birds. Condor 73: 376–379.

Ritchison, G. 1979. Social organization in winter flocks of Black-capped Chickadees. Loon 51: 121–126.

Robbins, M.B., M.J. Braun, and E.A. Tobey. 1986. Morphological and vocal variation across a contact zone between the chickadees *Parus atricapillus* and *P. carolinensis*. Auk 103: 655–666.

Robins, J.D., and A. Raim. 1970. Late winter movements and social behavior of the Black-capped Chickadee. Jack-Pine Warbler 48: 66–72.

Robinson, S.K., and R.T. Holmes. 1982. Foraging behavior of forest birds: the relationships among several tactics, diet, and habitat structure. Ecology 63: 1918–1931.

Rogers, C.M. 1987. Predation risk and fasting capacity: do wintering birds maintain optimal body mass? Ecology 68: 1051–1061.

Rohwer, S., and P.W. Ewald. 1981. The cost of dominance and advantage of subordination in a badge signalling system. Evolution 35: 441–454.

Root, O.M. 1961. Cowbirds vs. chickadees. Massachusetts Audubon 46: 43.

Root, R.B. 1964. Ecological interactions of the Chestnut-backed Chickadee following a range extension. Condor 66: 229–238.

Røskaft, E., T. Järvi, M. Bakken, C. Bech, and R.E. Reinertsen. 1986. The relationship between social status and resting metabolic rate in Great Tits (*Parus major*) and Pied Flycatchers (*Ficedula hypoleuca*). Anim. Behav. 34: 838–842.

Roughgarden, J. 1983. Competition and theory in community ecology. Am. Nat. 122: 583–601.

Royama, T. 1966. Factors governing feeding rate, food requirement and brood size of nestling Great Tits, *Parus major*. Ibis 108: 313–347.

Rydén, O. 1978. The significance of antecedent auditory experiences on later reactions to the "seeet" alarm-call in Great Tit nestlings, *Parus major.* Z. Tierpsychol. 47: 396–409.

Saitou, T. 1978. Ecological study of social organization in the Great Tit, *Parus major* L. I. Basic structure of the winter flocks. Jpn. J. Ecol. 28: 199–214.

Saitou, T. 1979a. Ecological study of social organization in the Great Tit, *Parus major* L. II. Formation of the basic flocks. J. Yamashina Inst. Ornith. 9: 137–148.

Saitou, T. 1979b. Ecological study of social organization in the Great Tit, *Parus major* L. III. Home range of the basic flocks and dominance relationship of the members in a basic flock. J. Yamashina Inst. Ornith. 9: 149–171.

Saitou, T. 1979c. Ecological study of social organization in the Great Tit, *Parus major* L. IV. Pair formation and establishment of territory in the members of basic flocks. J. Yamashina Inst. Ornith. 9: 172–188.

Saitou, T. 1982. Compound flocks as an aggregation of the flocks of constant composition in the Great Tit, *Parus major* L. J. Yamashina Inst. Ornith. 14: 293–305.

Saitou, T. 1988. Winter flocks with overlapping home ranges in the Great Tit. Acta XIX Congr. Int. Ornithol.: 2391–2406.

Samson, F.B., and S.J. Lewis. 1979. Experiments on population regulation in two American parids. Wilson Bull. 91: 222–233.

Sasvari, L. 1979. Observational learning in Great, Blue and Marsh Tits. Anim. Behav. 27: 767–771.

Schneider, K.J. 1984. Dominance, predation and optimal foraging in White-throated Sparrow flocks. Ecology 65: 1820–1827.

Schoener, T.W. 1982. The controversy over interspecific competition. Am. Sci. 70: 586–595.

Schoener, T.W. 1983. Field experiments on interspecific competition. Am. Nat. 122: 240–285.

Shalter, M.D. 1978a. Localization of passerine seeet and mobbing calls by Goshawks and Pygmy Owls. Z. Tierpsychol. 46: 260–267.

Shalter, M.D. 1978b. Mobbing in the Pied Flycatcher. Effect of experiencing a live owl on responses to a stuffed facsimile. Z. Tierpsychol. 47: 173–179.

Shedd, D.H. 1983. Seasonal variation in mobbing intensity in the Black-capped Chickadee. Wilson Bull. 95: 343–348.

Sherry, D.F. 1982. Food storage, memory and Marsh Tits. Anim. Behav. 30: 631–633.

Sherry, D.F. 1984a. Food storage by Black-capped Chickadees: memory for the location and contents of caches. Anim. Behav. 32: 451–464.

Sherry, D.F. 1984b. What food-storing birds remember. Can. J. Psychol. 38: 304–321.

Sherry, D.F. 1989. Food storing in the Paridae. Wilson Bull. 101: 289–304.

Sherry, D.F., and B.G. Galef, Jr. 1984. Cultural transmission without imitation: milk bottle opening by birds. Anim. Behav. 32: 937–938.

Sherry, D.F., and B.G. Galef, Jr. 1990. Social learning without imitation: more about milk bottle opening by birds. Anim. Behav. 40: 987–989.

Sherry, D.F., and A.L. Vaccarino. 1989. Hippocampus and memory for food caches in Black-capped Chickadees. Behav. Neurosci. 103: 308–318.

Sherry, D.F., A.L. Vaccarino, K. Buckenham, and R.S. Hertz. 1989. The hippocampal complex in food-storing birds. Brain Behav. Evol. 34: 308–317.

Shettleworth, S.J. 1983. Memory in food-hoarding birds. Sci. Am. 248(3): 102–110.

Shettleworth, S.J., and J.R. Krebs. 1988. Spatial memory in food-storing *Parus* species. Acta XIX Congr. Int. Ornithol.: 2094–2099.

Sibley, C.G. 1955. Behavioral mimicry in the titmice (Paridae) and certain other birds. Wilson Bull. 67: 128–132.

Sibley, C.G., J.E. Ahlquist, and B.L. Monroe, Jr. 1988. A classification of the living birds of the world based on DNA-DNA hybridization studies. Auk 105: 409–423.

Silverin, B., P.A. Viebke, and J. Westin. 1989. An artificial simulation of the vernal increase in day length and its effects on the reproductive system in three species of tits (Parus spp.), and modifying effects of environmental factors—a field experiment. Condor 91: 598–608.

Simberloff, D. 1983. Competition theory, hypothesis testing and other community ecological buzzwords. Am. Nat. 122: 626–635.

Skutch, A.F. 1961. Helpers among birds. Condor 63: 198–226.

Slagsvold, T. 1975. Critical period for regulation of Great Tit (Parus major L.) and Blue Tit (Parus caeruleus L.) populations. Norw. J. Zool. 23: 67–88.

Slagsvold, T. 1984. Clutch size variation in birds in relation to nest predation: on the cost of reproduction. J. Anim. Ecol. 53: 945–953.

Slessers, M. 1970. Bathing behavior of land birds. Auk 87: 91–99.

Smiley, D. 1964. Another nine-year-old chickadee. Bird-Banding 35: 267.

Smith, C.C., and O.J. Reichman. 1984. The evolution of food caching by birds and mammals. Ann. Rev. Ecol. Syst. 15: 329–351.

Smith, C.L. 1964. Old chickadee. Bird-Banding 35: 124.

Smith, D.C., and J. Van Buskirk. 1988. Winter territoriality and flock cohesion in the Black-capped Chickadee, Parus atricapillus. Anim. Behav. 36: 466–476.

Smith, H.G. 1989. Larger clutches take longer to incubate. Ornis Scand. 20: 156–158.

Smith, H.G., H. Källander, and J.-Å. Nilsson. 1987. Effect of experimentally altered brood size on frequency and timing of second clutches in the Great Tit. Auk 104: 700–706.

Smith, H.G., H. Källander, and J.-Å. Nilsson. 1989. The trade-off between offspring number and quality in the Great Tit, Parus major. J. Anim. Ecol. 58: 383–401.

Smith, H.G., and J.-Å. Nilsson. 1987. Intraspecific variation in migratory pattern of a partial migrant, the Blue Tit (Parus caeruleus): an evaluation of different hypotheses. Auk 104: 109–115.

Smith, J.N.M. 1978. Division of labour by Song Sparrows feeding fledged young. Can. J. Zool. 56: 187–191.

Smith, J.N.M. 1981. Does high fecundity reduce survival in Song Sparrows? Evolution 35: 1142–1148.

Smith, J.N.M., P. Arcese, and D. Schluter. 1986. Song Sparrows grow and shrink with age. Auk 103: 210–212.

Smith, K.G. 1986. Winter population dynamics of three species of mast-eating birds in the eastern United States. Wilson Bull. 98: 407–418.

Smith, M.C.L. 1947. Recovery of chickadee bands from a Screech Owl pellet. Bird-Banding 18: 129.

Smith, S.M. 1967a. A case of polygamy in the Black-capped Chickadee. Auk 84: 274.

Smith, S.M. 1967b. An ecological study of winter flocks of Black-capped and Chestnut-backed Chickadees. Wilson Bull. 79: 200–207.

Smith, S.M. 1967c. Seasonal changes in the survival of the Black-capped Chickadee. Condor 69: 344–359.

Smith, S.M. 1972. Roosting aggregations of bushtits in response to cold temperatures. Condor 74: 478–479.

Smith, S.M. 1973. An aggressive display and related behavior in the Loggerhead Shrike. Auk 90: 287–298.

Smith, S.M. 1974a. Factors directing prey-attack by the young of three passerine species. Living Bird 12: 55–67.

Smith, S.M. 1974b. Nest-site selection in Black-capped Chickadees. Condor 76: 478–479.

Smith, S.M. 1976. Ecological aspects of dominance hierarchies in Black-capped Chickadees. Auk 93: 95–107.

Smith, S.M. 1980a. Henpecked males: the general pattern in monogamy? J. Field Ornithol. 51: 55–63.

Smith, S.M. 1980b. Demand behavior: a new interpretation of courtship feeding. Condor 82: 291–295.

Smith, S.M. 1984. Flock switching in chickadees: why be a winter floater? Am. Nat. 123: 81–98.

Smith, S.M. 1985. The tiniest established permanent floater crap game in the Northeast. Nat. Hist. 94(3): 42–46.

Smith, S.M. 1987. Responses of floaters to removal experiments on wintering chickadees. Behav. Ecol. Sociobiol. 20: 363–367.

Smith, S.M. 1988a. Social dynamics in wintering Black-capped Chickadees. Acta XIX Congr. Int. Ornithol.: 2382–2390.

Smith, S.M. 1988b. Extra-pair copulations in Black-capped Chickadees: the role of the female. Behaviour 107: 15–23.

Smith, S.M. 1989. Black-capped Chickadee summer floaters. Wilson Bull. 101: 344–349.

Smith, S.M. 1990. Winter replacement rates of high-ranked chickadees vary with floater density. Pp. 453–460 in J. Blondel, A. Gosler, J.-D. Lebreton, and R. McCleery, eds., Population Biology of Passerine Birds, an Integrated Approach. NATO ASI Series, vol. G-24. Springer-Verlag, Heidelberg.

Smith, S.M., M. Duryea, and M. Graaskamp. 1990. Possible habituation to predator models by free-living Black-capped Chickadees, Parus atricapillus. Acta XX Congr. Int. Ornithol. (Suppl.): 374.

Smith, S.T. 1972. Communication and other social behavior in Parus carolinensis. Publ. Nuttall Ornithol. Club No. 11.

Smith, W.J. 1977. The Behavior of Communicating. Harvard Univ. Press, Cambridge.

Snipes, K.P., T.E. Carpenter, J.L. Corn, R.W. Kasten, D.W. Hirsh, D.W. Hird, and R.H. McCapes. 1988. Pasteurella multocida in wild mammals and birds in California: prevalence and virulence for turkeys. Avian Dis. 32: 9–15.

Snow, D.W. 1956. The specific status of the Willow Tit. Bull. Brit. Orn. Club 76: 29–31.

Snow, D.W. 1967. Family Paridae. Pp. 70–124 in R.A. Paynter, ed., Checklist of Birds of the World, vol. 12. Museum of Comparative Zoology, Cambridge, Mass.

Southern, W.E. 1966. Utilization of shad as winter food by birds. Auk 83: 309–311.

Speirs, J.M. 1963. Survival and population dynamics with particular reference to Black-capped Chickadees. Bird-Banding 34: 87–93.

Spicer, G.S. 1987. Prevalence and host-parasite list of some nasal mites from Birds (Acarina: Rhinonyssidae, Speleognathidae). J. Parasitol. 73: 259–264.

Springer, M., and C. Krajewski. 1989. DNA hybridization in animal taxonomy: a critique from first principles. Q. Rev. Biol. 64: 291–318.

Steen, J. 1958. Climatic adaptation in some small northern birds. Ecology 39: 626–629.

Stefanski, R.A. 1967. Utilization of the breeding territory in the Black-capped Chickadee. Condor 69: 259–267.

Stephens, D.W., and J.R. Krebs. 1986. Optimal Foraging Theory. Princeton Univ. Press, Princeton.

Stephens, D.W., J.F. Lynch, S.E. Sorenson, and C. Gordon. 1986. Preferences and profitability: theory and experiment. Am. Nat. 127: 533–553.

Stewart, I.F. 1963. Variation of wing length with age. Bird Study 10: 1–9.

Stone, E.R., and M.C. Baker. 1989. The effects of conspecifics on food caching by Black-capped Chickadees. Condor 91: 886–890.

Strong, D.R., Jr. 1983. Natural variability and the manifold mechanisms of ecological communities. Am. Nat. 122: 636–660.

Sturman, W.A. 1968a. Description and analysis of breeding habitats of the chickadees *Parus atricapillus* and *P. rufescens*. Ecology 49: 418–431.

Sturman, W.A. 1968b. The foraging ecology of *Parus atricapillus* and *P. rufescens* in the breeding season, with comparisons with other species of *Parus*. Condor 70: 309–322.

Sullivan, K. 1984. Information exploitation by Downy Woodpeckers in mixed-species flocks. Behaviour 91: 294–311.

Sullivan, K. 1985. Selective alarm calling by Downy Woodpeckers in mixed-species flocks. Auk 102: 184–187.

Tallman, D.A. 1987. Abnormally colored juvenile Black-capped Chickadee molts to normal basic plumage. Wilson Bull. 99: 721–722.

Tanner, J.T. 1934. A melanistic Black-capped Chickadee. Auk 51: 240.

Tanner, J.T. 1952. Black-capped and Carolina Chickadees in the southern Appalachian Mountains. Auk 69: 407–424.

Tarbell, A.T. 1983. A yearling helper with a Tufted Titmouse brood. J. Field Ornithol. 54: 89.

Taverner, P.A. 1949. Birds of Canada. Musson Book Co., Toronto.

Terres, J.K. 1940. Birds eating tent caterpillars. Auk 57: 422.

Tiersch, T.R., R.L. Mumme, R.W. Chandler, and D. Nakamura. 1991. The use of flow cytometry for rapid identification of sex in birds. Auk 108: 206–208.

Tinbergen, J.M. 1987. Costs of reproduction in the Great Tit: intraseasonal costs associated with brood size. Ardea 75: 111–122.

Tinbergen, J.M., and J.H. van Balen. 1988. Food and multiple breeding. Acta XIX Congr. Int. Ornithol.: 380–391.

Tinbergen, L. 1960. The natural control of insects in pine woods. Arch. Neerl. Zool. 13: 265–379.

Van Tyne, J. 1928. A diurnal local migration of the Black-capped Chickadee. Wilson Bull. 40: 252.

Veghte, J.H., and C.F. Herreid. 1965. Radiometric determination of feather insulation and metabolism of arctic birds. Physiol. Zool. 38: 267–275.

Verbeek, N.A.M. 1962. On dew bathing and drought in passerines. Auk 79: 719.

Waite, T.A. 1987. Dominance-specific vigilance in the Tufted Titmouse: effects of social context. Condor 89: 932–935.

Waite, T.A., and T.C. Grubb, Jr. 1987. Dominance, foraging and predation risk in the Tufted Titmouse. Condor 89: 936–940.

Walker, J.E.S. 1972. Attempts at fledging of a runt Great Tit. Bird Study 19: 250–251.

Walkinshaw, L.H. 1941. The Prothonotary Warbler, a comparison of nesting conditions in Tennessee and Michigan. Wilson Bull. 53: 3–21.

Wallace, G.J. 1941. Winter studies of color-banded chickadees. Bird-Banding 12: 49–67.

Wallace, G.O. 1967. An aggressive display by a Tufted Titmouse. Wilson Bull. 79: 118.

Wallace, G.O. 1970. Winter flock structure and behavior of the Carolina Chickadee. Migrant 41: 25–29.

Walsberg, G.E. 1986. Thermal consequences of roost-site selection: the relative importance of three modes of heat conservation. Auk 103: 1–7.

Ward, R. 1966. Regional variation in the song of the Carolina Chickadee. Living Bird 5: 127–150.

Ward, R., and D.A. Ward. 1974. Songs in contiguous populations of Black-capped and Carolina Chickadees in Pennsylvania. Wilson Bull. 86: 344–356.

Warren, R.P., and M.A. Vince. 1963. Taste discrimination in the Great Tit (*Parus major*). J. Comp. Physiol. Psychol. 56: 910–913.

Waterman, J., A. Desrochers, and S. Hannon. 1989. A case of polyandry in the Black-capped Chickadee. Wilson Bull. 101: 351–353.

Weise, C.M. 1971. Population dynamics of the Black-capped Chickadee. Univ. Wis. Milw. Field Stn. Bull. 4: 6–11.

Weise, C.M. 1979. Sex identification in Black-capped Chickadees. Univ. Wis. Milw. Field Stn. Bull. 12: 16–19.

Weise, C.M., and J.R. Meyer. 1979. Juvenile dispersal and development of site-fidelity in the Black-capped Chickadee. Auk 96: 40–55.

Weisman, R., and L. Ratcliffe. 1987. How birds identify species information in song: a pattern recognition approach. Learn. Motiv. 18: 80–98.

Weisman, R., and L. Ratcliffe. 1989. Absolute and relative pitch processing in Black-capped Chickadees, *Parus atricapillus*. Anim. Behav. 38: 685–692.

Weisman, R., L. Ratcliffe, I. Johnsrude, and T.A. Hurly. 1990. Absolute and relative pitch production in the song of the Black-capped Chickadee. Condor 92: 118–124.

Wesolowski, T., L. Tomialojc, and T. Stawarczyk. 1987. Why low numbers of

*Parus major* in Bialowieza Forest—removal experiments. Acta Ornithol. 23: 304–316.

West-Eberhard, M.J. 1975. The evolution of social behavior by kin selection. Q. Rev. Biol. 50: 1–33.

Wetherbee, K.B. 1933. A chickadee changes color of tail. Bird-Banding 4: 160–161.

Wetherbee, O.P. 1950. Chickadee in convulsion. Bird-Banding 21: 61.

Wharton, W.P. 1964. Nine-year-old chickadee. Bird-Banding 35: 41.

Wheeler, T.A., and W. Threlfall. 1986. Observations on the ectoparasites of some Newfoundland passerines (Aves: Passeriformes). Can. J. Zool. 64: 630–636.

Whiting, R.M., Jr. 1979. Winter feeding niche partitionment by Carolina Chickadees and Tufted Titmice in east Texas. Pp. 331–340 *in* J.G. Dickson, R.N. Conner, R.R. Fleet, J.C. Kroll, and J.A. Jackson, eds., The Role of Insectivorous Birds in Forest Ecosystems. Academic Press, New York.

Wiens, J.A., J.T. Rotenberry, and B. Van Horne. 1985. Territory size variations in shrub steppe birds. Auk 102: 500–505.

Williams, L. 1941. Roosting habits of the Chestnut-backed Chickadee and the Bewick Wren. Condor 43: 274–285.

Willis, E.O., D. Wechsler, and Y. Oniki. 1978. On behavior and nesting of McConnell's Flycatcher (*Pipromorpha macconelli*): does female rejection lead to male promiscuity? Auk 95: 1–8.

Withiam, M.L., D. Lemon, and C.P.L. Barkan. 1988. Pair-bonds, social behavior, and the use of space in wintering Black-capped Chickadees (*Parus atricapillus*). Abstract No. 58, Wilson Ornithological Society Centennial Meeting, June 8–12, 1988, Rosemont, Penn. Wilson Ornithological Society, Ann Arbor.

Witkin, S.R. 1977. The importance of directional sound radiation in avian vocalization. Condor 79: 490–493.

Witkin, S.R., and M.S. Ficken. 1979. Chickadee alarm calls: does mate investment pay dividends? Anim. Behav. 27: 1275–1276.

Wrege, P.H., and S.T. Emlen. 1987. Biochemical determination of parental uncertainty in White-fronted Bee-eaters. Behav. Ecol. Sociobiol. 20: 153–160.

Ydenberg, R.C. 1987. Foraging vs. territorial vigilance: the selection of feeding sites by male Great Tits (*Parus major* L.) Ethology 74: 33–38.

Ydenberg, R.C., and J.R. Krebs. 1987. Trade-offs and territorial defence. Am. Zool. 27: 337–346.

Yunick, R.P. 1980. Timing of completion of skull pneumatization of the Black-capped Chickadee and the Red-breasted Nuthatch. N. Am. Bird Bander 5: 43–46.

Yunick, R.P. 1981. Skull pneumatization rates in three invading populations of Black-capped Chickadees. N. Am. Bird Bander 6: 6–7.

Zimmermann, U., and E. Curio. 1988. Two conflicting needs affecting predator mobbing by Great Tits, *Parus major*. Anim. Behav. 36: 926–932.

Zonov, G.B. 1967. On the winter roosting of Paridae in Cisbaikal. Ornitologiya 8: 351–354. In Russian; quoted in Calder and King 1974.

# Index

*Library of Congress Cataloging-in-Publication Data*

Smith, Susan M., 1942–
    The Black-capped Chickadee : behavioral ecology and natural
history / Susan M. Smith.
        p.   cm.
    Includes bibliographical references and index.
    ISBN 0-8014-2382-1 (alk. paper). — ISBN 0-8014-9793-0 (pbk. :
alk. paper)
    1. Black-capped chickadee.   2. Parus.   I. Title.
QL696.P2615S55   1991
598.8'24—dc20                                            91-55072